BOMBERS
of the West

BILL GUNSTON

BOMBERS
of the West

LONDON

IAN ALLAN

First published 1973

ISBN 0 7110 0456 0

© W. T. Gunston 1973

Published by Ian Allan Ltd, Shepperton, Surrey,
and printed in Great Britain by
Morrison & Gibb Ltd, London and Edinburgh

Contents

Preface

I HAVE written books on many topics, because publishers have been good enough to ask me to. But I have written *this* book because I wanted to. Instead of having—to use the old RAF slang—to "gen up" on the subject, the content of this book is in my bones.

Ever since I was a boy, in those peaceful days when neither Von Ohain nor Whittle had built a jet engine, I have been well placed to see the whole world of aviation. It is a vast world, embracing not only the entire spread of modern technologies—including biochemistry, medicine, geophysics and many other disciplines that are far from immediately obvious—but also such contrasting topics as the management techniques for giant programmes, the economics of the airborne alert and the economics of the packaged-tour holiday.

In particular, I have been able to talk to the people who use modern aircraft, to the engineers who create them and to the various interposed layers of government officials who serve as a lubricant or sometimes as sand in the works. To me such talk reveals the very life-blood of a splendid and exciting subject. It is so much a part of my life that I am frankly unable to guess whether the totally non-aviation person would find this book of interest or not. But it interests me. The story of a modern aircraft, like true love, never runs straight but instead mirrors all the perversity and paradox of an imperfect world. It is replete with ulcer-making problems, disaster, wry humour, sheer brilliance and sheer stupidity.

I have poured out each tale just as I feel it to be, "warts and all". I have tried to be objective, and not to prove any particular class of people foolish or any particular nation incompetent. There is a world of difference between the nervous exhaustion of trying to make an immensely challenging new aircraft, that will meet the customer's shifting requirements within an impossible time-scale and a hopelessly optimistic budget, and the somewhat easier task of criticizing these efforts with the benefit of hindsight. It is common nowadays for young reporters on the mass media to pour unadulterated scorn on practically anyone who has to bear responsibility. Yet perhaps this is no worse than the behaviour of their counterparts 20 years ago when the instant reaction to a new aircraft programme was adulation and wonder. My intention has been to tell it like it is, or was, which ought to be a middle course.

I am grateful to G. Freeman Allen and John W. R. Taylor, who suggested that this first volume ought to deal with bombers. The bomber probably exerts a wider and sharper fascination than most other categories of aircraft, and modern bombers can be judged against the changing background of nuclear and conventional warfare and the rapidly increasing difficulty of penetrating hostile airspace. So difficult is this basic duty of "penetration" that 15 years ago every expert I knew had no doubt in his mind that manned bombers would soon be obsolete. They would have been flabbergasted to read the last chapter in this book.

There are plenty of other books on bombers, ranging from dry official reports, pilots' notes, classified evaluations and deep theoretical studies, through superficial histories for "spotters", terse descriptions and numerical data, and stories that concentrate on detail differences between one aircraft and another of the same type, or upon squadrons and aircrew and bloody wartime missions. What I have tried to do is to record the biography of each aircraft, explaining why it was developed, what it was meant to do, why it came out the way it did and what happened to it in the course of its life. I think I am right to have assumed that most readers will already have a nodding acquaintanceship with the aircraft concerned, and will readily be able to look up the wing span, or any other data, if they so desire. I have tried to avoid too many figures which could easily have detracted from the story.

If this volume proves successful I shall enjoy writing companion histories of other types of aircraft. In some of these categories it would be possible to include aircraft of the Soviet Union, but to my great regret I cannot do so in this first book. The Russian bombers are of exceptional technical interest, and their long individual stories of development would undoubtedly make fine reading, but to attempt to include them in this book would have meant too much supposition and guesswork. It used to be a joke among my colleagues that any approach to the Russians was always met by a sepulchral voice saying "That story, eet ees not very interesting . . .". Hopefully we'll be able to dig out those stories—which undoubtedly are interesting—while the people involved are still with us.

So I cannot include the Russians, but I can acknowledge the immense help I have received from officials, Top Brass, chief designers and many other active and retired friends who have been good enough to read these chapters and make helpful suggestions. With their aid I have been able to eliminate most of the errors, and hopefully all; but I shall welcome critical comment from any source.

Haslemere, 1973   BILL GUNSTON

BOMBERS
of the West

Glossary

On the principle that it is better to offend an air marshal by telling him RAF stands for Royal Air Force than to leave a reader groping in the dark (hopefully not over those particular initials), the following are some of the abbreviations, places and jargon that might otherwise cause difficulty.

AAEE Aeroplane & Armament Experimental Establishment, Boscombe Down, England.

AAM Air-to-air-missile.

ACAS Assistant Chief of the Air Staff (UK).

ADC Air Defense Command (USAF).

AFB Air Force Base (US).

AFSC US Air Force Systems Command.

AMA Air Materiel [sic] Area (USAF).

AOC Air Officer Commanding (RAF).

ARDC US Air Force Air Research and Development Command, became AFSC.

Armée de l'Air French Air Force.

ASM Air-to-surface missile.

AWACS Airborne Warning and Control System.

BMEWS Ballistic Missile Early Warning System (US/UK).

bomb/nav A crew member or electronic system fulfilling the functions of bomb-aiming and navigation.

Boscombe Boscombe Down, Wiltshire, location of the AAEE.

BS Bomb Squadron (USAF).

BuAer US Navy Bureau of Aeronautics, became NASC.

BuShips US Navy Bureau of Ships.

BW Bomb Wing (USAF).

CA Release Release by the Controller, Aircraft, for operational service (UK).

CAS Chief of the Air Staff (RAF, RAAF).

CEP Circular error probability, a measure of bomb or missile accuracy.

CEV Centre des Essais en Vol. Brétigny (Fr).

CFAS Command des Forces Aérienne Stratégique (Fr).

c.g. Centre of gravity.

CSCS Cost/schedule control system (US).

DEI Development Engineering Inspection (US).

DCOS Deputy Chief of Staff (USAF).

DoD Department of Defense (US).

DTIA Direction Technique et Industrielle de l'Air (Fr).

ECM Electronic countermeasures.

Edwards AFB in Mojave Desert, California, location of USAF and NASA flight-test centres.

Farnborough UK government (not RAF) airfield in Hampshire, location of original RAE.

FLIR Forward-looking infra-red.

FLR Forward-looking radar.

FY Fiscal Year (1 July to following 30 June) (US).

GAP Ground-alert posture (US).

GFE Government-furnished equipment (US).

GNP Gross national product.

hi High-altitude portion of an offensive mission.

IAS Indicated air-speed.

ICBM Intercontinental ballistic missile.

IOC Initial operational capability (US).

IR Infra-red.

ITP Instruction to proceed, authority to industry to start work in advance of a contract.

LABS Low-altitude bombing system.

lo Low-level portion of an offensive mission.

MAP Ministry of Aircraft Production (UK, became MoS).

Mintech Ministry of Technology (UK, became MoAS).

MIRV Multiple independently targeted re-entry vehicles (for an ICBM).

mission profile Written or graphic description of the planned variation in aircraft altitude throughout an offensive mission.

MMH/FH Maintenance man-hours per flight hour.

MoA Ministry of Aviation (UK, became Mintech).

MoAS Ministry of Aviation Supply (UK).

MoD Ministry of Defence (UK).

MoS Ministry of Supply (UK, became MoA).

MTBF Mean time between failures.

MTO Maximum take-off weight.

NACA National Advisory Committee for Aeronautics (US, became NASA).

NAS Naval Air Station (US).

NASA National Aeronautics and Space Administration (US).

NASC Naval Air Systems Command (US).

NATC Naval Air Test Center (US).

NPL National Physical Laboratory (UK).

OCU Operational Conversion Unit (RAF).

OR Operational Requirement (UK).

Pax River Patuxent River, Maryland, location of the NATC.

penaids Penetration aids, such as ECM, decoys, feint manoeuvres, chaff and anti-radar missiles.

Pentagon Building near Washington DC, headquarters of the DoD.

PFRT Preliminary Flight Rating Test, of an engine (US).

profile Mission profile.

RAE Royal Aircraft Establishment, located at Farnborough, Bedford and Aberporth (UK).

RAAF Royal Australian Air Force.

RAF Royal Air Force (UK).

R&D Research and development.

RDT&E Research, development, test and engineering (US).

Reqt. Requirement (UK).

RFP Request for Proposals, from US military customer or DoD to industry.

SAC Strategic Air Command (USAF).

SAM Surface-to-air missile.

SecDef Secretary of Defense, head of the DoD (US).

SEP Specific Excess Power.

signature Characteristic reflection of radar energy by each type of aircraft.

SLAR Side-looking aircraft radar.

SLBM Submarine-launched ballistic missile.

SOR Specific Operational Requirement (US).

SPO System Project Office (USAF).

SST Supersonic transport.

STOL Short take-off and landing.

TAC Tactical Air Command (USAF).

t/c ratio Ratio of wing thickness (top to bottom) to chord (front to back).

TFR Terrain-following radar.

USA United States Army.

USAF United States Air Force.

USN United States Navy.

WADC Wright Air Development Center (US).

VSI Vertical speed indicator.

WPAFB Wright-Patterson AFB, location of WADC.

Wright-Patterson, see WPAFB.

WS Weapon System (US).

WSPO Weapon System Project Office (US).

English Electric Canberra

TOWARDS the end of World War 2 the Luftwaffe operated the world's first jet-propelled bombers. In July 1945 Sir Roy Fedden and his investigating team from the MAP found not only the shattered German airfields but even straight stretches of the Autobahns littered with them, the newly built Arados having at the last moment been abandoned by their crews for want of fuel. Over the subsequent two years the US industry, though contracting violently and racing after civil business, showed that it had lost no time in combining new axial jet engines with impressive bomber airframes. The culminating shock was the Boeing XB-47 (p. 126) which even in a coarse newspaper illustration could be seen to be of extraordinarily bold design. Throughout 1948 I heard that English Electric were at work on a jet bomber in Britain, but it seemed to be taking a very long time. In February 1949 a B-47 crossed the United States at 608 mph. In view of the monster B-36, the eight-jet Northrop "flying wing" and three other types of American jet bombers, I began to feel that Britain was being left behind. It was a feeling quite alien to me, and I found it disturbing. Where were our jet bombers? Was the Lincoln (originally called the Lancaster Mk IV) the best our industry could produce? I left the RAF with such questions ringing in my ears.

Suddenly, in May 1949, our new jet bomber was revealed; and, if it were possible, I felt worse than before. The English Electric A.1 was the most ordinary looking jet bomber it was possible to imagine. It was also the smallest. Admittedly it was clean and streamlined, and painted a nice glossy turquoise blue, but the immediate impression that the prototype, VN799, made on me was that it certainly couldn't carry very much, was unlikely to have more than a "European" range, and that, as it seemed to have escaped our notice that swept wings made aircraft go faster, it was likely to prove deficient in speed. A former colleague in Bomber Command—and liable to be put on a charge if he flew too much, for this was a time of the most severe rationing of everything, including RAF fuel—had actually seen the A.1 in the flesh, and was desperate to find out all about it. I could only tell him, rudely, that it had to be designed like that so that pilots like him could fly it.

Pilots like him could indeed fly it, and therein lay part of the strength of this classic design. In 1949, as I vainly looked for something British that had swept wings and at least ten engines so that I could again hold up my head in public, I had not the slightest idea that this modest aircraft would be one of the greatest success stories in British aviation, and sought after by air forces all over the world for a quarter of a century. Still less did I dream that it would be built under licence in the United States. If ever I am asked to give an instant appraisal of some new flying machine I remember the prototype Canberra and how terribly wrong first impressions can be.

It was in 1943 that the Air Staff and MAP first held a conference on jet bombers. The subject was so in the melting pot, because of the tremendous yet imponderable effects of jet propulsion and the rumoured atomic bomb, that the main conclusion was that it was all very difficult. One major thread of development concerned the "high-speed day bomber", and this was to have jet engines. A second concerned the "gas turbine heavy bomber" and this was thought of as a 350 mph machine with dozens of propeller blades. A third was the "giant bomber" which, as the B-36, was already under development in the United States in order to bomb Germany after a possible British collapse. Bristol were the main giant-bomber firm, but this project gradually merged into the civil Brabazon in 1943. As 1944 dawned there were a dozen drawing boards from Weybridge to Preston on which appeared three-view drawings of future bombers. D. L. Ellis, later of English Electric, told me "It was simple to sketch a wide range of convincing proposals on the basis of two or four Nenes, or the axial engines under development at Armstrong Siddeley or Metrovick; and the weapons bay and fuel volume for a given mission could also be calculated. But when it came to such basic questions as what shape you make the wing or where you put the engines, we were all stumped by the sheer profusion of possible answers. What's more we didn't have a high-speed wind tunnel, and didn't know how to build one."

In 1944 English Electric's Aircraft Division at Samlesbury, near Preston, in Lancashire, was churning out the last of 2,145 Halifaxes (more than were built by any other company) and tooling up to build the Vampire jet fighter for which de Havilland had no spare capacity. Neither of these big and important programmes involved much design and development, but in 1944 W. E. W. "Teddy" Petter had joined the division as chief engineer and, at the MAP's invitation, built up a design team that has today grown to become the pre-eminent military aircraft team in Europe —and I am not forgetting Hawker and Dassault. Petter had come from Westland Aircraft, where his last project had been a tactical jet attack aircraft requested by Sir Ralph Sorley, the Controller of R&D at the MAP. As soon as he arrived at the embryonic design office in a bus garage in Corporation Street, Preston, Petter laid plans to commit the division to the development of the first British jet bomber, using the notes and data from his low-level study at Yeovil. There was no hurry in official circles. In stark contrast to the desperate haste in Germany, the Air Staff considered no jet bomber could be produced in time to influence the war. If one is winning a war it is possible to enjoy the luxury of such a decision; if one's back is against the wall it is sometimes possible to work miracles simply by adopting a different attitude and seemingly impossible time-scale. This book has a lot to say about time-scales. All the American prototype jet bombers were completed in considerably less than the time taken to produce the prototype of the smaller and simpler A.1. One is driven to conclude that by 1944 Britain no longer felt it needed to hustle; certainly the Labour Government elected in 1945 deliberately encouraged this attitude in order to save money on armaments.

Although Petter's team in 1945 included some outstanding engineers—one of whom was Freddie Page, now chairman and managing director of the BAC Military Aircraft Division—it was puny compared with those of the Americans. Fedden, two years before his mission to probe Germany, had produced a monumental report on the US industry in which he laid stress on the massive strength of American design and engineering staffs. This part of the report was promptly called "Fedden's folly" by a smug British industry which jumped to the conclusion that the eminent engine designer had been taken in by American exaggeration. For 12 years after the war Britain managed to persuade itself both that it led the world in aviation and that it could do so with a mere handful of engineers. It was considered distastefully unsporting or unpatriotic to point out that it was this shortage of engineers that made British firms take nearly twice as long over a big programme as their rivals in the United States or Soviet Union. When details of the English Electric jet bomber programme were revealed not one critic ventured to ask why the prototype had flown two years after much bigger and more complex US bombers that were started at the same time.

At least Britain was spared the high-speed day bomber, the gas-turbine heavy and the giant. Specification B.3/45, which Petter had a hand in drafting, called for "a two-seat high-altitude bomber equipped with jet engines and a radar bomb-sight". The last item was vital, for it was to allow accurate bombing without seeing the target. This was the first of several important specifications strongly influenced by the success of the Mosquito (a design which in 1940 escaped total rejection only by a hair's breadth) in relying solely on flight performance to avoid being shot down. Gone were the heavy and complex turrets and gunlaying systems of World War 2. By 1945 the most forward-looking members of the Air Staff had decided to standardize on jet bombers with no guns at all, a philosophy at variance with that of the US Air Force even when the latter service bought a strategic bomber having supersonic performance

15

(the B-58, p. 185). Petter wholeheartedly concurred with the omission of defensive armament, but he still took a year to decide on the basic shape.

In 1944 Rolls-Royce were busily scaling up the two-stage centrifugal superchargers of the Merlin and Griffon piston engines into forms that would serve as the compressors of gas turbines. The first scale, to a mass flow of 20 lb/sec, gave the world the Dart turboprop, which is still in production in 1973. The second, to 230 lb/sec, was planned to bring forth a turbojet more than twice as big as the Nene—then the most powerful engine running—with a sea-level thrust of 13,000 lb. In June 1945 Petter decided to design the whole bomber around one of these giant engines. He was captivated by the possibility it offered of achieving a clean un-cluttered aerodynamic design, with the engine exactly fitting the circular-section fuselage, but in July he had to admit defeat. With the centre fuselage full of engine he had nowhere close to the centre of gravity to put the bombs. Rather regretfully Rolls-Royce abandoned their great project and agreed with Petter that a superior layout would be the more con-ventional one of a 6,500 lb thrust engine on each wing. Such thrust was easily within the compass of the Nene derivative later called the Tay, but Rolls were anxious to get into the axial-compressor business where they could see the future lay. They decided to embark on the AJ.65 (axial jet, 6,500 lb thrust), and Petter's bomber was thenceforward planned around two of these much slimmer engines which were at first fitted inside the roots of the wing. This revised design was one-eighth lighter.

There was never any doubt the specification could be met because, unlike the more challenging requirement cooked up for a larger bomber in 1946, B.3/45 merely called for the bomb-load of a Mosquito (4,000 lb), with the hope that this would be exceeded, and the radius of action of a Lancaster (800 nautical miles) with full load. Petter told me he did not ignore wing sweep, but from his earliest calculations considered the specification could be met with 13,000 lb total installed thrust "and with this level of thrust sweeping back the wings and tail would have been pointless, and would only have added weight". The A.1 was what has later become known as a "state of the art" design, a term which means that innovations are avoided in the hope of getting an operational product quickly. With the XB-47 Boeing did precisely the opposite, as described later in this volume; but as they had nine times as many design engineers as English Electric's Aircraft Division the B-47 and the British bomber entered service in the very same month in 1951.

Nowhere did the conservative philosophy show itself more clearly than in the wing, which was completely unswept, very broad indeed in chord, and although of a high-speed laminar aerofoil section had a thickness/chord ratio at the root of 12 per cent, a value which, taken in conjunction with the enormous chord, allowed the wing to be quite deep and thus lightly built from thin-gauge light alloy. An early English Electric brochure described this wing as having been "planned to give the highest possible altitude performance and lowest fuel consumption". This is not strictly true. Petter told me in 1953 "Yes, we would have gained more height and range with a greater span, but the weight of the wing would have gone up and the load factor would have come down. The wing we chose was a fair compromise which in conjunction with a very low wing loading conferred excellent altitude performance in a simple, cheap, easily built aircraft." But I never ceased to be amazed that the marvellous altitude performance of the Canberra with more span was never realized in Britain, except in a fainthearted way with the PR.9 reconnaissance version. It was left to the Americans to do what the basic design cried out for, and that was to develop special high-altitude versions with twice the span. Until about 1957 it would have made sense even in bomber versions, as presently described.

Apart from having axial turbojets, Petter's design was unusual among British aircraft in having a pressure cabin, and especially a pressure cabin covered by a huge canopy moulded from a single sandwich of Perspex acrylic plastic. During the war some late marks of Mosquito had had lightly pressurized cabins, and a bolder arrangement was tried in the high-flying Wellington V and VI, but making the whole nose of the new jet in the form of a pressurized cabin for the pilot and navigator was at the time considered quite radical. There was to be no bomb-aimer, for the heart of the aircraft was to be a very advanced radar bombing system of the type then being successfully realized in the United States. In fact, this system was the biggest gamble in the whole programme, but it was not Petter's problem. He was merely given a volume, weight and electrical power load, and told that in due course trucks would arrive from Tele-communications Research Establishment (later the Royal Radar Establishment) at Malvern carrying a lot of black boxes.

On 7 January 1946 four prototypes were ordered, all with AJ.65 engines, radar bombing system and wings devoid of fuel. By this time the design team were engaged in moving eight miles west to the former American base at Warton. Late in the war I happened to be at nearby RAF Kirkham when a Liberator from Warton crashed into a school at Freckleton, just over the road from the airfield, causing what may have been the worst air casualties of the war. But when Petter's men arrived the great base was deserted. All they had to do was repress the central heating, for in those days the British liked to be cold.

Existence of the programme was revealed in September 1947, when the Minister of Supply, George Strauss, said the new machine would have "about twice the speed of current bombers". This was fair where the RAF was concerned, although Mr Strauss did not mention that the US Air Force (formed from the Army Air Force in that very month) was armed with the B-50 capable of over 400 mph with full combat load. Another thing he failed to mention was the timing, and by September 1947 it looked as if this could go seriously awry. The cause was not the aircraft but the engines and systems, both of which were giving trouble. The Rolls-Royce AJ.65 ought not to have been a great challenge, because in most respects it was conservative, but in those days an axial compressor was a rather hit-and-miss undertaking because of the immense complexity of the aerodynamic and aeroelastic problems. If it turned out to be a miss it was a long and hard row to hoe, and in the case of the AJ.65 it missed. Despite such palliatives as variable-incidence guide vanes and blow-off valves, the new axial compressor steadfastly misbehaved; and Rolls were also unhappy with the big single-stage turbine that drove it. By the autumn of 1947 one of the four aircraft was earmarked for conversion to the Rolls-Royce Nene as an insurance. I thought this a smooth piece of Derby salesmanship. The one thing Petter wanted to avoid was a pair of fat centrifugal engines, yet this was just what he might have ended up with, and it meant adopting conventional engine nacelles centred on the wings like a Meteor instead of having everything buried inside a clean airframe as he had wished. Nobody explained why he was not offered as an alternative the more powerful and slimmer Metrovick F.9, which the following year took on a new lease of life as the Armstrong Siddeley Sapphire. Perhaps the answer lies in the fact that this superb axial engine, the design of which went like a bomb, was not wanted by Metropolitan-Vickers who were in 1947 trying to get out of the aviation business entirely; and the Hawker Siddeley Group had not yet taken it on. Fortunately it all came right in the end: Rolls made the Avon compressor work and they threw out the clumsy turbine and used instead two more lightly loaded stages. Later still they made a much better Avon with the compressor of the Sapphire, but by this time practically all the Canberras had been built.

Until mid-1948 Petter's team toyed with civil airliner derivatives of the A.1. All were low-wing projects, some of which specified pre-packed baggage bins for quick turn-round; the only problem was that the conservative airline industry was nothing like ready either for jet propulsion or pre-loaded baggage bins. Later Vickers, Avro and Handley Page tried to launch airliner derivatives of their much bigger jet bombers. Britain was so unable to perceive the importance of making the best use of design strength that we kept on with three four-jet bombers plus three lots of derived jet airliner projects and concurrently bought jet transports from elsewhere. Petter gave up for the obvious reason: he had hardly enough engineers to do the bomber, let alone a jet airliner. And, as a sideline, he had begun to tackle a (dare it be whispered?) supersonic aircraft. At this time his engineering staff were fewer in number than Boeing had on hydraulics alone.

Despite all this the A.1 was so straightforward a design that the erecting shop at Warton put it together without too much trouble, and on 5 May 1949 VN799 was towed out into the bright sunshine. In the United States they enjoy ceremonial rollouts, with at least the local senator if not the President himself telling the vast crowd all about their great new creation and what it means to the state and the nation. At Warton the A.1 rollout set the pattern since followed by every British aircraft I can recall: a photographer did record the scene and the only crowd comprised three blokes who happened to be crossing the tarmac at the time. Both engines had the front cowls off and big bell-mouth intakes for ground running, so the sleek aircraft was hardly seen at its best. A few days later the official Ministry of Supply (new name for the MAP) head-on and side-view photographs were taken; contrary to usual practice these were not taken in the rain, nor was the aircraft surrounded by ladders and pails.

In 1947 English Electric had been fortunate in getting W/Cdr R. P. Beamont as chief test pilot. Roly Beamont, whose wartime exploits are legendary, spent 1948 checking out as many as he could of the 1,400 Vampires made at Samlesbury, while preparing himself for the A.1. In May 1949 the great day came, and he wasn't a bit perturbed that it was Friday the 13th, telling edgy Petter, "Why worry? It's a nice day, and we're serviceable." The flying programme began well and got better. Soon Bee was demonstrating that here was a bomber quite unlike the highly loaded Americans. He could fling it into a tight turn on take-off, orbit within the airfield while accelerating and then go into a loop, a roll or anything else he felt like. Thousands saw the new aircraft at the SBAC show at Farnborough in September 1949—a marvellous show which to a Britisher seemed like summer after a long winter, with the Viscount, Apollo, swept-wing prototypes and the Comet herself all real and smelling of kerosene. And it was Bee who electrified everyone by demonstrating a bomber in a way no bomber on Earth had ever been flown before.

By this time it had been named the Canberra. The British practice of giving aircraft names is a two-edged weapon. Canberra was the last of an era in which bomber names had to be cities. It did not come easily off the tongue, any more than would English Electric Auckland or Ottawa, and it led one to believe there was interest in the new bomber down under. This was too right. In the summer of 1949 the Australian government chose the new jet to succeed the lumbering Lincoln at the Government Aircraft Factories (GAF) at Fishermen's Bend, Melbourne. They also decided to engine it with the Rolls-Royce Tay centrifugal jet which they thought Commonwealth Aircraft could make more easily that the still slightly doubtful Avon.

They were pleased to discover that the airframe could hardly be simpler. Even the funny air brakes, in the form of a spanwise row of "fingers" that could be extended into the airstream, 12 under each wing and nine above, were easy to make. They were driven by a very ordinary hydraulic system, the electrics were 28 volts DC, the cabin was pressurized by engine bleed, and Dowty were happy to supply the only bit the Australians would have found difficult: the Liquid Spring in the twin-wheel nose gear. From the start English Electric had adopted an extensive mould lofting technique in which almost every part of the airframe was developed to a two-dimensional shape and accurately laid out on sheets of sensitized aluminium. There were about 600 such loft plates to the whole airframe. As the Australian version, the B.20, differed in some respects from the RAF machine (but fortunately not, after all, in engines) the GAF were sent loft plates drawn in non-reproducing ink on which their own engineers then inked in the parts to make a B.20. This use of lofting to assist others to make the aircraft had not been anticipated; it proved a marvellous bonus in Britain in 1950 and in the United States a year later, and this was even more unexpected.

As the Canberra was about as conventional as a jet bomber could be, its flight development was expected to be fairly painless, and so it proved. Bee romped through contractor's handling and then lost VN799 to the AAEE at Boscombe Down where Ministry pilots put it through 30 hours of initial assessment in 18 days. Up at Warton D. L. Ellis, who had said nobody knew how to build a transonic tunnel, found the answer himself. In July 1948 the first transonic tunnel in the British industry roared into life, driven by the ejector effect of aircraft jet engines. Such tunnels are costly in fuel bills but are cheap and quick to build and so suited the needs of the time. A further cause for satisfaction was that when the second aircraft, VN813, flew on 9 November 1949 its Nene engines were an insurance that seemed unlikely to be needed. But the programme was in deep trouble for reasons unconnected with the basic aircraft. On 12 November 1947 Specification B.5/47 had been issued for the production machine, and in March 1949 English Electric received an ITP on production machines. Jigging and manufacture went on at a cracking pace, and in July came the first definitive order, for 90 Canberra B.2s, 34 PR.3 reconnaissance aircraft and eight T.4 trainers, to be built in that order. Unfortunately the B.2 was not at all what the Air Staff had originally specified. It lacked the vital radar bombing system. In Petter's words, "From the start I had been troubled by the radar bombing system. I had considerable doubts about it in the early project stage. In 1949, with the four prototypes virtually complete and production gathering momentum, we had to make provision for a visual bomb-aimer in the nose, a third member of the crew. We threw out all the elaborate black boxes and put back wartime equipment. Had we done so earlier the Canberra would have reached the service earlier in a more useful condition." The failure to produce a radar bombing system for the Canberra was one of those monumental errors too big to get into the papers, and the poor public knew nothing about it.

Fortunately the collapse of the original two-seat radar Canberra was seen in time for the production programme, in both Britain and Australia, to be affected only slightly. The first production version was the B.2, to a revised visual-bombing specification B.5/47. The pilot stayed where he had been in the four prototypes, six inches left of the centre-line in an "office" reminiscent of that in a bomber Mosquito but more roomy. Behind him the navigator was moved from the centre-line hard up against the left wall, and the bomb-aimer seated on his right so that he could crawl round past the pilot to his old-fashioned bomb-sight in the transparent nose. English Electric flew the first of two B.2 prototypes (VX165 and VX185) on 23 April 1950. The first production Canberra (WD929) followed on 8 October and deliveries began early in 1951, to 101 Sqn, Bomber Command. Getting the Canberra into service ended a very trying period for the RAF.

In 1945 everyone wanted to forget about new armaments, and to the new Labour government this feeling was welcome. Nothing was done to stop a sharp run-down in RAF and aircraft-industry strength to very low levels indeed, based on a vague hope that the services of these organizations would not be wanted. The Berlin airlift of 1948–49 brought an agonizing twinge of doubt, and then on 25 June 1950 war broke out in Korea. In a matter of hours there was a situation that can only be described as panic. The simple fact was that the RAF did not possess one modern bomber, and English Electric could not build more than about five per month (they had delivered four-engined Halifaxes at the rate of 100 a month). After desperate meetings of the Cabinet the decision was taken to increase arms production by every possible measure. Economy was thrown to the winds. Almost overnight the Canberra was ordered from Avro, Handley Page and Short & Harland in Belfast, and its Avon engine was ordered from Bristol, Napier and Standard Motors. All these firms were in turn thrown into a panic trying to get hold of any labour with any productivity skills, tooling and raw materials. Short managed to fly Canberra B.2 WH853 on 30 October 1952, Avro flew WJ971 on 25 November and HP flew WJ564 on 5 January 1953. Later in 1953 an armistice was signed in Korea and Avro and HP were stopped at the 75th aircraft; Short went on to build other versions, as described later. It does not need special wit to see that a nation ought to avoid trying to make up for lost time by tooling up three big factories to boost output for one year.

Thus, in an extremely uneconomic way, production of the Canberra B.2 was raised to 13 per month. The first batches had sides and undersurfaces glossy black, but the colour was changed to greyish blue in 1952. When 101 Sqn became operational in May 1951 they were a picked bunch and had few major problems, even though they were the first British unit with axial engines. I flew with 101 and 9 Sqns and found it the proverbial piece of cake. High over Germany S/L Southall told me "Even in this bright moonlight there isn't a fighter could get near us. Even when we have proper jet night fighters I don't think we'll be intercepted." Back at Binbrook one felt relaxed, unlike the old days when crews had to shout into each other's earholes for hours afterwards.

In 1952 I visited 231 Operational Conversion Unit, at Bassingbourn. Here it was a rather different story. Experienced pilots were busy converting very inexperienced National Servicemen on to these fine machines. Although the Canberra could hardly have been more undemanding it was very worrying to find pupils flying straight into the ground a mile or two beyond the airfield. Meteor pilots were doing the same thing even more frequently. Eventually the cause was traced to a powerful "seat of the pants" sensation experienced by the pilot and the conflicting readings of the flight instruments when overshooting in bad visibility when external cues were absent. Instructors discovered pupils determinedly trying to keep the nose down and avoid stalling, even though their VSI told them they were accelerating on the level or actually diving. It did no good for an instructor to shout at a pupil "Believe your instruments", because the vital artificial horizon progressively mis-read under the sustained high horizontal acceleration possible with the powerful new jets. It seems a pity that, although English Electric reported on this characteristic, and warned that it should be watched in training, it should have caused many tragic write-offs. Pity, too, that the side-by-side dual-control Canberra T.4, built to a 1949 specification (T.2/49), should not have reached 231 OCU until 1954. Today military pilots would not consider that the Canberra had a high ratio of thrust to weight, and they use flight instruments which do not rely on the pendulous weights that caused the false readings; but at the time the problem was real enough.

It is also odd that the first photo-reconnaissance Canberra, the PR.3, should have been developed to a 1946 (!) specification yet not introduced until 1953. Apart from trading bombs for a set of traditional visible-light cameras, the PR.3 carried extra fuel in the bomb bay and needed only pilot and navigator. In October 1953 a PR.3 specially equipped for fast gravity fuelling won the speed section of the race from Heathrow to Christchurch, New Zealand, covering 12,270 miles in nine minutes under 24 hours.

Canberras had been setting world point-to-point records long before this. The first was on 31 August 1951 when a B.2, with Bee at the helm, flew from Aldergrove, Northern Ireland, to Gander, Newfoundland, in 4 hr 18 minutes at over 481 mph against the wind. The aircraft was being delivered as a pattern machine to what was then the Glenn L. Martin Co. of Baltimore, who the previous 19 April had signed a licence agreement with English Electric to make Americanized versions for the US Air Force. This deal, coming as it did at a time when the British felt they had a sort of "world lead" in aviation, tended to be smugly accepted as proof of that lead instead of marvelled at as a remarkable achievement. Martin was a big and proud firm. It had aircraft in production as diverse as civil airliners, ocean patrol bombers, big flying boats and carrier attack aircraft. It had flown two prototype six-jet bombers which lost out to Boeing. In 1949 it had flown the first XB-51 three-jet attack bomber which looked one of the most advanced aircraft of its day and the direct antithesis of the supremely ordinary Canberra.

George Bunker, who joined the company as president in 1952, told me how they felt when the US Air Force told them instead of the XB-51 they were to make the British Canberra. "Frankly, we were disgusted. Building a foreign plane was something our industry had never done [he should have said "almost never"] and a lot of us took it almost like a personal insult . . . Glenn Martin was in his last year as board chairman; it seemed a poor reward for a lifetime of service to the US military . . . but gradually the Air Force convinced us there was nothing personal in it. They simply thought the Canberra a fine plane, just what they wanted for the Korean war. They wanted us to tool up for a very high rate. The program was to be a big one, and it looked like trouble-free work which we badly needed. By the time I joined Martin English Electric's Glen Hobday was making us all fall for the British, and Roly Beamont had amazed everyone at the Middle River plant by the way he flew the ship he brought over. We had no real difficulty turning your Canberra into our B-57 and I think it gave us fewer problems than any other major program this decade." Bunker impressed me. He was the man who, when the last Canberra was out of the door, said Martin had "sloughed off its emotional attachment to the airplane" and was henceforth in the rocket business.

Nevertheless Americanization was perhaps a bigger job than it need have been. Martin's v-p for sales, Jess Sweetser, said "Out of 2,800 engineering changes I reckon 2,700 have been made just to comply with US standards . . . there's been a massive waste of effort here; how's about our two countries trying to get together a bit?" (Today I think the "waste of effort", on Phantoms, Harriers and other Anglo-American types, has been even greater in terms of cost; but we're still trying to get together.)

Probably the biggest improvement made in the B-57 was the rotary bomb door. The bomb bay was enclosed by a large door carried on rotary pivots at each end. All the internal stores were mounted on the inside of the door which was hydraulically flicked through 180° for bomb release. The scheme worked wonderfully; curiously, it was never transferred to British Canberras and was not used in Britain until the Buccaneer, flown in 1958. Other changes in the B-57 were aerodynamic and mechanical improvements to the flying controls, the addition of underwing stores pylons and, before the main production started, the fitting of eight 0·5 in guns in the wings. Engines were British Sapphires of early vintage which were hurriedly Americanized by Curtiss-Wright as the J65—with a lot of headaches—and put into volume production by Wright and Buick at a 7,200 lb rating for the B-57, A-4 Skyhawk and F-84F Thunderstreak. They had some of the first cartridge starters ever made in the United States, and starting early B-57s caused each engine to squirt out dense black smoke that enveloped the whole flight line. Although someone pointed out such a smoke-screen might be useful in wartime, and also give a good idea of the surface wind, smokeless propellant was welcomed in 1953, some months after the first Martin-built machine flew on 20 July.

To achieve the desired rate of output Martin subcontracted a great deal of the B-57 in the way that has become standard for big programmes. Martin were delighted at the photo-lofting technique and distributed copy plates to all subcontractors. But one firm whose plates must have been a bit off-focus was Kaiser, because their first set of ailerons refused to fit Martin's wings. English Electric rushed over ailerons from Preston which fitted perfectly, and these were in use on the first B-57 flight. Subsequently Martin made a total of 403 B-57s in a programme smaller and slower than planned because of the Korean cease-fire. All but the first 75 had a completely new forward fuselage seating pilot and navigator in tandem beneath a huge upward-hingeing canopy, and all except the final batches were delivered in an overall finish of glossy black that has seldom been applied to any other US type except the wartime P-61 Black Widow. Compared with contemporary Canberras the B-57s were at least as nice to fly and marginally faster.

Why did the Pentagon buy the Canberra, the first foreign aircraft made for the US government since 1918? The short answer is "because it was right, and nothing else was". The Korean campaign had from the outset called for a close-support tactical strike aircraft having the performance of a jet, good load-carrying capability, short field length, long range and endurance and the volume and systems needed for the inclusion of advanced radars and other half-baked sensing and navigational devices to enable it to find battlefield targets at night or in bad weather. The British Canberra was exactly right on every count, even though it had been designed for something quite different. No US aircraft available off-the-shelf could come anywhere near it. For example Martin's own XB-51, seemingly a far more advanced and impressive machine, was not only several years away from service but it needed double the field length, was much less flexible and versatile and promised to cost twice as much.

To me the funniest part of the whole story is that in mid-1953, when Martin were just getting into their stride with producing the B-57, the Korean war ended. The US Air Force cut back sharply on the programme and, perhaps inevitably, polarized their thinking around global conflicts with the Russians and spent astronomic sums on global bombers and missiles. The vital need for a short-field jet attack machine, carrying all the sensors needed to find and hit battlefield targets at night or in the rain, seemed so humdrum in comparison it was almost forgotten. Then when war flared up again in Vietnam the US Air Force found itself armed to the teeth with totally unsuitable aircraft. Suddenly the pendulum swung right over in the other direction and throughout the 1960s the Pentagon hummed with "LARA" and "Coin" attack proposals and other projects all too simple and too small to do the job. Finally after Westinghouse had developed a low-light TV system and laser ranging, and Texas Instruments had developed a new multi-mode radar and infra-red detection system, the whole lot were at last put together with suitable armament in the B-57G, first flown by Martin (now called Martin Marietta Corporation) in 1969. By this time the B-57 had been out of production some 13 years and good airframes were scarce.

Martin and later General Dynamics also produced very much altered versions of the B-57 intended for reconnaissance at extreme altitudes. The final variants were incredible machines that could outclimb a U-2, with span double the value selected by Petter and engines three times as powerful: but they are not bombers, so their story must wait for another time.

Meanwhile, back in Britain in 1952–53 Canberra B.2s were being built in four plants at the rate of 13 or 14 a month. By modern standards this is impressive, but it really betokens a crippling rundown in the productive capacity of the aircraft industry. During the war much larger four-engined heavies had been made at the rate of 400 a month despite material shortages and disruption caused by enemy action, and on top of a tremendous workload overhauling and repairing aircraft already in operational service. By 1952 the plants had been run down and the labour dispersed, and the government seemed genuinely surprised to find it so. Sir George Nelson, chairman of English Electric, was one of those called to explain to Sir

Winston Churchill, who had become Prime Minister in 1951, how bad the situation was. Churchill was horrified, and within two weeks, in March 1952, announced the "Superpriority" scheme whereby certain named aircraft programmes had absolute priority for scarce labour, machine tools, raw material and anything else. In the case of the Canberra this did help a bit because it removed one or two bottlenecks in manufacture caused by shortage of material (notably high-strength steels) and machining capacity. But labour was a desperate problem, and remained so; and Superpriority could do little to speed the development of the urgently needed swept-wing machines. Altogether the period is indelibly etched in my memory as the last time an intelligent government thought it could swiftly increase production by legislation.

There is a further basic fault in the British procurement policy of the time which, hopefully, has been cured. The Treasury seemed to have no interest in the overall expenditure but to exert an intense interest in what was being spent each week. As a result everything was bought on the penny-pinching "drip feed" system. This was not too bad with items like "trousers, blue-grey, airman", but for advanced aircraft it was disastrous. It meant the manufacturer had to make out a case for every trivial item of expenditure, and was even unable to buy items having a long lead-time, such as special alloy raw materials which were in short supply and on which months of work would have to be done, until each aircraft had been ordered. It was rather like the housewife who saves money by buying everything in the smallest possible quantity. At the end of the year the other kind of housewife, who bulk-buys and has a deep freeze, has not only enjoyed a higher standard of living but has also spent less. The argument appeared either not to be noticed by the Treasury or else not believed. So in 1949 English Electric received an order not for the RAF requirement of 400 Canberra bombers, but for 90. Then they received an order for a further 75 in 1950. Ultimately 430 were made of the original B.2 model alone, and altogether 925 were built in Britain, but the benefits of big production were largely nullified by the procedure of buying in penny numbers. Today multi-national collaborative programmes are sometimes held to give a much bigger initial production run, enabling the manufacturers to plan ahead properly. In fact the big change is simply that, in order to take part in such a programme, the British system has had to be changed. If the Canberra had been a collaborative venture Britain would have bought 400 at the start, to everyone's benefit.

An initial buy of 400 would have enabled both the industry and RAF to build up their emasculated strength with complete assurance. As it was, Bomber Command was as run-down as the industry and from 1950 until 1953 its personnel were sorely extended in assimilating Canberras and in training aircrew and tradesmen. But by late 1952 it was possible to divert a few Canberras to other purposes, and since that time the Canberra has been the most versatile and useful flying test bed and research aircraft in the world. Except for the monstrous Gyron, there is scarcely a single British turbojet for aircraft propulsion developed since 1952 that has not been tested in the Canberra. One of the earliest conversions, flown in August 1952, was the first pair of flight-cleared Olympus. On 4 May 1953 Wally Gibb took this aircraft quite effortlessly to a new world altitude record of 63,668 feet, and on 29 August 1955 he reached 65,889 feet. Slightly less effortlessly, but with consummate skill, Mike Randrup of D. Napier & Son beat this on 28 August 1957 when he coaxed an ordinary Canberra fitted with a Double Scorpion rocket pack to 70,310 feet. It was tantalizing to think what could have been done with a Canberra having twice the span, Olympus 300s and a Double Scorpion. Apparently the RAF, unlike the US Air Force, have no requirement to fly high.

A brief aberration occurred in the Canberra story with the B.5, a one-off conversion of the second prototype B.2, VX185. In 1948 the Air Staff decided it would be nice to have special target markers equipped with extra radar and preferably cleared to fly faster at low level. Conversions were ordered of the Canberra and Valiant. The Canberra B.5 made provision for lots of avionics that never materialized, but it was built to the visual specification B.22/48 and so sensibly retained a flat aiming panel under the nose. It had integral fuel tanks in the wings and introduced the 7,500 lb Avon 109 with a triple-breech starter in an enlarged cylindrical bullet fairing; with the original engine any failure to light up at once meant a wait of several minutes while an erk found something to stand on and then changed the cartridge. The B.5 was not built in quantity, but the new engine and extra fuel were logically transferred to the original B.2 to produce the B.6, and this began to replace the earlier mark in 1954. Like the B.2 it found modest export sales and served as the basis for much further development. Short Brothers, by then the only second-source, made 30 of the total of 129. The equivalent reconnaissance version was the PR.7, and this in turn was developed by Short into the most advanced of all British Canberras, the PR.9, but this is again outside the scope of this book.

On 23 July 1954 English Electric flew the first B(I).8, an aircraft that greatly extended the versatility of the Canberra in the way Petter had envisaged. At last the Air Staff came away from their vision of a crew sitting remotely in a radar-packed machine at 50,000 feet and issued a requirement for an interdictor intended to operate at low level in visual contact with the ground and packed not with radar but with guns, bombs and rockets. In some ways the B(I).8 parallels what Martin did with the tandem-seat B-57B, except that in the British machine the pilot climbs in through a door on the right side and takes his seat on the extreme left under a fixed offset canopy, the bomb/nav, the only other crew member, being seated in the nose. Beneath the wings are two 2,000 lb store pylons. Under the rear half of the bomb bay projects a pack containing four 20 mm Hispano guns, of the same basic type as Marc Birkigt designed in 1917, plus enough ammunition for almost a minute of continuous firing. In the forward bomb bay a tactical nuclear weapon can be carried, with a yield greater than that of the "nominal nuclear bomb" assumed in designing the RAF's first four-jet bombers in 1947 which was 10 feet in diameter and 30 feet long! The first B(I).8 was a rebuild of the B.5. It was followed by 74 for an eagerly waiting RAF (mainly 2nd TAF in Germany) plus useful export orders including no fewer than 66 for India. Pity this machine, which combined the versatility of practically all the marks of Mosquito in a single aircraft, was not introduced earlier. A particular virtue appreciated by pilots is its improved field of view. It would have been even better if it had sensors to find battlefield targets at night or in bad weather, but this would have "doubled the cost of the programme" (said the RAF).

While waiting for the B(I).8 some 2nd TAF squadrons, notably No 213, received the B(I).6, a B.6 fitted with the gun pack and underwing pylons but retaining the old crew layout. This was a sensible conversion from two points of view. Not only did it help 2nd TAF fulfil its low-level mission, while losing nothing in high-altitude effectiveness, but it also reflected the gradual decline in the "penetrability" of the high-altitude bomber. When the Canberra was designed, the jet engine and atom bomb had given the bomber a quite extraordinary increase in effectiveness, but by 1955 the development of guided weapons had—predictably—begun to turn the tables. It was in 1955, just as the expensive force of high-altitude V-bombers was beginning to be formed, that the RAF finally accepted that the high-altitude bomber was fast becoming a suicidal way of delivering explosives, except possibly in so-called "limited" or "brush-fire" conflicts. Low-level trials with specially instrumented Canberras began in that year and by 1956 it was policy to equip all RAF bombers with a fatigue meter, mounted as close as possible to the centre of gravity, through the glass window of which could be read the number of times the meter had exceeded specified positive and negative accelerations in the vertical plane, thus giving a rough idea of the number and severity of the bending reversals imparted to the airframe. This "life" meter is quite separate from the normal-accelerometer fitted to the pilot's instrument panel to prevent him pulling more than $4\,g$ in manoeuvres ($4\,g$ is the service limit, although the structure is designed for $7 \cdot 5\,g$).

In the case of the Canberra it was concluded that in the atmospheric turbulence common in Western Europe an ultimate airframe fatigue life of 20,000 hours should be possible with no major structural modification. But the element of uncertainty in such figures is so great that a scatter factor of 40 was applied, resulting in a "safe life" (whatever that means) of 500 hours' low-level operation. At the end of this time the airframe is either rebuilt, for the RAF or an overseas customer, or scrapped. Even quite early Canberras generally have about half their safe life still unused, because the average crew can stand no more than a few minutes at a time at 450 knots at sea level! In special trials Canberras of the Ministry of Aviation went far beyond the allowable g accelerations in 1960–63 in the course of "limit finding" tests to explore just how much light alloys and human beings can stand. Missions were flown at full power at low level over the Libyan desert at ambient temperatures exceeding 100° F to provide statistical data for the TSR.2 programme. I don't think anyone suggested trying to use these particular Canberras again.

One of the difficulties of attacking at low level is that if you drop a nuclear weapon you blow yourself up. Thinking this would be unpopular with aircrew the US Air Force and Minneapolis-Honeywell jointly devised the low-altitude bombing system (LABS) which transferred to bombers the automated, computer-controlled flight-trajectory technology already developed for all-weather fighters. Also known as toss-bombing, LABS involves programming an airborne computer with precise details of target location in relation to an identifiable ground landmark. Near the target the computer is placed in sole charge of the flight control system and at the appropriate place it pulls the bomber up into a firm zoom climb, releasing the weapon at a programmed point so that it carries on arching up in a steep ballistic parabola to a height of several thousand feet. The bomber keeps pulling round in a traditional Immelmann turn, finally rolling out from the inverted position and going back more or less the way it came. It should have at least a minute, worth about eight miles to a Canberra, before the bang. Honeywell began to deliver LABS to the USAF in 1954, while research continued to see whether the "forward toss" was better than the "over the shoulder" technique. By 1955 LABS was urgently being developed in Britain, but, although the problems had already been solved once, the British hardware ran behind schedule and in January 1956 £267,580 was spent on Honeywell equipment to fill the gap.

Even today it is not possible to comment at length on nuclear weapons, but from the earliest days of such devices it has been British policy to be self-sufficient. I believe that the only time this policy was waived was when US tactical bombs were supplied in 1954 and issued to Canberra squadrons in the absence of a British weapon of this size. The same bombs were eventually passed on to the Valiant squadrons that replaced the

Canberra force assigned to NATO (Saceur) in 1958–63. So far as I know none was ever dropped. But during the Suez crisis early in November 1956 Canberras dropped live h.e. on Egyptian targets in an episode which would have seemed less unsavoury had not American pressure forced it to be unsuccessful. In contrast, no such emotion was generated by Canberra strikes against guerillas in Malaya, which 45 Sqn did from 1957 to 1960, nor the sudden dash to Kuwait in 1961 nor the prolonged Canberra presence in Cyprus.

From 1955 the Canberra gradually faded from the scene in Bomber Command and assumed different burdens in the Near and Far East in specially equipped conversions such as the B.15 (with Decca Doppler, among other things) and B.16. Dozens served as special trials test beds, radar trainers and, even today, as patient towers of all sorts of targets. Perhaps one day there will be an opportunity to relate more of the countless stories of the deeds of Canberras in every corner of the globe. Here just one must suffice. In 1957 two aircraft were taken from 76 Sqn at Hemswell, fitted with Double Scorpion rocket engines and flown out to Christmas Island in the remote Pacific to sample nuclear-test fallout at extreme altitudes. In April 1958 F/Ls De Salis and Lowe had to make a hurried exit from one at over 56,000 feet, which may be the greatest height from which a crippled aircraft has ever been abandoned. Both men free-fell to 10,000 feet, suffering acutely from intense cold which initially was 97° F below zero. De Salis' stabilizer chute hit something as he ejected, and for "several minutes" he was semi-conscious in a wild spin with his arms flung out above his head. Lowe fell face-down for what "seemed like a day and a half" before his main canopy deployed. They must have thought it ironic that by this time the Canberra had become a low-level aircraft.

High level or low, the Canberra has made a contribution to Britain's defence many times greater than I think could have been predicted in 1949, even though in my view the basic airframe cried out for really bold and imaginative development, with a high-lift wing, fan engines and advanced sensors, that could today have made it the world's pre-eminent tactical attack aircraft and taken the whole world market for machines in the USAF "AX" category through the 1980s. Even with the timid development it actually received the Canberra proved incredibly hard to replace in its native land, and the TSR.2, AFVG and F-111 are names most Britons would rather forget. At last, as I write, the MRCA is fast taking shape under the hands of the men who made the Canberra, and their sons. And the BAC Military Aircraft Division in Lancashire has earned close to £100 million in exports of the one jet bomber every air force on Earth could operate.

Short SA.4 Sperrin

THIS WAS planned to be Britain's first big long-range jet bomber, to succeed the Lincoln in RAF Bomber Command. It didn't turn out that way. It never reached the RAF at all, but the work of Short Brothers and Harland Ltd in creating it was technically competent and in some ways outstanding. In including the Sperrin I can begin a critical commentary on British big-bomber philosophy throughout the crucial immediate post-1945 years, so that the same ground does not all have to be retraced in the stories of the V-bombers (Valiant, Vulcan and Victor).

Standing well back to take in the whole scene it is possible to assess the work of the three major victors of World War 2. The Soviet Union had an immense leeway to make up, and accomplished more than ten years of it in one jump by copying the American B-29 and putting it into production in a remarkably short time. Then they very quickly achieved production with a twin-jet tactical bomber and could have done the same with a big four-Nene aircraft, but chose to wait until a very large axial engine became available in 1952. They also elected to put the British 1943 idea of a "gas turbine heavy bomber" into practice and in doing so combined huge turboprops with swept wings; the result ought to have been a disaster but instead was a resounding success, as the Tupolev Tu-20 "Bear" testifies.

In the United States there was such a wealth of talent, manpower, money and energy that five impressive USAF jet bombers flew between March and December 1947. All were quite unlike each other. The first and most conventional was picked for rapid production as a stop-gap, and the last and most radical soon showed itself as the best. Meanwhile studies went on with a much bigger global jet bomber which finally emerged in 1952 when suitable engines were available. At the broad policy level there were practically no mistakes, no waste of money and no duplication.

In Britain the dynamic nation of World War 2 seemed to be rather tired. To recall the atmosphere of the times, the RAF draft sent from my station to help work the London docks (which were on strike) was held up for 12 hours because the train driver could get no coal. When they finally arrived at Hornchurch in bitterly cold weather there was no fuel to heat the hangars in which they were billeted, and the inadequate messing facilities ran out of food (and nobody could buy any from a shop unless he had the right coupons). In the aircraft industry harassed designers tried to create splendid jet bombers in soggy wooden huts in the rain while wondering how their shapes would behave in a transonic wind-tunnel, if there existed such a thing (there didn't, because the ones in Germany were pinched by our Allies). There was inadequate labour, inadequate material, inadequate money and above all inadequate incentive. The industry's weakness, and inability to keep pace with fast-moving aircraft technical development, tended to be masked by the fact that there was nothing much demanded of it. The government, preoccupied with the National Health and Ground Nuts schemes, hated spending its pennies on military aircraft. Little was done, and that slowly.

In September 1947 an official statement, unsigned but apparently having the authority of the Secretary of State for Air, announced that "A contract was placed 2½ years ago for a medium-range bomber with two 'straight' jet engines, having a speed approximately twice that of current reciprocating-engined bombers". This was, of course, the Canberra, and either the author of the statement thought the date of the specification was the date of the contract or else he tried to mislead the public by a year. The announcement continued, "A second contract was placed a year ago for a longer-ranged heavy bomber of performance otherwise very similar to the twin-engined machine; this aircraft will be powered by four straight jet engines". This, referring to the Sperrin, again was the date of the specification, not that of the contract which was signed only three months before the announcement. And it concluded, "Demand by the Air Staff during the past 18 months for still higher performance in terms of speed, range and operating height have led to further careful studies by the Ministry of Supply and design teams in the aircraft industry. To effect these last improvements it will probably be necessary to adopt some unorthodox shape of wing . . ."

I doubt if anyone at that time would have credited that, whereas the conventional four-jet bomber would never go into production, not one but two types of "unorthodox shape" bombers would go into full production and operational service, preceded by yet another type which seemed rather a good idea as well. Bearing in mind that such aircraft represented an enormous technical challenge, and that the British industry's meagre resources were already thinly spread over a great profusion of military and civil projects of all kinds, it is not to be wondered at that the three V-bombers plus the Sperrin sorely extended the industry still further, took a long time, cost about twice as much as a single programme for the same production total, and led to usable end products just at the time that high-altitude bombers began to be regarded as no longer viable in the face of missile defences.

It is simple to think up all sorts of reasons for what was done. In 1947 unorthodox shapes were regarded as new-fangled and unproven. Nobody remembered that Büsemann had reported on the high-Mach improvements possible with swept wings before the war, in a published paper that had been on file in the Air Ministry for nine years. Nobody had done any swept-wing research in Britain during the war, and in 1945 the tiny UK team that tried to comb Germany for interesting aeronautical developments found the plums already picked. They did bring back some crates full of paper on which were printed tunnel test results on swept and delta wings. In the US all such things were greedily devoured and soberly put to good use, but in Britain there was an odd psychological blockage. The German data had been gathered by Germans for Germans, and there was no reason to suggest that any of the figures were suspect. Yet the immediate reaction of almost all British experts was that it was all "futuristic" (whatever that means), had no immediate relevance and would in any case all have to be done again in Britain (when we had somehow provided ourselves with the equipment to do it). Sir Sydney Camm, an outstanding fighter designer who had most to gain from such data, dismissed it all with a mixture of anger and laughter. Bomber designers were less outspoken but I do not know of a single one who was impatient to put an "unorthodox shape" into the sky.

So it is not difficult to excuse the planners who in 1947, the year the B-47 flew, decided it would be a good idea to order Britain's first big jet bomber with straight wings. In introducing major new technological developments it is supposedly less risky—if one can afford the extra time and cost—to make haste slowly and progress in stages rather than in a giant leap. Specification B.14/46, conceived in 1946 but issued on 6 October 1948, which gave Britain the Short SA.4 Sperrin, was a sound insurance policy intended to give Bomber Command a jet-propelled "heavy" at the earliest possible date. The only thing really wrong with it was the timing. In the United States the equivalent requirement was drafted in 1943, and the resulting hardware emerged in 1947. For example, the Convair XB-46, which on early 4,000 lb axial engines could reach 565 mph and carry a 20,000 lb bomb load, flew on 2 April 1947. The first SA.4, which was 1 mph slower and carried the same bomb load, flew on 10 August 1951. So the crucial question is not "Why did Britain order the SA.4 in 1947?" but instead "Why did Britain not order it in 1943?" It would have done quite nicely with centrifugal Tay engines in 1946 and could have begun to replace the Lincoln in 1948. As it was, our giant slippage in advanced aircraft began during the war, and probably stemmed from the fact that everyone involved was interested only in things that could end the war, whereas in the United States people could see beyond it. Indeed, why should not a jet bomber have had relevance to World War 2? It did in Germany.

B.14/46 specified a big aircraft, with a permissible weight of 140,000 lb, capable of carrying a "special bomb" weighing 10,000 lb and measuring no less than 10 feet in diameter by 30 feet long, to a target 1,730 miles from a base "anywhere in the world" at great height and speed and capable of taking evasive action and deploying radar countermeasures. It was to be fitted with an "advanced H₂S system" for navigation and bombing, with a stand-by visual sight in the nose, an ejection seat for the pilot, to be used after the "rapid" bale-out of the rest of the crew (who did not have such a benefit), and an absence of any new or difficult features in order to facilitate "rapid quantity production" and "easy maintenance". For the obvious bomber firms it was difficult to know how far they should commit themselves to what ought to be only an interim design. The chief designers—George Edwards of Vickers, Stu Davies of Avro and R. S. Stafford of Handley Page, all appointed in 1945—had to decide whether to go flat out for the supposedly easy B.14/46 or try for the more difficult but potentially bigger prize with the "unorthodox shape" they knew was coming. All three had a go at B.14/46, but the firm that was chosen was Short. I still have a feeling this was not because their submission was the best—although the Ministry of Supply said it was—but because they wanted Vickers, Avro and HP to be free to tackle the difficult one.

Short Brothers were in the throes of moving from Rochester, Kent, to Queen's Island, Belfast, next to the shipyard of Harland & Wolff with whom they had become associated. In 1947 most of the works had gone, but the design staff under C. P. T. Lipscombe and David Keith-Lucas were still on the banks of the Medway. In addition to a profusion of versions of the Sunderland, Sandringham, Seaford, Solent and Shetland flying boats, and the new Sealand amphibian, Sturgeon and SB.3 land-planes, the experimental Sherpa and a few other types, the project staff were busy with proposals for the B.14/46 bomber, the N.7/46 jet fighter and the SA.5 transport. I am not sure whether a whole man could be assigned to the bomber, but he did a good job. And lack of men was matched only by lack of facilities. Although they were "the first builders of aircraft in the world", the company had never possessed a wind tunnel—not even a slow one. Models of the bomber could have been taken to the RAE at Farnborough or the NPL at Teddington, but this would have meant waiting in the queue for several months. Lipscombe did what others have done since: he used his flying-boat towing tank as a hydraulic analogy tunnel and pulled through the water suitably distorted models from which he could get measurements approximating to those obtained with the true shape in a stream of air. And to argue that one look at the SA.4 betrays the fact that it was designed without a tunnel seems to me unkind.

There really was little room to manoeuvre. The wing had to be an ordinary shape, and it was a foregone conclusion it would have a 12 per cent thick laminar-flow section. It had to be mounted well above the mid position in order to leave room for the cavernous bomb bay, and the front end of the fuselage was dictated by the big pressure drum for the five crew members (although perhaps one might not have expected the fat tube leading down like an elephant trunk to the visual bombing windows). The whole underside of the nose was to be full of the "advanced H_2S" which helped provide an excuse for the enormous flying-boat proportions of the hull. Fuel was contained in 22 bag tanks, eight of them in the fuselage. Superficially the most startling feature was the way the four early 6,500 lb Rolls-Royce Avon axial engines were carried on steel-tube space frames above and below the wing in unique double-deck nacelles, but really there was nothing radical here. Much more bold was British Messier's 4,000 lb/sq in hydraulic system and fine bogie main landing gear, which broke much new ground and incidentally helped that supplier make similar contributions to the Britannia. The main gears folded inwards, and I doubt if any other jet bomber could have an inspector inside the undercarriage bay to check the sequencing of the various items during the retraction and extension. Another feature used on the Britannia was the fully manual servo-tab control system. At first Lipscombe schemed powered flying controls but, perhaps because of the awful experience with the electric rack-and-pinion controls of the Shetland (and these were very early days for powered flying controls), he finally made the cockpit controls drive long cable-runs to screwjacks connected to the surface tabs. Ever since the Sperrin I have cherished a belief—or at least a wish to believe—that on subsonic aircraft powered controls are an admission of failure. The only major source of risk in the whole aircraft seemed to be the widespread high-strength light alloy (75ST to DTD.687) which was already known to shatter when overloaded instead of showing a nice elongation. But the ruling stresses were kept remarkably low for a jet bomber, and I particularly liked the way all the skin rivets were inserted into hot-dimpled countersinks and then milled flush.

As a result VX158 may have looked like a great whale but her standard of finish was excellent. A contributory factor was that all her main portions were constructed in production jigs at Queen's Island, the MAP having been quite happy to pay for production tooling before the first flight in order to speed eventual quantity deliveries. This was not done with the three V-bombers, yet the SA.4 was the only one of the four types never to go into production. Moreover, the urge to get this interim machine quickly into service, as a replacement for the Lincoln, was thwarted by a four-month delay in the issue of drawings caused by the move to Belfast and then by further fiddling delays in the winter of 1950–51 while VX158 was assembled, tested, pulled to bits, put on road trailers, trucked to Alder-grove (today's Belfast Airport) and then put together again. It was not until 10 August 1951 that Tom Brooke-Smith was able to begin the flight-test programme, and by this time the company knew that the Vickers 660—which had beaten the SA.4 into the air—was being bought instead.

This was tough on the Short team, whose product always seemed to me better than it looked. Flight trials went swimmingly, and when one recalls the interminable problems Gloster had with the ailerons of the Meteor it is possible to see that conventional airframes need not be trouble-free. There were just a few vibrations and buffets that were quickly cured, one lot of trouble stemming from the old-fashioned bomb doors and another from the junctions between the jet nozzles near the wing trailing edge where small boat-tails were added in a way that had to be done 12 years later with the nacelles of the VC10. The flying-control screwjacks ceased to be irreversible when coated with a thin film of ice, and diving at 18,000 ft/min caused atmospheric pressure to rise so fast that the fuel cells collapsed. But on the whole Brooke-Smith, Wally Runciman and Jock Eassie found the SA.4 most agreeable, even on the 6,500 lb engines. Its standard of serviceability was well-nigh perfect, and quite incredible for a machine subjected to so little "development"; Hugh Conway, when he was chief engineer at Belfast around 1955, said to me "how do you 'develop' an aircraft that won't go wrong?" VX158 per-formed well at the 1951 SBAC show and later, when it had been named for the Sperrin mountains of its native Ulster, it appeared in an odd paint scheme of mainly black and dark grey that hardly conformed to any official scheme.

VX161, flown on 12 August 1952, was the second and last Sperrin, although a third airframe was tested to destruction in a mighty static test frame at Belfast. Subsequently 161 did sterling work at Farnborough, Boscombe and Woodbridge backing up the Ashtons in flight development of radar bombing systems, navigation devices and weapon carriage and release, some of the more dramatic trials involving free drops of concrete models of Blue Boar and other proposed fearsome weapons (but not Blue Steel). Meanwhile 158 was picked as the only aircraft that could readily fly de Havilland's monstrous Gyron turbojet. Short put a Gyron in the left lower position and Eassie flew it on 7 July 1955; with the Avon above it at flight-idle it just about balanced the two right-hand engines at full power. On 26 June 1956 Eassie flew with Gyrons in both lower positions, only to lose the right main-gear door over the Irish Sea. A replacement was obtained by cannibalizing 161, which never flew again, and abandonment of the Gyron in May 1957 terminated 158's life also.

Short Brothers, whose major shareholder is the British government, received only a few pounds in scrap value for the tooling that was to have given birth to Britain's first fleet of heavy jet bombers. Like so many British programmes the Sperrin did it all the hard way, found out all the answers and then saw all but a few of the answers discarded unused. Had the design run to a timetable four years earlier this bulky yet tractable machine could have transformed Bomber Command, and would probably have found export sales as well. As it was, perhaps the best thing about the programme is that the total bill from start to finish was only £3·5 million, which today would not pay for the technical manuals.

Vickers-Armstrongs Valiant

VICKERS, who from 1918 had been a major supplier of heavy bombers to the RAF, saw production of the Wellington continue right through World War 2 in a way that few aircraft could rival. But their Warwick lost out competing with four-engined "heavies", and their somewhat unconventional Windsor appeared too late in the war to see production. From 1944 Rex Pierson at Weybridge directed studies of jet bombers, and these continued the following year under the bright new chief designer G. R. (later Sir George) Edwards. GRE showed such attributes that he later rose to become head of British Aircraft Corporation and in my view the pre-eminent figure in the whole British industry. In these difficult days I hope he has time to derive comfort picturing white Valiants rolling off the line, because, like the Viscount with which it ran parallel in timing, this was one of the very few British aircraft programmes since 1945 that was well planned, well managed and delivered the goods on time. And, like the Viscount, it nearly died at birth.

The turmoil in bomber design caused by jet propulsion and the atomic bomb (to use the language of the time) was rivalled by that due to the evolution of electronic systems permitting bombers to navigate without reference to the ground yet with a theoretical accuracy of the order of 100 feet. As long as the war lasted little was done to put all these developments to use—although, curiously enough, the Brabazon Committee was expressly convened to look ahead to the period after the war and plan new civil aircraft. Perhaps the planners genuinely hoped no military aircraft would be wanted when the war was over, but this is hard to credit. Whatever the reason, the Americans ordered their first jet bombers in 1943 and we ordered ours long after the war. We seemed to find the idea of a big high-Mach jet so daunting that years were spent merely thinking and talking, while the Americans were building. In the end, our definitive V-bombers, the Vulcan and Victor, were on the whole better than the American first-generation bomber, the B-47; but the thousandth B-47 was delivered before either of the British bombers was cleared for service, and the USAF counterparts of the Vulcan and Victor in terms of timing were the global B-52 and the Mach 2 B-58. In any case, by this time the notion of the big jet bomber serenely proceeding on its mission high in the stratosphere was due for swift erasure from the battle plans of the major powers. A missile could knock it down too surely.

Surface-to-air guided missiles were actively developed, to the point of guided test firings, in Germany during World War 2. So, for that matter, were air-to-air missiles. Obviously the Air Staff took these facts into account in drawing up Requirements for new bombers after World War 2, but I have never been able to discover how they did so. The general consensus of opinion among the people involved to whom I have been privileged to talk is that it was simply thought that new bombers could be developed quicker than effective missiles, so that it would be well worth while planning major high-altitude jet bomber programmes for the RAF in the expectation that these would have a useful lease of life before missiles made them obsolete. Thus the new bombers were a race against time. Yet there seemed a strange belief throughout Britain that there was all the time in the world. At the 1949 SBAC show I picked up a leaflet issued by the host establishment, the RAE, which explained, "Pure jet engines, swept-back wings, the possibility of supersonic speed and the achievement of high-altitude flight over great ranges are all unknown quantities, and it is too early to predict how they will affect future aircraft design". At this time supersonic flight was commonplace in the United States, the Sabre and Mig-15 were in squadron service in great numbers, and the B-47, a fully-swept 100-ton bomber, was in large-scale production. It is tempting to think the snail's pace of development in Britain was due to lethargy, but in fact a contributory root cause was a shortage of engineers and an even worse shortage of transonic tunnels and other research equipment.

This crippling environment of inadequacy was superimposed on a fundamental timescale that differed from those in the USA and Soviet Union. In the latter countries new airframes designed for high Mach numbers were flown at the earliest possible date, and production aircraft programmes were based on whatever engines and systems looked like being available in the same timescale. In Britain nothing comparable was done, apart from an extraordinary concentration on tailless and all-wing aircraft which were an aberration. There was nothing to prevent a British counterpart of the B-47, and the fact there was no such aircraft was because the British were still doodling on paper when the B-47 was in the air. And in this category of aircraft the main doodles were triggered by Specification B.35/46, issued in March 1947, which was an historic document. Whereas B.14/46, which resulted in the "conventional" Sperrin, laid down numerical targets for bomb-load and performance, B.35/46 merely called for "at least twice the speed and twice the over-target height" of current bombers (by which was meant the Lincoln), together with greater range and bomb-load. There was an overwhelming feeling that not enough was known about what might be achieved, and that the best specification would not include many numbers but would emphasize the freedom of design staffs to go all-out for the ultimate attainable. The basic lack of knowledge, of course, was only to be expected in a country without proper research facilities, but we did at least have six or more firms capable of tackling such a specification and of offering each other the sharpest possible competition. In a land having a single aircraft-manufacturing organization this vital incentive would be difficult to provide, to put it mildly, and a B.35/46-type document could lead to disaster.

As it was, Sir Roy Dobson of the Hawker Siddeley Group (and Avro in particular) professed to think unprintable things about Sir Frederick Handley Page, and Sir Fred heartily reciprocated. Vickers' strong men did not indulge in personalities, and GRE was too busy anyway. At Hatfield aloof de Havilland knew they would beat everyone at anything they chose to demean themselves by noticing, while Bristol and Short just wanted work. All these firms were involved in the discussions that led to B.35/46 and all submitted proposals. Nobody chose any form of propulsion other than four of the forthcoming axial engines buried in the wing roots. It was almost as if this most challenging branch of engineering was influenced by mere fashion. Boeing, who had more engineers and more research tools than all six firms combined, could produce data by the ton to show that a long-range bomber came out best with a high-aspect-ratio (slender) swept wing with engines distributed across the span in pods. In contrast the British parametric studies all seemed to start with the engines buried inside the wing as if this should be taken for granted instead of arriving at the best configuration as the result of comparing all possible arrangements.

As a result nobody will ever know what would have been the optimum high-subsonic bomber realizeable on paper in 1947. Probably nobody will ever know which of the B.35/46 submissions was really the best. The crippling lack of technical strength was manifest most directly in the fact that the Air Staff were unable to make a choice. Instead they picked the two most unconventional designs, the delta of Avro and the "crescent" wing of Handley Page, in the vague belief that one of these might show itself demonstrably superior. In the event the Air Staff never was able to choose between the two, in a way described in the histories of these aircraft, the Vulcan and Victor. This was bad enough, because it diluted the scarce industrial talent and approximately doubled the workload not only in the industry but also in the RAF, besides adding greatly to the cost and taking longer. On top of this, the Short bomber was already under contract as a low-risk insurance. As if this were not enough, the Air Staff kept having a second look at the unsuccessful Vickers design and suddenly thought it would be nice to have this one as well.

When the facts are starkly set down like this the lunacy of the whole situation is obvious, but at the time the procurement machine in the

Ministry of Supply found no difficulty in justifying its actions. Although the British government wanted to have nothing to do with costly armaments, it was a time of great and increasing danger, with British forces drastically cut in strength and generally armed with obsolete weapons, yet facing Communist forces of immense size led by governments that seemed implacably hostile. The provision of effective jet bombers having not even been started until long after the war, everything possible had to be done to guarantee that the RAF would get such equipment as soon as possible. The Short bomber was needed as an insurance. The Avro and HP designs seemed best in the long term. The Vickers design was very nearly as good, and promised to take a shorter time to develop, so it looked a better insurance than the Short machine. But, as the latter had already gone a long way, it was preferable to continue it. I repeat, these are the official arguments. It seems remarkable that contracts were not also placed with Bristol and de Havilland, just so that nobody should have felt left out.

This sort of thinking was a hangover from the days when new designs took a few weeks and cost a thousand pounds or so. Insurance policies and duplicated programmes were not uncommon, in case one manufacturer should fall down badly. In the era of jet engines and the uncharted realm of performance they made possible, the officials were afraid of making a hideous mistake. They appear to have been obsessed by the thought that they could commit the RAF to a new bomber that at some later time would prove to have crippling faults of a deep-seated nature that could not be cured. But it is difficult to see how such a state of affairs could have come about. If aircraft are fundamentally wrong it usually shows on paper. I can think of nothing in the structure, aerodynamics, propulsion or systems that could remain unknown to a late point in the programme and would then cause the whole design to be abandoned. The worst cases I can think of are three. In the F-111 many problems, of which the most severe was weight escalation, caused a shortfall in performance. In the Electra a hidden tendency of the propulsion system to pull the wings off was overcome by sheer technical capability in a matter of weeks. In the Comet 1 a tendency of the fuselage to rip open could have been swiftly rectified in exactly the same way but instead was treated as a huge national disaster. These three aircraft were really successes, and the abandonment of the Comet 1 was due to British psychology and certainly not because its fault was incurable. I feel the Air Staff and MoS were guilty of a gross error of judgement in ordering four big jet bombers. The belief that by so doing they were avoiding an unknown disaster that was most unlikely to happen should have been outweighed by the absolute certainty that they were throwing away any possibility of achieving parity in timing with the Americans (and, as was later discovered, the Russians). We appeared to prefer something fractionally better in very small numbers much later.

Even at the time, when it was most unusual and unpatriotic to question anything in British aviation, some people did have the nerve to ask why so many different aircraft, each far more complex and expensive than anything previously attempted, were being bought for the same job. The answers were not helpful. Duncan Sandys, Minister of Supply, said, "My answer is that in equipping an air force, as in racing, it is risky to put all your money on one horse, or to try to spot the winner too long before the race". George Ward, Under-Secretary of State for Air, said, "The Vulcan and Victor must be put to the test of squadron service so that it can be decided, in the interests of efficiency no less than of economy, whether to concentrate on one or both of them". Later, in 1955, Reggie Maudling, Sandys' successor, thought up a new reason: it was better to continue both bombers "than to transfer production of one aircraft to the factory of the other, which would result in widespread disruption". But the following year Air Commodore Rod Banks urged, "It should now be possible technically to assess each and choose that showing the superior overall advantages and future stretch capabilities". I suggested he ought to have said this in 1950, not 1956, and he replied, "I did". Fortunately, the cataclysmic shake-up in the British aviation scene in 1956–62 has probably ensured that no similar episode will ever occur again. As a tax-payer, I should not relish supporting three totally different Concorde programmes, even though the SST initially posed a higher technical risk than the V-bombers.

In all this long preamble the Vickers Valiant, subject of this chapter, has barely been mentioned. This is typical of the Valiant. It was seldom in the limelight, because a good programme is seldom news. It was started later than the Short Sperrin, flew earlier and was of much more advanced conception. I do not quarrel at all with the decision to drop the Sperrin in favour of the Valiant; but, on the day in 1950 when the decision was taken, Short ought to have been instructed to drop the Sperrin, production tooling and all, and bring all their effort to bear in helping to develop and manufacture the Valiant. And, by this time, a clear choice should have been made between deltas and crescents. That it was not was largely made possible by the competent performance of Vickers in actually providing the RAF with a modern deterrent force. They had had long enough to wait. Until the Valiant came, the only "heavies" in Bomber Command had piston engines, and the best equipment was the B-29 which was regarded as obsolescent in the US Air Force. The big Boeings had been supplied, for free, under a "Mutual Arms Aid" agreement of January 1950 (what we gave the Americans, to make it mutual, was not apparent). Arthur Henderson, Air Minister, said we should only need the B-29s "for a year or two, until our own new heavy bombers are ready". Pressed to say whether he meant his words to be taken literally, he feigned anger: "I am sure you do not expect me to give you the exact date . . . you must understand that the government have laid their plans well in advance, and our new aircraft will very soon be ready". Politicians probably hate being reminded of things they said; Henderson's year or two turned out to be five, and it is difficult to believe that the schedule was not known to him.

In fact Vickers-Armstrongs (Aircraft) Ltd did marvellously well in making the wait only five years. When the Air Minister talked of "a year or two" they had only been working on the Valiant just over a year, and they began deliveries approximately six years after receipt of the prototype contract. This was only a year longer than Boeing's performance with the B-47, and compares with eight years for the Vulcan and almost ten for the Victor. All three V-bombers enjoyed the Superpriority status (p. 26), and although the Vulcan and Victor were of more advanced design than the Valiant, requiring considerably more engineering development in airframe construction and systems, this was partly counteracted by the fact that Vickers had to find numerous answers first and thus helped the two aircraft that came later. Overall, although it is impossible to prove, I think the gross effort Vickers had to put into the Valiant was not greatly inferior to that needed to produce the initial production versions of either the Vulcan or Victor. It was the performance of Vickers that took much of the pressure off Avro and HP, who would otherwise have been in an extremely difficult position.

But nobody took any pressure off Vickers. From the outset their Type 660 was regarded, often rather unfairly, as simple and easy and therefore quick to develop, whereas the Avro 698 and HP.80 were regarded as terribly futuristic and likely to encounter all sorts of problems. Specification B.35/46 was considered a great challenge, and the Avro and HP proposals were supposed to meet it fully. The Vickers 660, although it offered combinations of range and bomb-load much greater than anything possible with the Lincoln, or even the B-29, could not equal the values predicted for the Avro and HP studies. The latter, of course, were somewhat ephemeral because they were based on such intangibles as the specific fuel consumptions of engines that did not yet exist. But the best is often the enemy of the good, and in January 1948 the Avro delta and HP crescent were chosen and the Vickers proposal was thrown out.

At this time the Viscount had yet to fly, and BEA had just ordered a fleet of Ambassadors, apparently killing the project stone dead; and there was a limited future for the Viking family. GRE knew how important the 660 was to Weybridge, and he privately refused to take "no" for an answer. He kept his foot in the MoS door and in March 1948 achieved his first giant success by making the officials change their minds. There can be very, very few occasions in the history of military aircraft procurement where such a thing has been achieved. The official explanation in this case was simply not credible; it was that the 660 was at first rejected "but was later discovered . . . to meet practically all the requirements . . .". If this were indeed true, the mind boggles at the superficiality of the original evaluation. What is far more likely is that the capabilities of the 660 were fully explored as soon as the proposal was submitted and that its marginal inferiority to the more radical projects was finally, and rightly, judged to be outweighed by its promise of quicker development.

Time was indeed the essence of the justification of the Vickers programme, and GRE was screwed down to a contract that stipulated a first flight not later than 1951 and an airborne production machine not later than 1953 (a far sterner challenge). To take care of the fact that the design did not meet all the requirements of B.35/46 a new specification, B.9/48, was written around it. In April 1948 two prototypes were ordered, one powered by Avon engines and the other by Sapphires. Work went on around the clock at Weybridge and also at nearby Fox Warren. Like de Havilland's Salisbury Hall, Fox Warren was a secure establishment where secret prototypes were built under A. W. E. "Charlie" Houghton. Backing up the programme was the best range of research facilities in the British industry, which by 1949 included a tunnel capable of reaching Mach 0·94 in a 3ft × 2ft working section and a huge altitude chamber in which could be reproduced the very low pressures and temperatures of the stratosphere. Today such things are taken for granted but a quarter century ago they were almost un-British. Rex Pierson laid the groundwork and by the time of the 660 research was managed by Major P. L. Teed and Barnes (later Sir Barnes) Wallis, possibly the only engineer since Whittle to be well known to the general public. On the manufacturing side Weybridge was strengthened by great new machine tools, such as skin mills, Hufford stretch-presses and many other expensive facilities.

Its "interim" role tended to obscure the fact that the 660 was in 1949 not only one of the biggest and heaviest aircraft ever planned in Britain but also one of the fastest, its design Mach number of 0·84 being superior to that of a Meteor F.8. Yet it was almost wholly conventional, and its unusual features were simply because Vickers chose to do things that way. Its basis was a high-mounted 12 per cent laminar-flow wing with the merest whiff of sweepback but having the vital modification of a peak-suction line (which broadly corresponds with the line of maximum thickness) sharply extended forwards at the root. This greatly improved lift/drag ratio, and it was later introduced to the wings of the Vulcan and Victor, but it meant that the distance from the inboard engine intakes to the jet nozzles was almost 40 feet. Throughout the 1950s designers argued over the merits of these buried engines with very long ducts against Americans who supported the short external pod hung below and ahead of the wing. National pride was at stake, and otherwise sensible (which means impartial) engineers adduced all sorts of reasons connected with drag, aeroelasticity, crash landings, turbine-disc bursting, fire risk, accessibility and many other factors to show that their scheme was the best. At this distance in time my own view is that the V-bombers were all designed with big wings in which it was possible to bury the engines, while the American aircraft were hung from thinner and more highly loaded wings in which engines could not have been buried; and, as the US designs tended to need longer runways, they were marginally more efficient in cruising flight.

Some of the earliest large British jet projects were even planned around buried centrifugal engines (so was the Comet, of course, but these were of the direct single-entry type), but by the time the V-bombers were planned designers could look ahead to the more slender axials. In 1949 it was decided to power both the 660 prototypes with the Avon, initially at the RA.3 rating of 6,500 lb but with the airframe stressed for projected later Avons of at least 9,000 lb thrust. Surprisingly the 660 was planned to use bag tanks, throughout the wings and upper part of the fuselage, even though integral tankage ought not to have posed a development risk. On the other hand, pressure fuelling through sockets at shoulder height in the low-slung fuselage was a welcome innovation.

The finely streamlined fuselage was of basically circular section. The whole nose was full of the biggest radar ever planned for a British aircraft, and accommodating it not only meant the visual bombsight had to be somewhere else but also caused the front bulkhead of the pressure cabin to be a huge disc externally concave instead of the usual convex. Production of the pressure cabin was subcontracted to Saro; it accommodated captain and co-pilot side-by-side with two navigators and the wireless operator (later called the air electronics officer) facing aft at a lower level behind them. All five crew entered through a door on the left side which, like the two aft compartment windows, was of the near-elliptical "neutral hole" shape found by Vickers (but not by the Comet designers) to give minimum stress around its edge. Under the pressure cabin was a streamlined bulge for visual bomb aiming, while on top was a much larger bulge forming a canopy over the pilots (a similar bulge was used on the Viscount, but the fairing behind it made it less obvious). The top of the canopy could be blown off by firing 26 explosive bolts, which simultaneously uncoupled the pilot control columns and pulled them forwards to clear the way for the Martin-Baker Mk 3A seats. But the other three chaps had no ejection seats. They were supposed to get out by undoing their seat harness and suit connectors, and walking over and opening the main door, as well as a hinged windbreak ahead of it without which exit at high indicated airspeed would have been, in official language, "difficult". Alternatively, the right rear window frame could be unlocked and allowed to blow out. A similar scheme was followed in the Vulcan and Victor. As shortly described, the first time a V-bomber was abandoned the only casualty was a pilot; but by 1958 a Vulcan incident had triggered a storm of controversy throughout the RAF, the Ministry departments and the industry centred around the provision of ejection seats for all crew-members. They didn't get them.

Although the design of the 660 was planned to avoid unconventionality, one feature stands out a mile in retrospect as most unusual. Like the Focke-Wulf 190 before it, the great Vickers bomber was practically all-electric; and to a considerable degree this was because, in the person of Harry Zeffert, Weybridge had the greatest electrics king in the British industry (and, as I write, still does). His choice was to fill the bomber from stem to stern with 112 volts of direct current, supplied by a $22\frac{1}{2}$ kW generator on each Avon capable of giving full power even at flight-idling revs. It was hardly surprising that the system broke acres of new ground; and perhaps it would be rude to be surprised at how little trouble it caused. The wing was full of Acme-screw electric actuators for the double-slotted flaps (split flaps under the jet-pipes, of course) and airbrakes, while the greatest of all retracted the main landing gears. The undercarriage was of Vickers design but subcontracted to Rotol. Each main gear comprised two wheels in tandem on separate legs of S.99 steel, retracting outwards like a couple of Liberators. The actuator incorporated a huge electric motor driving a ball-screwjack, a smaller half-power motor for stand-by and a shoal of limit stops, switches and protective devices. For years Rotax used a beautiful cutaway drawing of this package in their advertising. One marvelled at the complexity of it, and wondered if this was an advantage over an hydraulic jack. Similar precision engineering went into the powered flying-control units, by Boulton Paul, but these variable-delivery package-type units were the forerunners of thousands, and led straight to VC10 and Concorde.

When I wrote this chapter in 1972 I asked Harry Zeffert, who is still in BAC (which absorbed the aviation part of Vickers) whether he had any second thoughts on the Valiant. I cannot do better than quote him: "It should be appreciated that the tremendous advantage gained by going to high-voltage DC gave us the lightest cable weight related to the number of functions performing on the aircraft that has ever been achieved in any aircraft before or since, and this in spite of the fact that the normal mass of hydraulic spaghetti found in every other aircraft was completely absent throughout. The engine nacelle contained a generator – period. Everything else was done electro-hydraulically right at the point where the function was required. If, therefore, one considered the main undercarriage as a complicated piece of mechanism, it should not be done in isolation since, had we had an hydraulic jack, though this would inevitably have been lighter in its local application, the total weight of engine-driven pumps, distribution pipes and fluid, including tanks and pressure vessels, would have been far more and required much more in the way of maintenance—and, in any case, would have been festooned with the same limit switches and electrically controlled valves, etc." So, no regrets.

In the winter of 1950–51 all these new devices, plus quite a lot of machined skin and new dielectric structure (but nothing like as much as for a production machine), converged amid the fir trees at Fox Warren and were built into WB210. The major sections were trucked to the new company airfield at Wisley, swiftly assembled and flown there by Mutt Summers (he was determined to do this before he retired) and Jock Bryce on 18 May 1951. This made the first target date look easy, and from the first the flying at light weight from Wisley's grass went well. After three flights WB210 was based at Hurn, near Bournemouth, while Wisley was given a runway. WB210 was polished light alloy all over, and so devoid of excrescences it was almost uninteresting. The only discontinuity in its smooth skin seemed to be the narrow "letter box" intakes, fitted with a row of vertical straighteners just before the first flight, which in a 1949 paper by D. L. Ellis were said to surpass all other intake shapes for aerodynamic efficiency yet which have hardly ever been used since. Even the second prototype, WB215, abandoned them for separate bulged holes with a larger area sized to feed not only the 7,500 lb Avon RA.7s actually fitted but also the 9,500 lb RA.14 proposed for production aircraft (and well able to match the engine ultimately used which was even more powerful). Early in 1952 the 660 was officially named Valiant, starting an odd fashion that British strategic bombers had to have names beginning with V, perhaps (though I was never able to confirm this) because in 1944–45 this letter and its Morse equivalent had symbolized Allied victory. On 11 April 1952 WB215 flew. What Vickers didn't count on was that by this time it was the only Valiant left. On 12 January 1952 WB210 had been engaged in shutdown and relight tests over the Hampshire coast in connection with noise measurements for the projected V.1000 military transport. One Avon suffered a wet start and caused a fire in a bay where no detection equipment had been judged necessary. By the time it was discovered the wing was thought to be about to come off. All five crew got out but S/L Foster, the co-pilot, was killed; nobody will ever know how his ejection seat came to hit the Valiant's tail.

On 20 April 1951 Vickers had been given an initial order for five pre-production Valiants, with RA.14 engines, and 20 production machines cleared to higher (175,000 lb) maximum weight and with 10,500 lb Avon RA.28 engines. The company had also earlier received an order for a "one-off" in some ways paralleling the Canberra B.5. The Air Staff made a case for a special target-marking version of the Valiant to fly at much greater indicated airspeeds, in other words very fast low down. To meet the requirement Vickers had to effect a major structural redesign. The so-called Pathfinder, Type 673, flew nicely in time for the SBAC show, on 4 September 1953. Painted glossy black overall, it could be seen to have a longer forward fuselage and a bogie-type main undercarriage retracting backwards into long fairings projecting behind the wing in the style that became the trademark of Tupolev. The new main gears were needed both to cope with the increased gross weight and also to allow the wing to be made with an undersurface of heavier-gauge skin with no cut-outs. WJ954, which probably added about 20 per cent to the overall develop-ment workload, was in my view the finest Valiant ever built. Its most startling advantage was that at sea level it could safely fly at a thrust-limited 552 mph, whereas the standard Valiant was held to an airframe-limited 414 mph. It was intended to lead to a definitive aircraft, also called the Pathfinder, to propel which Rolls-Royce submitted their paper study for the RB.80 by-pass jet; thus the whole Conway turbofan programme stemmed from a stillborn aircraft. But the really ironic feature is that the Pathfinder is exactly what the RAF later wanted, instead of a high-flying bomber. When they discovered this, and made the Valiant behave like the Pathfinder, its airframe didn't like it, as we shall see.

Engines of the black B.2 were 9,500 lb RA.14s, and these were also fitted to the five pre-production machines which took shape during 1953 in the new production jigging which, because steel was hard to get, was mainly of concrete. Assembly was arranged on two lines in a new building at Weybridge, across the airfield from the humming Viscount shops. Completed aircraft were to be flown out, and although by this time Brooklands had a runway it was a mere 3,900 feet in length and bounded by the steeply banked former motor racing track at each end. But Jock Bryce, Brian Trubshaw and their colleagues had no qualms, and when WP199 finally emerged Jock lifted her out like a bird on 21 December 1953, giving GRE a relaxed Christmas with the crucial "production aircraft" deadline in the bag. WP199 showed the longer jetpipes and huge radar of the production machine, but still lacked plenty that subcontractors had yet to deliver. Finished in silver, it soon appeared with the 1,645 Imp. gal. underwing tanks first fitted to the second prototype and with which it was at one time intended to fly in the England–Christchurch race in

October 1953. Unfortunately the Air Staff suddenly got cold feet and had the entry scratched at the last moment, to the disappointment of everyone except F/L R. E. Burton, who won the race in a Canberra.

By 1953 Vickers had the first of five production contracts. I think the Air Staff issued these in dribs and drabs in the evergreen hope that each buy would be the last and that they could switch to Vulcans and Victors. But Vickers had to keep on plugging the gap, and buying long-lead materials and parts for orders that came at the eleventh hour, in true British style (how Tom Gammon, who was works manager, must have envied Boeing, whose B-47s were ordered in batches of hundreds). All the production machines had the 10,000 lb Avon 201 or 204 (RA.28), which was then the smallest and lightest turbojet of this thrust in the world (indeed I remember one bitter day at Weybridge when a B.1 turned in an aggregate calculated thrust of 43,850 lb). The small-batch ordering was compounded by a tendency to keep changing the specification, something that from 1950 to 1965 bedevilled almost every RAF combat-aircraft manufacturing programme. In 1954 the B(PR).1 was slotted into the line at intervals, with removable equipment for strategic reconnaissance and survey; further down the line the plain B.1 petered out and was replaced by the B(PR)K.1 with cameras and a Flight Refuelling hose-reel pack in the bomb bay; finally the whole production switched to the BK.1 with provision for the same pack plus a probe in the nose, but no cameras.

Production during 1954 was of the plain B.1 (Vickers Type 706). On one beautiful day Bill (his baptismal name and not short for William) Aston let me accompany him on the shortest flight without a snag that I ever made. By this time the Valiants were coming off the line in white anti-nuclear-flash paint all over, with pale blue serial numbers (later these reverted to black, probably after deep calculation that they wouldn't get very hot anyway). We were airborne in much less than half the available distance and probably could have crossed the Brooklands boundary at 1,000 feet had not Bill had to stuff the nose down towards Wisley, where we landed, after a leisurely circuit, just over two minutes later on a runway that in comparison seemed endless. Several production machines that needed modification were even flown back into Brooklands.

CA Release came in January 1956. First production deliveries went to 232 OCU at Gaydon, a lovely Warwickshire airfield now deserted by the RAF. Then S/L R. G. W. Oakley, who for three years had been detached to Vickers and would have flown the Valiant in the New Zealand race, was appointed CO of 138 Sqn, the first British V-force unit. It was also based at Gaydon, and straight away set about emulating Strategic Air Command in becoming an élite force of grizzled veterans. National Service aircrew had no chance of getting into the V-force. At first pilots had to have a

49

whole string of exceptional qualifications, including 1,750 hours in command and a tour on Canberras. Later the sights were lowered. The original intention was that all aircrew and senior ground staff would stay in the V-force, and probably in the same squadron, for five years. (Today the RAF would be taking a chance if they tried to plan ahead for five weeks.) Yet another innovation, and a good one, was that the RAF introduced the US-style crew chief, in charge of ground crew assigned to a particular aircraft throughout its career. He even had a jump seat on board, and flew with the bomber on overseas assignments.

Overseas trips there were in plenty, because Britain still had global commitments. And the thought of V-bombers being dispersed to short remote airstrips led in 1949 to the idea of boosting them into the air with rockets. The earliest B-47s had been fitted with various rocket assistance packs based on cheap rechargeable bottles, but the British V-bombers had to have something more interesting. To permit operations at maximum weight from short tropical bases "under the most adverse conditions" the Valiant was to be provided with two formidable Scarab rockets clipped to the rear fuselage. Later, in 1950, these were replaced by much more costly DH Super Sprite motors running on high-test peroxide and kerosene and rated at a mean thrust of 4,200 lb for 40 seconds. These were arranged to thrust through a long steel probe, but potentially dangerous difficulties led to the rockets being relocated under the main engines with a different attachment system. To save money it was decided the rockets should be re-usable. They were packaged into nacelles built like miniature aircraft fuselages and containing: a long steel strap to give a 300 lb pull to stabilize the pack after release; negative-incidence foreplanes to rotate the pack positively nose-down after the strap had pulled free; the cleverest parachute system GQ had then created; and a complicated arrangement of automatically inflated air bags to cushion the landing. Developing the system kept hundreds of expensive people busy for more than four years, besides twice coming within a hair's-breadth of writing off a Brigand trials aircraft. It finally flew on a Valiant in July 1956, a month after it had been announced that the bomber would "be able to use" it. Then, when the whole development had been funded, rocket boost was quietly dropped and never used (no storm in the papers, no questions in Parliament).

But the Valiant was used, and no mistake. A particularly busy day was 11 October 1956. In the morning, while Weybridge rolled out one of that month's four new BK.1s, aircraft of 138, 148, 207 and 214 Sqns detached to Luqa, Malta, and a flight of 138 carrying live high-explosive bombs made an operational sortie against Egyptian military targets in support of the Anglo-French intervention at Suez. Thereby achieving all sorts of "firsts" that 138 would rather forget, the Valiants demonstrated pinpoint accuracy that was possibly not helped by the embarrassed crew of one aircraft being given nice homings by the airfield they were about to bomb. An hour or two later on the other side of the world the crew of B.1 WZ366 went to bed much relieved after dropping Britain's first live airborne nuclear weapon. It detonated over Maralinga, South Australia, "within 110 yards of the aiming point".

By this time the B(PR).1 (Type 710), B(PR) K.1 (733) and BK.1 (758) were all in service, and their crews were highly proficient. Valiant detachments had begun to score well in the annual bomb/nav competition of Strategic Air Command, and I shall never forget a Bomex exercise when the assigned targets were "a 58 inch manhole cover on Bovingdon airfield, the centre of a tower on the Little Ouse and part of the corner of a building near Kirkwhelpington Mill, Northumberland". I asked a navigator/bomb-aimer whether such targets were not more for public-relations than practical use, and got a sharp lecture in reply. This taught me that, with the Valiant, the RAF learned how to drop a bomb at Mach 0·82 at about 50,000 feet so that the point of release was correct to within a few feet.

Doubtless 49 Sqn could achieve this precision as well as anyone, but their big job of 1957 did not really call for it. They were given the task of dropping Britain's live thermonuclear weapons. An H-bomb, the thing that humanity most fears but has learned to live with, is a very different proposition from a plain fission bomb. It was for the H-bomb that the Valiants were painted white, and fitted with other special equipment including crew vizors with lenses which darken in the presence of brilliant light. Not only this, but the actual dropping of the bomb is no mere removal of a pin. Instead the aircraft has to be flown to its airframe limits, and immediately after weapon release the pilot manually performs a maximum-rate turn through 90° to reach a safe radius at the time of detonation. If he pulled round too hard he would do a high-speed stall, with consequences which any pilot can work out for himself. RAF aircrew have for generations been used to situations calling for skill, precision and sheer cool nerve, but for the Valiant BK.1s of No. 49 shining brilliantly white amid the waving palm trees of Christmas Island this was a new situation where a mistake could turn the aircraft into a charred lump in mid-air.

In the event everything went like a bomb. The first drop was on 15 May 1957, when XD818 took off with W/Cdr K. G. Hubbard in command. The megaton-yield weapon was accurately dropped towards a theoretical aiming point on Malden Island, and the Valiant was over ten miles away when it detonated after a free-fall to 10,000 feet where the barometric fusing was triggered. Further tests, with more powerful bombs, were made on 19 June and 8 November. No nuclear weapon has been dropped by the RAF since. Hopefully, it never will.

Meanwhile other squadrons were busy elsewhere. Exercises and competitions with SAC continued, strategic missions were flown in the evaluation and test of the Dewline (distant early-warning radar system), and hundreds of thousands of miles were flown in development and training with advanced navigation systems in the absence of ground aids. In May 1958 a Valiant began the flight trials of the Blue Steel "stand-off bomb", the long-range air-to-surface thermonuclear missile that was later to be issued to Vulcan and Victor squadrons. Much later, in March 1963, when Valiants were becoming obsolescent, the first production machine was used to flight-test the Pegasus vectored-thrust turbofan engine, which nicely fitted into the bomb bay. In March 1958 operational trials with flight refuelling were begun by 214 Sqn. The excellent probe-and-drogue system used had been develeped in the 1940s by Sir Alan Cobham's Flight Refuelling Ltd., and in 1949 a USAF B-29 equipped with three hose reels pumped kerosene to three Meteors of Fighter Command simultaneously. Then, having satisfied themselves the system worked, the RAF did nothing with it, and carefully ordered fleets of new bombers and fighters—even the Mach 2 Lightning, with a limited range on internal fuel—in which a probe was conspicuously absent. The result was a generation of aircraft fitted with a crude probe as an afterthought. The Valiant was one of this generation, and 214's aircraft grew not only a probe but also an unsightly pipe to carry the fuel from the probe round the outside of the pressure cabin to the tankage. Only the BK.1 was equipped for receiving; other Valiants had no probe, although the B(PR)K.1 could carry a hose reel and, like the BK.1, transfer just half of its total of 10,000 Imp. gal.

The last Valiant, XD875, flew out of Brooklands on 27 August 1957 and was delivered on 24 September. Vickers had built 108 production aircraft plus two prototypes and the Mk 2. From Nos. 6 to 108 each aircraft had been delivered on or ahead of time. They equipped nine bomber and tanker squadrons, plus No. 543 photo-reconnaissance squadron. In 1963, with the later V-bombers in strong service, the four remaining Valiant strike units—49, 148, 207 and 214—were assigned to Saceur, forming a tactical wing based at Marham to operate in support of the NATO nations. From December 1963 their missions were flown mainly at low level, the task for which the B.2. was designed. It was hardly surprising that in July 1964 fatigue cracks were found in the front and rear wing spars of one aircraft, with many more being discovered the following month. Consideration was given to a structural rebuilding, but the estimated cost per aircraft was not far short of the new price when they were ordered.

Safe-life calculations followed, with minimal repair and modification, and when the scatter factor was applied it was found that many of the aircraft —which had logged 2,000 to 2,500 hours—had already gone far beyond it. So in December 1964 all Valiants were grounded, except for four assigned to special programmes, and would remain so "except for a national emergency". After an urgent investigation of alternative courses of action the decision was taken in January 1965 to scrap the whole force. Denis Healey, Minister of Defence, said, "This is causing considerable embarrassment for us with our NATO allies". It also caused considerable embarrassment to the rest of the RAF, whose thirsty fighters and bombers suddenly had nothing to thrust their probes into. Naturally the public were told nothing of the number of aircraft involved, the costs of re-sparring or the costs of scrapping. The Press decided to think it a scandal that the aircraft should suddenly crack, failing to realize that they had so long been used in a way never considered at the time of their design, and also failing to notice that one week earlier the US Department of Defense had spent just over $300 million to extend the useful life of the later versions of B-52, which were cracking beautifully.

So over a few weeks the whole force of Valiants was "reduced to produce". It is policy to try to recover as much as possible by selling bits as well as raw materials, but I have been unable to track down a single item from the Valiant force that was sold in this way (can the radars, instruments and engines, and those splendid Rotax actuators, all have been sold at so much a ton?). Soon only XD816 was left, flying from Wisley on Mintech trials; and I hope it finds its way to a museum. If I had to choose two British military aircraft programmes of the past 25 years that I consider successes, one would be the Valiant. In February 1965 George Brown said the "total cost of Valiant research, development and production" was "about £67 million". When the aircraft was new George Ward, Under-Secretary of State for Air, said the price per copy was "unlikely to exceed £350,000". In fact, the average unit cost was not greatly in excess of this, and you could have had a fully equipped Valiant for much less than the price of an RB.211 engine. And if they had all been Mk 2s they might still be in business.

Hawker Siddeley Vulcan

ONCE UPON a time there was a great dream called Britain's Lead in Aviation. Although less enduring than *Pax Britannica* it made headlines for a dozen years, and reached its pinnacle during a few days in September 1952 at the annual show of the Society of British Aircraft Constructors. This was a feast for everyone from hardened aircraft designers to schoolboys. Some thousands of the latter carried piles of brochures in a large folder given away by the Hawker Siddeley Group, on the cover of which was the proclamation "1952—DELTA YEAR". Inside, it explained that future aircraft would have wings shaped like triangles. To prove it, the Group's factories had put into the sky gaily coloured research aircraft, the Avro 707s; a great all-weather fighter, the Gloster GA.5 (Javelin); and an even greater bomber, the white-painted Avro 698. Roly Falk's demonstrations of the 698 at Farnborough that week had an impact rivalled by very few other occasions in the history of flying machines. Everyone was on their toes in incredible excitement. The 698 looked like the triangular sail of a mighty yacht, and it cruised round the huge crowds in tight turns at a height of about one wing-span. With the Comet in BOAC service, and a dozen other marvellous things to show off, it was probably the proudest moment for the British industry in all its history.

This overwhelmingly impressive new shape in the sky was the first tangible fruit of the B.35/46 specification already described in the histories of the Sperrin and Valiant. This specification was deliberately couched in terms that invited the industry's designers to push their proposals right to the limit of "the state of the art". Meeting it was never expected to be a quick job. In 1947 the Ministry of Supply and Air Staff thought it would take seven years. In fact in the case of the Vulcan it took 9 years 8 months from receipt of specification for the first aircraft to join a squadron, and this was better than the performance of Handley Page who also tendered successfully. Whether these times were good or not depends on what is considered normal. By American or Russian yardsticks anything over five years must be considered poor, but in Britain there were many handicaps and many plausible excuses. Avro could point out that, when they received their copy of B.35/46 in January 1947, their Lincoln—a re-worked Lancaster—had been in service less than 18 months. Probably the root cause of the slow British timing was the absence of work on advanced jet bombers until long after World War 2, coupled with a lack of transonic research tools. Indeed, in January 1947 Roy Chadwick, Avro's technical director, had to start from scratch.

He could easily have proposed something not far removed from a jet Lincoln. He could equally reasonably have sketched an ordinary sort of aircraft, such as the American jet bombers that flew early in 1947, provided with a small degree of sweepback on the wings and tail. This would have resulted in something like the Valiant, and it is rather ironic that before very long the increment in performance between such an aircraft and the "ultimate subsonic" machine he actually strove to create did not matter anything like as much as the Air Staff had imagined when they drafted the specification. In 1946 the planners thought a bomber flying at Mach 0·8 at 45,000 feet would be easy and cheap and strictly interim, while a B.35/46 type bomber flying at Mach 0·9 at 50,000 feet would be almost impossibly difficult yet so much more valuable that it would be worth waiting years longer for it and paying a far greater price. Yet by the time the Vulcan entered service in the summer of 1957 there were hundreds of missile batteries at least nominally at readiness in the United States and Soviet Union whose commanders would have claimed that they could shoot down either bomber with equal ease. Later I will go into this question of what became known as "penetrability" in more depth. For the moment we can rack our brains with Roy Chadwick as he looked down from the Lancaster portrait on the wall and tried desperately to come up with a better idea than the obvious ones.

His team tried all the obvious ones, then spent weeks on a project with 45° sweep that came out at twice the 100,000 lb weight limit the Air Staff had suggested, and then took a long look at an all-wing design. Northrop's enormous XB-35 had given a pointer to what could be done, and was soon to fly in jet form; and Avro's sister firm of Armstrong Whitworth had flown an all-wing glider and was soon to fly an enlarged jet version, the AW.52. An all-wing bomber seemed obvious, because bombs take up little room. The project staff at Chadderton, between Manchester and Oldham, soon produced a drawing of a fine all-wing bomber; but it was still well over the suggested weight. As there was nothing else left to leave out, some designers would have called it quits; but Chadwick next investigated the effect of sharply reducing the aspect ratio by making the wing broader but stubbier. Quickly sketch succeeded sketch, all for shapes lighter than any previous ones, and gradually the process of maintaining sweepback, reducing tip chord to get good induced drag for maximum range, and above all filling in the gap at the back between the swept trailing edges and the short body, led to the pure triangular shape characterized by the Greek letter delta.

This was not a new shape. Alexander Lippisch and others in Germany had conducted extensive high-speed tunnel tests on delta models since 1942, and in California Convair were building a high-subsonic delta aircraft. But what was born at Avro was a triangular wing that flew by itself, with no excrescence save fins and rudders on the tips. The crew were under a canopy at the forward apex, the fat middle part contained two or four engines and the bombs were housed between the engines and the main landing gears (or asymmetrically on one side of the aircraft only, with fuel on the other). Unlike earlier all-wing aircraft, this one had an enormous wing chord near the centreline so that even with a laminar 12 per cent thick section there was enough depth for a man to walk upright inside the wing. This seemed important in 1947, because designers were very concerned with the gains that seemed possible with such aerodynamic advances as eliminating the fuselage and laminarizing the wing. They would certainly have been surprised to be told that 25 years later the fastest, longest-ranged aircraft would have the biggest fuselages ever built and no laminarization. On top of this the stubby triangle was a beautiful shape structurally, allowing thin material gauges to be combined with modest stresses.

In May 1947 Avro submitted their delta to the Ministry of Supply. The figures seemed right, but in the environment of the Lincoln and Shackleton it had a frightening element of fantasy about it, as though the sober project team had proposed one of the paper models that boys chuck around class-rooms. Chief designer Stuart "Cock" Davies (now of Dowty) later said, "It is one thing for a junior technician to push an unconventional idea, but for a designer with Mr Chadwick's past history of success to risk his reputation on such a venture was an act of high courage which was not perhaps sufficiently recognized". And when he said this any recognition would have been too late, because on 23 August 1947 Chadwick was killed in an Avro Tudor in the accident which at last spurred legislation making it impossible to connect aileron controls the wrong way round.

In November 1947 the Avro submission was accepted, and an ITP (instruction to proceed, but without a contract) for two prototypes was received in January 1948. By this time the pure triangle had become much altered. The tip fins were replaced by a conventional vertical tail on the centreline, and realization of the need for low thickness/chord ratio, which today seems obvious but apparently was not in 1947, made the Avro engineers reduce the thickness of the wing and add a fuselage prcjecting far ahead of it to house crew, radar and part of the fuel. Equally significant was the discovery by the Royal Aircraft Establishment at Farnborough (really a re-discovery, see p. 82) that the wing ought not to be a plain triangle. Instead the line of peak suction on the upper surface should be swept sharply forward over the inner portion of the wing by bringing the thickest part of the section closer and closer to the leading edge. This would have meant an impossibly bluff shape had the whole inner leading edge not comprised the biggest intakes ever designed, to feed the four Bristol BE.10 engines buried in side-by-side pairs with the weapon bay between them. The result was a tip section that was fairly conventional and about 8 per cent thick, and a root section almost twice as thick in terms of t/c ratio and shaped like a wedge. So thick was this root that it encompassed the nine-foot diameter of the fuselage, which was something odd for the fastest aircraft then being designed in Britain.

It was only prudent that the radically new shape of the Avro 698 should quickly be explored with small-scale test aircraft, and the silver Avro 707 (VX 784), to Spec. E.15/48, was flown by Eric Esler at Boscombe Down on 4 September 1949—the day on which Bill Pegg first flew the Brabazon. Relative to the 698 the 707 had an oversize body and manual controls, but it flew nicely and no obvious cause could be found for its crash, killing Esler, on 30 September. Although the nature of the crash lent weight to those who said deltas were tricky at low speeds, the three hours it flew at least showed the basic shape was tractable. Unfortunately the cart had got before the horse in that the very advanced wing of the 698, with its startling changes in section from tip to root, had progressed far beyond the plain delta shape of the 707. As the basic idea of a small-scale research aircraft is to get things right before the full-scale design is frozen, Avro quickly obtained authority to build a replacement. But even then the wing of the blue 707B (VX 790) flown by W/C R. J. "Roly" Falk, superintendent of flying, on 6 September 1950, was nothing like the shape previously agreed. Not until the so-called "high-speed" 707A (WD 280), painted orange, built to Spec. E.10/49 and flown by Falk on 14 July 1951, did the research aircraft catch up with a wing that usefully resembled that of the bomber. As the prototype 698 was by this time far advanced in construction the whole purpose of the 707 programme degenerated into secondary things, such as discovering that the nose gear ought to be lengthened to help the aircraft take off. And, as so often happens, a lot of time was spent investigating problems with the research aircraft that had little or no direct relevance to the 698. Falk flew hundreds of hours investigating the pitching oscillations of the 707 caused by out-of-phase movement of the manual elevators. Thousands of measurements were taken of the pitch damping, which was very poor, even though the 698 was to have irreversible powered flight controls prohibiting out-of-phase movements. In the early days of high-subsonic flying I suppose every bit of knowledge was worth paying for, but on a strict funding basis I think it is hard to justify the construction of scaled research aircraft unless they give results that can be usefully applied to the full-scale aircraft. Perhaps the real purpose of the 707 series was to reinforce confidence in the basic delta shape and allow Falk to become familiar with its handling.

Avro received the contract for two prototype bombers in March 1949. By this time it was decided the BE.10, now named the Olympus, would probably not be ready in time and the first aircraft, VX770, was ordered with 6,500 lb Avons, just over half the thrust Avro had assumed for the ultimate Olympus. First drawings were issued to the shops in May 1950. The design was already highly refined, and, apart from lengthening the nose leg and turning the jet nozzles downwards or outwards to minimize trim change with power, very little was cranked in from the supposedly supporting 707 programme. Yet, quite apart from the shape, the 698 abounded in bold features. Its hydraulics operated at 4,000 lb/sq in, like those of the Britannia and several other British aircraft designed before 1950, giving a lighter system than the 3,000 lb/sq in hydraulics that are still used in the latest American aircraft. Boulton Paul's power units for the rudder, inboard elevators and outboard ailerons were a great advance on any earlier surface actuators. Dowty's main landing gear was quite outstanding, with four twin-tyred wheels on a levered-suspension bogie carried on a giant casting of magnesium alloy. Magnesium was also used for much of the structure and skin of the tail, made by Armstrong Whitworth. The air brakes were narrow strips, four extended above each wing and two below, which could be rotated until at 90° they added 250 per cent to the aircraft profile drag. These brakes were among the regions chosen by Davies for manufacture in light-alloy honeycomb, which after exhaustive research into methods of reliable manufacture and inspection gave superbly light yet rigid structures that were used more extensively in the later Vulcan B.2 and in the supersonic Avro 720 and (in steel) in the 730.

In June 1952 Avro received a production contract. Managing director Sir Roy Dobson said, "We know we have the most efficient long-range bomber design in the world", which was possibly true although I doubt if they could really have put numerical values to the world's long-range bomber designs. Privately he doubted rival Handley Page would get a production contract, whatever Sandys might say about not backing single horses. He claimed Avro's airframe was "almost 10,000 lb lighter" than the HP crescent, despite being stressed for a higher ultimate gross weight and more powerful engines, and he said it would fly over its targets "at least 5,000 feet higher". (To all of which Sir Fred's chief designer, R. S. Stafford, equally privately opined that Dobbie had got his figures the wrong way round, thus setting the stage for the farcical situation in which both machines were continued to the bitter end.) The Avro managing director also drew attention to the immense effort that had been put into the 698 design, "which can be picked up for free by the world's airlines". By 1953 his company was trying to interest possible customers in the Atlantic, a Vulcan with an enormous new passenger fuselage; and Sir Fred had offered them his double-deck HP.97. Potentially both aircraft were at least the equal of the later 707 and DC-8, but for various reasons which affect the bomber story only in a negative way, Britain (by which I mean BOAC) chose to show no interest in such aircraft until they could be bought from the United States.

In mid-August 1952 VX770 was rolled out at Woodford, Cheshire, whence the bits had been taken earlier in the year by road so that even with light tarpaulins as screens everyone could get a clear idea of what sort of beast it would be. Named Vulcan just before the roll-out, the aircraft was flown by Falk on 30 August, in nice time to log enough time to appear at Farnborough a mere two days later and amaze everyone. The delta shape, with neither tailplane (or foreplane) or flaps, could not pretend to be efficient in terms of maximum lift coefficient (although Avro had discovered the unexpected advantage that, at least in the wind-tunnel, it did not stall but still gave 90 per cent of its peak lift at the fantastic inclination of 60°). But Roly's flying showed that even this drawback, combined with the low engine thrust, was far outweighed by the wing loading of some 20 lb/sq ft during the light-weight early trials; for comparison, the B-47 began life at more than four times this loading, and at maximum weight each square foot of the Boeing wing had to support more than 150 lb. There could be no greater antithesis than these two jet bombers, both built at about the same time to do the same job. History suggests the highly loaded wing was right, if you have SAC-size runways.

Basically, low wing loading was the key to the Vulcan's manifest advantages. Today nobody would build a subsonic delta, and this is partly because designers can assume longer runways and choose much more highly loaded wings which offer superior cruising efficiency. And, although today's wings would be made of stronger and heavier slabs of metal, they could cancel this out by being much smaller than the 3,400 sq ft of the Vulcan. I first realized the depth of the Vulcan wing when I saw the front spar of VX777, the second prototype, and compared the aperture for the intake duct, about five feet deep, with the nine feet or so of the spar web. Inside the wing was space not only for the engine installations but also for the main gears, several items of equipment known by colourful code names which may even today still be classified, and much more fuel than the aircraft needed. The leading edge and a few other parts were constructed in envelope jigging, a technique pioneered by Fairey in which the component is assembled inside a surrounding jig envelope in order to attain the highest accuracy and surface smoothness. Apart from the items

59

from AWA at Coventry already mentioned, almost the whole Vulcan was made at Chadderton, and the rigorous new standard of airframe accuracy brought to light the fact that there was slight subsidence due to old mine workings which kept moving the jigging a few "thou" at a time. I hope the works is still there.

Before long the precision jigging for the leading edges had to be done again. The one big contribution made by the 707 programme was that the 707A could encounter mild high-frequency buzz in the outer wings when pulling g at high altitudes. The buffet was a problem partly because it could induce fatigue and, in particular, because later Vulcans with more powerful engines would fly faster and higher and encounter it more easily. So the Phase 2 wing was devised in which the outer leading edge, from 48·5 per cent semi-span to the tip, was extended forwards by adding a new thinner, downward-drooped leading edge. The same sort of thing was having to be done to literally dozens of high-subsonic designs, and even a few supersonic ones such as the F-102 and Crusader. The Vulcan was one of those where the extra bit was kinked, so the net result was a wing that swept sharply at 52° to 48·5 per cent semi-span, 10° less sharply to 78 per cent and then at the original angle to a slightly broader tip. It was tested on one of the two 707As in 1954 and on 5 October 1955 on the second prototype Vulcan. It is rather surprising that the problem could not have been discovered earlier, and the reason seems to be the fact that not until the second half of 1951 was a 707 flown that in some way resembled a Vulcan and behaved like one. So when the Phase 2 wing was devised, production aircraft were on the line and in the air, and 16 leading edges had to be thrown away.

VX777, the second prototype, was fitted with Bristol Olympus 100 engines rated at 9,500 lb and flew on 3 September 1953. Again just in time for the annual SBAC show, 777 flew there with its sister which had been re-engined with Sapphires, apparently in a move by the Hawker Siddeley Group to get their engine into the programme (it had already been chosen for the Victor). But Bristol Aero-Engines had an obviously superior power-plant in the two-spool Olympus, which was cleared for production in 1954 as the Mk 101 with a rating of 11,000 lb. These were about to be fitted to VX777 when it made a forced landing at Farnborough in July 1954, for reasons unconnected with propulsion, and did not fly again until December. The first production B.1, XA889, painted in the silver finish then pre-scribed, emerged early in 1955 and flew on 4 February. At that year's SBAC show the second B.1, fitted with nearly all its operational equipment, was daily rolled by Falk at quite low level. He had confided earlier that he had been certain he could roll the Vulcan since the start of the flying programme, and that the fighter-type pilot cockpit with side-by-side sticks instead of wheels made extreme manoeuvres sheer pleasure. XA889 was delivered to Boscombe for acceptance trials in March 1956, by which time deliveries were being made to MoS test establishments of aircraft with engines rebladed to the Mk 102 standard rated at 12,000 lb. Initial CA release came in May, and the first delivery to the RAF was made to 83 Sqn in September. But the first unit to form was the Operational Conversion Unit, No 230, likewise at Waddington, which became operational on 22 February 1957. No 83 Sqn followed on 11 July, with engines further up-rated to Mk 104 standard at 13,000 lb. Between then and April 1959 Avro delivered a total of 45 Vulcan B.1s, equipping an élite force comprising 27, 44, 61, 83, 101 and 617 Sqns, all in 1 Group.

From the start both the Vulcan and its outstanding engines put up a splendid performance in service, with exceptional reliability and freedom from both minor and major snags. The measurement of maintenance man-hours per flight hour, and other numerical indexes of service performance, were then not routine procedures in the RAF, but with the Vulcan an attempt was made to quantify some of the obvious yardsticks and see how at least the three V-bombers compared, if not the other RAF combat types. On most counts the Vulcan B.1 put up figures that were unrivalled, and even today, when every index of performance is fed to computers—taking a giant leaf out of the book of the airlines—its record remains a good target at which to aim. Of course, true to British tradition, the data are all kept secret.

Like all the other RAF jet bombers the Vulcan carried no defensive armament. The two pilots were seated high up under a large jettisonable canopy which was totally opaque apart from a circular window on each side, and the rather poor natural lighting was countered by what seemed to me the best artificial lighting of any flight deck. The two pilots sat side by side in rather tight matiness, especially if they were big men, but the two navigators and air electronics officer had plenty of room lower down and behind. Just behind the mighty nose radar was the expected ventral blister for visual bombing, and between this and the nose gear was the pneumatically operated entrance door, with jettisonable stairway, which when open created a dead-air region for the emergency exit of the three lower-deck men. Immediately aft of the pressure cabin was the fuselage fuel bay. Behind this the weapons bay lay between the two massive wing-spar bridge pieces, and at under 29 feet was shorter than that of the rival Victor but just adequate for the nuclear bombs that were on paper when the 698 was designed. Unlike the Sperrin, Valiant and Victor, which were all bombed up by cable hoists from or past the upper fuselage keel, the Vulcan stood so high it was loaded from trolleys by hydraulic jacks working directly on the bomb beams. In the conventional role its maximum load was the small one of 21,000 lb, comprising three Avro septuple carriers. No B.1 was ever fitted to carry any load externally except in R&D programmes.

The first long overseas flight began on 9 September 1956, when XA897, one of the initial batch, left Boscombe on a diplomatic and training mission to Melbourne (where the Olympic games were about to be held) and New Zealand. Everything went in true Vulcan style until the arrival back at London on 1 October. XA897 picked up the Heathrow localizer and got well set up on the glide-path to runway 10L in low overcast and torrential rain, with surface visibility varying from about 500 to 2,000 feet. My colleague Mark Lambert, waiting under an umbrella, knew the important flight was making a full GCA, possibly the first "for real" ground-controlled approach ever made by a Vulcan. The Heathrow controllers are jealous of their superlative reputation, and they talked down their unusual visitor meticulously. But, although Mark couldn't see it at the time, the bomber hit the ground hard in a field of cabbages at Longford, some 3,000 feet short of the runway, wiping off its main gears and forcing up its elevators, critically damaging their power units. Suddenly Mark saw the great delta, rearing up at a totally wrong angle like a giant ray leaping from the ocean, with sudden streams of smoke as full power came roaring on. With painful slowness it reached apogee of about 200 feet. Then, with a bang, off flew the canopy, followed by the ejection seats of S/L Howard and his co-pilot, Air Marshal Sir Harry Broadhurst, then AOC Bomber Command and now deputy chairman of Hawker Siddeley. While they were saved by the faultless Martin-Baker machinery, the rest of the crew were killed as the Vulcan scattered itself across the airport, lining the horizon with flickering flames.

On 20 December "a full statement" was made in the Commons by the Air Minister. It explained nothing; on the contrary it asserted the almost unbelievable facts that: there had been no GCA malfunction; no height correction was passed to the pilot; and the talk-down was continued normally *after the aircraft had hit the ground*. Frank (now Lord) Beswick called it "A most unsatisfactory report". Sir Harry said it had seemed a perfectly normal approach "until the ground suddenly appeared in the wrong place". The general secretary of the Institution of Professional Civil Servants concluded that the LAP controllers had been "used as a scapegoat". Indeed, it was soon conclusively demonstrated that the official figures were nonsense in height, distance and speed (some didn't even tally mathematically). I wondered if the height controller had found a second blip on his display—but caused by what? This puzzling incident was instrumental in triggering off a campaign that had earlier been simmering in the Valiant force: the men at the back wanted ejection seats.

Long trials were made with various schemes of aft-facing Martin-Baker seats in a Valiant, culminating in an ejection by W. T. Hay on 2 July 1960. But nothing more was done along these lines.

Ultimately Handley Page, despite his failure to merge with someone, was given a contract for new, swivelling seats for all operational V-bombers. The seat was provided with an ML Aviation pneumatic cushion to "blow the occupant out of the seat even under conditions of high acceleration". What he did next was still up to him. On 30 January 1968 a Vulcan crashed in Rutland; both pilots ejected but the two navigators, the AEO and a nav. instructor were all killed. The coroner hoped that "those in authority will take immediate steps to provide the other members of the crew with means of escape equal to those of the pilot and co-pilot". The Ministry of Defence said the "cost of a redesigned crew station would amount to £100,000 per aircraft", and implied that nothing would therefore be done. The figure was never explained in parliament or anywhere else, and if anyone had questioned it they would have been told it was secret and so could not be discussed. When the F-111K was cancelled, Roy Mason (Minister of Defence, Equipment) said it would "put a new burden on the Vulcan force". As this might have to operate in the arduous low-level role until 1978 he was "looking again" at the crew escape situation. MoD were even persuaded to reveal the V-force casualty figures. Between 1955 and 1968, four Valiants, five Victors and seven Vulcans had been lost in flight. Of the 71 aircrew killed, 72 per cent had been rear men, only a little higher than the 66·6 per cent to be expected if all had equal chance of escape. And there the matter rested.

Not included in the RAF figures was the first prototype, VX770. As previously noted, this was re-engined with the Sapphire 6 and then in 1956 was lent to Rolls-Royce at Hucknall for use as the test-bed for the very important Conway by-pass engine (what we would today call a very timid turbofan) that was on order for the Mk 2 Victor and on offer to the airlines for use in the 707 and DC-8. Four 15,000 lb-thrust RCo.7s were installed and VX770 flew again on 8 August 1957. On 20 September 1958, when it had completed valuable flight development, the Conway-Vulcan was a star attraction at the Battle of Britain display at Syerston, Notts. Making a fast run down the runway the whole aircraft appeared to explode, with bits shooting ahead out of a vast ball of fuel. The cause was traced to structural failure of the wing. It seemed ironic that the first Vulcan ever built should so dramatically have highlighted the dangers of low-level operations with so big a wing designed for the stratosphere.

Meanwhile, Avro (Hawker Siddeley from 1962) kept on with improving the B.1 and developing the much better B.2. One of the dead-ends in development was the use of a jettisonable, re-usable rocket pack to boost

63

take-off performance in adverse conditions. If ever a bomber didn't need such things it was the Vulcan, but as de Havilland Engines were producing Super Sprites for the Valiant (which were never used) and Spectres for the Victor (likewise) they were also asked to fit the Spectre package to the Vulcan. Compared with the rather primitive Super Sprite, the Spectre was a considerable advance, with a neat turbopump, very compact design and, in the fighter version for mixed-power intercepters, thrust controllable in one second from flight-idle to 8,000 lb. In 1957 a Vulcan B.1 was provided with Spectre pack attachment fittings, but the trials were never held and the whole Spectre programme was abandoned, with a write-off of £5·75 million, in October 1960.

More productive, but incredibly late starting, flight refuelling finally reached the Vulcans in 1959. I remember a Ministry of Supply press conference early in 1953 when someone asked if the V-bombers would be equipped for the FR probe and drogue method. There were a few quick exchanges of meaningful looks and then came the reply, "The V-bombers have exceptional range, but it would be possible for this method of aerial refuelling to extend this range". Unhelpful, but it showed the officials had heard of the technique. Yet most of the V-bombers were built without a receiver probe, or else given a crude lash-up installation as an afterthought. The Vulcan's probe was relatively neat, and the first contact took fuel from a Valiant tanker in May 1959. Subsequently the whole force was thus equipped. In June 1961 one of 617's aircraft flew from Scampton to Sydney in 20 hr 3 min (573 mph), refuelled by Valiants over Cyprus, Karachi and Singapore.

By this time most of the Mk 1 aircraft had been painted in anti-flash white and brought up to B.1A standard by adding an electronic counter-measures system in a bulged and extended rear fuselage. This made the Vulcan look more conventional, with an obvious fuselage at both ends. The B.1 Phase 2 wing modification, which left the original triangle unchanged aft of 12½ per cent chord, was so clearly advantageous that Avro were considering a further extension of it as early as 1955. J. R. Ewans, chief aerodynamicist and from June 1955 chief designer, knew that more would have to be done to allow the airframe to utilise the remarkable thrust-growth that Bristol were promising from the Olympus. By 1954 work at Patchway was well advanced on the Olympus BO1.6, a redesigned engine with one stage fewer on both the LP and HP compressor spools yet, because of its great increase in mass flow, likely to start life giving more than 15,000 lb thrust. Anticipated growth of this engine would need a new wing.

While Avro drew this wing, strategic conferences were held by the Air Staff and MoS to decide whether the manned bomber would play a significant role in British defence planning throughout the foreseeable future or would swiftly be rendered obsolete by long-range missiles. The opinion was sought of the US Department of Defense, although one could have got as good an assessment by reading *Aviation Week* or *Flight*. It appeared that no missile had flown having a range greater than 300 miles, but that the NA Navaho winged cruise missile was expected to fly 5,500 nautical miles. Later the Atlas ICBM was to fly the same distance. The decision was taken in principle to develop a British long-range ballistic missile, using US technology, and to continue development of the British Avro 730 supersonic bomber, although it was generally thought this might well become obsolete before its development should be completed. But subsonic bombers appeared to have a future until 1960, unless claims for missile systems such as Nike-Hercules should prove true (they were). After that time the ballistic missile was thought to be dominant. To fill the gap until Blue Streak was ready, Avro and HP were given an ITP to go ahead with Mk 2 versions of the Vulcan and Victor, with improved wings and engines much more powerful than anything envisaged at the time of their original design.

So Ewans finished his new wing and flew it on VX777 on 31 August 1957. This began a cost/effective programme, but one which yielded its main fruits in greater range from a given airfield; the increment in speed and height really didn't matter, especially as before long the stratospheric wing was having to operate at tree-top height where the main objective was not more wing area but much less. Compared with the B.1 the B.2 wing carried the Phase 2 idea much further, with an increase in tip span and chord achieved by redesigning the whole wing outboard of 48·5 per cent semi-span with increased area, much reduced t/c ratio, a downward-cambered leading edge and a sweptback trailing edge carrying two very big elevons inboard on each side and two small honeycomb-filled ones outboard, instead of inboard elevators and outboard ailerons. This new wing enormously opened out the boundary of altitude and acceleration to match the limits attainable with four of the new Olympus engines. The latter, having for a while hovered around 16,000 lb, were in January 1958 cleared for production as the Mk 201 at 17,000 lb, with plenty of stretch still to be realized. Handling of the B.2 was distinctly better even than that of the Mk 1 Vulcan. Like the Mk 1, stalling was prohibited in service because in a determined stall at fully aft c.g. there was lateral and directional divergence at about 25° angle of attack which could have got the aircraft into most irregular situations in inexperienced hands; but for anyone to stall a Vulcan by accident seems practically impossible. Probably the sole undesirable quality was that, despite its powered controls, the Vulcan needed artificial pitch-damping. A duplicated system was fitted to the B.1, but in the B.2 the natural damping was actually negative over a small range of Mach numbers so the pitch dampers were quadruplicated.

Instead of placing a fresh order the decision was taken to introduce the improvements as early on the line as possible. The 46th and subsequent aircraft (XH533 *et seq*) were accelerated at the expense of the tail end of the B.1 line, so that the last B.1 (XH532) did not fly until more than six months after the first B.2 had flown on 19 August 1958. Almost 90 Mk 2 aircraft were delivered, the first service delivery being XH558 to 83 Sqn on 1 July 1960. Consideration was given to converting all the RAF B.1 Vulcans but the decision was negative. The retrofit costings came out at a level well over half the new price of the first B.1 batch, partly because Britain was firmly bent on inflation. I was once assured that at the end of the programme, in 1965, the price of the bare airframe, costing much less than half the price of a fully equipped B.2, had risen beyond the total unit cost of the first batch of Mk 1 aircraft. But the rival Victor escalated even more swiftly, starting off in 1952 cheaper than the Vulcan and ending up in B.2 form more costly.

Unlike the Victor, which served as a strategic reconnaissance and tanker aircraft, all RAF Vulcans served only in the strategic strike role. Although in practice the United Kingdom was ceaselessly involved throughout the Vulcan's life in troublesome minor conflicts embracing most of the territory from British Honduras to Hong Kong (going east), the aircraft was explicitly regarded as the prime deliverer of the "British deterrent" in the major nuclear conflict that never happened. Long before even the B.1 entered service it was uneasily thought that perhaps the development of defensive guided missiles might render this task difficult. When specification B.35/46 was drawn up, the general idea was that the resulting bomber would have a performance so high as to be practically invulnerable; in modern parlance it would have "high penetrability". As it was a very classified subject in the early 1950s I was never able to discover the reasoning. The surface-to-air missile did not appear to be subject to any limitation in performance or manoeuvre comparable with those then afflicting manned aircraft, and it appeared logical to design such missiles to shoot down bombers flying at least as fast and high as the V-bombers.

In 1955 I showed a picture of a Nike-Ajax, a very early anti-aircraft missile, to a senior aircraft procurement official. The picture showed a test firing against a B-17, and when I asked how vulnerable a V-bomber would be against such a weapon I was told, "Not at all . . . when the V-bombers are in service they will offer very different targets from a B-17 flying straight and level, and probably fitted with devices to help a missile hit it instead of devices to make it miss". In July of that year I had a long talk with engineers at Western Electric and Douglas Aircraft, who were prime contractors for the Nike series, and came away with a different picture. Their view was that the Ajax, a strictly interim weapon, would have "almost 100 per cent lethality against any subsonic aircraft coming within its slant range". The much bigger Nike Hercules, then coming into volume production, extended this lethality to "almost 30 times as big a volume of sky". They agreed that the subject of countermeasures, a vast and sensitive area about which I learned in fascinating detail that night, might yet prove a tough nut to crack in some of the forms then being explored in the United States; conversely, although in some of those forms the bomber would appear to vanish and reappear elsewhere, confusing the defences, the electronics and hardware would be so extensive there would be no payload left for bombs. They expressed the view that they considered it unlikely that the V-bombers would carry counter-measures more sophisticated than those to be used by Strategic Air Command, and they were unanimously of the opinion that any SAC aircraft that ventured within 60 miles of a Hercules would unfailingly be destroyed, unless it was hugging the ground. They had a big commercial axe to grind; but I believed them then and I still do.

V-force countermeasures are undoubtedly still a classified subject, but when one considers the profusion of tricks that can be played by a B-52 (p. 154) it is probably not a transgression of security to suggest that the American engineers' view of 1955 was right. So one looked in vain for an explanation of the great importance apparently attached in British bomber procurement in the second half of the 1950s to a little bit more speed and a little bit more height. There was undoubtedly an attempt to spread a vague view that aircraft with good altitude performance could fly so high that missiles would find it difficult to reach them. Indeed I heard an RAF Chief of the Air Staff say as much at a luncheon. When Gary Powers' U-2 was shot down over Sverdlovsk on 1 May 1960 there was a vigorous American attempt to discredit the Soviet story that the aircraft had quite effortlessly been shot down by a missile battery. The highly intelligent periodical *Aviation Week* suggested that it was common knowledge along the Pentagon grapevine that the U-2 had suffered a flame-out and then been shot down after it had descended far below the level at which "it has for years been cruising invulnerable, high above the range of Russian missiles". As the U-2, even with J75 engine, could not get higher than 90,000 feet, one tried in vain to reconcile this contention with the official US Army "fact sheet" on the Nike Hercules which gave the missile's ceiling as "in excess of 150,000 feet". And by this time Hercules was obsolescent.

Obviously, with expenditures of hundreds of millions of pounds or dollars to be justified, there was a strong inclination of the aircraft men and the missile men each to reach their own conclusion, so I should not have been surprised that the answers I got varied so immoderately. Where did truth lie? It certainly did not lie somewhere in the middle, because, while early missile systems were initially temperamental, so were the early countermeasure and decoy systems. I think if one makes a crude judgement today the answer comes out about 4:1 in favour of the missile; in other words, the missile claims were 80 per cent true and the bomber claims only 20 per cent. Thus, by 1960 the bombers were being forced down to tree-top height and replaced by ICBMs and missile-firing submarines.

Of course, not all the globe is yet infested with surface-to-air missiles. Such systems are as costly as bombers, and tend to be disposed fairly close to important bomber targets, such as major cities or the bombers' own airfields. So it was natural to continue the work begun in 1940 in Germany and devise pilotless missiles, much more penetrable than the bombers, which could carry the bombers' loads through the final, heavily defended region and accurately deliver them to the target. The relatively small missile could not fly all the way, so the bomber was still needed to carry it most of its journey with high accuracy. But the problems were considerable. The World War 2 bomber-launched missiles had a short range, just enough to keep the bomber away from most of the defensive guns, and over a range of the order of five or ten miles it was quite practical to use "command guidance", the missile being steered to its target by radio signals from a special control unit worked by the human bomb-aimer who "piloted" it to the target visually. But with missile defences the bomber might be unwise to approach closer than 30 or even 100 miles—old Hercules, for example, had a slant range of over 86 miles—and brief reflection of what such a distance looks like, even from 50,000 feet, suffices to rule out command guidance for any target smaller than a big city. This in turn meant a clever missile, able to navigate by itself.

Such a development was a far cry from a mere guided bomb, but it was the latter that Sir Hugh Pughe Lloyd, AOC Bomber Command, had in mind in 1952 when he said, "We've got to get away from this free-falling bomb business as quickly as possible". During World War 2 there had been apocryphal tales of the USAF Norden bomb sight which could "put a bomb in a pickle barrel"; and the RAF Pathfinders consistently achieved great precision in Oboe-guided target-marking. But the run-of-the-mill standard of bombing was seldom better than a circular-error probability of 500 feet, and with jet bombers flying twice as fast and twice as high it looked as if accuracy was going to deteriorate sharply. In fact the reverse happened. New hardware and better training brought such an improvement that Bomber Command's 9 Sqn, flying the Vulcan B.2, regularly achieved circular-errors only 15 per cent as large as they did when they first equipped with the Canberra. Indeed, in participating in the Laurence Minot trophy and the annual SAC competition, Vulcan B.2 squadrons have since 1960 achieved higher accuracy than a crack Lancaster unit could have hoped to attain in 1945. So the guided bomb was one of the British weapons cancelled before too much had been wasted on it, and no such thing was ever produced for the V-force.

Instead by 1953 the emphasis had swung sharply in favour of the air-to-surface missile capable of flying a long way, and thus allowing the bomber to stand-off some 150 miles from the target (hence the British terminology of "stand-off bomb", a contradiction in terms). The first such device to be test-flown was the American Bell GAM-63 Rascal, a delta-winged transonic beast propelled by a three-chamber liquid rocket engine. This was dropped like a hot potato by the USAF, but the basic configuration appealed to Britain and was used as the starting point for Blue Steel. All British guided weapons, associated ground and airborne electronic systems and certain other highly classified devices of this generation were identified by code names of this kind, in which the first word (actually a surname rather than a christian name) was a colour. The naming system was partly complex and partly random, and Blue Steel was one of the few recipients that kept its code name in operational service (Red Top was another). And in the case of Blue Steel the airframe really was largely of steel, but hardly blue. I always thought steel a mistake; today's faster Concorde is light alloy.

After what Dobbie called "a personal crusade to get it started", the prime contract for Blue Steel went to Avro who as well as doing the Vulcan were about to launch forth on a supersonic mixed-power inter-ceptor and a supersonic bomber, to say nothing of developing the Shackle-ton and undertaking three other major project studies. For a missile launched by a bomber and supported by a wing in the atmosphere at only just over Mach 1 a rocket engine seemed an odd choice, but Arm-strong Siddeley's team at Ansty, led by Sid Allen, took time off from the Snarler and Screamer aircraft rocket engines and several other major programmes to develop the two-barrel Stentor, with a big boost chamber and a smaller one for the long cruise part of the mission. Twist-and-steer control was provided by ailerons and canard foreplanes, a thermonuclear bomb was packaged in the forward fuselage and the most difficult job of all was developing the first inertial navigation system in Britain.

Choice of inertial guidance was the one right and forward-thinking decision taken with this missile. The year was 1954, and it was still not universally agreed that such a system would be needed for all future strategic winged vehicles to enable them to navigate with precision without help from the ground and without sending out tell-tale radar emissions (as did Green Satin, the Vulcan's doppler navigation system). One form of inertial navigator contains an Euler pendulum, a rotating mass with a period of swing of 84 minutes, identical with that of a plain pendulum having a length equal to the radius of the Earth. This holds a very freely pivoted frame exactly horizontal relative to the Earth beneath, no matter how the Blue Steel (or whatever it may be fixed in) flies from A to B. On this frame are mounted gyros and accelerometers more accurate than any previous mechanisms ever made in metal, with tolerances measured not in "thous" but in microns. Making such things introduced industry to the ultraclean room, with not merely filtered air but compulsory nylon smocks and mob caps on the head and feet, and total prohibition on such filthy things as pencils and rubbers with their intolerable pollution (environmental preservationists would have loved it, but in those days they hadn't been invented). Totally insulated from vibration and temperature changes, the environment was just about good enough for hardware accurate to within a few wavelengths of light. When everything was bolted to the pivoted frame it could be made to integrate, or continuously add together, all the accelerations imparted to the frame along the longitudinal, vertical and lateral axes, thus enabling the calculating part of the system to keep an exact record of the frame's position in relation to any prior position. All that was then needed for a perfect, self-contained navigation system was to know exactly where the frame was at the start of its mission and where the target was in relation to it.

This put sudden urgency into global mapping and geophysical surveying, in the course of which it was found that, while the continents were mapped to a fair degree of accuracy, the position of, say, a point on Carswell Air Force Base in Texas in relation to a point in Moscow was not known to within ten miles. I have chosen a US base because the Americans made all the running in this field, the main original pioneers being Northrop Nortronics and Autonetics division of North American Aviation. In 1956 Dobbie confided that Avro had had a desperate need for prototype inertial guidance equipment for the Blue Steel. For over a year he had got nowhere using official channels. Then he "went over to see Kearfott Corporation, bought an inertial gyro on the spot and had it in my mackintosh pocket as I came through customs at Heathrow". This broke a long stumbling-block at the Weapons Research Division at Woodford, and the Elliott inertial system went ahead fast. The story of Blue Steel, a supersonic canard delta, cannot yet be told in detail but it has its own share of excitements. The first full-scale missile flew in 1958, being dropped from a Valiant and powered by a Double Spectre engine. The Stentor-engined missile flew in 1960, and in January 1962 a fully equipped operational missile was flown at Woomera from XA903, the only Mk 1 Vulcan to be Blue Steel converted. Many of the Mk 2 bombers were delivered unable to carry the missile, presumably because of the difference in timing. In 1962 they were progressively given cut-away inner bomb doors and other modifications to allow them to carry Blue Steel semi-externally, where its drag reduced performance "by only two per cent". Later B.2s were matched to Blue Steel from the start, needing minor modifications for use with internal bombs.

A sortie with Blue Steel involves an outbound sector with the bomber and missile navigating individually and each monitoring the other. The bomber's accuracy becomes progressively superior with the passage of time, as it had doppler, astro, radio and radar (and an old-fashioned pair of drift sights), and from 1968 it also had a Sperry heading reference system. So immediately before missile release the coupling umbilical fed the Blue Steel with precise data on geographical position, height, speed and acceleration. Then, with a long blast of flame, the 35-foot missile shoots ahead as the Vulcan pulls up out of its way.

Like the Vulcan, Blue Steel was designed to be a high-altitude vehicle, and it was the rocket engine's indifference to altitude that led to its choice. Navigating to its target is not inherently difficult, because inertial errors tend to be proportional to flight-time and Blue Steel doesn't take long at Mach 1·6. But the missile also tries to confuse the defences by following a pre-programmed trajectory all the way from sea level to 100,000 feet (or back again), with a few changes of course as well—to say nothing of countermeasures. It also presents a small radar cross-section for the defenders to detect (but still far larger than the more modern SRAM, p. 181). Even today Blue Steel would prove quite penetrable. In the Vulcan's low-level role, described at the end of this story, the Blue Steel has to be modified to Mk 1* standard in order to avoid hitting the ground when dropped from the speeding bomber. Low-level trials at Weapons Research Establishment at Woomera, South Australia, went very well indeed against simulated strategic targets, although I wonder how much more difficult they would have been in mountainous terrain? Air Marshal Sir John Grandy, then Bomber AOC, said "Obviously one cannot release Blue Steel from an altitude of ten feet", but in fact the Stentor fires at the point of separation and I believe a "toss" from 50 feet is practical in an operational situation. There was to have been a completely redesigned Mk 2 Blue Steel, with a 450-mile range, but it was cancelled in 1959 after £825,000 had been spent.

One reason for the cancellation was that Blue Steel was considered obsolescent. Another was the fast development of the native ballistic missile Blue Streak. And a third reason was that for more than two years

71

the DoD in Washington had been busy with something quite new, an ALBM (air-launched ballistic missile, see p. 169). In his *Report on Defence 1960* Minister Harold Watkinson wrote "It may be decided not to rely exclusively on fixed-site missiles as the successor to the medium bomber with the stand-off powered bomb . . . possibilities of mobile launchers, whether aircraft or submarines, for long-range delivery of nuclear warheads are being investigated". Contrary to what he wrote, it was not the launcher that was to deliver the warheads but the ALBM they were to carry and fire. The British government gave every indication that they had suddenly heard about the American Skybolt, which the technical press had been discussing for over six months.

Watkinson called it "a breakthrough in missile deployment" and the Secretary-of-State for Air confirmed "We are taking a close interest in Skybolt, which . . . should be ready for service in about the right timescale". But Col. Glines of the US Air Force told me "Your government seems to think it can buy Skybolt off the shelf. Our research people are slightly embarrassed; the concept itself is still not fully explored, and may be radically altered or even found to contain a fatal flaw." In fact the response of DoD was to try to pressurize Britain to support the highly frightening proposed NATO Multi-Lateral Force of surface ships looking like merchant vessels (each flying 15 flags?) with a cargo of Polaris missiles at instant readiness.

But the British had the bit between their teeth and suddenly saw the future with encouraging clarity. Prime Minister Macmillan hurried off to tell the good news to President Eisenhower at Camp David. Britain, having stopped the Mk 2 Blue Steel, had now also decided to scrap its ballistic missile, Blue Streak, and was eagerly reviewing the possibility of using instead the American Polaris and Skybolt. "I was greatly influenced," records Mr Macmillan, "by the fact that we in Britain already had a bomber force. . . . I reached the view that if the Americans would sell us the Skybolt missile . . . it would get us through a long period of years with least disturbance." By this time it was beginning to look as if governments formed of cultured amateurs were beginning to find defence a difficult subject, and something that would get the nation through "a long period of years" was like manna from Heaven. Blue Streak's cancellation as a weapon was announced on 13 April 1960, and Peter Thorneycroft was sent off with his carpet bag to sell it as a space launcher. But with a supposed waste of £65 million the news exploded like a Blue Streak warhead, and on 27 April the great Blue Streak censure debate overflowed with rhetoric. Defence Minister Watkinson allayed all the fears: "Skybolt is the perfect and almost invulnerable replacement for it. . . . We have had people integrated in the Skybolt team for a considerable period.

... The initial specification drawn up by the United States included the requirement that Skybolt should be capable of being carried in Mk 2 V-bombers as well as in the B-52 ... the US government have taken a firm decision to press on with the development of Skybolt with the highest priority." By June Watkinson was able to announce that the American ALBM was "ideal for the Vulcan; for the Victor we may have to consider a British weapon . . .". I had the rest of the year to ponder the credibility of Bomber Command deploying two ALBMs until I was assured that there was "no question whatever" of an all-British missile of this type being produced for the Victor (p. 78). So why did the Minister say there was?

Prime contractor for the Skybolt airframe and for assembly and test was Douglas Aircraft, and it was to the warmer climes of Long Beach that a Vulcan B.2 of 83 Sqn flew on 29 January 1961 for preliminary survey and compatibility tests; then it spent some time at chilly Wright-Patterson AFB in Ohio, the HQ of Systems Command where Gen. Bernard Schriever possessed all the powers of technical management that Britain hardly seemed to realize it lacked. In July 1961 AEI were awarded the main UK industrial contract, for the Vulcan/Skybolt interface equipment including an analog/digital converter. This was needed to enable the bomber to tell the missile its exact spatial co-ordinates and velocity at the moment of launch, and Skybolt understood only digital language with discrete "bits" of information. By this time Hawker Siddeley had effected most of the hardware modifications necessary to mate the missile to the bomber, with a single Skybolt carried well below each wing on a pylon housing part of the interface equipment. A British thermonuclear warhead was also being busily developed, but I suspect the team (probably at Aldermaston) found the available space and weight rather tight, and the timescale short. The UK was also requested to make a contribution to the Skybolt R&D cost, but I never found anyone who knew the proportion.

As related in the story of the B-52, Skybolt ground to a halt in December 1962. By this time there had been a number of flight trials, and compatibility testing with the Vulcan B.2 had been successfully completed, and the official MoD line was that the Vulcans would be operational with the missile in the winter of 1964–65. When the programme was stopped there were plenty of political commentators who complained that President Kennedy had done it because he disliked Allied deterrent forces. This was undoubtedly true; he would have preferred to clear the nuclear arena for summit negotiations with the Soviet Union, and after Suez he may even have thought Britain should not be trusted with too many megaton yields. In fact JFK acted on the considered advice of his new SecDef, Robert S. McNamara, who professed to have plenty of reasons for not buying the

Skybolt in quantity. The President was even briefed to say it was "in a sense, the kind of engineering that is beyond us".

Whilst one must accept a presidential utterance as a true statement, I formed the view at the time that Skybolt posed no problems requiring any contravention of this Earth's natural laws for their solution, and that if DoD had wanted to deploy the missile operationally the programme could have been successfully completed. Terminating it generated surprisingly little heat in the United States, and in any case that country could claim that the new concept of "assured destruction" was amply provided for with such systems as Minuteman and Polaris (JFK was soon to make his famous pronouncement "enough is enough is enough"). But in Britain the foundation of our defence appeared to have been knocked away in a fashion that had never previously happened in the island's history. Politicians can generally derive great comfort from the public's short memory, but even the proverbial landlady in Wigan remembered the glee with which Skybolt had been greeted as the nation's saviour, permitting the cancellation of Blue Streak a bare 2½ years before. This time there was no ready-made "perfect and almost invulnerable replacement", and not even a cover story.

On 10 December 1962 the Minister of Defence, who was now Peter Thorneycroft, met McNamara after having been briefed to take "a tough line" insofar as he could. He said afterwards he had "made the British position eminently clear", which as a political euphemism is hard to beat. McNamara said Britain was welcome to carry on with the whole Skybolt programme if it wished; the US industrial contractors would be empowered to reach new agreements with the UK government, or the latter could move the whole thing to Britain. Alternatively, Polaris and Hound Dog were both nice missiles, and Britain might like to buy them in the happy knowledge both were fully developed. In a hectic evaluation the combination of Vulcan B.2 and Hound Dog was judged to be a non-starter. The SAC air-breathing missile had twice the range of Blue Steel, and certain other advantages, but was otherwise no great advance; whereas Skybolt was to have been a totally different animal, a ballistic missile that could not be knocked out by an enemy strike against its launcher which could be anywhere in 100 million cubic miles of sky.

On 19 and 20 December Mr Macmillan met JFK at their historic Bermuda conference. Two days earlier the President had said that Skybolt could still go ahead (I thought the engineering was beyond them?), but "We have put $500 million into it already. The question is how much it is worth to the British and ourselves, where there are competing claims for our money." I do not think Mr Macmillan argued very much. As the world knows, he came away from Bermuda having opted for Polaris, with a British warhead, thus transferring responsibility for delivery of the UK deterrent away from the RAF entirely. Arguments in a thousand RAF messes were heated that night, and to show what could be said by those in retirement Air Marshal Sir Philip Joubert proclaimed "President Kennedy wants to ensure the political and diplomatic collapse of Britain". More specifically, A/Cdre Sir Arthur Vere Harvey, MP, asked "What about the British personnel in California, several hundreds with wives and children, who expected a tour of $2\frac{1}{2}$ years and have bought cars and furniture on hire purchase?" It was a new experience to find somebody worrying about British subjects in California! In any case nearly all of them were not in that state at all but at Eglin AFB in Florida. This state is no cheaper to live in and probably helped jack up the British part of the Skybolt bill to no less than £27 million. When Julian Amery revealed this figure he said it was all due to "modifications to the Vulcans, support and training". Nobody in the Commons made the point that this was not far short of the original R&D bill for the Vulcan itself. Opposition MP Patrick Gordon-Walker merely commented that it was "absolute madness to rest the whole of the nation's defence policy on one weapon made by a foreign country". Meanwhile the staff at RAF Coningsby pushed into the corner the hardware they had been preparing to fit the base as the nucleus of the Skybolt force. In 1965 they were busily preparing it as the first station to receive TSR.2. In 1967 they were dashing about to have everything ready to receive the first F-111K squadron, and in 1969 they actually got into business as 228 OCU (Phantom). I must ask the MO if he had any psychiatric cases.

In the immediate aftermath of Skybolt there was an odd sense of vacuum, but in fact the Vulcan B.2 had continued in production the whole time, switching in 1962 to the 20,000 lb Olympus 301, with an LP zero-stage, which had flown in the outer positions on B.2 XH557, the engine development Vulcan, on 19 May 1961. By 1963 the whole B.2 force had been re-engined with the 301, making the Vulcan one of the very few military aircraft to double its propulsive power in the course of its life (another was the Spitfire). Coupled with this splendid engine came the dramatic change in V-force operating altitude, from the highest attainable to the lowest.

By 1955 the admitted lethality of surface-to-air missiles was alleviated by the fact that at least the first two generations of such weapons provided defensive armour having a chink at the bottom. Most of them operated by detecting and following electromagnetic radiation either in the form of a pencil beam from a surface radar or in scattered reflections from the aerial target. Unless mounted on a high tower or mountain, surface radars could not see down to the visible horizon. The last few degrees were too mixed up with "clutter" from the surface and from other sources of scattering or distortion to be of much use for precision guidance (today this has been largely overcome, mainly by making the radar ignore the fixed clutter yet remain sensitive to any moving target). By mid-1955 both SAC and TAC had carefully explored how aircraft ranging in radar cross-section from the F-104 to the B-52 could exploit this region of radar blindness by racing to a surface target at the proverbial "nought feet", or as near as it was possible to fly in safety.

Obviously there are so many major variables that there are no simple rules. How low one can fly depends on the design stressing of the airframe, the indicated airspeed, the presence or possibility of obstructions and, to a very great degree, on the terrain and even on atmospheric turbulence. The British naval specification NA.39, which resulted in the Buccaneer, produced the first aircraft designed for high-subsonic penetrability at low level. But Blue Steel and Skybolt kept the pressure off the V-bombers until 1962. Then the fact had to be faced squarely: either the V-bombers had to operate at nought feet or they could be thrown away. In the stories of the Canberra and Valiant details have been given of how those aircraft stood up to the arduous task. But what about the Vulcan, designed for the stratosphere and held to a sea-level IAS of about 455 knots? Could it reasonably be modified to come tearing in on the deck at full power, pulling up to skate over a hill, banking steeply to follow a curving valley and then, after an hour of such exhausting, breathtaking penetration, suddenly pulling up at $4g$ into a LABS attack, tossing away a thermonuclear weapon to such a height that the Vulcan could escape far beyond its terrifying fireball? I put this to Maurice Brennan, who at the time had the title of "chief designer, Manchester, Avro-Whitworth Division", and secured his firm opinion that the task could be done so long as one didn't have to start with the Vulcan.

In fact he did have to start with the Vulcan. Even mighty SAC was having to meet the same problems with its B-52 force. In 1964 the short-lived Avro-Whitworth team (which for once brought under one name those who had constructed the Vulcan airframe) received an important contract to modify for low-level operations all the Vulcan B.2 aircraft in Bomber Command. Obviously the whole thing was a massive compromise. Ideally they should have jacked up the nose radar (modified for terrain-following) and the countermeasures in the tail and run a new Vulcan between them with about one-third as much wing span. But funds were available for a less ambitious scheme; indeed Air Minister Hugh Fraser conjured up a memorable phrase when he described the modification as "negligible in the extreme". In fact it was not quite so miniscule in cost, because it did include a terrain-following radar (but not a head-up display). Details are secret, of course, but I have long wondered whether the big-winged Vulcan might actually gain in penetrability by flying a little slower and lower than, say, an F-111 at Mach 1·2?

At Wittering in February 1964 a demonstration was staged of both the Vulcan B.2 and Victor B.2 operating in the low-level role, carrying the new low-level Blue Steel Mk 1*. And this is the sort of thing the Vulcans are still capable of doing. The last B.2 was not delivered until January 1965, and from then until 1973 the type equipped nine squadrons, called Bomber Command until 30 April 1968 and Strike Command thereafter. Two of these units are, at the time of writing, "permanently based" in Cyprus at Akrotiri. Greek fishermen must by now be hardened to having four Olympus 301s, with throttles wide open, pass overhead at mast height. It's supposed to keep the peace.

Handley Page Victor

DURING World War 2 there ran through the British aircraft industry a strong current of revolution where the shape of aircraft was concerned. Designers wanted to put the tail in front of the wing, or on the tips of the wing, or leave it off altogether; and not a few wanted to leave the fuselage out as well. Despite their long and rather conservative—or perhaps I should say Puritan—traditions, Handley Page were in the front rank of the revolutionaries by the end of 1941. Dr Gustav Lachmann, who at that time was interned, reasoned that a swept-wing tailless bomber could at one stroke overcome the problems of drag and of c.g. position with heavy tail armament. This, of course, was four years before sweepback was considered in Britain for any other reason. The company built a private-venture research aircraft called the Manx (Manx cats have no tails) which after many modifications flew at Radlett in August 1943. This shape was chosen for various bomber and transport studies, some of which by the end of the year were jet propelled. All were wholly revolutionary except that all conformed to the assumption—taken for granted without question —that the only place for the engines in a multi-jet aircraft was inside the wing roots.

Fortunately no metal was cut. As the European war drew to a close, most of the design and engineering staff of 200–220 were working on the strictly conventional Hermes and Hastings transports. In June 1945 the new chief designer, Reginald Stafford, went on the Fedden Mission to probe Germany. In October his younger colleague Godfrey Lee, whose title was research engineer, was chosen by Ken G. Wilkinson, now managing director of Rolls but then at the RAE, to probe tailless research in Germany, which was considered important enough to warrant a mission all to itself. Lee found plenty of tailless studies, but what had him brimming over with excitement when he returned to Cricklewood were the new shapes of wing intended for high Mach numbers. Unlike many—if not most—British firms, HP took to the new ideas like a duck to water. Within two months their jet bomber had been swept, and not at the 30° that was the norm but at a bold 45°. Today tailless shapes, and the delta, can be seen to have been an aberration in subsonic aircraft, but in the 1940s it seemed quite in order to cast aside the configuration that had been, and remains to this day, almost universal.

By the spring of 1946 the project had vertical fins and rudders on the wing tips, supplemented by a vestigial central fin carrying a tailplane to trim out the pitching moment due to wing flaps. In late 1946 the project study was wrapped up and sent to the MAP, but the Air Staff were immersed in the big, far-seeing B.35/46 specification for just such a machine. HP were one of the firms sent this document on the first day of 1947 and they coolly set about trying to meet it. Like everyone else, they could not at first do so. Fortunately, in direct contrast to Avro, their first year made the project more conventional. By mid-1947 it had grown a proper body and tail. Powered by four 7,000 lb thrust Rolls-Royce AJ.65 or Metrovick F.9 engines it had a gross weight of 90,000 lb and would have carried 10,000 lb of bombs a still-air range of 5,000 miles at 520 mph at 50,000 feet—HP thought. This was staggeringly good, and would have met the requirement. The project was numbered HP.80.

Unlike Avro the tiny Cricklewood team calculated that they could make a slender, highly swept wing that was also light, whereas Avro's calculated weights were way outside specification until they hit on their fat triangle. Competition between the two firms was friendly, although sharp as a razor, and the personal feud between Sir Frederick HP and Dobbie of Avro always seemed to be put on for an audience rather than sincerely felt. It was quite early in 1947 that the MAP agreed the two firms should continue to pursue divergent configurations. It would give a modern British official heart-failure to recall that at that time there were six British projects for four-jet "heavy bombers" (as they were then called), of which four flew and three saw service in numbers. The total design and engineering staff at Cricklewood in 1947 continued to number barely 250, of whom at least half were working on other projects; for comparison Boeing had about 5,500. To handle the new bomber the HP project team was split into an aerodynamics group under Lee and a structures and systems group under Charles F. Joy, both reporting to Stafford.

Lee had become intensely interested in the variations on simple swept wings that he had found among the German reports. Blohm und Voss's kinky W and M shapes looked startling, but seemed to be dead ends. Arado, on the other hand, really seemed to be on to something. Dipl-Ing R. E. Kosin, their chief aerodynamicist, had devised a "constant M_{crit}" wing that curved like a scimitar from root to tip. Kosin supervised the building of such a wing to be test flown on one of the several non-standard Ar 234 jet bombers. But the British troops who captured the plant, before the wing could be destroyed or mated with the fuselage, failed to appreciate the wing might be of interest to anyone and it was scrapped. What was this notion of constant M_{crit}?

As the speed of an aircraft is increased, the point is reached at which the local flow velocity becomes sonic (equal to that of sound in the surrounding air) over convex surfaces such as the upper part of the wing where the velocity is locally accelerated. A small, fairly weak shockwave forms at the rear of the supersonic region, causing possible boundary-layer breakaway and much increased drag. This occurred in 1947-type aircraft at a free-stream Mach number of about 0·75 (three-quarters of the local speed of sound) to 0·8. Further increase in aircraft speed caused more shocks to appear at other places, while the original ones migrated further aft and became stronger. These are the basic transonic phenomena. Very little was known about it all, and in Britain there were few facilities for finding out, but the fundamental design goal appeared to be to delay shock formation by minimizing bulges, convex curves and the thickness of the wing and tail. The airspeed at which a shock first forms is called the critical Mach number (M_{crit}), and in 1947 this was just becoming a very important criterion in the design of fighters and bombers (in modern supersonic aircraft it is virtually ignored). What Lee's team set out to do was to devise a shape for the HP.80 that would have a constant M_{crit} all over. In other words, all the parts that accelerate the airflow, such as the nose, wings and tail, were intended to accelerate the flow the same amount everywhere, so that all would form small shockwaves simultaneously with no place being especially bad. This seemed to be a route to minimum transonic drag, but with no wind tunnel in which to test a model it called for a formidable amount of exhaustive mathematics (and there were no computers either).

Most of the visible results of this philosophy were not odd in appearance, although obviously the nose was pointed and had smooth curves. But in the case of the wing, and to some extent the tail, the design objective gave the aircraft not only a very successful aerodynamic and structural form but also a distinctive shape. The basic aim with the wing was to combine considerable sweep and aspect ratio with good stalling behaviour. Swept wings tend to stall first at the tips and, as these are well aft of the c.g., the result is pitch-up: the aircraft is longitudinally unstable from the onset of the stall and rears up dangerously. With a low aspect ratio, as would be the case with a fighter, the problem is contained. But for a long-range bomber the demand for high lift/drag ratio calls for a wing of quite high aspect ratio with considerable span and slender tips. The Cricklewood designers reasoned that Kosin's wing provided the key to an elegant solution.

For the HP.80 the wing was aerodynamically divided into three sections from root to tip on each side. The inboard portion was made to sweep back at a very sharp angle, 53° at the quarter-chord line, and thus could be made relatively thick and therefore light. The root t/c ratio was no less than 16 per cent, a typical figure for a piston-engined bomber and providing space for fuel, engines and main landing gear. But at the tip the sweep angle was only 22° and the t/c ratio only 6 per cent, the weight penalty here being small as the structure was much smaller. The contrast between the root and tip was so great it was not thought practical to join the two at a single giant kink, so the semi-span was divided into three equal sections with three degrees of sweep all blending into each other. Later for practical reasons the tip was extended inwards to halve the width of the middle portion.

This wing had a mean sweep of about 30° and stalled rather like a 30° wing but with no pitch-up and with the great advantage of a light yet capacious inboard section. Compared with the B-47 (p. 126) the resulting HP.80 had almost the same weight, the same span and the same parasitic drag, but with the further great advantage of 50 per cent more wing area. And there were other major benefits. Possibly the greatest was the beneficial way the wing responded to increased flight loads. With a plain swept wing, "pulling g" in manoeuvres causes the tips to bend upwards, reducing their incidence and thus lift. This makes the aircraft pitch-up, as it does at the stall, and reduces the manoeuvre margin. With Handley Page's wing this tendency to twist was prevented by a strong opposing torsion from the inner wing. Thus, by accident, the HP.80 wing had "aero-isoclinic" properties: it held its incidence unchanged no matter how much it was bent upwards by flight loads. The same held for the tailplane and elevator. In this it gained the same goal as was sought by the aero-isoclinic wing flown on the Short Sherpa in October 1953. This replaced ailerons and elevators with pivoting wing tips of the kind pioneered by Prof G. T. R. Hill's Pterodactyl aircraft of 1924–36. But the HP.80 wing had conventional ailerons, and here again there was a bonus in that the ailerons were not far behind the flexural axis, as in ordinary swept wings, but slightly ahead. Thus they did not suffer from control-reversal caused by twisting of the wing that was a plague with other aircraft having slender swept wings.

Handley Page called their bomber's wing a crescent shape, and it was thereafter the most characteristic feature of the aircraft. Ideally I think a more rigorously correct name would have been a cusp; a crescent ought to have a smooth curve from tip to tip, with zero sweep at the centreline, as in HP's earliest aircraft of 1910–11. Whatever its name ought to have been, this wing was undoubtedly the most efficient high-subsonic wing on any drawing board in 1947, and the only one to have progressed distinctly beyond the points reached by the German designers in 1945. The rival wing of Avro scored good marks for structural rigidity, internal capacity (far more than was at first needed) and weight, but I am certain Dobbie erred when he claimed, in 1953, "We know we have the lowest drag". Lee calculated the original Avro 698 wing had about 120 per cent of the transonic drag of their crescent, and in any case later development of the Vulcan did all it could to turn itself into a high-aspect-ratio crescent. Indeed, in 1949 W. S. (later Sir William) Farren and S. D. Davies came down from Avro with MAP blessing to have a full briefing on the rival Handley Page wing.

I think the Cricklewood designers armed themselves well with theoretical knowledge. For example the other V-bombers were already on the drawing board when information from the RAE suggested their wings ought to be modified at the root to bring the line of maximum thickness sharply forward, thus bringing the two-dimensional suction peak closer to the leading edge to avoid loss of effective sweep inboard. But when Lee visited Göttingen in 1945 he discussed this very topic with the true originator, Ludwieg, so the HP.80 was right in this respect from the start. Ludwieg's classic paper actually contained a mathematical error, and the first correct treatment for the root of a swept wing was a bundle of foolscap half an inch thick produced by Stefan Neumark at the RAE. The HP.80 wing sections were worked out by S. B. Newport using the NPL method of Prof S. Goldstein; R. W. Annenberg did the lift distribution, taking account of camber, twist and flaps according to another NPL classic, the lifting-surface theory of V. M. Falkner; chief flutter man was J. C. Baldock; and F. T. Davies managed the vast work of stability and control, including theory for powered flying controls, yaw damper, roll damper, autopilot, Mach trimmer and other things that were most futuristic before 1950. Multhopp's method was used to deal with the flaps, which were an area-increasing type rather like the Fowler.

On the leading edge HP would naturally have liked to fit his own slats, but this appeared so difficult with so thin a section that instead the outer wings were fitted with a hinged leading edge that could be drooped by hydraulic actuators to improve lift at low speeds. At first the nose flaps were made automatic, a lift-coefficient sensor being arranged to signal a powerful hydraulic accumulator system that slammed the flaps down on both sides very rapidly. Later it was discovered with other types of aircraft that some fixed droop was acceptable at high Mach numbers, and when the nose flaps were fixed partly down the success was complete; the drag increment could not be measured, and the stall was still satisfactory. Even later, in 1955, Doc Lachmann hurried to California to find out how Ed Heinemann had managed to fit slats to his thin-winged Skyhawk, but I don't think HP ever considered changing course at this late date.

Another area where the ideal solution eluded the team was in the vexed matter of crew escape. As other stories in this volume indicate, not one of the big British jet bombers found a happy answer to the problem of getting all five men out unfailingly and fast, and many aircrew died in consequence, especially after the missions came down from the stratosphere to tree-top height. Handley Page, perhaps helped by the inherent boldness of their design, looked at some bold schemes. In October 1947, having made the problem worse by putting a central tail on, they investigated the possibility of making the whole nose jettisonable, with explosive rams to push it clear and four hinged side panels to stabilize the severed nose as the rest of the stricken bomber reared up immediately behind it. This got as far as trials with a scale-model glider. The nose fins and parachute were to be activated immediately after separation by long cables hanging along the fuselage. Shortly before the trial a fitter helpfully shortened these untidy-looking cables, with the result that when the jettison was triggered they all broke and the nose dropped like a stone. End of experiment. In any case the need to fill the bottom of the nose with a huge radar made this idea more and more difficult, and after the MoS had decided against fitting five upward ejection seats, with five blow-off hatches in the pressure-cabin roof, it was decided to leave the three rear men to try and get out as best they might through the side door.

HP received a full design contract on 1 January 1948, by which time the aircraft looked broadly as it does today. Four Metrovick F.9 Sapphire turbojets, each rated at 7,500 lb, were to be buried in the wing roots. Immediately outboard of them were the extremely neat main gears, with four twin-tyred wheels on each leg, retracting forward into chordwise boxes. The contractor for this gear, Electro-Hydraulics, achieved a total installation weight of 3·3 per cent of the HP.80 gross weight, and did even better with the later Victor B.2. Testing in the new RAE high-speed tunnel, and high-lift testing in the NPL compressed-air tunnel (until it caught fire), confirmed the basically correct shape although at a late stage it was decided that more fin area was needed and that this could best be done by moving the horizontal tail to the top of a very slightly taller vertical surface and in addition giving it dihedral. This further improved the appearance at a time when the T-tail was novel. HP had hoped to use an "all-flying" slab tail, but later decided to house the actuators in a fixed delta-shaped portion.

As soon as the configuration seemed roughly settled it was agreed with the MoS that it should be test flown on a radio-controlled glider, and in a matter of weeks the latter had been built as the HP.87. Early British experiences with remotely piloted vehicles were uniformly disastrous, despite the long history of regular use of radio-controlled target aircraft such as the Queen Bee and Queen Wasp. The HP.87 was taken to the RAE and flown straight into the ground in singularly ill-chosen weather. Fortunately the decision had already been taken to build a much more ambitious manned jet aircraft to test the unusual aerodynamic features of the Handley Page bomber, and specification E.6/48 called for a high-speed research aircraft on a scale of about one-third. It was particularly wished to explore the behaviour of the wing at high speed and at low speed with leading and trailing edge flaps depressed, as well as the stability and control with the high-mounted slab tailplane. It was soon evident that Handley Page were too overloaded to build the aircraft, and the job was given to Blackburn who saved time and money by using a fuselage similar to that of the Supermarine 510 sent up from South Marston. All the detail design was done at Brough although HP naturally had to keep a close watching brief. By June 1951 VX330 had been painted glossy blue and white, rolled out and photographed for the MoS. For obvious reasons the ministry chose to release the exact side view in which the secret crescent wing could not be seen, and an artist airbrushed the shadow (surely a rare phenomenon on Humberside!) to make it look like that from a plain swept wing. Then the press release was sent out including one of the other views showing the wing and shadow perfectly.

The aircraft was trucked to Carnaby and flown there on June 21 by G. R. I. "Sailor" Parker. I expect he entered "Blackburn YB.2" in his log-book because that is what his company called it; Supermarine called if the Type 521 and most people refer to it as the Handley Page 88. Despite its doubtful ancestry the HP.88 was nice to fly, but it rather followed the British tradition of making flying scale models as different as possible from the full-scale machine. The wing was the original shape with a high aspect ratio and three equal stages of sweep. HP wanted to try out the wing in its simplest form and were afraid a bad root intake might unfairly damn the whole concept; in any case the bomber's intakes had not been quite settled, so the root of the wing bore scant resemblance to the very characteristic root of the bomber. The nose flaps were of the type the company considered ideal aerodynamically, yet for the bomber a simpler, lighter and cheaper type was adopted. The trailing-edge flaps were also quite different, and the tailplane was a slab pivoted on a colossal acorn fairing some way down the fin. Even the air brakes were quite unlike those of the bomber in shape and location.

There were two other things that didn't help. The first was that, like the delta Avro 707, the HP.88 was timed about two years too late to be of much help to the bomber because the latter was not merely designed but also well advanced in construction. The second was that during a fast low-level pass down the runway at Stansted on 26 August 1951 the HP.88 broke into pieces in less than a second. Handley Page pilot Duggie Broomfield could never have had any idea of what happened. Indeed it took the boffins a full two years to find out. The one who got the complete answer was our old friend Neumark, the Pole at RAE who had solved the swept-wing root problem. He traced the cause to an obscure servo-instability in the tailplane control system, involving the bob-weight that on the RAE's own recommendation had been incorporated as a safety measure. When the V-*g* recorder was salvaged it was found to read ± 12 *g*. So the best things about the HP.88 were that its tailplane control system was not representative of that of the bomber (naturally) and the whole programme cost only £1·6 million.

So WB771, the first of the two HP.80 prototypes ordered in 1949, had to learn the hard way. This was a pity, because in my view I think the design was marginally the best of all the world's bombers of the post-1945 decade, and HP were so small they needed all the help they could get. But the MoS took the view that there was all the time in the world. On the three public utterances by Ministers to the HP.80 in advance of first flight only one thing was stressed each time. This was that the specification was such a challenge the aircraft would take a very long time to develop. I'm afraid it did not strike me at the time, as it did later, how fundamentally wrong this policy was. This is because, quite apart from the question of whether the RAF or the country needed the aircraft, time can be correlated fairly accurately with money. I can think of nothing more unnecessary, and unhelpful to the taxpayer, for anyone—least of all the customer—to lay great stress on the very long-term nature of an aircraft programme. Who decides what constitutes a reasonable time? In both the military and commercial fields a programme is likely to have rivals, and those in other countries may follow different ground rules and management procedures, and have a greater sense of urgency and more rapid funding. To impress one's public with how long a programme is going to take is to impress the same thing on the contractor, while knocking away the ground from under the feet of anyone who wishes to hurry. Almost all of Britain's most saleable aircraft of the jet age took longer than they need have done—through lack of money, management expertise, materials, man-power and motivation —and thus cost more and lost markets. If HP had had 50,000 dynamic employees the government attitude might have done little harm, and the Victor would have been with squadrons in 1953 or 1954. In the circumstances it was lunacy.

Indeed Sir Fred himself said in his address to shareholders for 1953 what a pity it was that "big programmes" could not be ordered into production straight away, so that the manufacturer could get in all the materials, production jigs and tools, special manufacturing and test equipment, and the thousands of bought-out components. It was hardly difficult to guess what he was talking about. Britain's most advanced bomber programme crystallized in my mind as a chaotic army of people trying to make critical bits of futuristic structure by using a hand tool on a workpiece held in a bench vice, while other hordes of harassed white-collar workers argued endlessly on telephones with subcontractors whose bits had failed to arrive. When I began to frequent Cricklewood I realized the truth was all this and more. A little while after HP himself had made his eminently reasonable suggestion—which I am sure was not in the least influenced by the fact that Dobbie was telling everyone HP would never get a production order at all—I happened to have the opportunity to question the current Minister of Supply on the topic. The exchange was brief: "Is it really impossible for an aircraft such as the HP.80 to be ordered into production straight away?" Minister: "I'm afraid it's absolutely impossible. Even to suggest such a thing betrays a complete ignorance of what is involved in developing a modern aircraft." "Do you think the Americans are foolish to do it with the B-52?" Minister, after a second's icy pause "I suppose you are one of those people who think everything American is wonderful?" A few months later we had more enlightenment. The *Select Committee on Estimates* noted Sir Fred's remarks, and explained "Unfortunately the present economic situation seems to prevent the MoS from following this desirable policy". As far as aviation was concerned the truth was that not following such a policy had caused the economic situation. By 1954 Sir Fred had called for "efficient, mechanized, mass production" of the Victor so often one began to think he had a vested interest. But Britain never wavered from its purpose and steadfastly dribbled in funds piecemeal, often on a monthly basis, to support a consequently dribbling programme.

Today the Victor looks quite ordinary, but when I think of the major assemblies of WB771 assuming a shape more like a V-2 rocket than an aircraft I feel again the thrill experienced even by schoolboys throughout the land as they waited for the first flight and the release of pictures in the weeks prior to the 1952 Farnborough show. But not only was the HP.80 running later than the Avro 698: the MoS set things back further by decreeing Radlett airfield inadequate for the vital first flight, and the aircraft had to be dismantled and taken to Boscombe. To preserve secrecy the huge load was shrouded by a white sheet, draped over a frame making it look like a boat, and with the bold legend GELEYPANDHY SOUTH-AMPTON stencilled on each side. I wondered whether a vast shrouded shape emerging on to the highway from the Boeing works and labelled "GENIOB" would at once be reported to the Kremlin as a new frigate? Maybe we sought to cause confusion among Her Majesty's enemies by getting the spelling of the anagram wrong.

At the Farnborough show in September S/L H. G. Hazelden said there had at one time "not so long ago" been the expectation of getting it to the show, like the Avro 698. Today it needs a mental effort to appreciate how he must have been feeling at the prospect of being responsible for all the initial flight development of the almost recklessly futuristic HP.80. Apart from the Avro bomber, which Roly Falk handled with such élan, there was no aircraft in Britain anything like so advanced in design, not even among the fighters or research machines. Compared with the Avro delta there were at least as many unknowns and certainly more to go wrong as far as flight controls and moving surfaces were concerned. In addition the chosen engine, the Metrovick F.9, by 1952 called the Armstrong Siddeley Sapphire, was extremely powerful but not proven by production or service. Two early Sapphires at 7,220 lb rating had thrust a Meteor to a startling world rate-of-climb record, and Hazel himself had flown a prototype Hastings with early Sapphires in the outer positions in order to become familiar with the new axial engines. The Sapphire 6, with a rating of no less than 8,300 lb thrust, was very new indeed and had merely done a bench type-test and some flying in a Canberra.

But at Farnborough 1952 Hazel radiated confidence, and even expressed the view that there was nothing the Avro bomber could do that could not be done at least as well by the HP.80—"although maybe not at quite such an early stage in its flight programme". I rather read between the lines that he thought Roly was being pressurized to show off a little too flamboyantly in a prototype that was supposed to be vital to the nation. Sir Fred produced several splendid biblical quotations about the superior qualities of they that cometh after, and on the Handley Page stand in the indoor exhibition was a breathtaking display of the proposed HP.97. This was a projected airliner with a double-bubble fuselage seating 150 and with a very convincing high-subsonic wing root passing through the lower bubble with a pair of Sapphires on each side. I was told this had nothing to do with the HP.80, so the enemy agents who were foxed by GELEY-PANDHY were doubtless equally put on the wrong scent by the placard stating that the HP.97 could cruise the 3,455 miles to New York at 580 mph carrying a payload of 50,000 lb—and there were lots of other figures. In fact, of course, the HP.97 was identical with the HP.80 apart from the more capacious body, and the security people at the MoS must have had terribly mixed feelings when they saw how nonsensical the security rules were.

Having mentioned the HP.97 I will keep the reader on tenter-hooks waiting for the first flight a little longer and sound off at some length at the proposed civil conversions of the Victor and Vulcan. Hawker Siddeley's project was the Avro Atlantic, using almost exactly the same wing and power plant group as the Vulcan B.1 but with a very large single-deck fuselage seating up to 131 passengers five-abreast. The delta layout was not so well suited to a civil transport as was the less radical crescent, although most of its problems have had to be overcome in the Concorde.

87

Certainly today several things can be seen clearly that in 1952 were hidden or distorted. One is that high-subsonic performance should not have meant radical aircraft shapes but merely an extension of the traditional shape with modest sweepback and greater structural strength. A second is that national performance in producing competitive transport aircraft depends not so much on the manufacturing industry as on the major national air carriers, and on how well they specify for the future. And a third factor is that the introduction of jet propulsion to air transport is by far the biggest single advance the airline industry has made. Full discussion must await another occasion, but hindsight shows that Britain could not have mismanaged the strategic situation more completely. In the United States the Boeing bombers were totally unsuited for any conversion to civil transport use (although with the B-47 Boeing tried on paper for years), and until the JT3 came there was no suitable engine. The HP.80, however, was ideally suited for redesign as a civil transport. Its potential was exactly right, and in the original planning of the HP.97 and of the more refined HP.111 transport of 1958 it was established there were no unexpected major difficulties. Had the HP.97 gone ahead at full speed, with proper programme management, massive industrial backing (which would have meant bringing in other firms) and perceptive support from BOAC and the government, there is no reason to doubt that it would have taken something like £500 million away from the 707/DC-8 market. As it was, neither HP nor BOAC had the stature or foresight to take the proposal seriously. The result was a national mistake so huge that nobody noticed.

In 1952 BOAC was so wrapped up in the Comet and Britannia it could not see the limited potential of these aircraft, and I cannot blame them because neither could the government four years later. As for the government, this had little manpower to spare for looking ahead to the next decade. Most of its staff were busy with far more important things, such as holding 14 committee meetings with the Air Council to choose a name for the HP.80 and then solemnly coming to the conclusion that, like the aircraft itself, the name must be kept secret until after the first flight. Whitehall has a basic rule that everything must be kept secret unless there is a definite reason for disclosure, whereas in Washington it is decreed in writing that the reverse must apply. I recall a semi-serious telephone conversation with an official who confided that the name of the Avro 698 began with "Vul"; I thought he said "Bal" and pondered on Balmoral. As for the HP.80, he said "Vic" and there was a choice of two obvious names. I picked the right one, to be told "On no account must the name be traced back to me". Hopefully today's administration has a different idea of what is important and what is trivial.

In any case the name was soon revealed because Hazel flew WB771 on

Christmas Eve 1952. Despite the fact the engines were derated to 7,500 lb, he took off in less than 1,500 feet, or roughly one-quarter of the distance available at Radlett. One was driven to the belief that the aircraft had been sent to Boscombe through sheer ignorance and an unwillingness to accept the maker's calculations. Anyway Hazel had a splendid Christmas, saying when he landed "It was all so effortless, it's difficult to see why we were so apprehensive". The silver Victor demonstrated such fine handling at low speeds I thought it would be bound to win over the white delta which appeared to need a tailplane (better still a foreplane) and powerful flaps, and which could not equal the Victor's maximum lift coefficient or low drag. According to the Breguet range formula the Victor was superior, and it also had a bigger bomb bay and sat lower on the ground. Yet when HP received the first production order, signed shortly before the prototype flew, Dobbie professed surprise and disgust which seemed to be real.

When HP got this order, for a small batch of 25, he had practically no Victor production tooling and a factory jammed to the doors with Canberras. Eventually the Korean war came to an end in mid-1953 in time for the second half of his contract for 150 Canberras to be cancelled, avoiding difficult overlapping of the two programmes. At the beginning of 1953 the Victor was added to the list of aircraft enjoying "superpriority", but Sir Fred found a quotation which precisely suited the situation in which ten programmes were all chasing the same shortages and all using the superpriority label against each other. He also suggested it would be helpful if he got a proper order, and it was abundantly clear he did not have a high opinion of the MoS procurement machine (I never met anyone who did, but most people hid their feelings). The one good thing in the Victor programme seemed to be the hardware itself, which had the misfortune to be bought by an inept government from a too-small firm.

Structurally the Victor was as remarkable as it was aerodynamically. The main portions of the airframe were made from sandwich skins comprising inner and outer light-alloy sheets spot-welded to a top-hat corrugated light-alloy core. Handley Page did a vast amount of work perfecting this system, which made for a strong and stiff structure with a simple underlying framework and outstandingly accurate and smooth outer profile. At the start every weld was X-rayed, but stringent quality control allowed the production Victor panels to be random-sampled, usually on a 10 per cent basis, and defective welds were done again. This reduction of inspection from 100 to 10 per cent was crucial in making the process financially attractive.

The fixed part of the wing and the nose flaps were wholly of sandwich construction, as were the landing-gear doors and tail. One of the remarkable accomplishments of the HP designers was to run the strong wing box entirely ahead of the engines, whereas in the Valiant and Vulcan the engines were inside it and in the Canberra they were in front of it. This allowed the most highly stressed part of the aircraft to be uncompromised by big access doors, and it eased maintenance, kept the vital wing box away from fire or burst-turbine damage and made it easier to switch to a different and bigger engine. The upper and lower wing-box skins were corrugated spanwise, while most of the other skins had chordwise corrugations, the result being stiffness or flexibility where each was wanted and with practically no ribs. Much credit goes to stressmen R. H. Sandifer and F. Tyson. The whole wing bristled with ingenious details and with neat little forgings, diffusion doublers, finger plates and special fixtures giving great strength and also good fatigue-life, which was something not considered in RAF bomber design at that time. But if the aircraft was to be built only in penny-numbers it was all nonsense, at the taxpayer's expense.

Early in 1953 the contractual MoS specification, B.128P, was finally completed, and the design of the Victor B.1 agreed. It was a time when the British aircraft industry was characterized by good modern military and civil aircraft all running desperately late and coming off the line either not at all or else at a pathetic rate. The only exceptions were the old Meteor and Vampire and the original B.2 version of the Canberra which was built by four companies simultaneously. But the splendid Victor was obviously going to run true to the form of the rest of the industry, and it was almost solely because HP had about one-quarter as many people, both for R&D and production, as the programme needed. By mid-1953 the crescent and the delta were not quite such vague unknown quantities as they had seemed even a year earlier. It would have been possible to have run competitive trials between the two aircraft, despite the fact neither yet had its production engine, and decide which one to deploy operationally. Had this been done the result would have been more of the better bomber sooner, and at a lower unit price because of the doubled production run. Because it was not done we had fewer of both bombers later, and at increased cost. The reasons why it was never done were pathetic; they appear in the story of the Valiant.

But throughout 1953 the Victor prototype made good progress, it being completely unharmed (apart from the 16 main tyres) on the spectacular fourth landing when the parking brake was inadvertently left on. A few seconds before this happened a young amateur with a camera had taken a fine picture of the aircraft on the approach which revealed all sorts of things supposed to be secret and carefully hidden in the two officially released views which everyone had seen hundreds of times. Maj Oliver Stewart published the picture in his magazine *Aeronautics*. Anyone who knew those days will agree that he risked being sent to the Tower, and no publication dared to copy him. I do not recall any other case of a security breach of this kind. And of course Oliver was quite right when he said "Anyone could take that photo". Handley Page, I think, were rather pleased, because WB771 with everything out and down was an impressive sight in the era of the DC-6. By mid-year it had cleared handling, flutter and systems, as well as many special trials for crew escape, braking parachute and other systems. It several times flew four missions in a day, and once six.

In August 1953 the Secretary of the US Air Force, Harold E. Talbott, visited Radlett and Hazel took him for a ride. Nobody tried to read any special significance into the visit, although the V-bombers were the only front-rank British combat machines not supported by the US taxpayer through "off-shore procurement" (a policy designed to help friendly air forces and aircraft industries, which ceased smartly when those industries began to offer the US commercial competition). Mr Talbott's official agenda in London included off-shore procurement, and I think the MoS merely wanted to show him an impressive British aircraft. Anyway, he made all the right noises: "That crew compartment has all five men together, something we don't seem to have in my air force . . . it's real chummy in there, I guess the pilot and co-pilot could have a nice game of gin rummy if they wanted . . . flying this ship is just as easy as a baby carriage." I could not tell from Hazel's impassive countenance whether the last remark was welcome or not, but the important American had put his finger on an excellent characteristic of the Victor that HP had been forbidden to reveal: it landed itself! In most aircraft the ground rising under the tail kills the tail downwash and causes a nose-down moment that the pilot must oppose by "holding off". With the Victor the tailplane was about half the normal size and high off the ground, so the effect was near zero; on top of this with a swept wing there is induced downwash at the root and upwash at the tips, and killing this gives a nose-up pitch. Hazel said, "Get it properly set up on the approach and I promise you will make a perfect landing if you just leave it alone". Years later I suggested something of the sort to 15 Sqn, one of the first users, to open polite conversation at the bar. A very cultured flight lieutenant replied, "Not *quite*, actually . . .", and I felt I had dropped a clanger. It seemed they had been so inculcated with proper procedures not one of them had tried to land hands-off, and they regarded the idea as rather a silly stunt. In fact such favourable landing characteristics are a major asset which many a wounded skipper in World War 2, and many a B-47 pilot, would have appreciated.

At the Coronation Review of the RAF at Odiham in June 1953 WB771 was booked to fly past at 288 knots, while Dobbie (who else could do such a thing?) had managed to get "460 knots" printed in the official programme alongside the prototype Vulcan. This was the design airframe limit at sea level, and in June 1953 I do not believe the prototype Vulcan had been cleared to reach it, nor do I believe it was possible on the thrust of 6,500 lb Avons. But I will admit Roly came past faster than the Victor, which was well throttled back. And on the last day of the year, at a speed lower than 288 knots, WB771's port inner flap came off, fortunately not at low level and not with full flap on. The cause appeared to be high-frequency buffet from the engines, by this time at the 8,300 lb rating. Worse was to come. On 14 July 1954 WB771, still the only Victor HP had managed to complete, was doing a low-level run down the main runway at Cranfield in the course of ASI position-error trials. Without the least warning the tailplane (temporarily borrowed from the second aircraft) came off the fin, just as it had on the HP.88, and within one second the Victor impacted at the intersection of the runways. Handley Page's splendid and immensely valuable prototype had made its contribution to Britain's shocking post-war record in which, out of 60 military prototype and research aircraft built between 1945 and 1955, 46 crashed and one was damaged beyond repair while being trucked to the airfield. In the case of the Victor, the fin/tailplane structure looked admirable from the viewpoints of both static strength and fatigue, the aircraft had flown under 350 hours and it was flying straight and level. At the inquest on R. V. Ecclestone and his crew of three the MoS expert witness testified, "This complex failure could not reasonably have been anticipated". This is probably fair, for to err is human. Handley Page were afraid of tail flutter and went to unusual lengths to guard against it, especially at the fin/tailplane joint. But sometimes fate seems to be quite equally determined. Wind-tunnel tests were done with a flutter model, and a vital stiffness was in error. Calculations were done based on ground resonance tests on WB771, and an aerodynamics term was wrong. Flight tests were done with rudder jerks and the engineers were misled by a difficult record interpretation. What fate did was make all three (incorrect) answers approximately the same, confirming that all was well. Sometimes you just can't win.

In contrast to contemporary American programmes, in which fast progress was made at the possible cost of greater need for modification by the "Cook/Craigie plan" under which production was started before anything had flown, the Handley Page programme moved at a snail's pace and the crash of 771 left the company with nothing to fly until Hazel finally got the second prototype, WB775, into the air on 11 September 1954. Soon afterwards Charles Joy told me his conviction that the company could have moved much faster, but that the overriding message from the customer was "take all the time in the world, be careful, be cautious".

Their objective, he said, was to save money, but he heartily agreed that the best way to do this would have been to move quicker. He confirmed that the production price of a Victor back in 1952 might not have been very different from the "slightly more than £350,000" disclosed in that year by Air Minister George Ward; now, in the fall of 1954, it was double that figure, and most of the production run had yet to be ordered. Most distressing of all was his feeling that he did not thoroughly understand the loss of 771 and that the rather crude reinforcement added to the second Victor was a "botch-up born of ignorance".

On the same occasion I was able to assess the massive wealth of projects engaging the company's attention. I had a good look at the Vampire fighter fitted with a carefully manufactured "glove" around its wing containing thousands of holes for boundary-layer suction. This was by far the biggest item of hardware in a long-term programme to produce a laminar-flow aircraft that would be much more efficient, and burn less fuel, than the traditional turbulent species. From 1949 until the final collapse in 1969 Handley Page doggedly persevered with laminar-flow projects, which never appealed to a conservative airline industry, still less to air forces, who have never lacked explanations of their preference for thirsty, shorter-range machines. Another project group at Cricklewood were engaged in transport and low-level versions of the Victor, another team were working on a wholly new design for a low-level bomber with a small wing, while another was busy with a supersonic bomber. Nobody appeared to question the fact that the company had about one-quarter of the number of engineers needed to do the Victor alone properly, because the industry had grown up using project teams that could be counted on the fingers. Godfrey Lee and F. R. C. Hounsfield were leading a team (that could not have numbered more than half a dozen) on slender delta wings, which were applicable not only to the proposed bombers but also to supersonic airliners the firm were working on for good measure. Hounsfield had been the moving spirit behind the impressive high-speed tunnel, powered by three Nene jet engines, constructed at Radlett in 1952. It began operations just in time to play no part in the design of the Victor, but Lee was delighted at the results obtained with models of slender deltas. Lest it be thought this amazing proliferation of challenging projects was tiresome to the MoS, who might have been concerned at the fact that in eight years the Victor programme had yielded two aircraft, it is a fact that practically all of it was paid for by MoS contracts.

Nevertheless, the Victor programme always made a little progress each day (I think). The Sapphire-Hastings had been used to investigate the crew bail-out problem, never properly solved. I thought the best method would be to push dummies out of the door of WB775, but instead a replica door was built in the rear fuselage of the Hastings and a representation of the Victor wing and intakes painted further aft in the correct location. Then chaps bailed out while a photographic aircraft flew alongside. This seemed fine except for the facts that the Hastings was limited to 175 knots, the airflow was utterly unlike that round the nose of the Victor, the door was on the wrong side and the painted intake was not likely to suck people in. I asked why tests could not be done with the real Victor, and to my great glee received a reply which implied it would be much too dangerous. In the end the solution adopted was merely to lengthen the forward fuselage by 40 inches (the reason given was that this would "improve the c.g. range" which had demanded half a ton of ballast in lieu of the radar in WB771), so that the door was not hard up against the port intake, and make the door hinge at the top, open outwards and draw out a windbreak at the front. I felt at the time the door could have been a strong corrugated sandwich structure hinged diagonally to act as a powerful airflow deflector, with a slat and flap if need be, but maybe this would have been too effective for a customer who seemed to tackle the vital lifesaving problem in a singularly ineffectual way. But at least the bombing trials conducted at Orfordness range in June 1955 showed that something could get out of a Victor safely.

During 1955 the first production batch, ordered in 1952, were at last taking shape in the erection shop at Radlett. The first Victor B.1, XA917, flew on 1 February 1956. Unlike the prototypes, which from 1953 had been finished in an unofficial scheme of silver, grey, black and red (a livery also applied to the Short Sperrin), the first production batch were matt silver, with big black serial numbers. The production engine was the Sapphire 202, of ASSa.7 rating at 11,000 lb, which accounted for the sprightly performance demonstrated by test pilot Johnny Allam (not to be confused with John Allan, deputy chief designer and one-time project engineer on the HP.88). The B.1 also introduced the longer nose, and a broader but shorter vertical tail without the unsightly dorsal fillet containing a combustion-heater intake. Carefully metered engine bleed henceforth handled all the airframe de-icing, except for Napier Spraymat electric panels in the engine intakes, with cold air taken in through intakes on each side of the extreme nose which began life as NACA flush apertures and then, on some aircraft, were changed to big bulged scoops that looked draggy but weren't. In fact the drag of the Victor was commendably low, and below that of any other British four-jet bomber. The shape was obviously right too, because on 1 June 1957 XA917 put its nose down a few degrees and made a magnificent sonic bang, becoming easily the largest aircraft to have flown at the speed of sound (about Mach 1·1, HP thought) at that time.

It was reported that the bang was made during a delivery to the Victor Operational Conversion Unit, No 232, at Gaydon, but in fact proper deliveries did not begin until November 1957, eleven years from the start of the programme and about two years behind the original tentative schedule. Deliveries to an operational unit followed in April 1958, the recipient being No 10 Sqn at Cottesmore. During the summer No 15 Sqn began to convert, and No 543 at Wyton received the first of the small batch of the B(PR).1 reconnaissance version. By this time HP had received all their orders for the Mk 1 Victor, amounting to 64 aircraft, and were hard at work on the much more powerful Mk 2. They were also busy with meeting new requirements in the final half of the Mk 1 buy, the B.1A having numerous equipment and systems changes as well as a visibly obvious change in the blunter tailcone housing the same countermeasures package as was fitted to the corresponding Vulcan. The Mk 1 aircraft of 10 and 15 Sqns were in 1958–60 brought up to Mk 1A standard, and one of these, XH648, was photographed dropping 35 standard 1,000 lb bombs in five tight sticks of seven (compared with three sevens which was the limit for the Vulcan). Both aircraft, of course, were designed to carry nuclear weapons of the same size; the extra volume of the Victor's bomb bay was yet another bonus due to the crescent wing, which brought the spar box far forward at the root and allowed the whole cross section behind it to be available for weapons and fuel.

As in the case of other British military aircraft the Victor spent the first ten years of its life with no flight-refuelling probe, but by 1958 the land where the technique was pioneered was taking pride by revealing that "the design of the Victor makes provision for the incorporation of flight refuelling". Either it was never specified in B.128P or else the Treasury wanted to waste money by insisting it was "incorporated" by modifying the aircraft after they were built. It was not until 1960 that trials with XA930 proved the probe system, a typically horrid non-retractable thing like a cross between a jousting lance and a unicorn's horn that to the pilots looked like a 16-inch gun fixed to the cockpit roof. XA930 also proved the installation of a 1,400 gal unjettisonable tank under each wing, which became standard on operational Victors, as well as the use of a pair of 8,000 lb thrust de Havilland Spectre a.t.o. rockets in streamlined nacelles fixed under the engine bays which most certainly did not. Thus the Victor became the third V-bomber type to consume some tens of thousands of man-hours, to say nothing of hardware, being cleared to use rockets to shorten the take-off run for a reason that was never explained and was evidently unnecessary.

To complete the story of the Mk 1 Victor, even though it overlaps chronologically with the Mk 2, the decision was taken in 1960 to convert

all operational Mk 1 Victors to serve the dual roles of strategic reconnaissance and tanker as soon as they could be replaced in the bomber
force by the Mk 2. There seemed to be no need to hurry. The standard
RAF tanker was the Valiant, which was available in ample numbers to
meet the needs of the strike and fighter squadrons. Not until July 1964
was the second production Victor, XA918, flown again after a protracted
conversion at Radlett to the BK.1 configuration. It had its bomb bay filled
with rigid transfer fuel tanks, a Flight Refuelling Mk 17 hose reel was
fitted in a retractable mounting immediately to the rear and a Mk 20B
windmill-driven hose-reel pod was attached beneath each outer wing. No
great problems were encountered, but it took more than six months for
XA918 to reach the stage at which the first tentative hook-ups could be
made by Lightning F.2s of 19 Sqn at Leconfield, using the wing hoses
only. I got the impression that the programme might never have made
any progress at all had it not been for the sudden panic caused by the
fatigue problem of the Valiant and the grounding of that aircraft in
December 1964. The RAF woke up one morning to find it had no tankers,
apart from XA918 which had never made a contact. In the resulting
pandemonium Handley Page were almost stopped from doing anything
else but urgently rush through Victor tankers. To try to get them converted quickly the interim job left out the centre-line pack and added just
the wing pods for a "two point system", first flown on BK.1A XH620
on 28 April 1965. The definitive "three point" aircraft began with XA937,
flown on 2 November 1965. After the demise of the Valiants in 1964 the
RAF got a tanker again in June 1965, when two-point machines began to
reach 55 Sqn; the three-pointer began to reach 57 Sqn in February 1966.
During the frightening tanker gap, lasting over six months, it was very
considerate of Her Majesty's enemies not to stir things, because the only
way fighter aircraft could have been got to the scene of the crime would
have been as deck cargo. The RAF did not even have a freight aircraft
in which fighters could have been carried dismantled, apart from the Beverley
which needed flight refuelling itself to fly beyond the Isle of Wight.

Thus we come to the Victor B.2, which, like the corresponding improved
Vulcan, dates from 1955. In that year, when there was but a single prototype Victor in the world, the MoS decided it was worth spending a lot of
money to make subsonic bombers fly a little higher over their targets.
Studies showed that with four Olympus 6 or Conway engines the Victor
could gain 8,000–10,000 feet, while at the same time carrying a heavier
load further and slightly faster. My view, expressed in the Vulcan story,
is that it was all nonsense; in the missile age nobody gains much security
by coming over a target a bit faster or a bit higher. With the benefit of
hindsight one can see that the choice should not have been the Mk 2

versions of the Victor and Vulcan, nor even a choice made between them, but the smart termination of both programmes and the urgent development of one of the low-level bombers that had been projected since 1952. Unfortunately the Air Staff could not see this, and tried hard to pretend that anti-aircraft guided weapons either didn't exist or else were not very lethal. In any case in 1955–56 Britain was falling over backwards to "build on success" in aviation. Three government spokesmen pointed to the Viscount, Comet and Britannia as saleable products on which the nation should concentrate, instead of thinking about such a silly thing as a big jet. The same thinking affected the Air Ministry. The Vulcan and Victor were good things on which to build. They became very angry if anyone suggested that any conceivable future mark of these fine aircraft would be practically as vulnerable as the Mk 1.

HP were awarded the B.2 development contract in 1955 and the chosen engine, the 17,250 lb thrust Rolls-Royce Conway RCo.11, was ordered in April 1956. Had this not been so I think it unlikely Rolls-Royce would ever have sold an engine to buyers of the Boeing 707 and Douglas DC-8, so the Victor B.2 did do the nation some good. The main philosophy was more power, more fuel, better systems, more span and additional mission equipment, the main item under the last heading being the Blue Steel stand-off bomb. The most important advance was the new engine, which weighed about the same as the Sapphire and burned fuel at about the same rate yet gave almost 60 per cent more thrust. It was about five inches fatter. This might have been accommodated without major change to the engine bay, but the fact that the total engine mass flow had gone up from 180 to 280 pounds per second meant much bigger inlet ducts which in turn meant a completely new inner wing. It was eventually decided to add part of the extra span at the root, 30 inches being added on each side here and the same on each tip, to increase the span from 110 to 120 feet. So big were the new inlet ducts that they had to project beneath the lower surface of the wing in a form of chin box. And where they passed through the spar there was no room for any web at all. Instead the spar loads, increased because of the greater weight and span, were transmitted through massive spectacles forged on the High Duty Alloys 12,000-ton press from slabs of DTD.683 alloy about six feet square. Further problems stemmed from the sensitivity of the Conway, then a very advanced high-pressure engine designed rather near the surge-line, to inlet velocity distribution. Here again the Victor helped the civil jetliners by getting the installation right, and it took two years.

In the matter of systems the main advance was improved ancillary power. The Victor B.2 had a much more powerful hydraulic system, a much more powerful electric system (paralleled a.c., generated by a

50 kVA alternator driven by a Bradford-built Sundstrand drive on each engine), a Blackburn Artouste gas-turbine APU in the starboard wing fed by an electrically operated scoop, and a pair of big Rotax turbo-alternators fed by hydraulic ram-air scoops in front of the restored dorsal fin. It made one wonder how on earth the Mk 1 had ever managed.

As the electrical load on the B.2 was not more than 20 per cent greater than that for the Mk 1, a lot of the added power was belt and braces for emergencies, although the a.c. system did have far better reliability. It fed a new e.c.m. equipment in the tailcone, with six peripheral aerials looking like an old radial engine with a helmet-type cowling. Further very precise a.c. supplies were needed by new mission equipment that I still cannot discuss. Another improvement was the fitting of a combined yaw/roll damper, instead of a single-axis yaw system, because increased stability problems were expected at heights around 60,000 feet.

A fairly big structural change was the redesign of the weapons bay and its doors to mate with the Blue Steel. Eventually a way was found to keep cut-away doors which closed above the missile so that the aircraft could fly without the weapon and still be reasonably streamlined. The performance penalty with Blue Steel on was later given as "two per cent"; I think the penalty without the missile would have been rather greater. Provision was also made for converting the B.2 to carry ordinary free-fall bombs of both nuclear and "iron" varieties, but the conversion took a day and a half and was not normally a task for the user squadron.

Development of the B.2 predictably took almost as long as the original B.1, and it cost more. The engine programme was not helped by the crash of the Conway-Vulcan on 20 September 1958, and in the report to shareholders for that year Sir Fred explained a poor trading result by pointing to the problems with both the Mk 1 and Mk 2 Victor. Aircraft were "delayed by the installation of new equipment", there was "a large number awaiting modification", enormous sums were "locked up in work in progress", much more money was needed to "finance production", and (cryptic, this) "the cost does not cover the whole expense". In short, the situation was absolutely normal for the UK airframe industry. Eventually the first B.2, which was simply the next aircraft in the serial list after the last B.1, was hustled into the air by Johnny Allam on 20 February 1959. It was XH668, and, as was the case with the Vulcan, B.2 and B.1 aircraft were assembled at Radlett together for two years, the last B.1 (XH667) not being delivered until February 1961.

By this time Rolls had run true to form and developed the RCo.17, with a guaranteed rating of 19,750 lb and an average output of 20,600 lb, and this was the engine chosen for production as the Conway 201. With four of these XH668 was a truly remarkable aircraft in terms of flight performance, for it had far more thrust than any 707 and usually flew at about half the weight. By June 1959 it had been delivered for handling trials to Boscombe, where its crews were envied—until 20 August. On that day it simply didn't come back. As it was Britain's very latest and most powerful bomber there were all sorts of wild rumours, and one wondered if it had been delivered to the highest bidder. But careful scrutiny of radar plots indicated a probable descent into the Irish Sea somewhere off Pembroke. It seemed odd to me that this valuable aircraft should not have been kept under careful surveillance at all times, but there was an almost complete lack of information. No radar had seen the descent or sea impact, nobody on land or sea had seen it, nobody knew the exact time of the disaster and there had been no radio transmission. Psychologically it seemed like the Comet 1 all over again. Eventually small bits of flotsam were found, a fleet of small ships was gathered that ultimately numbered 12 vessels of the Royal Navy and 27 chartered trawlers, and an exhaustive dredging process began. By the end of 1959 they had brought up 592,610 pieces, representing about 70 per cent of the aircraft. By October the decision had been taken to tank-test the pressure cabin and many other items. Eventually this extraordinary accident was traced to failure of a simple piece of standard equipment followed by a curious sequence of unlucky circumstances, but it took about a year to elucidate.

It is hard to think of anything more damaging to an aircraft programme than a completely mysterious fatal crash. HP never slowed production, but entry to service was certainly delayed by the long and painstaking investigation and the whole programme was set back about nine months, having previously lost about the same time in 1956–59. The second B.2, XH669, flew in September 1960, just in time for Farnborough and one of the occasions when the SBAC show certainly acted as a spur rather than a hindrance. The fact that 669 was sent to 232 OCU at Gaydon the following month suggested slight impatience on the part of the customer, but the rest of the run were following at their proper intervals and it looked like a clear run home. In December 1961 XH674 went straight from Radlett to the Avro Weapon Division at Woodford where it began compatibility trials with the Blue Steel missile. Everything seemed to go very well once the big weapon had been coaxed under the Victor's low-slung belly. By this time there was known to be little future in flying high, and like the Vulcan the Victor B.2 was painted in green and grey and pressed into service in the low-level role. It could release Blue Steel at the nominal 200 feet altitude and also do toss bombing with h.e., although I do not believe any live weapon was ever dropped from these aircraft. The first operational unit was 139 "Jamaica" Sqn at Wittering, which received its first B.2 in February 1962. Deliveries were then made to 100 and 57

Sqns (but not to any of the users of the Victor B.1 or 1A), completing the offensive Victor force in 3 Group. When fully equipped, 139 held a great open day for the press. A flight demonstration was put on by a B.2 which was flung into a very tight turn on take-off. On the second time round he turned, very low, at an even sharper bank angle and slipped straight down to hit the ground in a ball of fire. Many of the most experienced journalists left this out of their story.

It was already clear that there would be no more Victors, that the Vulcan would be the principal carrier of the British deterrent (equipping not just three squadrons but nine), and that Sir Fred was being regarded as a stubborn old has-been who obstinately refused to sell his company to a bigger one as the government wished. Obstinate he certainly could be, but he had a powerful desire to leave his great firm in good shape and had no inherent objection to a merger if the terms were fair. It is not generally known that Handley Page Ltd could have been happily merged into another British group (not BAC or HSA) under terms satisfactory to Sir Fred and his board. Then on 2 August 1960, in the middle of the negotiations, the MoA clumsily cancelled the last ten Victors and the deal fell through. I ought not to blame the MoA because they merely passed on the reduced requirement of the RAF, whose view was that Skybolt would increase the number of targets that could be taken out per aircraft from one to three, thus reducing the number of aircraft necessary for the RAF deterrent force.

Some observers said Skybolt was difficult to fit to the Victor. Defence Minister Harold Watkinson incredibly muttered something about having to develop "a British weapon" (presumably in the ALBM category) for this aircraft. But Reginald Stafford, by now on the HP board, said his studies led him to precisely the opposite view. I then lived near him in Middlesex and he once gave me a lift home from Cricklewood in his car, saying he was deeply concerned at the political manoeuvring afflicting the industry. "I know", he said, "that the Victor is as suitable as a carrier of Skybolt as any aircraft in the world. But the government wants to believe otherwise and I am not allowed to say a word in public." He suggested there were petty officials who believed the old lion had lost his teeth and could have his tail twisted. But he had not yet lost his voice. Within a week Sir Fred considered he had nothing to lose by speaking his mind in a way that was conspicuously absent from the speeches of other planemakers. "You have my assurance", he said, "that the Victor 2 can carry Skybolt without needing either wing strengthening or undercarriage modification. Already it has flown with the equivalent in weight and drag of two Skybolts under its wings. These facts are known to our defence chiefs." Trying to frame my question in such a way as to preclude prevarication I put in a formal request for confirmation of the fact that there were technical difficulties in mating Skybolt to the Victor. The MoD did not answer it, but instead replied, "It is unlikely that Skybolt will be carried by the Victor". It seems difficult in Britain ever to take a decision and then announce it. I still do not know the answer: presumably either the Victor was at last judged inferior to the Vulcan (pity we didn't find out earlier), or it was out of favour because the government wanted to spite HP (which was certainly true), or there were indeed compatibility problems (despite HP's denial) or there was some yet further reason.

This was the end of the road as far as new aircraft were concerned, and XM718, the last B.2, was delivered on 2 May 1963. But there was a big job ahead in modification and conversion. It was discovered at this time that adding large streamlined fairings above the trailing edge of the wing, to house the "Window" anti-radar chaff (thin strips of foil released by the million to blot out the bomber's radar reflection), which in the B.1 was accommodated under the nose, did not increase drag but reduced it. They behaved as "Küchmann carrots" or "Whitcomb bodies"—fairings to reduce transonic drag-rise and seen prominently on the CV-990 airliner. So in 1963–64 these were added to all the Mk 2 Victors, but not to the Mk 1 aircraft, making them look rather as if they had been designed by Tupolev's bureau. A much bigger conversion programme was the B(SR).2, with a bomb bay full of fuel and extensive equipment for multi-sensor reconnaissance. As the grounding of the Valiant had left the RAF short of strategic reconnaissance aircraft, not fully met by the stop-gap conversion of the Mk 1 Victor, the B(SR).2 became a vital part of the national armoury. Compared with the Valiant it had "40% more range and 15% higher ceiling". The first conversion, XL165, flew on 23 February 1965, and deliveries to 543 Sqn began in September. The SR variant could "map with radar an area of 750,000 square miles in six hours". It was also reported—in June 1966 by the Central Reconnaissance Establishment— that "four can map the whole Atlantic in six hours". Unfortunately the Atlantic is almost 32 million square miles, so I hope the RAF establishment of the SR was not based on such faulty sums. (As I write this it looks as if the mistake has been discovered, because there is now talk of an SR conversion of the Vulcan B.2 as well.) Years earlier, in about 1962, people around Radlett had noticed a Victor B.2 flying with what looked like the longest and slimmest drop tanks ever seen, about 40 feet long and shaped like a pencil. Each pod was a splendid side-looking aircraft radar (SLAR) for which I believe the code name was Red Neck, but it was one of at least two systems that, surprisingly, were left out of the final SR.2.

The last variant was the K.2 tanker, which replaced the K.1 in the Air Refuelling force which had in the meanwhile moved from Honington to

Marham. Compared with the K.1 it carries slightly more transfer fuel and is marginally better equipped. HP did all the design for the conversion but never received the conversion contract. On 8 August 1969 the bankrupt firm called in the Receiver, became a subsidiary of the K. R. Cravens Corporation of St Louis and finally shut up shop for good in February 1970. The government were concerned only to the extent that they wanted someone to convert the Mk 2 tankers, and eventually, in 1970, a contract was signed with Hawker Siddeley Aviation. By 1972 the 29 Victor K.2s were at last being converted at the lair of the Vulcan at Chadderton and at Woodford, where the work is managed by K. C. Pratt who in happier days was in charge of the vast Victor structural and systems test programmes. Until at least 1980 these 29 tankers will bear a heavy burden in support of whatever global mobility the Queen's armed forces possess.

In human artifacts as complex as modern aircraft it is difficult, and probably foolish, to try to give slick appraisals. If I allege that, simply because of its shape, the Victor ought to be a more efficient long-range aircraft than the Vulcan, this could be hotly denied by the former Avro people and by today's Vulcan crews. And the latter can point out that, even though in 1961 the AOC Bomber Command called the Victor "The best medium bomber in the world", by that time the decision had been taken to concentrate on the Vulcan. If this decision had been taken ten years earlier Britain would have saved something in excess of £100 million, which in those days was a lot of money.

Dassault Mirage IV

THE IMAGE of France under General de Gaulle was one of a nation determined to make an exceptional and deliberate effort to increase its stature. One could argue endlessly about whether an objective concerned with a nation's standing in world politics really can do some good, in making people want to work harder and take greater pride in their accomplishments, or is foredoomed to failure in warping national judgement and diverting resources from things that really matter. In particular, vehement arguments can be sustained over the decision of the French government to develop nuclear weapons and strategic delivery systems for them. Such a task was bound to make a mighty drain on the national budget for very many years. I have heard left-wing "students" in Paris angrily taking it for granted the decision was by Le Général, but in fact it was taken long before the nation called him. The original architect of the *Force de Frappe* (strike force) was Pierre Mendès-France, the most left-wing French leader in my lifetime. In 1954 his administration committed France to a goal of credible nuclear strength which has consumed many thousands of millions of new francs; but, with scant help from others, the goal has been attained.

In the third national *Loi de Programme* (five-year defence plan) of 1955–59 most of the money was voted for the development of a fission bomb, the engineering of the bomb into a compact air-portable form and the R&D for a bomber to carry it. In the final two years of this *Loi* funds were also voted for initial research into a thermonuclear (hydrogen) bomb and into ballistic missiles to carry the original fission bomb over ranges of the order of 2,000 miles. In the fourth *Loi* of 1960–64 money was voted for the fleet of operational bombers, for a land-based IRBM, a submarine-based SLBM, the submarines to launch the SLBM and further development of the H-bomb. In the fifth *Loi* of 1965–69 funds were provided for operating the nuclear bombers, for building the IRBM and SLBM force and for initial deployment, as well as initiating H-bomb testing. The current *Loi*, 1970–74, provides for operation of all three delivery systems and the start of production of the thermonuclear weapon. By any yardstick this is an incredible achievement. I will leave it to defence experts to decide whether the whole thing has been cost/effective, but it is missing the point to argue whether it gives France any sort of parity with the United States and Soviet Union. One must not forget that France is less interesting to an aggressor. It was Dassault's eloquent General Gallois who told me that, "making the most pessimistic assumptions, the French nuclear bombers could destroy ten Russian cities; and France is not a prize worthy of ten Russian cities". Or, in de Gaulle's own words, all France need do was "arracher un bras à son agresseur pour qu'on la respecte". Thus, according to this argument, their deterrent really does deter; indeed, by 1961 the *Force de Frappe* had been renamed the *Force de Dissuasion* (deterrent force).

This change of name precisely reflected the change in the public-relations thinking of the United States, which began with the Dulles concept of massive retaliation—which France could never hope to emulate —and shifted to the more constructive notion of deterrence, the existence of power so terrifying that aggressors would come to heel without the need for any fighting. The motto of the US Strategic Air Command has always been "Peace is our Profession" and, however much the Left may dislike SAC and its motto, they cannot deny that the concept has worked perfectly for 25 years. This thinking has dominated the French during the past 20 of those years. In the early 1950s the French had three options: leave nuclear deterrence to others; take part in a collaborative programme within the framework of NATO, and certainly leaning heavily on Britain; or go it alone. There is obviously something in the French make-up that resists accepting the belief that there is anything beyond the capacity of the nation. Critics have called it "delusions of grandeur", but today's French-man would say any "grandeur" died with their colonial empire. Their nuclear weapons have been undertaken for very clearly-thought-out, cool-headed reasons. And, from the original decision to undertake the development of nuclear weapons, the French have spurned the idea of any form of collaboration in this field apart from buying certain items of foreign hardware or manufacturing licences which, while saving time and money, were never crucial to their programme. In de Gaulle's own words, they will never trust their defence "and, therefore France's very existence, to a foreign, that is to say an unreliable, protector".

So France set out on her giant task of creating a viable deterrent, with nuclear weapons, bombers, ballistic missiles, underground control centres and even red telephones, to say nothing of a fleet of giant submarines armed not with Polaris but with the home-grown MSBS. But plenty of voices were raised in opposition, and finding the best course of action was often far from easy. The primary task, however, was to create an airborne vehicle to deliver the French nuclear bomb. At once the aircraft designer needs to know where it is to be delivered. Despite their profound distrust of the Anglo-Saxons, the French have—outwardly, at least—given the impression they consider their main threat to be posed by the Soviet Union. This is a very big country and it is quite a long way even from France.

Hitting it in an aerial attack based on the technology of the mid-1950s calls for quite a big bomber, no matter whether it flies at subsonic or supersonic speed. Even with the use of flight refuelling, the likely missions were so long that until 1955 the French were daunted by the probable cost of producing a bomber to fly them. France was being slowly bled white by the war in Indo-China, had large commitments to NATO and was in addition having to find well over NF 10,000 million (about £800 million) for the mere R&D preparatory to building a nuclear bomb. Until the middle of the decade their deterrent force seemed to me to be a gigantic will to do something that was patently beyond their capabilities (in this I was simply quite wrong, but a lot of Anglo-Saxons had formed a falsely limited view of French economic strength). The only plausible answer appeared to be Sud-Aviation's Super Vautour, a stretched Vautour (Vulture) with Atar engines rated at 10,500 lb thrust and an operational radius at about Mach 0·9 of 1,700 miles.

In 1955 forty Vautour IIB bombers were ordered to serve as the nucleus of the Command des Forces Aériennes Stratégique (CFAS). These were based on the original Vautour airframe and incapable of fulfilling much of a strategic role. In fact they were meant only to help prepare the way for future bombers to serve fully operationally. But, having got them, could they do a valid operational job? Discussion of the way these Vautours might be used in the event of a genuine emergency led to the gradual acceptance of an idea which has not often been used as the basis of a military force. The reasoning was logical enough. If there were a nuclear war there would be no Paris, no France, nothing to come back to. So the long out-and-return mission could be forgotten and replaced by a one-way trip. What France really wanted was a bomber having the highest performance and maximum penetrability that could deliver the French nuclear weapon to designated targets. What happened after that was immaterial. Surviving aircraft might succeed in landing in the Soviet Union (or wherever the target was) or in Finland, Turkey or some other nearby country. This dramatically reduced the size and cost of the delivery vehicle. In the teeth of bitter opposition from many Armée de l'Air generals, who variously disputed the concept of a one-way mission, doubted the financial ability of France, doubted the credibility of the proposed deterrent or simply opposed the very idea of nuclear warfare, the Socialist government of Guy Mollet in May 1956 drew up a specification and passed it to the Direction Technique et Industrielle de l'Air (DTIA). It called for a bomber capable of carrying a bomb 5·2 metres long and weighing three tonnes over a distance of 2,000 km without air refuelling, but to have provision for such replenishment. To the surprise of many, it also demanded the ability to fly at supersonic speed.

There was really only one horse in the race. Although Sud-Aviation and Nord-Aviation both submitted studies which could claim to be based on existing supersonic aircraft, Dassault submitted a detailed proposal for the Mirage IV which looked overwhelmingly attractive on both technical and cost grounds. Its great advantage lay in the fact that it stemmed directly from a twin-engined night-fighter that was proposed early in 1956 as a direct scale-up of the Mirage III day fighter. There are often major benefits in simpler development to be gained by scaling a successful design, although it is not quite as simple as the technically illiterate person might suppose. As both the smaller and larger aircraft will fly in the same atmosphere a "Reynolds number" correction has to be applied to the scaling process because of the viscosity of the air. As many items built into the aircraft are not scaled but stay the same size (obvious examples are people, ejection seats and radar aerials for a given wavelength) the scaling process must be modified to accommodate them. And the square/cube law, which states that doubling the linear dimensions results in four times the area but eight times the weight, is always approximately adhered to although it can be partly countered by the fact that a bigger structure can be made in a more refined way. Sometimes a design team have proposed to scale a successful design and produced a complete failure. Dassault's enlarged Mirage looked a winner from the start.

The original Mirage had been twin-engined; a light research machine, based on a specification for a short-range "light fighter", it flew on 25 June 1955 on the very modest thrust of two Viper turbojets which Dassault proposed to make under licence for various applications. The immensely more capable Mirage III supersonic fighter used a single, far more powerful Atar with reheat. For the Mirage IV Dassault simply scaled up this aircraft by about 50 per cent in linear dimensions, equivalent to a gross weight between two and three times as high, and made provision for two Atar engines side-by-side. The Atar played a central role in all Dassault's military designs at the time. SNECMA, who began with a basically German design in 1948 that would barely give one ton of thrust, had by 1956 begun to build the prototype Atar 9, a refined supersonic engine that later gave 11,000 lb dry and 16,000 lb with full reheat, and was cleared to flight Mach numbers greater than 2. This light, slim and keenly priced engine was the foundation upon which Dassault built his vast success with the Mirage III fighter, and it was also the basis for the night fighter that was developed into the bomber. The proposed bomber had a span of only 37 feet, a length of 67 feet and a weight of about 55,000 lb. Dassault tentatively predicted a flight Mach number of 2, because the prototype Mirage III had reached 1·6 with a much earlier Atar fed by fixed-geometry intakes. Dassault received an ITP for a flight prototype and a static-test airframe in April 1957. The company's main design office and prototype factory is at Saint-Cloud, on the north-west outskirts of Paris. It has been perpetually overworked ever since 1950, but from April 1957 St Cloud has been non-stop pandemonium.

In six months Dassault had a detailed specification, a structural mock-up, a systems mock-up and a mock-up cockpit for pilot and navigator in tandem, but Jean Rouault, the engineer in charge of the vital bomb/nav system, had still not secured a final avionics schedule from the customer. The ideal would have been a self-contained inertial navigation system, updated by radar, astro or doppler methods, and linked with a blind-bombing and mapping radar. Obviously, despite the high supersonic speed the Mirage IV was also going to need the very best in the way of electronic countermeasures in order to defeat the new generations of surface-to-air missiles being developed in all major nations. Rouault's small staff were intensely interested in the systems carried by the Convair B-58, the only existing example of a supersonic bomber. The American technical press obligingly kept everyone fully informed on such matters— had there not been this source of information it is interesting to speculate on how far the French could have relied upon official NATO sources— and Dassault and their electronics subsidiary EMD, together with the main radar supplier CSF, anxiously investigated the limits of what appeared to be possible. It was not until 1960 that all hope was abandoned of providing production aircraft with an inertial system, because the attraction of such a system kept it in the picture against the severe handi-caps of French lack of experience, inability to make IN-quality hardware, political bars to US suppliers, the take-off delay while the system warmed up and was aligned, and the probability of poor reliability and MTBF. Today the French have inertial guidance in missiles as small as Pluton (and it may fly today with the Mirage IV, for all I know) but I think they were wise not to attempt it in 1957. Instead they took the search radar of the Alizé anti-submarine aircraft, the only good French airborne radar then available, turned it into the Cyrano 2 with a continuously rotating aerial above a circular radome that scarcely broke the bottom line of the fuselage, and went to Marconi in Essex for a good doppler radar. The British company produced the AD.2300 to Dassault's specification, and were even allowed to supply it from the UK. Panoramic radar plus doppler amply met the specification of the Armée de l'Air.

There were not many other imported items. Martin-Baker's seats, Flight Refuelling's nose probe and Marquardt's emergency ram-air turbines were all made in France. The airframe, though resembling a scaled Mirage III, was actually considerably more advanced and incor-porated machined and chem-milled planks, tapered sheets, a small amount of titanium, and integral tankage almost everywhere including the leading portion of the fin. Although Dassault made all of the prototype, 01, a consortium was set up for production Mirage IVs consisting of Sud-Aviation (wings and rear fuselage), Breguet (fin) and Dassault (front fuselage and flight-control system). Messier made the challenging bogie landing gears, which for a large tailless delta have to be tall yet hinged inside the extremely thin wing. I believe the Mirage IV wing, with a thickness/chord ratio of 3·8 per cent at the root and 3·2 per cent at the tip, is the thinnest ever built in Europe and one of the thinnest in the world. Today, of course, a supersonic bomber would not be a tailless delta but would have swing-wings, or a tailplane or a foreplane, but the Mirage IV was probably a correct choice in 1957. Any alternative would have posed too great a technical risk and taken too long.

Superficially the Mirage IV seemed the world's easiest route to a Mach 2 bomber, yet many Armée de l'Air generals continued to consider the aircraft much too small, deficient in range and obviously inadequate because it could not fly the return trip. One general who most certainly would not knock the Mirage IV is Roland Glavany. In 1954 he took five years' leave from the Armée de l'Air to serve Dassault as chief test pilot. It was Glavany who conducted the vital early flight testing of the Mirage III, and on 17 June 1959 he climbed the taller ladder to the cockpit of Mirage IV–01 and flew that bigger aircraft at Melun-Villaroche. The prototype bomber had looked complete by Christmas 1958, which admirably illustrates what Dassault can achieve with a mere handful of men at St Cloud. Systems testing at Melun took some months, and then Glavany began taxiing and short hops—one lasting 3,000 feet—on the Melun runway which in those days was 9,160 feet long. On 17 June Glavany logged an hour, accompanied closely by the tandem-seat Avon-powered Mystère IVN as chase-plane, reaching 325 knots at 12,000 feet. On its second flight, accompanied by a Mirage III to give scale, Glavany flew the bomber along the Le Bourget runway before a Paris air show crowd of 600,000. In view of the urgent need to press ahead with development it seems remarkable that the first seven flights were all mere exhibitions and demonstrations. One was given before de Gaulle himself, and that austere gentleman knew why some of the pressure had gone off the development of Mirage IV–01. He thought it nothing like big enough for the glory of France!

When he was called by the nation to lead them into the Fifth Republic in 1958 one of the first things Charles de Gaulle did was take a close look at the *Loi Programme* and the plans for nuclear deterrence. He eagerly agreed with the generals who thought the Mirage IV, with its inability to fly home from its targets, small and inadequate. Despite frantic danger signals from some who added up the likely costs, de Gaulle got the Cabinet to agree on a strategic bomber able to fly both ways, and capable of much more rapid global deployment without flight refuelling. The DTIA wrote a new specification and early in 1959 Dassault began working three shifts. The team at St Cloud were almost always overtired and a typical working week for a senior engineer was 80 hours. In those months in the spring of 1959 some actually did crack up with nervous exhaustion. Work never totally dropped on the Mirage IV, but the new project, which was tentatively called Mirage IVB, was more than twice as big in terms of design effort. At first the gross weight was put at 165,000 lb, but by March 1959 it had settled at 140,000. Likely engines were the British Olympus and Conway and the American J75. Very quickly the decision was taken to adopt the J75, because this was already fully developed as a supersonic military power-plant with afterburner. But buying it from Pratt & Whitney was out of the question; it had to be made in France.

In a matter of days a top P&W delegation from Hartford came to Paris to talk to the French government and to the national engine company SNECMA. The proposition was that SNECMA should procure a manufacturing licence for the JT24 (J75B), an engine even more advanced than that fitted to the F-105 Thunderchief. Two of them would impart 56,000 lb thrust to the Mirage IVB at take-off, and urge it to a flight Mach number of 2·4. Pratt & Whitney already knew the US Departments of State and Defense would not object, for the J75 was far from a new engine, but they looked a long way ahead. To them the formidable French bomber looked anything but an assured programme, and their astute brains pictured the scene as it might be a few months hence with the bomber cancelled for want of funds and no deal left with the French. In a matter of days they sewed up a nice arrangement with the French, whom they virtually had over a barrel. The main essential was that Pratt & Whitney were given 10·9 per cent of SNECMA, and as SNECMA was a nationalized group this was a remarkable thing. On top of this they tied up SNECMA with Pratt & Whitney engines for military and civil fields, and in particular permitted the French company to study their advanced technology, look at the new JTF10A turbofan that later was the successful candidate for the TFX (F-111) and also act as the main P&W overhaul centre in Europe. For the immediate future, they promised to provide full propulsion support to the Mirage IVB.

The team sent over from Connecticut hardly had time to meet their French colleagues when the whole programme collapsed, in July 1959. None of this was announced at the time, and in fact all the French had really done was revert to a smaller bomber using flight refuelling, but to the Dassault design staff the situation was fairly chaotic. You don't switch from a 26,000 lb-thrust aircraft to a much heavier 56,000 lb-thrust one at the drop of a hat, and it is not very easy to jump back to an intermediate one with 31,000 lb. This must have been an excruciating time for the French, because the essence of their programme was effective use of resources to create their Mach 2 bomber as quickly as possible. Changing horses in mid-stream was not really welcome. In fact, the first change, to the IVB, seemed to me to carry with it an unacceptable risk. The proposed aircraft was not far short of the B-58 in calibre, and I frankly thought somebody had bitten off more than he could chew. In fact, so I am assured, the total cost of the IVB programme would not have been greater than the total cost of the adopted programme. This was to deploy a force of slightly enlarged bombers, using a new version of the Atar rated at about 15,500 lb (a theoretical sea-level figure with full reheat), supported by a fleet of 12 Boeing KC-135 (707-type) tankers. With two spare aircraft to take care of attrition this meant buying 14 big tankers similar to those used by SAC, and the key factor in the abandonment of the Mirage IVB was the receipt by the French government of sanction for this purchase by the US State Department. In view of the condemnation in Washington of French nuclear weapons, this approval seemed remarkable. Maybe the Americans were just being pragmatic—after all, a French friend asks me, "What was to stop us buying a dozen 707s outside the United States and transforming them into tankers?"—but it still seemed to imply tacit approval of the French deterrent.

One very big factor in favour of the flight-refuelling solution was that it automatically provided France with a force of very capable long-range military transport aircraft which had previously been conspicuously lacking. Even without the need for a large airlift to South-East Asia the French still had a requirement for some global logistic capability, much of it directly concerned with nuclear-weapon testing, and the KC-135 was ideal for the purpose. Without modification the standard tanker would accommodate 145 passengers or 50,000 lb cargo above the floor. The only major change the Armée de l'Air decided to make to the KC-135 was to convert the refuelling boom to the British probe/drogue system which had been adopted as standard by the French services. A study was made of using the SAC boom/receptacle method, but this would have made it impossible for the bombers to refuel each other by means of a "Buddy pack", which simulated operations showed to be highly desirable.

The bomber finally chosen was designated Mirage IVA. Wing area was increased from 670 to 839 square feet, and gross weight from 55,000 to about 70,000 lb. Only a day or two after the big IVB was dropped, Glavany began serious flight development and took 01 beyond Mach 1. So well had Dassault's élite crew done their job on the systems rig that the powered flight-controls worked almost faultlessly, and indeed were left wholly untouched on the first four flights. The aircraft continued to be exceptionally trouble-free. The first flight of the resumed programme had been the eighth. On the ninth Glavany reached Mach 1·53. On the fourteenth, still in July 1959, he held Mach 1·9 in level flight on the power of the two Atar 9B engines each rated at about 13,200 lb with maximum reheat. From the start 01 had supposedly definitive intakes with translating half-cone centre-bodies positioned by an automatic control system. Most of the systems were very much state-of-the-art. Electrics were a mix of d.c. and raw (unsynchronized) a.c., the main source of pneumatic power was compressor bleed, and the hydraulics used mineral oil at 3,000 lb/sq in. Even so there were enough complications for plenty to go wrong, and the almost weird absence of snags—in my view—is evidence that luck can be good as well as bad. In the F-111 millions of dedicated man-hours were met by technical difficulties like a succession of stone walls; in the Mirage IV a handful of men, individually not endowed with super-human attributes, created a Mach 2 bomber that worked like a charm. To a large degree the key to success was Dassault's basic philosophy of doing what they knew already, and sticking their necks out as little as possible.

In the autumn of 1959 Glavany's five years were up; he returned to his beloved Armée de l'Air, and René Bigand took over the reins. The proto-type spent some weeks on the ground between the first and second series of flight tests having a thorough inspection and a number of modifications. The most obvious change was a major reduction in aspect ratio of the vertical tail. This was generally reported at the time as a reduction in area by cutting off the top, but it was actually an increase in area gained by extending the chord, adding more than was taken away by a small reduction in height. The rudder power unit, originally in the fuselage, was moved half-way up the fin in a streamlined fairing like that seen on Concorde. Provision was made for a finless 550-gal drop tank under each wing, and a significant modification was the large recess under the fuselage between the engine ducts in which nestled a ballistic simulation of the bomb. Mirage IV-01 went from strength to strength. By the end of 1959 it had sustained Mach 1.85 at 59,000 ft, reached Mach 2 on the level, manoeuvred at 818 mph at 10,000 ft and explored the flight envelope with the bomb absent and a gaping cavity underneath. It had also flown at night, been sampled by service pilots at CEV Brétigny and started development with an observer on board.

On 18 September 1959 Dassault received a contract for three pre-production Mirage IVA aircraft. The award would have been placed earlier on the splendid behaviour of 01, but not until September 1959 was it safe to assume the bomb was going to work. Even at that time there was a high element of risk in the weapon programme, but a "pré-serie" order could not be delayed further without hurting the aircraft schedule. Mirage IVA-02, 03 and 04 were the definitive size, with length increased to 77 ft 1 in, but with an interim gross weight of 65,000 lb. Engines were to be the definitive Atar 09K, (originally 09D) with a steel compressor, having the first two stages transonic, better able to soak at Mach 2 temperature. A unique feature of this new Atar is that at Mach 1·5 the engine is allowed to overspeed beyond the normal limit of 8,400 rpm, to a peak speed of 8,700 rpm at Mach 2. This would be equivalent to a sea-level thrust with full reheat of about 15,430 lb. In fact the 09K was not fitted until aircraft 04, the first two pre-production aircraft at first having 09C engines generally similar to those of early Mirage fighters. The first pre-series aircraft, 02, flew on 12 October 1961. When it emerged one could see that the Mirage IVA introduced further alterations, the most notable being an increase in the depth of the fuselage, change in the geometry of the main landing gear and of its attachment to the wing, further increase in fin area by addition of a long braking-parachute box below the rudder, and modifications to the airborne systems. Aircraft 02 was still a long way short of the definitive article, but early in 1962 it was detached to the weapon and trials range at Colomb-Béchar in southern Algeria where it dropped simulated nuclear bombs. It has been said it was constantly watched by Egyptian officers hiding behind the surrounding sand dunes. They could hardly have kept hidden, nor watched both the airfield and the distant bombing range, and I doubt that such activity really yields much useful information. Aircraft 03 flew on 1 June 1962 and was fitted with the definitive navigation system and FR probe. Aircraft 04 flew on 23 January 1963 and was practically representative of the production aircraft.

The fact that there was going to be a production aircraft dated from April 1960. France's first, and very clumsy, fission device was successfully detonated at a remote test site at Reggane in the Sahara on 13 February 1960. Amid a storm of criticism (which today would be a thousand times greater) the French then assembled a "transportable nuclear device" and successfully tested it on 1 April 1960. On 4 April the French government announced that "a first batch" of 50 Mirage IVA bombers was being purchased, the funds being provided in the NF 4,137 million (about £300 million) for combat aircraft in the *Loi Programme*. What did not appear in the credit vote was some NF 450 million for the 14 Boeing KC-135F tankers. When these were delivered, from 1963, they made a great difference to the CFAS and allowed the Vautours to be used in training and test roles rather than as combat tankers for the Mirage IVA. The decision was also taken to equip every alternate Mirage IVA to serve as a tanker, with a "buddy" type pack under one wing. These packs were procured from Flight Refuelling's French licensees. The air refuelling procedure was developed in numerous contacts between aircraft 03 and the first KC-135F in 1963, using powerful lights on the tanker to facilitate rendezvous in bad weather without tell-tale radio transmissions.

Not the least of the remarkable features of the Mirage IV programme is that it involved only four RDT&E aircraft of which only three were truly representative of the production aircraft. The prototype, 01, was so free from trouble that its original assignment of proving the basic aerodynamics and systems was finished on 15 September 1960. Four days later René Bigand showed the potential of the aircraft by doing what Dassault had long wished the Mirage IV to do: he captured the world 1,000 kilometre circuit record. Bigand flew at about 48,000 feet twice around a circular course at a radius of about 50 miles around Paris, passing roughly over the home base at Melun. His time was just on 33 minutes, yielding a speed of 1,131 mph. This was almost precisely the same as Peter Twiss's world record in a straight line with the FD.2 four years earlier (an event which confirmed Dassault in building the Mirage III). But the Mirage IV-01 was kept at full throttle for well over half an hour, on internal fuel only (less capacity that the IVA), and this was more significant than the speed. As I have emphasized several times in this book, speed had ceased to be important in determining the penetrability of bombers by 1960. Countermeasures, radar cross-section and low flying were becoming infinitely more important, and what the Mirage IVA wanted most was not speed but range. Lack of range continued to be the weakest feature of the aircraft in the eyes of Armée de l'Air generals from Chief of Staff Stehlin downwards. (Stehlin, who bore the responsibility of creating the Mirage deterrent, was solidly behind this task; but that did not stop him from privately wishing its fuel capacity was greater.) And the very idea of the French nuclear deterrent remained anathema to many deputies—not only to the Communists—in the Assemblée Nationale. De Gaulle scraped through a vote of confidence on the Mirage nuclear force by just 77 votes on 18 October 1960. The newspapers said it would have made little difference if his administration had been defeated on this crucial issue, because the general would have ruled subsequently as a dictator under the emergency provisions of the French constitution.

In 1962 aircraft 01 was handed over to the CEV for trials with almost all the elements of the bomb/nav system in advance of those flown with the bigger pre-series aircraft. Subsequently it was used for crew conversion and was destroyed in a crash on 13 February 1963. By this time the three pre-production aircraft were all at work, and the first eight production aircraft were visible at the Dassault plant at Bordeaux-Mérignac where the aircraft were assembled. The definitive bomb had been made and tested, and its nominal yield raised from 60 to 70 kilotons. None of these bombs was ever announced as having been dropped from a Mirage or any other aircraft, although the statement was issued that it "could be dropped unarmed 20,000 metres without exploding". This ought not to be news. Much earlier the Americans had learned how to make nuclear weapons that could crash at supersonic speed, much faster than their free-fall terminal velocity, or cook inside a white-hot burning aircraft, without doing worse than release radioactive products. There was no official liaison at all between the US Atomic Energy Commission or its bomb producers, such as Douglas Aircraft and Sandia Corporation, and the French. Indeed, American propaganda found itself ranged alongside that of the Soviet Union in doubting and discouraging the French nuclear-weapon programme. As a result many people were very surprised at the French taking on a task of such great magnitude. They were even more surprised when in November 1963 Minister of the Armed Forces Pierre Messmer announced that "Taking no notice of foreign protests . . . France will not only continue the development of fission bombs but will arm herself with thermonuclear weapons as well." I admit that this frightened me. I considered the French just sufficiently insular in their Gaullist vision of greatness to test their proposed H-bombs in the Sahara. They did consider this, but reason prevailed (some would not even agree here) and a new test site was prepared in the South Pacific, where at least there was no chance of the atmosphere suddenly collecting a million tons of radio-active desert.

Never in recent years have a nation's leaders waited for an aircraft with such mixed feelings as did the top Frenchmen await the first production Mirage IVA. Several French "top brass" continued to be totally unimpressed, and to doubt the credibility of the very deterrent itself. Officers in rival services grumbled because the CFAS, like its prototype in the US Air Force, was thought to be consuming colossal sums and making everyone else go short. In fact CFAS never swallowed more than one-quarter of the smallest defence budgets France had known since 1789; about 3–4 per cent of the GNP. In any case, to de Gaulle the needle-nosed bomber was the supreme expression of French power, French independence, and French ability—including the new ability to thumb his mighty nose at American military domination and even at the NATO alliance. It was almost entirely because of this little delta-winged bomber that de Gaulle was able, early in 1966, to walk out of NATO and send scores of thousands of Americans and other NATO troops out of France.

According to the original 1960 schedule there should have been seven production Mirage IVAs in 1963, 22 in 1964 and the remaining 21 in 1965.

In fact, although the manufacturing pace was soon at the programmed level, the whole schedule ran about six months late. The first production aircraft flew on 7 December 1963 and the number deployed at the end of 1964 was given by M Messmer as "15 to 20". But these were now operational aircraft, with highly experienced crews and a massive force of hardware and men supporting them. The operational force is organized into nine squadrons of four aircraft, there being three squadrons at Mont de Marsan (80 miles south of Bordeaux), three at Istres (the big test airfield near Marseilles), and three at St Dizier (125 miles east of Paris). The four aircraft of each squadron operate as two pairs. Both take off at maximum weight, one with a bomb and empty external tanks, the other with maximum fuel. Both later make contact with a KC-135 which tops them up to a weight of around 76,000 lb, considerably above MTO weight. The two aircraft continue to fly together until, at a calculated point, the all-fuel Mirage refuels the one with the bomb. Like this the effective radius is very considerably in excess of 1,500 miles even allowing for part of the profile being flown at a sustained Mach 1·7. The tanker, of course, lives to fly another day, but the notion of a one-way trip is still deeply ingrained in the Mirage squadrons of the CFAS.

Indeed many of these very professional crews are doubtful that they would ever get into the air if nuclear war should burst upon the world. They take it for granted there is a Soviet missile for every Mirage IVA airfield in France. It was in a desperate bid to increase the dispersal of the CFAS that Dassault were told in 1962 to clear the Mirage IVA with rocket-assisted take-off to reduce the full-load field-length from 11,000 feet to about 6,000 feet. Each Mirage today has provision for a row of 12 SEP solid-fuel rocket motors firing diagonally down below the wing flaps. I would consider a gross-weight take-off on a short strip using these rockets a hairy procedure, and it is not often done in training. In 1963, as the Mirage IVA neared operational service, use of rockets was only one of several ideas studied to make the force less vulnerable. One was to disperse to selected unpaved strips hastily reinforced with steel mesh, a six hour job, or with sprayed-on chemical agents, taking only two hours. Another was hardened dispersal, and several designs of blastproof hangar were studied before reluctantly deciding that no financially practical scheme could survive a near miss with even a nominal 20 kiloton warhead such as can be carried by tactical artillery rockets or naval missiles launched from just off the French coast. In any case, today I am told that vulnerability of the Mirage IVA force on the ground is "no longer of interest" in view of the existence of the land-based and submarine-based ballistic missiles.

What remains significant was the acceptance of the belief that even a Mach 2 aircraft is vulnerable at high altitude, and during 1963 the decision was taken to plan most Mirage IVA missions at low level. At first Dassault proposed a major upgrade in the aircraft by fitting twin SNECMA TF106 reheat turbofan engines, which were the first fruit of the 1959 deal with Pratt & Whitney. These engines would have demanded a redesigned fuselage, but Dassault pointed out that ideally a low-level bomber ought to have a new airframe anyway. The Mirage IV-106 filled an impressive brochure in December 1963. It was designed for Mach 1·2 at sea level, for LABS toss-bombing of the 70-kiloton bomb and for eventual deployment with an ALBM, a proposed French version of Skybolt. The IV-106 was to have a gross weight of 105,000 lb and to be fitted with terrain-avoidance radar, and possibly blown flaps and a foreplane rather like the "moustache" of today's Milan fighter. It was a foregone conclusion it would be too costly for France, and I gained the impression it was being proposed partly because SNECMA had the TF106 and could not find a home for it.

In the event Dassault did get a repeat order for the Mirage IVA, as described shortly, but for a batch almost identical with the original aircraft. By 1963 the French, like some other nations, were heatedly debating whether or not the bomber was fast becoming obsolete. For example in 1961 the US Secretary of State, Dean Rusk, in confirming his administration's plan for a NATO force based on Polaris missiles, said, "Manned bombers are already little more than museum pieces". And in 1963 M Le Theule, Assemblée Nationale Rapporteur on the military budget, announced that the Mirage IVA would "cease to be credible" by 1970 at the latest. He pointed out that the proposed French MSBS naval ballistic missile, to be deployed aboard at least three all-French submarines, would probably "not become operational before 1973". There would thus be a dangerous gap between the end of the Mirage IV as a credible delivery system and the take-over of the deterrent by the navy. After deep study the French government came to the conclusion that it ought to develop a land-based IRBM with all possible speed. Le Theule described such a weapon as "cheaper and less vulnerable" than the Mirage IVA or any other bomber. Today almost everyone close to the subject of strategic delivery systems would shake their heads at such a slick solution, and refer M Le Theule to the arguments contained in the B-1 story (p. 262) on the several huge advantages of bombers. But it was the missile today called SSBS, now in service in lonely silos on the Plateau d'Albion in southern France, that took the money that might otherwise have gone to buy the Mirage IV-106 or even later bombers. The French have developed their two strategic missiles, the SSBS and the submarine MSBS, for little more than 1 per cent of the sum expended by the United States on Atlas, Titan, Minuteman and Polaris over the same period of 1955–70. But even this is a massive sum, equal to about £100 million, and it is debatable whether the missiles were worth it. SSBS silos are undoubtedly highly vulnerable, and so is an MSBS force when it numbers so few ships. I am told the vulnerability is a secondary issue; the importance of these missiles is that they force any aggressor to show his hand (*déclarer*) in a pre-emptive attack on them. At least the Mirage force, four aircraft of which are permanently at three-minute readiness with a bomb on board, might be able to "flush" in time to avoid being hit on the ground. It is unlikely the missiles could be "flushed" without being sent all the way to their pre-designated targets, and in the moment of crisis these might be the wrong targets.

In 1963 I would have bet the 50th Mirage IVA, bits of which were then beginning to become visible, would be the last. But in 1964 an additional 12 aircraft were ordered. They differed from the original 50 in numerous generally minor ways, almost all of them modifications to the structure, flight controls and avionics in order to fit the aircraft to a low-level role. In parallel the DTIA and Dassault managed a comprehensive fatigue-test programme to establish a safe life for the Mirage IVA in the new low-level role. By this time there were many new avionic and systems developments in France that could be relevant to the Mirage, among them an inertial platform and the excellent new Antilope radar by Electronique Marcel Dassault that gave outstanding picture-brightness and sharpness in ground test and was being considered for later use in the Mirage bomber force. But money remained extremely tight. When one considers the total vote in a typical five-year *Loi Programme* is less than £1,000 million for all purposes, it seems incredible that the French had created a Mach 2 strategic force by the mid-1960s and were well on the way to having an SLBM force and an IRBM force—things that I think most "reasonable people" would have considered quite beyond the ability of the nation to do single-handed. Taken together with Concorde, the biggest space programme in Europe and a host of other advanced combat aircraft, there is no doubt the French were walking a financial tight-rope. And whereas in the late 1950s de Gaulle would have swept impatiently aside any trivial quibble about the cost of the French deterrent, by 1964 the mere running cost of the CFAS was a cause for deep concern, and major improvement to the aircraft a matter for careful consideration. Later the decision was taken to introduce nearly all the modifications that characterized the final 12 aircraft retroactively into the original 50 so that the whole force should have a low-level capability. The cost was officially described as "minimal"; the alterations were confined to equipment, Dassault's structure being designed for the "lo" role from the start.

From the outset the Mirage IVA had been symbolic of France, and associated with the highly national élite force. But Dassault would not have been Dassault if he had not pondered on possible markets for the Mirage IV elsewhere. There were difficulties that he did not have to contend with in selling the Mirage III fighter. One was that it was a highly classified aircraft, and he could not openly discuss it with possible pur- chasers. (Indeed when I began to write this chapter I sought the co- operation of Dassault in checking my facts and was curtly turned away because, even in 1972, the aircraft is not to be discussed.) Another problem was that, as originally conceived, the Mirage IVA was a highly specialized delivery vehicle. It was planned as a high-altitude carrier of a single free- fall nuclear bomb. Not many countries have such bombs, and few would have been interested in funding a major engineering and flight-test pro- gramme to turn the Mirage IVA into a general-purpose carrier of iron bombs, reconnaissance systems and all the other hardware for use in a versatile spectrum of roles which alone could justify its great expense.

To a non-nuclear country there did not seem a great deal to commend the Mirage IVA as it was originally designed (though it could be modified to carry heavy conventional loads), yet from 1960 until 1963 the Australians were on the verge of buying it. The need for a new RAAF bomber was obvious. Their Canberras were among the earliest of all the many variants of that evergreen aircraft, and were getting long in the tooth in more ways than one. Just to the north the Indonesians had dramatically changed the strategic balance of power by putting into service at least 25 Tu-16 ("Badger") bombers, each in the class of the Valiant and fitted to carry stand-off missiles. The Aussies began shopping for anything that was called a bomber and could fly at about Mach 2, but were halted pretty sharply by the price, especially in the case of the B-58 (which they doubted they could cope with, anyway) and the Vigilante (which was their favourite). By 1961 their attention had become polarized on the Mirage IVA. I suggested to a visiting staff officer from Canberra that the Mirage was nonsense in the context of non-nuclear war over enormous distances, and received the guarded reply ". . . well . . . Old Scherg is just about sold on Dassault expertise and can't see anything else in sight. Do you have any ideas?" Air Marshal Sir Frederick Scherger was then CAS down under, and a good and popular one. Never before had his country con- sidered buying such expensive hardware, for any purpose, and it thought very hard indeed to try to be certain it did not make a mistake. When I was asked for my suggestion I naturally murmured something about TSR.2 and was told "We really would like to buy TSR.2, if you ever build it, but frankly we can't take the risk. We want to buy proven hardware." This was no bad idea, but like so many good intentions it was soon forgotten. The scintillating star of the swing-wing F-111 made Old Scherg and everyone else forget the Mirage IVA, with results that were worse than anyone could reasonably have anticipated. And I cannot blame the Australians because it happened in Britain as well, but in the reverse order.

In 1964 nobody in Britain had the slightest need to think about the Mirage IVA, but as the October general election loomed nearer many began to wonder what would happen if the Labour Party formed the new government and carried out their oft-repeated threat of bulldozing TSR.2 off the face of the Earth. The Labour planners themselves had no doubt at all: they would buy the super F-111. But the planemakers, including Dassault, began to wonder whether there might not be some way of preventing this sell-out to the United States and betrayal of the policy of European collaboration (these are rather shrill words, but this is what was being said at the time). The closer anyone got to Messrs Healey and Jenkins, who in October 1964 were respectively appointed Ministers of Defence and of Aviation, the more obvious it was that any such wish was a waste of time. Their fixation on the F-111 could have served as the proto-type for the viewpoint "My mind is made up; don't bother me with the facts". At that time the F-111 facts (which were not really facts at all) looked marvellous, and they tended to make it very difficult for anyone in Whitehall to give serious or objective consideration of any other long-range strike and reconnaissance aircraft to replace TSR.2.

When the British aircraft was finally killed in April 1965, as described in a forthcoming volume *Attack Aircraft*, the only planemakers with instant proposals were McDonnell with the swing-wing Phantom S and Hawker Siddeley with successively improved versions or developments of the Buccaneer. These aircraft might have been cost/effective. McDonnell were prepared for much of the Phantom S to be built in Britain, by such companies as Short and BAC who had already begun production of major assemblies of the original fixed-wing Phantoms for the RAF and RN. They reinforced their argument with the undeniable interest of the US Navy, which was becoming rapidly disenchanted with the carrier-based F-111B. But ministers do not like giving the impression of having made a mistake. The Whitehall view of the trouble with the F-111 was not one of urgent concern but a smug belief that American might would simply trample it to death, and that, in any case, it was confined to the F-111B version that was nothing like the proposed F-111K for the RAF. Hawker Siddeley got nowhere either, being curtly reminded that the Buccaneer was not quite a Mach 2 aircraft and thus useless for the RAF strategic reconnaissance mission (the RAF appeared to believe that flying at Mach 2 would stop their high-flying reconnaissance aircraft from being shot down). By the summer of 1965 it looked as if the planemakers had retired hurt.

Then in July came the most persistent assault of all. It was mounted by a united front consisting of Dassault, BAC and Rolls-Royce.

Fitting Spey reheat turbofan engines to the Mirage IV was the key to what on paper looked an extremely interesting aircraft. The only thing that surprised me was that the three partners took so long to get round to it. They had certainly heard of each other. In 1960 Rolls had put an Avon into a Mirage III, and the two companies were deeply intertwined in jet-lift development. Since May 1965 Dassault and BAC had been ostensibly working together on the "AFVG" variable-geometry combat aircraft. A Spey-Mirage IV could have been roughed out on the back of an envelope and a very convincing brochure written in a couple of weeks, but the idea was not formally proposed until 16 July 1965, when the three companies made a presentation at the Ministry of Aviation attended also by representatives of the Ministry of Defence. The proposal was certainly worth thinking about, unless one's mind was tightly closed.

Replacing the Atar 09K by the Spey 25R raised the take-off thrust with reheat from a little over 30,000 lb to 41,700 lb, while reducing specific fuel consumption by 30 per cent. This enabled the gross weight to be raised by 14 per cent to 80,000 lb, either by carrying more fuel or more bombs. And there was room for more fuel, because the bigger engine ducts needed a three-inch addition to the depth of the fuselage, and the increase in engine weight was balanced by a two-foot increase in body length ahead of the wing. The rest of the airframe was almost identical with that of the final 12 Mirage IVAs. There would, I think, have had to be local increase in skin gauge over much of the fuselage and wing, but it looked as if the existing forgings could be retained. The proposal on the airframe was that BAC would make the front and rear fuselage at Weybridge and either ship these to Dassault or, for political reasons, assemble the Mirage IVS at Weybridge to where Dassault would ship the wing, mid-fuselage and tail. Nobody in BAC seemed to notice that none of these parts were actually made by Dassault, but I expect Dassault noticed!

So far the Mirage IVS looked plain sailing, but what about the avionics? The equipment of the French bomber, though thoroughly effective and workable, was at least a generation earlier in concept than the superb TSR.2 systems, which were fully integrated by Harry Zeffert on a most impressive rig at Weybridge and were all installed in the third flight article which had been within a month of flying when the programme was cancelled. The biggest job, both in formulating the Mirage-Spey proposal and in turning it into hardware, would clearly be integrating a new nav-attack system into the airframe. There were various reasons, both technical and in programme-timing, why the Mirage IVS should not merely be fitted with the TSR.2 systems lock, stock and barrel. Instead it was proposed to fit the TSR.2 reconnaissance package and then build into the aircraft a mix of avionics already developed for the Phantom, Hawker P.1127 and 1154 and Buccaneer, and proposed for the Buccaneer 2*. The key component was the radar, and here the obvious choice was the very promising Antilope already mentioned, which by 1965 was flying in a Vautour. It was the preferred solution of BAC, although the TSR.2 radar by Ferranti was rather later in concept (and correspondingly less well advanced in development, though flying in a Buccaneer).

Altogether the Mirage IVS looked a thoroughly sound proposal, yet it could easily be criticized. It needed a longer run than did the F-111, and a paved runway, though the need for STOL using rough surfaces was nothing like as acute as the Air Staff had thought five years earlier. The operational strike radius and ferry range were slightly shorter than the brochure figures for the F-111. The whole thing looked like being a big development job that was starting at a time when there were already many F-111s in the air. And how could a hastily contrived botch-up be the equal of the most carefully planned multi-role aircraft in history? At the 16 July briefing it was obvious how things were going to be. The MoA technical staff had not been told to close their minds; they considered the proposal "warrants further investigation". But the higher one went, the more closed their minds became, and I can quote (but had better not name) one senior official who told me, "The F-111 is the only possible answer, and nothing must be allowed to interfere with this conclusion". Denis Healey professed not to know that the Mirage was already a low-level bomber, and insisted "a very great increase in development would be needed to give it that capability". And according to BAC the problem was "the Air Marshals, who want the very latest". This odd statement was certainly not aimed at former CAS Sir Dermot Boyle who had become BAC vice-chairman. He very rationally pointed out the Spey-Mirage could "offer substantial cost/effectiveness gains over the F-111 for a minor adjustment of the requirement".

In fact the Anglo-French aircraft would have met practically every one of the RAF's needs in full, and the points where it fell short—which really boiled down to field length—were of secondary importance. Quick studies at St Cloud and Weybridge confirmed the feasibility of the whole aircraft, with all the proposed avionics installed and coupled up to their proper power supplies and cooling. With very minor changes external pylons could be added for 14 bombs of 1,000 lb or equivalent loads of other stores. In a clean configuration it was estimated the speed at 200 feet altitude would be 860 mph, and the dash performance at altitude 1,500 mph, both figures considered conservative. In my own view the 860 mph could have been a rather rough ride, because although the low aspect-ratio delta is a good wing in the lo penetration role, the area of the Mirage IVA wing seemed too large for comfort. But the Armée de l'Air pilots, and their airframes, were quite used to it by 1965. And when the Ministry of Defence finally had to go through the motions, and send over an evaluation team, the RAF pilots who flew the Mirage IVA at low level were favourably impressed. It was not lost upon them that even the Atar-powered aircraft had a considerably greater operational radius, at any level, than any supersonic aircraft in the RAF, and a much greater endurance at Mach 2. They flew from Glavany's base, Mont de Marsan, and there are few flatter regions of land or sea than 200 miles around this airfield, with the marked exception of the Pyrenees where there was not then a low-flying area. The RAF team, which had never before made flights at such sustained speeds at all altitudes, came back and wrote a report which was factual and objective; I hope it didn't hurt their careers. Simultaneously an MoA cost and technical evaluation team went to St Cloud, asked a few questions about productive capacity and pricing policy and then went away again. I expect they stayed long enough to find out that the French bits of the Spey-Mirage were not made by Dassault, but their probe was a pale shadow of what a US team, or even a genuinely interested British one, would have done. BAC commented the investigation was "not in very great depth . . . relatively superficial".

One of the minor handicaps under which the proposed industrial consortium laboured was that, as is often the case where Whitehall is involved, there was no input from the customer. It would not have done any harm to have conducted a proper evaluation in depth of the Spey-Mirage with the full co-operation of the RAF. This would have facilitated the preparation of a detailed standard of aircraft known to meet the customer requirement. Instead BAC and Dassault had to grope in the dark, and they naturally assumed the last known standard which was TSR.2. They were also kept in the dark regarding numbers of aircraft and rate of delivery. Assuming a total of 50, with all R&D written off against their price, allowances for contingencies and profit at 10 per cent, the price was estimated at £2·321 million per aircraft; for 110 the unit price was put at £2·067 million. Both figures were below the price to Britain of the F-111K, and it is relevant to note that BAC and Dassault expected to sell the Spey-Mirage to the Armée de l'Air and to such other countries as India, the RSA, Israel (if de Gaulle permitted) and even Sweden or Peru. Such sales would obviously have helped prevent escalation in the price.

Late in November the MoD made the odd statement that, equipped to full RAF standard (a standard kept secret from the builders), the Mirage IVS would cost "not under £2 million". It seemed unhelpful to make so obvious a remark, and it may have been designed merely to horrify the public. On 3 December *The Times* published a strange leading article which took an uninformed swipe at the Anglo-French proposal and then advocated "an immediate order for between 40 and 50" of the F-111. Sir Archibald Hope wrote that the eminent paper's criticism of the Mirage IVS would not withstand an impartial examination. Then Sir John Slessor, another ex-CAS (Sir Dermot Boyle came in a little earlier), wrote to the *Telegraph* that the "Choice of a new aircraft for the RAF cannot be determined by political or industrial considerations . . .". I would love to listen to this proposition being debated! In any case in the United States they make it as firm a rule as they can never to buy combat aircraft from abroad, and I'm sure Sir John would have hated it if the Wellingtons and Lancasters of 5 Group in 1942 had all come from a factory in Tibet.

So far the British government had said nothing, although it was obvious they did not want the bother of having to think about anything but the F-111. I thought their policy would be to say nothing at all about the IVS, except perhaps for about seven terse words which might be wrung out by a Parliamentary question, but to my surprise on 13 December 1965 Roy Jenkins sounded off at some length. "It would be idle to pretend", he said of the Spey-Mirage, "that it has the range, the speed, the weapon load or the capacity to operate from unprepared strips which the 111 has. In addition, with the Spey fitted and the required nav/attack system developed, it would not in our view—I wish it were otherwise—be available for service until at least two years after the 111. . . . It falls between the Buccaneer and 111, but in cost is much nearer the American aircraft. . . . To develop . . . the Spey-Mirage and to bring it into service in the early 1970s might—and I do not say more than might—create more of a barrier to an effective RAF demand for the Anglo-French Variable-Geometry aircraft than would a slightly earlier purchase of the 111." With the benefit of hindsight I can now be "idle" and "pretend" that the Mirage IVS would have been slightly faster at all levels than the F-111K, and would have had at least an equal range (Mr Jenkins did not apparently know the extent of the F-111 deficiency in range); as for weapon load, the F-111K loads were never published but I do not believe they would have been very much heavier or more varied than those of the IVS, which by December 1965 ranged up to 20,000 lb. As for the ability to operate from unprepared strips, I think history has shown that this is not very important, and I have yet to see an F-111 actually doing it.

By 1966 I would have thought the British and French would have given up, but they did throw one final fling on 20 January by flying British pressmen to see Mirage IV production at Bordeaux. Most of them just thought it would be a nice day away from the office; I doubt if a single one entertained for a moment the idea of writing a pro-Mirage story, although most of the "quality" papers did repeat their hosts' arguments without much comment. G/C Sammy Wroath for Rolls-Royce pointed out how well the Mirage engine programme would follow on the Phantom programme for a virtually identical power-plant, and lead to big economies in the RAF. J. Begue, of Electronique Marcel Dassault, outlined the radar options and gave the timing of the programme for the Antilope, with production in either France or Britain. Pierre Thirliet, technical director, foreign sales, of Dassault, gave a good briefing on the IVS including an account of the long Armée de l'Air experience of simulated low-level missions in gusty conditions with the IVA. And Allen Greenwood, then military sales director of BAC, wrapped everything up and carefully showed how the partners had "answered every major point that has been made against this vital Anglo-French project".

Of course, they couldn't win. One reporter wrote that his "day at the Dassault factory . . . failed to convince me that the Anglo-French aircraft is as good a proposition as the US F-111", while the man from the *Telegraph* said of the F-111 "There is no doubt that this plane is in a class of its own and its performance far superior to the Mirage". Comment like this was hardly surprising, but I was not prepared for what Julian Ridsdale MP, had to say at Westminster: "The Mirage is a high-flying aircraft designed to drop nuclear bombs yet it is claimed that it can be converted from this high-flying role to the more demanding conventional one of low-level strike and reconnaissance . . .". And on 22 February 1966, in the *Defence Review*, the Spey-Mirage was presented in most odd terms: "It is a high-level nuclear bomber for temperate climates with the capacity for low-level conventional strike in tropical climates. It would have been made largely in France . . . Britain alone would have had to bear the whole R&D cost. . . . It would not have been available until at least two years after the F-111. . . . Its cost would have been greater. . . ."

I hope the reader will forgive me if I do not take each point and pick it to pieces, but this was a period when, in aerospace at least, I could never accept anything the British government said at face value. I have no doubt the Queen's ministers really did think the F-111 the best hardware for Britain, and I am sure they would say today they were merely reflecting the view of the Air Staff. But did we have to blind ourselves to any alternative? Was it necessary for relationships to deteriorate to the point at which the following could appear in a press release: "It is quite clear to BAC that the French are astonished at the statements made in the House of Commons and elsewhere about the Mirage and which are contrary to the readily ascertainable facts. They regard these misrepresentations, which seem to them to be deliberate, as an inauspicious foundation for the Anglo-French co-operation which is the common political policy in

Britain"? One of the root causes was that the Labour government still smouldered against the British aircraft industry, which they considered had in some way perpetrated a giant confidence trick by trying to build the complicated combat aircraft earlier governments had ordered. I believe the Spey-Mirage was regarded as just a prolongation of the same confidence trick, but this time with the slightly jarring partnership of the French.

There was no reason to doubt the claims made for the Spey-Mirage, and no reason why this option should not have been examined a little more intelligently. It would have avoided the ill-will which led a French friend to tell me in 1972 "Les conséquences de la mauvaise foi Britannique ont pesé et peseront longtemps encore sur les rapports entre les deux industries". But taking a long-term view, this big programme at Weybridge would not have been helpful to another BAC team up in Lancashire. In 1965–67 this other team was also trying to work with Dassault—not on the Mirage but on the ill-fated AFVG. Today is has played the central role in creating the MRCA, and this will be more important in history than the Spey-Mirage would have been. So possibly this story ends in the right way, but for the wrong reasons.

Boeing B-47 Stratojet

VERY RARELY through the history of aviation a design team has come up with a design so advanced technically as to appear genuinely futuristic. Even more rarely have such designs been built. Sometimes they have proved dismal failures, but a very, very small number indeed have surged ahead and established a programme of the most profound importance to the manufacturer and to the user. In an environment that strongly favours proven methods and trouble-free operation, and therefore conventionality, the B-47 demonstrated its dramatic superiority over less radically advanced bombers. This superiority was much greater than even its designers had expected, and what had started as a rather frightening exercise that might prove to be inflexible, costly, difficulty to fly and operationally unattractive, ended up as the foundation of America's strategic power in the jet age and the most important single weapon in the world through the perilous years of the 1950s.

Altogether I find it difficult to begin this chapter without becoming sidetracked into superlatives, because the B-47 was one of the greatest aircraft of all time. It looked marvellous, especially as for the first five years the other shapes around it were the shapes of the piston era. Far from being difficult to fly, it could be handled like a fighter; and it impressed itself upon a new pilot like a Rolls-Royce, or perhaps I should say a Cadillac. The feel of the controls, the smooth taxying, the clarity of the R/T, all leave a wholly favourable impression undimmed by the passage of twenty years.

But it is thirty years since the story started. In 1943 the British were far too busy to think about jet bombers, but in September of that year, while Allied armies fought in a rainy Italy that had just officially capitulated, the US Army Air Force at Wright Field sent out an invitation to industry to propose just such an aircraft. There was no official requirement for a jet bomber, and no money had been voted under such a heading, so the invitation was an informal one. After a few weeks some money was found, but it was in an old sock labelled "reconnaissance", so the manufacturers were told thus to label their submissions (while taking care that what they really planned was a medium bomber). Boeing, though possessed of approximately the same number of design and project engineers (3,950) as the entire British industry, was hard-pressed developing the B-29 and a score of variants, the long-range aircraft that much later matured as the B-52, the great transport that became the C-97 and Stratocruiser, and several other aircraft from the evergreen B-17 to a STOL observation and liaison machine that seemed as out of place as a B-29 in the Piper works. The company's first essay into the jet age was rather pedestrian. Like a Beethoven symphony, inspiration did not come in a brilliant flash but by a painstaking process of improvement.

It seemed reasonable to begin with something like a B-29, which had an extremely efficient laminar-flow wing that was a known quantity and could in theory fly quite well at up to 450 mph. The Model 413 was a scaled-down B-29 wing carrying four of the proposed General Electric TG-180 axial turbojets that seemed likely to be the standard type of American jet engine for a good many years to come. At this time America's only practical experience of jet propulsion had been gained with the Whittle type of centrifugal engine, but the inherently better efficiency of the axial caused this home-grown but more difficult species to be specified in every one of the five jet bomber submissions that later became hardware. It was January 1944 when Boeing submitted the 413, to be promptly told there was not actually a requirement for a jet reconnaissance aircraft. What this meant was "Go away and do an even better jet bomber and we'll soon be in a position to fund a programme for it". For the next three months, scratching around among Pratt & Whitney and Wright for basic data on possible turboprops, Boeing studied two turboprop bombers and two jets. In March it chose one of the jets, the Model 424, to send to Wright Field. It was almost a scaled-down B-29, with a span of about 100 feet, carrying two pairs of TG-180 engines in underwing nacelles. In April the USAAF at last completed its detailed specification for a jet medium bomber. Most of the requirements were met by the 424. Possibly Boeing could have obtained a prototype contract for this aircraft. If it had, US military posture in the 1950s would have been significantly weaker. Three of the rival contenders, Convair, Martin and North American, did later go ahead with aircraft in the class of the Boeing 424. North American, helped by the fact it was using a piston-engined project as a basis, was first to fly. The XB-45 flew on 17 March 1947. As it promised to be a useful, trouble-free bomber, earlier in timing than any other Allied aircraft in its class, the USAAF bought the B-45 Tornado in inventory numbers, ultimately totalling 142. Convair's graceful XB-46, flown on 2 April 1947, was a one-off; so was the Martin XB-48, which had two three-engine underwing boxes and a bicycle landing gear. A fourth submission was the incredible YB-49, one of the Northrop series of all-wing aircraft and first flown on October 21 1947. Powered by eight of the universal TG-180 (later J35) engines, it was more nearly a rival to the giant B-36, but it too never saw production.

What was Boeing doing all this time? Typically, the company declined to sell the government what it considered an inferior aircraft. Although the image of the US industry was one of vast wealth in research equipment, in 1944 Boeing was in fact the only company with its own high-speed tunnel. Models tested in this tunnel in the summer of 1944 showed that straight-wing aircraft based on B-29 shapes were probably incapable of making use of the full potential of the new type of propulsion. In particular the 424 was unsatisfactory because of interference and high drag caused by the engine nacelles. Although acutely aware of the other four big jet bombers, Boeing decided to do much more thinking before building. The former board chairman, Bill Allen, was about to become president; Wellwood Beall (who retired from McDonnell Douglas in 1972) was v-p engineering and sales, while Ed Wells was chief engineer. Very soon Wells was to become v-p engineering, the new chief engineer being Lysle A. Wood. In the backs of their minds these men had a plethora of radically new shapes for jet aircraft, ranging from flying wings to paper darts. Somewhere among these shapes possibly lurked one or more that would partner the new engine and open a new vista of performance. But research data were almost wholly lacking, and it would be laborious gathering it.

For the present, as Boeing's B-17s were temporarily diverted from strategic bombing to support the new Allied bridgehead in Normandy in June 1944, the team at Seattle left the wing and tail alone and merely looked for a better place for the engines. One location that was interesting was inside the fuselage. Big piston-engined aircraft invariably had the engines outside, or else had to use long shaft drives, but the jet could be put close to the centreline inside the body, leaving the wing completely "clean". By the autumn the Model 432 had been judged the best layout. The thin laminar-flow wing passed through the deep, rather lumpy body well above the mid position, leaving plenty of room for a capacious bomb bay and for the landing gears (which were difficult to hang on the wing). On top of the centre section were mounted four turbojets, fed by large ducts from intakes on each side of the forward fuselage and with their jet pipes tilted up out of the top decking to terminate in aft-facing nozzles, the jet streams passing each side of the fin. Engineers will see all sorts of good features in this layout, but they will also see many bad ones. Today Boeing may forgive me if I say it looks terrible, but at least the company was breaking out and doing something quite new, which is what jet propulsion was all about. Similar untramelled thinking could be seen all over Germany, where in the extraordinary environment of immense research wealth, disintegrating research policy and a desperate need to create new weapons, scores of new jet designs—some good, some bad, but all quite unlike anything seen before—were tested in tunnels and even turned into hardware.

Famous as the first jet bomber to be built in Britain, the English Electric Canberra, seen here in B2 form, could today have been the world's preeminent tactical attack aircraft had the basic airframe been subjected to really bold and imaginative development.

Planned as Britain's first big long-range jet bomber, the Short SA4 Sperrin never saw RAF service and the total bill for the development programme was only £3·5 million, which today would not pay for the technical manuals. (*This oil painting hangs in the manufacturer's entrance hall in Belfast*)

Vic of V-bombers. First to enter RAF squadron service was the Valiant, nearest camera. The Vulcan (leading) was the first large bomber in the world to employ the delta-wing plan-form. Unlike the Valiant and Victor (furthest from camera) which served as reconnaissance and tanker aircraft, the RAF's Vulcans have served only in the strategic strike role to date.

Last of the three V-bombers ordered for the RAF, the Handley Page Victor was designed to the same general requirements as the Avro Vulcan.

When the French Air Force issued a specification for a high-speed strategic bomber to carry the newly-developed French atomic bomb, Dassault produced the Mirage IV by simply scaling up the basic design of the Mirage III day fighter.

One of the greatest aircraft of all time, the elegant Boeing B-47 was the foundation of America's strategic power in the jet age and the most important single weapon in the world through the perilous years of the 1950s.

Another of the greatest aircraft of all time —and in every sense of the word—the Boeing B-52 became SAC's "long rifle" and was the supreme expression of the long-range subsonic bomber in the pre-missile era.

First supersonic bomber put into production for the USAF, the delta-winged General Dynamics B-58 Hustler was also the first aircraft built from the start under the weapon system concept.

First all-jet attack aircraft designed for the US Navy, the McDonnell Douglas A-3 Skywarrior is still the biggest and heaviest aircraft ever designed for use from an aircraft carrier.

Although the North American Rockwell A-5 Vigilante will not go down in history as a great bomber, it still has its place in history due to the fact that it pioneered much brand-new technology.

Still regarded by many, rather literally, as a white elephant, the ill-starred North American B-70 Valkyrie Mach 3 strategic bomber established more "firsts" than any other "air vehicle" in history.

One of the greatest weapon systems in the world, the B-1 supersonic variable-geometry strategic bomber under development at North American Rockwell's Los Angeles Division incorporates the blended wing/body developed initially for the Corporation's submission for the F-15 fighter competition.

Late in 1944 Boeing got hold of a General Electric I-16, a Whittle-derived engine, and built it into a big outdoor rig to study the way the 432's four nozzles would curve over the wing and blast across the top of the fuselage. For the first time the thunder of a jet was heard at the most important builder of big aircraft in the world. In December Boeing completed its 432 proposal and submitted it to Wright Field, in competition with Convair and Martin. North American already had received the go-ahead for the rather smaller XB-45, while the giant Northrop XB-49 was not considered a direct rival but as an eight-jet conversion of the piston-engined XB-35, and intended for greater ranges. All these aircraft promised to be exceptionally costly to develop or to build in quantity. Although the Army Air Force paid for at least three-quarters of the prototype costs, money was tight and there were extremely strong incentives to minimize expenditure. An idea of the size of programme budgets is given by the fact that when, in March 1945, Boeing was awarded a Phase I study contract for the Model 432, involving full engineering design, component and system testing, wind-tunnel testing, at least one full-scale mock-up and all supporting material, the total came to a mere $150,000. The aircraft was given the designation XB-47.

This was the most crucial time for the programme. By this time Boeing knew pretty well how the rival bombers would perform. The XB-46 and XB-48 were the obvious, pedestrian way of doing it. The only unusual thing about either was Martin's bicycle landing gear, and this was going to be tried out on a Marauder. The XB-47 was much more unconventional, yet it hardly seemed likely to take the world by storm, and could even turn out inferior. In the summer of 1945 Boeing was caught between an indifferent design, a deep wish to do much better, the lack of a foundation for any better idea, and the timing of their own and their rivals' programmes. I have seen another design they tested at this time, in which the four engines were in the extreme tail. This seemed an ideal location, but how were the engines to be fed with air? The wind-tunnel half-model had intakes in the nose for the two inner engines and at the extreme tail-end for the two outers. Again, engineers will see all sorts of drawbacks. Boeing's only consolation is that nobody else seemed able to do any better.

As the Allied armies crushed Germany to final defeat, several technical missions were prepared in the United States to probe German weapon developments for ideas that could quickly be introduced in the war against Japan. The biggest of the missions was concerned with aeronautics. It included three bright young engineers from Boeing: George S. Schairer, chief of technical staff; George C. Martin, chief of structural design; and E. B. Kinnaman, later head of the vibration unit. They found plenty in Germany. The corresponding British mission, very much smaller and operating on a shoe-string, was led by that great engineer Sir Roy Fedden. He found himself on 22 June at Volkenrode, where there was an amazing high-speed wind-tunnel complex that had been quite unknown to Allied intelligence. Fedden was very interested in the technique of Schlieren photography the Germans had perfected to give a picture of air density and shock-wave formation. He also studied a small model of a swept-wing bomber that was ready for testing. That evening a handful of British and German enthusiasts, suddenly working toward a common objective, mounted the model in the tunnel and got the tunnel working (because, miraculously, there was electric power available). Suddenly, in breezed the three men from Boeing. I have no doubt they sized up the situation in a moment. Fedden was rather piqued to discover that next morning the swept-wing model could not be found.

When Schairer got back to the United States he had more than just a model. He had a suitcase full of research data on swept wings for flight at high Mach numbers, all of it the result of actual tunnel testing. Sweeping back the wings for high-speed flight had been considered by the NACA (predecessor of NASA), but their studies had not involved any tunnel testing. Back at Seattle work went on around the clock turning the 432 into the 448. The main difference lay in the fact that the wing and tail surfaces were swept sharply backwards; various angles were considered between 25° and 45° and the figure initially chosen was 30° at the quarter-chord line. It is worth recalling that in 1945 swept wings, and several other novel ideas the Germans were investigating, were matters of studied disinterest in Britain, and a number of eminent men—from leading designers of high-speed aircraft to men holding the rank of air marshal—thought the correct response was laughter. But at Seattle Boeing's board never doubted for a moment that the correct thing to do with their jet bomber was hold it up for months and give it sweep-back. Neither were there any dissenting voices at Wright Field, and the head of the Bombardment Branch, Col H. E. Warden, was a forceful advocate for sweep. Boeing did not abandon all work on straight wings, and it continued research with various section profiles and high-lift configurations, but 90 per cent of the effort was soon on the 448.

After a lot of discussion of how the contract should be arranged an agreement that the XB-47 should be based on the 448 was reached in September 1945. By this time Boeing had begun to obtain its own confirmatory research data on wings at sweep angles of 30° and 35°, and to explore their behaviour with flaps and leading-edge slats. At Los Angeles North American was redesigning its XP-86 fighter to have a 35° slatted wing, and at Buffalo Bell was hastily fitting a generally similar wing to a P-63 Kingcobra for research purposes. The wing was no longer the chief worry. Boeing was still unhappy with the engines, and the customer considered the arrangement "relatively vulnerable" and even "unsafe". There was a strong wish at Wright Field to get the engines out of their central location, which I think had been adopted just because the jet made it possible. There were plenty of alternatives, but one that came very late into the picture was the external pod. Wellwood Beall said, "We did not arrive at the pod without experimentation, for it is the least obvious configuration; and, as a matter of fact, it was more or less of an accident that we tried it at all". By September 1945 Boeing had considered using not four but six engines, as a temporary expedient until more powerful engines were available. In October the Model 450 emerged. Four TG-180 type engines were disposed in the slimmest possible double nacelles hung well below and ahead of the wing just inboard of 40 per cent semi-span. Two further engines were in single nacelles mounted one on each wing tip. In October 1945 Boeing proposed that the 450 should be the basis of the XB-47, and the Army Air Force agreed, asking Boeing the following month for a detailed proposal for two flight prototypes. By the end of the year the wing-tip engines had been brought some distance in from the tips, although they were attached directly below the wing and not hung on pylons. The sweep angle finally chosen was 35°.

By the end of the year not only was the design settled but Boeing had also agreed a detailed fixed-price contract for design, development, construction and testing of the two XB-47 aircraft, and all spare parts and special tools. In April 1946 the Phase II (hardware) letter contract was signed, in the amount of $8,352,457. (A corresponding contract today would be of the order of 50 to 100 times greater.)

What sort of an aircraft had Boeing proposed? Basically it was an extremely efficient bomber, with a wing of high aspect ratio to give, according to the Breguet formula, excellent cruising efficiency and low induced drag at a cruising lift coefficient of 0·35–0·45. The Boeing 145 laminar aerofoil section was very thin in the context of almost 30 years ago, and the combination of a very small cross-section, large span and the highest wing loading ever attempted combined to pose severe aeroelastic and structural problems. When the wing was designed, the thickest aircraft skin in the world was the 3/16th-inch used on Boeing's own B-29. For the Model 450 the bold step was taken of using tapered sheet, which at the time was not commercially available. The upper and lower skin of the wing box was 3/16th-inch thick at the tip but no less than 5/8th-inch thick at the root, roughly four times the usual skin thickness on the wing of a large bomber. This meant that the wing was heavy. Years later designers in Britain tried to meet the very difficult B.35/46 long-range bomber specification which imposed a suggested limit on gross weight of 100,000 lb, and they rejected small-section thick-skinned wings as too heavy. The key to the B-47 lay in the fact that Boeing was allowed to make the aircraft much heavier than 100,000 lb.

Even with this great mass of metal in the wing, the colossal flight loads were obviously going to make it flap up and down in a way that had never before been seen. There were stern-faced discussions concerning lateral control, fatigue, wing tankage and even such plain mechanical problems as how to stop the engine throttle linkages from changing the engine power as the wings flexed in rough air both in bending and in torsion. Later, when a B-47 wing was put into a static test rig in 1949, the tips were bent through an arc of 20 feet without the slightest damage, and even in normal cruising flight it was common to have flexure of five feet above and below neutral. This neutral position appeared to droop but in fact the wing had zero dihedral and the droop stemmed from the combination of sweepback and a 5° positive angle of incidence which had the effect of rotating the tips downwards. Parked, the wing really did have anhedral because it simply sagged. This was even though it never contained any fuel. Integral tankage was considered too much an unknown quantity, the space for flexible self-sealing cells was very restricted and there was enough room in the fuselage (it was thought) for all the fuel for the mission.

One extremely beneficial factor was the distribution of engine mass along almost the whole wing span. Calculations of aeroelastic behaviour were laborious before there were electronic computers, but in fact the exact positioning of the six engines was determined by the damping effect they exerted on wing flexure to avoid flutter, besides relieving the wing bending moment which would otherwise—with the entire load in the fuselage— have been formidable. Extensive tunnel testing was needed to find the optimum position for the twin-engine inner pods, which ended up with four feet of vertical space between the top of the pod and the wing, and so far ahead that a burst turbine would be likely to throw nearly all its fragments ahead of the wing box. The USAAF was concerned to reduce the drag of a windmilling engine, and the Model 450 specification provided for pilot-controlled shutters to hinge out of each intake periphery to seal off a failed engine. This remained a feature of the giant B-36D, which used its Boeing-built jet pods for only part of each mission, but it was removed from production B-47s.

One of the obvious problems with the B-47 layout was where to put the landing gear. By mid-1945 Martin had tried out the bicycle landing gear with a grossly modified Marauder—the "Middle River stump jumper" —and, after some hairy experiences, made it work and devised a pilot procedure for safe landing. The technique was to maintain a steady attitude on both take-off and landing, without trying to rotate or hold-off. In turn this meant landing at the speed for both sets of main wheels to touch simultaneously, which could be done provided the pilot worked out the speed beforehand appropriate to the aircraft weight, airfield altitude and ambient temperature. With the B-47 there was a big two-wheel truck at each end of the bomb bay, carrying the aircraft in a nose-high attitude giving optimum lift in a gross-weight take-off. The pilot could not haul the aircraft off even if he had wanted to—and I am sure many B-47 pilots wanted to, as they watched a fast-approaching boundary!—because the elevator could not rotate the aircraft about the rear truck, which was far aft of the c.g. On the ground the aircraft was kept from rolling over sideways by outrigger legs hinged to the inner-engine rear frames and retracting forwards into streamlined boxes under the pods. In flight these outriggers and the rear main truck could be extended at 305 knots IAS to act as an air brake for let-down at 7,000 or more feet per minute; they more than doubled the drag. But perhaps the biggest problems of all were simply speeding up the aircraft on take-off and slowing it down on landing.

The original TG-180 engines went into pre-production, with a 25-hour time between overhauls, in 1946. The builders were GE, who designed them, and also Allison, and, a little later, Chevrolet. The production engine was called the Allison J35, and its initial rating was 3,750 lb. Even with six engines acceleration was not going to be startling. Boeing calculated the first XB-47 would have an empty weight of 76,000 lb. (Production aircraft were much heavier. Excluding engines, radars and other Government-furnished equipment, the B-47E, described later, contained: 64,000 lb of light alloy, including 415 forgings; 20,000 lb of steel, mostly forgings; 2,000 lb of copper, brass and bronze; and 1,000 lb of magnesium. Americans love statistics.) Gross weight of the first prototype was 125,000 lb, with clearance to 162,000 lb if the airfield was long enough. With a wing loading of well over 100 lb/sq ft (gross wing area was 1,428 sq ft) and the very modest thrust it was obvious something would have to be done. The answer lay in the JATO (jet-assisted take-off) bottles developed by Aerojet-General from 1942 onwards. A battery of nine of these 1,000 lb-thrust rocket motors was arranged on each side of the rear fuselage, with their nozzles canted slightly outwards. On any but a bitterly cold day these motors gave more than 1,000 lb each, and up to 20,000 lb gross rocket boost could be counted upon for a firing time of 12 seconds.

Slowing up was a problem because the new Boeing bomber was about the heaviest, densest, most streamlined and fastest-landing aircraft ever built. Although it had superb wheel brakes, with four expander-tube drums on the front truck and two on the rear, all controlled by an anti-skid system that Boeing devised and then licensed to Hydro-Aire (to the latter's long-term benefit), the task they were set was unreasonably great. In the

133

case of a rejected take-off, or a maximum-landing-weight arrival on a wet or icy runway, the distances needed were more than twice the already formidable needs of a B-29. When in 1948 it seemed likely that the B-47 would be a widely used operational bomber, Boeing, after a great deal of experiment, used a German wartime design of ribbon-type braking parachute to serve as the basis for a fine canopy with a diameter of 32 feet, carried in a box under the tail and used in emergencies. Later its use became routine, and Boeing added a second 16-foot "approach chute" to increase drag throughout the landing. Streamed at about 1,100 feet altitude, it enabled the whole approach to be made at about 60 per cent power, balancing the extra thrust against the drag of the canopy. More than 20 years ago axial engines did not "spool up" like they do today, and if the pilot could start an overshoot with 60 per cent already showing he could afford to relax slightly. Of course, the approach chute had to jettison if an overshoot did have to be made, but I never heard of one failing to do so. By the time the B-47 reached the user it was not uncommon for both canopies to be fully deployed as the wheels touched the ground.

Flight controls were all powered hydraulically. Later Boeing was to develop much bigger and heavier aircraft with beautiful manual controls, but undoubtedly brute force (and not too much ignorance) was correct for the B-47. Each surface was driven by duplicated 3,000 lb/sq in jacks, with feel provided by torsion springs alone for the ailerons and torsion springs plus "q springs" (to give feel proportional to indicated airspeed) for the elevators and rudder. The resulting pilot control forces were outstandingly light and smooth, even though I believe this was the first such sophisticated flight control system ever developed. The only big unknown before first flight was exactly at what speed the ailerons would cease to roll the aircraft and would instead merely act as tabs to twist the wings the wrong way, causing control reversal. To ensure good lateral control at low speeds the outer segments of the large slotted flaps were arranged to act as flaperons by being linked with the lateral control system so that they retracted in unison with the up-going aileron. This provided a powerful lateral control in the vital high-lift regimes at take-off and landing, when the large rolling moment due to yaw of the swept wing (another recognized problem that Boeing was eager to explore) was expected to be greatest. I have no doubt that without the flaperon system the B-47 would not have been so viceless in engine-out and cross-wind conditions. Flap was mandatory for take-off, and a Klaxon was triggered if all engines went to take-off power with flaps retracted.

The basic philosophy with the flight controls was to use fully powered surfaces to combine adequate surface moment with attractive pilot forces, to make the surfaces irreversible as a protection against flutter (which was never far from the designers' thoughts) and to minimize problems associated with aerodynamic balance and deterioration of balance seals. At the same time the B-47 was designed so that it could be flown manually with control forces judged acceptable. The degradation in lateral control at increasing IAS was not expected to be a problem in normal use, but, if it was, spoilers (then a concept insufficiently developed to be incorporated from the start of design) were regarded as the likely answer. To make the stalling qualities of the swept wing acceptable, automatic slats were schemed for the entire leading edges. Fear that these might function asymmetrically led in 1946 to their replacement by powered slats fully opened during the initial extension of the wing flaps via a flap/slat transfer gearbox. The slats stayed on early production aircraft, but exhaustive stall tests in 1950 demonstrated that they were not needed and the slats were disconnected and bolted closed, and eliminated from the B-47B and subsequent aircraft.

Inside the circular-section, beautifully profiled body were housed the nav/bombardier in the nose and two pilots in tandem high under a giant bubble canopy, with the big K-2 bombing radar under the floor in a dark bulge on the underside of the nose, followed by a weapon bay capable of carrying any bomb in the US strategic inventory, with a succession of very large fuel cells above and to the rear. Total capacity in the first production aircraft was 14,980 Imp. gallons, compared with 5,500 for the B-29 and 1,510 for the B-17. This mass of kerosene weighed considerably more than a laden B-17, though the new jet had a smaller wing and only three men in the crew. This trend, more fuel and less crew, eventually happened in every major air force, but in the case of the B-47 it happened earliest and most dramatically. An incidental problem was that the great burden of fuel was distributed over about 50 feet axial length of fuselage, giving rise to c.g. and balance problems hundreds of times more serious than with the earlier bombers carrying smaller amounts of fuel in the wings close to the c.g. Correct fuel management was essential. Anyone who flew in a B-47 also learned that ham-fisted elevator movement could induce sloshing of the fuel that took what seemed like half a minute to die away, although this was of little consequence except on an overshoot with partial fuel at aft c.g. when tons of fuel could suddenly slosh towards the tail and give an inexperienced pilot a bad fright. At the tail end there was to be a radar-directed gun turret, but this was not ready in time to fly on the first B-47s.

I would like to wax lyrical about the systems and equipment, because although it looks dated today it was almost unbelievable in 1945, especially the completely new flush aerials (antennas) used throughout. But we had better deal with items as they arise in the story and get on with XB-47

No 1, bearing Army Air Force serial 1946-065, written on the tail as 6065. The first work order for hardware for this aircraft was issued in Boeing's Plant 2 in June 1946, and the essentially completed aircraft was rolled out on 12 September 1947. It was a fine sunny day, but employees were not given time off work and there was no ceremony, although the whole thing was done in some style and a select group of about 100 people watched and took pictures. By this time the programme was the direct responsibility of George C. Martin, the former structures man who had gone to Germany with Schairer and who had become XB-47 project engineer. Now also into the picture come Robert M. Robbins and Edward Scott Osler, the project test pilots. After ground testing had been completed they prepared on 17 December 1947 to fly 6065 for the first time.

Before that date there had been many first flights of aircraft that were bigger, or heavier, or of more advanced design, or faster, than anything done before, but no first flight that made such advances in every direction at once. I tried to put myself in the shoes of those two pilots and wondered if they were apprehensive. Today Bob Robbins heads the engineering organization at Boeing-Wichita, and he tells me "It is true that before I released the brakes to start the take-off roll I did ask God to help me for the next couple of hours, but I was not frightened. . . . For a year and a half we worked very closely with the engineers; in the Boeing wind tunnel we 'flew' the flutter model, which gave us an insight into the wing flexure modes and incidentally prevented us from being taken by surprise when we saw the unusual degree of flexibility that was normal for the B-47; I flew a B-29 fitted with a TG-180 mounted in the bomb bay which I could operate in flight, checking such characteristics as air starts and the acceleration from various power settings; we flew a B-29 specially equipped to simulate the approach and landing of the XB-47; we flew the 'Middle River stump jumper'; we felt the actual control forces 'flying' the tail of the second XB-47 in the Moffett Field (now Ames) tunnel, with power boost both on and off; we flew an F-80 jet at Muroc (now Edwards), and with it also experienced JATO take-offs; we rode an ejection-seat rig at Wright Field; we did almost all the ground-running of the engines; we conducted the most thorough taxi tests."

So on that 17 December, the 44th anniversary of powered flight, Robbins and Osler had confidence. Boeing Field then was 6,700 feet long, too short for a "hop" before actually flying, and becoming surrounded by urban development. Consideration had been given to barging the XB-47 some 30 miles north to the big runway at Whidbey Island NAS, and even to barging it all the way to California and thence overland to Muroc, but in the event a detailed plan was devised for a light-weight take-off from Boeing Field, with a possible swift return in dire emergency, and a fuel load just adequate to reach Moses Lake (Larson AFB), over the mountains in central Washington, where there was a 10,000 foot runway with good approaches. In the event the take-off was normal, a minor problem with flap retraction in the first two minutes was resolved, and with the XB-47 cleaned up there was enough fuel for a comprehensive exploration of flight behaviour with control power on and off in various regimes.

Throughout 1948 the XB-47 gained experience at Moses Lake, and I think the fact that the aircraft never made the headlines as having crashed was a matter of some surprise to a few rivals both in the industry and in the new blue uniform of the US Air Force. Another thing that did not make headlines was that the measured drag figures for No 6065 were barely three quarters of the calculated values that had previously been considered optimistic. Most aircraft demonstrate drag fairly close to prediction, and if there is a wide discrepancy it is invariably on the debit side. I cannot recall any other aircraft that beat prediction by more than 25 per cent. This was a matter of profound interest to the Air Force. Although no jet bomber of 1945 vintage appeared to be capable of performing the strategic missions that were required by the Air Force, the XB-47 had not only unparalleled speed but also the best range. There was every reason to anticipate much greater engine thrust, in so young and fast-moving a field as the aircraft turbojet, and altogether Boeing's bold venture into swept wings had by mid-1948 begun to look like the best jet bomber for the Air Force and a thoroughly sound and manageable delivery system. The second prototype, 6066, flew on 21 July 1948, with TG-180 engines, but after 25 hours was fitted with six of the brand-new General Electric J47-GE-3 engines each rated at 5,200 lb thrust. When figures for this aircraft had been digested the die was cast. On 3 September 1948 the Air Force ordered ten aircraft designated B-47A from Boeing's Wichita, Kansas, division. Here, at a Government-owned facility where 29,000 employees had earlier built more of the B-29 Superfortress bombers than any other source (1,644 plus the equivalent of 125 aircraft in spares), plans went ahead to serve as the sole production source of the new jet bomber. The initial ten of the B-47A model were confidently regarded as the first of many to be made in Kansas.

The B-47A was regarded as the service-test batch, which in earlier days would have carried a "Y" prefix. The ten built served to initiate Wichita into the manufacturing process, get the vast subcontracting system working smoothly, train Air Force aircrew and ground staff, and enable the optimum operating procedures and mission techniques to be determined, besides completing the development process of the aircraft itself. The A was very close to the second XB-47, although the decision had by 1949 been taken to incorporate as much combat equipment as would be ready within the tight time-scale. But I must break the story here for a digression into the way the B-47 was actually found to behave in flight.

It must be admitted that the B-17, and even the B-29, had allowed pilots to become very lazy with their rudder pedals. Knowing that pilots would come to the B-47 after many years flying these highly stable aircraft, Boeing were concerned at the B-47's yawing and rolling qualities and in particular at the possibility of suffering an unsymmetrical stall, which the company thought would be a disaster. Prior to first flight a simple yaw string was attached to the prototype. It was just 18 inches of white nylon parachute cord, fixed at one end to the centreline of the fuselage ahead of the pilot's windscreen and allowed to trail straight back, over a black painted line. This at once indicated the magnitude of any yaw (just as it does in modern sailplanes), and proved so useful it was kept on every production B-47—even though the stall was later found to be immaculate.

At modest speeds the XB-47s behaved well; indeed it was often said to "handle like a fighter", and although the rate of manoeuvre was not really fighter-like the radius of sustained turn was good. Every B-52 captain I spoke to in the 1955-60 period had flown many hours on the B-47 and invariably preferred the earlier bomber for sheer flying pleasure. It had much lighter control forces, and the B-47 driver also had a fabulous view perched high under the giant canopy through which he could see the Earth's surface directly ahead and straight down on both sides, the gently waving wings and pods and, with an effort, the tail. But at high IAS the rate of roll fell away to low values. At 400 knots it was barely 10° per second. At the maximum IAS of 450 knots the wing-twist was such that it was no easy task to roll the aircraft at all, though the speed for aileron reversal was above the placard limit and not considered a problem. A more unexpected phenomenon was Dutch roll, a combination of rolling and yawing (directional) oscillations that was soon found to be common in swept-wing aircraft at high altitude. Bill Cook, the project aerodynamicist, corrected this by devising a yaw damper, an artificial stability augmentation acting by applying controlled rudder deflections to cancel out undesired yaw. A yaw vane was put on the first XB-47 and soon made a standard feature to show the pilot the degree of yaw during asymmetric flight and, in particular, to drive home the need for firm rudder action in the event of engine failure. Today yaw dampers are common, but in 1948 it was a novel way of removing the last B-47 control problem inside its normal operating envelope. When it was fitted the Air Force considered the B-47 safe and ready to do an operational job.

Yet B-47 crews soon learned of a flight condition which made the lay public, to whom it was presented by gleeful newspapers, regard the aircraft as a literal death-trap. It was called "coffin corner". In every wing-supported aircraft the absolute aerodynamic ceiling is reached when, with the throttle wide open, the aircraft is flying on the verge of its stalling angle of attack. To attempt to climb further, by pulling back on the stick, merely causes a stall. The B-47 naturally could get into the same situation, but what made this aircraft different was that it was also possible to get into trouble by flying too fast. Flying straight and level at full throttle could not, I think, cause any problems; the J47 could run at 98 per cent rpm indefinitely and soon showed itself commendably reliable, if only for the reason that there were thousands in service. But at maximum speed the lowering of the nose, causing further increase in speed, or any attempt to "pull g" in a manoeuvre, resulted in pronounced buffeting and loss of stability. The symptom, often called Mach-buffeting, was characteristic of early jet aircraft which had the ability to fly fast enough to cause local supersonic airflow. Shockwaves formed, airflow broke away from the metal surface, turbulent boundary layers streamed away in great sheets and the aircraft and especially its control surfaces objected to the violent pummelling. It was largely because of the B-47 that aerodynamicists devised the technique of fitting vortex generators, or turbulators, which were small vanes about half as big as a playing card sticking vertically out of the surface of the aircraft at various angles to the airflow. Their task was to induce rotating vortices to re-energize the boundary layer, resist turbulent breakdown and keep the flow "attached". In December 1951 the first vortex generators were fitted to the B-47, and early in 1954 the final arrangement was standardized and quickly fitted to the many aircraft then built. It comprised a row of vanes along the top of the wing ahead of each aileron at about 25 per cent chord and a second row at about 35 per cent chord.

This greatly improved the ability of the B-47 to manoeuvre at maximum speed and altitude, but it did not remove coffin corner entirely. B-47 crews were not told to creep into this corner to see what it was like, but many did experience it. When right in the corner, the bomber was flying at full power yet on the point of stalling. As the wing loading of nearly all the production aircraft could reach 154 lb/sq ft, which was fantastic in the immediate post-war period and is still very high today, the B-47 needed extremely careful handling at high altitudes. It could do no more than just hold itself up with its nose well above the horizon and all six engines at high power. Any attempt to slow down or climb higher meant a conventional unaccelerated stall, which, though not dangerous, was accompanied by severe buffeting and caused great loss of height in the recovery. Obviously it was the last thing anybody would wish to do on an operational mission. So the pilot might be expected to keep both the power

levers and the control column well forward, but he was no better off here
either because that would cause Mach buffet and, if allowed to become
acute, could cause such severe flow breakaway and loss of lift/drag ratio
that the aircraft was said to suffer a "compressibility stall". I do not think
it was possible to cause gross destruction of wing lift by this means, and
the term coffin corner must have been coined by somebody with a nose
for good news headlines, but there is no doubt that the B-47, more than
any aircraft before or since, really could get its pilots into a situation
where they had to take care not to indulge in a single harsh control deflection. If all engines kept working there was never the slightest difficulty
on this score on an ordinary simulated mission, which at Mach 0·75 to 0·82
at a height rising from 32,000 to 38,000 feet as fuel was burned never
entered the dreaded corner at all. If you did go right into it you could
creep out again merely by reducing power and lowering the nose to hold
constant air speed on the way down, but it needed precision. British jet
bombers had relatively lighter weights, more thrust and bigger wings, and
were, in the vernacular, a piece of cake.

It was fundamental to the B-47 that it had more weight, less thrust and
a smaller wing, because that is how it was made to fulfil its mission so
well. Of course there has to be something in the debit scale-pan. In practice
coffin corner was no penalty, but the need for a first-class runway was.
When the B-47 was schemed nobody considered the possibility of long-
range guided missiles which could be zeroed-in on bomber airfields,
wiping them out by the score within minutes of some button being pressed.
For safe operation in temperate climates the B-47 needed a 10,000 foot
concrete runway. In tropical climates it was difficult to find a runway from
which it could take off at any weight above 150,000 lb. And the time taken
to get into the air was rarely brought below quarter of an hour, which in
the later day of the ICBM meant a B-47 was potentially a dead duck.
Even the external inspection before entering the aircraft took a conscien-
tious crew at least 10 minutes, and the whole process of getting airborne
was sprinkled with the usual checks and inspections. Today a future
bomber has to be designed so that the first man to reach the aircraft can
bang a switch on the nose gear which starts and checks everything by
computer while the crew are getting strapped in.

Back at freezing Moses Lake in the winter of 1948 such things would
have seemed as remote as flying to the Moon. By this time both the
prototypes had been flown by Air Force crews, and the low-powered first
machine had actually been turned over to the user for check testing on
8 July 1948, and delivered and accepted on 3 December. On 8 February
1949, still with the J35 engines, it was flown to Washington DC and took
advantage of a tail-wind to cover the 2,289 miles from Larson to Andrews

AFB in 3 h 46 min, at an average speed of 607·8 mph. This fact, coupled with the striking photograph that appeared in all the newspapers showing the arrow-like bomber streaking above snowy landscape, served to put the Boeing jet very much in the news, and it stayed that way for ten busy years. Later, in October 1949, 6065 was re-engined with the J47, which was then in full production for several aircraft and had been service-tested in the second XB-47. In retrospect it seems to me remarkable that these two prototypes should not only have served to clear the radically new flight controls and handling characteristics but also the engines, the whole range of on-board systems and quite a lot of the avionics (a word not then coined) and armament. Both prototypes could carry bombs. The large single bomb bay could carry the 10,000 lb device that served as the nominal strategic nuclear weapon in the immediate post-war period. In an overload condition it could carry also a single 22,000 lb conventional bomb, or other combinations of bombs with weights up to 20,000 lb. For defence the B-47 had been planned to have a radar-directed tail turret with two 0·50 in guns, controlled by the co-pilot (who was also called the weaponeer) who, with some difficulty, could swivel his seat round to face aft and watch the gunsight radar scope and, if he so chose, train and fire the guns manually. It took years to develop the B-47 turret and its radar, as related later, but trials began in 1949.

The first B-47A was rolled out at Wichita on 1 March 1950 and flew on 25 June. This long delay after roll-out reflects the fact that the aircraft, 91900, not only incorporated some structural revision, notably strengthening of the wing, but also carried almost all the combat equipment and electronics which were installed and checked in the fine weather out of doors on the flight line—which, very soon, was to grow in a way that far exceeded Boeing's wildest hopes. On the very day that the first B-47A flew, war broke out in Korea. It was an unexpected and remote war, but within weeks the United States was caught up in the conflict and discovering that most of its aircraft were still piston-engined and that the jets left much to be desired. As a strategic nuclear bomber the B-47 was not directly relevant to Korea, but the start of a shooting war more sharply polarized the world into the East and the West—which at the time was always referred to by the Americans as "the Free World". The Cold War became icy, the Dulles policies of Brinkmanship and Massive Retaliation coloured American defence thinking and the purse-strings were loosed for vast armadas of weapons. Suddenly the B-47 changed in stature from being a rather special and extremely expensive new bomber to become the primary instrument of American striking power in a perilous world.

During the summer and autumn of 1950 the pressure to clear a true production version for service with the USAF Strategic Air Command increased markedly, and meetings were held at the Pentagon and at Boeing's Seattle headquarters to discuss ways of accelerating rate of delivery. The first true production order had been placed in November 1948, as a letter of intent for 87 aircraft designated B-47B. Subsequent letter contracts were placed for these aircraft, five under the 1949 budget and the other 82 in 1950. But the Korean war made the Joint Chiefs of Staff think in terms of hundreds. Well before the end of 1950 the decision had been taken to bring in a second source, preferably a company that had not been an unsuccessful jet-bomber candidate. But the better the Air Force got to know the B-47, the more it liked what it saw, and the dramatic decision was taken in January 1951 to re-establish the BVD pool that had built nearly all the 12,731 Fortresses in World War 2. To most Americans BVD signifies a big-selling brand of underwear, but in this context it meant Boeing-Vega-Douglas. For the B-47 the name Vega (a Lockheed subsidiary) was not resurrected, and instead of Burbank the Lockheed B-47 plant was to be the former Bell factory built in 1943 at Marietta, Georgia, to produce the Boeing B-29. One of the biggest single manufacturing facilities under one roof in the world, it later gathered its own design and research teams as the Lockheed-Georgia Co. Likewise, whereas Douglas had built the B-17 at Long Beach, their B-47 operation was organized at the re-opened wartime plant at Tulsa, Oklahoma. The mighty team of Boeing, Douglas and Lockheed is one that can be claimed by no other peace-time product but the B-47.

The initial mass-production version, the B-47B, differed in minor ways from the A batch. As an operational and supposedly fully developed aircraft it had the K-2 radar and four reconnaissance cameras, but no tail turret. The last item proved difficult to develop, and in Britain the problem was circumvented by fitting no tail armament, which RAF operational research showed to be the correct answer for high-subsonic V-bombers. But in the United States the notion of the unarmed bomber remained unacceptable for many years, even though the doctrine of all-round defence was not persisted in. Doubtless for the jet era some *ad hoc* tests would have been done anyway, but the possibility of fitting guns only at the tail was discovered by accident. During B-29 operations against Japan the sporadic fighter opposition caused the 21st Air Force to remove all except the tail guns from many aircraft, turning them into B-29Bs with considerably better speed, range and altitude performance. It was fortuitously discovered that it was almost impossible to make a fighter attack on a B-29B going flat out except in a curve of pursuit from behind. Thus the Air Force and Navy accepted the quite severe performance and weight penalty of a tail turret not only in the B-47 but also in the B-52 (p. 154), B-58 (p. 185) and A-3 (p. 214); it is not inconceivable there could be tail armament in the B-1 (p. 262). This policy was followed by the Russians until well into the 1960s, but today I consider defensive avionics of far greater importance. In 1950 the only defence avionics comprised the crude strips of foil called window or chaff—which, of course, the B-47 carried. This was not too difficult to clear as a functional system, although even here there were problems in shoving it out into a 500 mph airstream and ensuring the correct scatter. But the tail barbette was a different matter.

According to the original plan all production B-47 aircraft were to be fitted with the A-2 radar-directed rear armament, starting with the first B-47A. Provision was made for the installation of the whole system in every airframe, but, as was commonly the case with the very new airborne electronic systems of 25 years ago, it could not be made to work. The chief fault with the A-2 lay in the servo loops, where the required manufacturing tolerance on the mechanical parts was beyond the state of the art at the time. A contributory factor was frequent failure of vacuum tubes (valves). The result was that the guns consistently oscillated badly and, after extensive flight testing in a B-47A, it was decided an acceptable system could not be delivered. The only short-term answer seemed to be to adapt the much simpler fire-control system that was operational with the B-36. The mating of this less advanced system with the B-47 was done by GE at Schenectady and Syracuse, with Avco's Crosley Division brought in as second source. Finally, on 23 May 1954, when about 800 B-47s were in service, Boeing was at last able to announce the bomber was "now equipped with a remotely controlled tail turret system capable of knocking down enemy intercepters in the night or in fog . . ." It was called the A-5 system, and was installed in the 455th production aircraft and all subsequent examples. The guns were two 20 mm, each with 70 rounds, in contrast to the two 0·5 in of the A-2 system. Subsequently Boeing rebuilt many of the unused A-2 turrets, matched them with a different radar and an optical sight to produce the B-4 fire-control system, and fitted this to aircraft Nos 180–454; later still these B-4 systems were replaced by the A-5, while in the main run of B-47E aircraft the A-5 was further developed into the MD-4 system with improved electronics. Tail guns were never simple, and SAC went through it all again with the B-52.

The other externally obvious characteristic that kept changing for years was the JATO rocket boost. The use of 18 separate solid motors was expedient, and gave reliable and highly spectacular departures which Boeing photographers made the subject of some of the most dramatic aircraft portraits ever taken. But it was expensive, logistically inconvenient and handicapped the aircraft by making it fly its mission full of empties. Extensive study was done on the use of various configurations of large liquid-propellant motors, but although these gave a higher specific impulse and were more convenient they were inadequately developed. Until 1953 one could see B-47s with numerous different arrangements of internal solid motors. One could also see a quite different arrangement which was first flown on a B-47B (50-0003, which should have been written on the fin as 00003 but, according to rules when the fiscal year ends in a zero, left a nought off). This aircraft conducted trials with a triple "horse collar" clipped immediately behind the rear landing-gear truck, on which could be attached various 1,000 lb JATO bottles up to a maximum (which was also the usual number) of 33. Not only did this give the crew a real push in the back, which was conspicuously absent from an unaugmented take-off at high weight, but the whole pack could be jettisoned after burn-out over a predesignated "safe" area. The pack was not normally recovered and so was by no means a routine fitment, but it would have been a requirement on practically every real mission if there had been a war with the Soviet Union, had it not been for the development of flight refuelling as described later.

It is probably fair to claim that there was nothing wrong with the B-47 that more powerful engines would not cure. The B-47B did have marginally more urge, imparted by J47-GE-23 engines. These were the first of GE's E-series J47, with a rebladed compressor handling more air at a slightly higher pressure ratio, and with many other changes including anti-icing and a high-altitude ignition system. Rated at 5,800 lb, the dash-23 enabled the B-47B to be cleared to take off at 180,000 lb, which compares very well with the empty weight of about 76,130 lb. But Boeing and the Air Force had for a long time looked at the possibility of fitting much more powerful engines. GE had their own J73, in the 9,000 lb class, but the choice fell on Allison, whose corresponding "second-generation" axial had been slipped into the budget as the J35-A-23. In fact it was not a J35 at all but a totally new design which, once funded, blossomed forth as the J71. It ran on the bench in April 1950, flew in an extensible pod under a B-45 and was earmarked as the engine for future B-47 models, as well as for various other aircraft both with and without afterburner. The 88th B-47B (51-2045) was set aside for conversion with four J71 engines, giving slightly more thrust than the six dash-23s for about 10 per cent less weight, considerably lower drag and at least 10 per cent lower fuel consumption. The first J71-powered B-47 was successively called the XB-56, YB-56 and YB-47C, but it never even got airborne and the B-56 production version was terminated in advance of contract. One reason was that the improvement conferred by the J71 was marginal (nothing like as great as fitting, say, a British Olympus), and there was actually an increase in total engine price. But a bigger reason was that in 1950 the urgent demands of the Korean war were for vast numbers of proven items. The decision was taken to build the thoroughly proven J47 not only at two GE plants (West Lynn, near Boston, and Evendale, near Cincinnati) but also at two big automotive companies, Studebaker and Packard (in 1942–46, of course, Packard had made the British Merlin). This decision had profound significance for the B-47. It kept the J47, a basically quite old wartime design, as the sole powerplant of all the vast fleets of B-47s (and many fighters), which in turn caused the J47 to become the most prolific aircraft gas turbine in history with a total run of more than 36,500 engines.

Total production of the B-47B amounted to 399, including the side-tracked "B-56" already mentioned, and these were the first to reach the squadrons of SAC. The first flew on 26 April 1951, just six days after the giant three-source production plan was publicly announced. Anyone in the planemaking business will be able to picture the work involved. The B-47 was the most technically advanced military aircraft in the world. Its 108 foot length was nowhere empty space, as had been almost every previous large bomber; wherever there was no fuel there was tightly packaged and complicated equipment. Lockheed and Douglas had to learn every nut and bolt from scratch, tool up two plants that had been closed since 1945, hire anybody they could get and train them not merely the detailed skills of, say, precision countersunk riveting but which end of an aircraft was which, and simultaneously set up vast offices, test and checkout departments and rehabilitate and greatly improve two airfields. But this is what keeps Americans from being bored, and with no outward ripple of difficulty Lockheed delivered eight of the last batch of B models and Douglas ten, all from parts fabricated at Wichita so that Douglas and Lockheed could set up fabrication and assembly departments simultaneously. By this time the B-47 programme was not only peacetime business on a fantastic scale but it was exceptionally widespread. It has been Boeing policy since World War 2 to subcontract widely. A typical unit price for an equipped B-47B was $2·5 million; of this 42 per cent went to subcontractors, and all Boeing (or Lockheed or Douglas) kept amounted to approximately 34 per cent of the price of the bare airframe, excluding engines, radar, systems and equipment.

Delivery of the B-47B began in May 1951, the same month that the RAF formed its first squadron of Canberras. This completed some five years of planning, inspecting and finally detailed flight evaluation by what was the Air Technical Service Command when the programme began and then, after the formation of the USAF, became the Air Materiel Command. The Bomber Flight Test Section, initially headed by Maj Guy M. Townsend, found the B-47 one of their happier experiences and incidentally found the B-47B could beat both the F-80 Shooting Star and F-84 Thunderjet in a straight run at full throttle, and turn inside them. The

145

first customer was SAC's 306th (Medium) Bomb Wing, at MacDill AFB, Florida. I was relieved to see the 306BW called "medium" because the B-47 had originally been officially classed a "light bomber" (whatever that means), despite its unprecedented weight. SAC never deigned to use anything called "light", and the partners of the 306th were the obsolescent B-29, the B-50 and the B-36, the first two called medium and the monster B-36 called heavy. Such classifications became meaningless in the nuclear age, a more important parameter being range. This leads into the one big area I have so far deliberately left untouched.

From the start of flight testing the Air Force was increasingly enthusiastic about Boeing's swept-wing bomber, but rather nonplussed about exactly how it might use it. The original jet-bomber competition was in no sense conducted in order to produce a strategic aircraft but merely to explore technical possibilities. Late in 1947 a paper competition was held for a medium bomber with longer range, to see if it would be possible to meet the needs of SAC with a jet, or more probably a turboprop. When all the submissions were in, in January 1948, the winner was judged to be Boeing's proposal for a bomber with four turboprop engines (this was quite separate from the turboprop B-52, p. 155). But by this time the incredibly low drag of the B-47 was making this much faster, and operationally more attractive, bomber a subject of renewed interest. By mid-1948 it had been decided that, with increased thrust, flight refuelling, and operating at increased gross weights, the B-47 could fulfil the SAC medium bomber mission. Without the flight testing of hardware this would never have been suspected, and the Air Force might have spent huge sums on uninspiring turboprop bombers. It was this that got the B-47 chosen for the inventory, and it ought to have impressed on the Air Force the false economy of taking decisions after paper studies. But for the B-47 to play an effective role in the Air Force it was essential to use in-flight refuelling.

Refuelling aircraft in flight, by various crude *ad hoc* methods, was the key to some outstanding endurance records before 1930, but as a reliable routine procedure for civil use it rested squarely on patient development in the late 1930s by Sir Alan Cobham. His company, Flight Refuelling Ltd., never attracted more than desultory interest from British services until after 1955 when it was realized that there was scarcely a single American bomber or fighter not FR-equipped, but in the United States it was a different story. By 1947 Cobham's method of fuel transfer, in which the receiver aircraft pushes a probe into a drogue trailed on the end of a hose unreeled from the tanker, was being urgently studied in competition with a completely new proposal by Boeing. The latter devised a Flying Boom method in which the receiver formated close below and behind the tanker while a crewman in the tanker tried to extend a tele-

scopic pipe into the bomber's "receptacle" socket. By 1948 the Flying
Boom was a 30 foot tube with a pair of aerodynamic control surfaces with
which it could be steered by a boom operator lying face down in a ventral
blister immediately ahead of the boom's pivoted mounting beneath the
tanker's tail. A good "boomer" could quickly aim at the receptacle and
then extend the telescopic boom straight into it, using a hydraulic motor
drive assisted by the internal pressure of the fuel, until it locked with a
fuel-tight seal. By 1950 this system was in SAC service with the KB-29P
(later the KC-97) tanker and the B-50D receiver. In that year the first of
two B-47As was converted with a boom receptacle, and the second was
converted in 1951 together with two B-47Bs which were respectively
modified as a hose-reel tanker and a probe receiver.

The subsequent evaluation was one of considerable importance, not
only to the B-47. The probe/drogue method was far from fully developed
and the Air Force judged that "unpredictable airflow variations" caused
the drogue often to deflect or oscillate just at the crucial moment, while
inability to keep the hose taut caused "whipping and snaking". In contrast
the rigid boom seemed precisely controllable, and could transfer fuel at a
considerably higher rate, No attempt was made to cure the deficiencies of
the British system, and Flight Refuelling Ltd were not in a position to do
much about it because the British officials who would have had to handle
the negotiations, and perhaps provide development funds, showed hardly
any interest in the subject. Had the US Navy adopted in-flight refuelling
at this time it is highly likely that this market also would have been won
by the Boeing method. Probably the boom was the best choice in 1951,
but the point should not be overlooked that the problems that eliminated
the probe/drogue were very soon cured as soon as anyone tried to do so.
With aerial refuelling the B-47B could be topped up to 202,000 lb, well
above the take-off limit and necessitating reduced manoeuvre factors. This
extended the range by 20 per cent and there is no doubt the point was not
lost on the Soviet Union when a flight-refuelled B-47B flew a simulated
mission over the geographic North Pole on 20 September 1951.

When delivered, every B-47B had a boom receptacle, but no guns. In
service the accident rate was commendably low (it was markedly better
than that of the conventional B-45 Tornado, and at the 10,000 operational
hour mark there had been only three fatal accidents compared with six
for the B-57—the docile Canberra!). SAC by 1951 had settled down as
a force which, despite its huge size, consisted of picked men to do a difficult
and demanding job. Only SAC had nuclear weapons at that time, and only
SAC had all the paraphernalia of underground command centres and red
telephones linked directly with the President of the United States. Only
SAC had aircrew who, to a man, seemed to be grizzled veterans of World

War 2 who always flew in scarlet baseball caps bearing the squadron number in bold white characters. Most of these crews numbered 11 or 15, and roamed about their vast bombers in true Flying Fortress tradition. The B-47, with only three men, offered less scope, but I still chuckle at one early experience when proper procedures were being worked out. Commander of the 306th BW was Col. Mike McCoy, and in 1951 he was riding in the bomb-nav station in the nose. The transparent nose-cap of the A model had gone, and apart from some small side windows there was only a periscope for external vision. This was a lovely thing, with powered elevation and traverse, but after a while McCoy hankered after broader vistas and a spell at the controls. "One of you guys come outta there", he called into his microphone, "I'm coming up." After giving the chap time to undo all the connections, and the fiddling seat-harness, McCoy started back upstairs. It was then that all three crew-members met in the narrow gangway. (In 1957 McCoy was killed at Pinecastle AFB, Florida, while practising for the annual SAC bombing competition. Today Pinecastle is McCoy AFB.)

This gangway was constricted at the best of times, and with a back-type parachute it was easy to knock a row of switches the wrong way. Yet it was regarded as waste space, and when in 1953 the much bigger B-52 was being prepared for production the tandem-seat layout of the two prototypes was abandoned in favour of side-by-side pilots in an airline-type flight deck. The original B-47 arrangement reflected Boeing's wish for minimum drag. In the air it was splendid, but on landing the co-pilot had almost no forward view, when it was essential to keep straight and laterally level, as well as in the correct nose-high pitch attitude. Cross-wind limits were low with the bicycle gear ($90°$ total of wind plus gusts, 25 knots), and Boeing nearly brought in a modification to allow both trucks to swivel slightly so that the aircraft could be crabbed on, as could the later B-52. Keeping straight involved steering with the front truck, with a $6°$ limit each side (one-tenth as much as in taxiing), while the outriggers just castored freely. Directional stability was greatly helped by the strong pull of the drag chute.

Although the gangway may have wasted space in the B-47's tight pressure cabin, there was enough left for an oven. It was an RAF joke at that time that all SAC bombers had soda-fountains capable of supplying every conceivable flavour of ice-cream. The propeller-driven bombers did contain ice cream, but I do not believe there was room for a soda-fountain in a B-47. Indeed, even an oven seemed odd to an Englishman who never even had a packet of sandwiches on piston-engined flights lasting three times as long as B-47 missions were supposed to, but possibly the advent of flight refuelling made some form of sustenance essential.

Much later, in 1955, a B-47E suffered a landing-gear malfunction at Nouasseur, Morocco, and the crew fixed it after 36 hours and three re-fuellings. Without food or drink the pilots would have been in poor shape for the landing.

In the winter of 1952–53 one B-47B, serial 51-2137, was bailed back to Boeing-Wichita and used for accelerated service tests in which 1,000 hours were flown in the shortest possible time. After it was all over one of the crew thought it had all been great fun, except for one really serious occasion when the oven malfunctioned: "We crossed three states and were well into a fourth before it turned out a single toasted cheese sandwich." Fortunately other incidents were nothing like so distressing, and most of the 121 missions were routine—so much so that Boeing said 2137 stood up to the hard work "like a million pre-inflation dollars" (which, as it was said in 1953, today sounds ironic). On one occasion, en route from Albuquerque to Wichita at 40,000 feet, a jet stream boosted the ground speed to 794 mph for almost half an hour; another such stream allowed 2137 to fly the 725 miles from Chicago to New York in 65 minutes, to the disbelief of listeners in various airport control towers. At 36,000 feet over Florida the absence of forward-looking radar caused 2137 to run straight into a severe thunderstorm, with no worse damage than five small holes due to lightning, and this demonstrated the remarkable ability of the B-47 fuselage to continue in a straight line while the wings took the punishment. Possibly the most unexpected event was the consternation caused one day over Ukiah, California. The B-47 left a characteristic vapour trail with the usual woolly white clouds of ice crystals interlaced by very thin lines of hard white where the crystal density was higher and much more persistent. In some conditions the trail broke into clear rings, each some 200 feet across, and when the good citizens of Ukiah saw these vivid white rings directly overhead, at a time when every news-bulletin had something to say about flying saucers, the result can be imagined.

During 1953 all the missing bits of operational equipment finally gelled, and to put them all together Boeing devised the B-47E, the main production version and possibly built in larger numbers than any other post-war strategic aircraft (the only one that could rival it is the Tu-16). The engine of the E was the J47-25, made by GE, Studebaker and Packard, and differing from the -23 in having a water-injection system giving 7,200 lb at sea level. With water and the 33-motor JATO rack the E was cleared to take off at 198,180 lb, and in flight it could be refuelled to 206,700 lb. The tail guns at last came out of the laboratory, as already related, the nose was revised to accommodate upward-ejection seats for the pilots and a downward-ejection seat for the bomb-nav in the nose, and the equipment was rearranged. The landing gear was stiffened, there were many

149

detail modifications and the undersides were painted with the newly developed anti-radiation white paint. To go with this paint, the two pilots were issued with photochromic spectacles which instantly darkened under the action of radiation from a nuclear explosion. Finally, but by no means least, the bomb bay and its ancillary services were modified to carry the first of SAC's thermonuclear weapons, which were no larger than the original 20-kiloton fission bombs had been.

With the E model the Air Force had its fully operational B-47. Boeing built no fewer than 931 at Wichita, Douglas-Tulsa built 274 and Lockheed-Marietta built 385. Such was the beneficial influence of the learning curve that almost every E cost less than $2 million, the average Lockheed price (the lowest) being $1·87 million. The first E flew on 30 January 1953. Subsequent production and service clearance were so rapid that between 3 and 5 June 1953 the 45 aircraft of the 306th BW, all of them of the E model, made mass formation flights from MacDill to RAF Upper Heyford on the first of many global rotational deployments. Oxford's dreaming spires, which had for years reverberated to the B-36D, generally found the swept-wing jet a pleasant relief. I find, as a complete layman, that people's behaviour varies greatly according to what society expects. Around 1956 I attended a dinner at Oxford at which the speech of Sir Maurice Bowra, one of the most eminent Britons of his time, was punctuated by the arrival of a complete B-47 wing. He told me he thought they had "exciting, evocative shapes" and that their sound was "rather thrilling". This was before the age of protest.

On 14 October 1954 the thousandth B-47 built at Wichita was rolled out, covered in stuck-on coins and folding money—"in a spontaneous move on the part of Boeing personnel"—which later was donated to the National Foundation for Infantile Paralysis. Wichita's last B-47E emerged in March 1956 "after 59 months of on-schedule deliveries to the Air Force", although the last few aircraft were not taken on DoD charge until 1957. The grand total of B-47 production is not easy to determine, because of the unusual number of sub-types and conversions, but according to DoD records it is 2,040; to emphasize how difficult it is to reach the correct figure, three standard published books on Boeing aircraft give the total as 1,941, 1,982 and 2,041, while I make it 2,067! Many of these were reconnaissance aircraft outside the scope of this book, the most important of these variants being the RB-47B which could be converted back to bomber configuration, the specialized single-purpose RB-47E, and the even more specialized RB-47H and ERB-47H which, carrying the ALD-4 system originally planned to be slung in a pod under the B-58, flew hazardous electronic reconnaissance missions all round (and often over, the Soviet Union and on at least two occasions fell before the guns of Migs.

There were various TB-47 trainers, DB-47s for launching and directing missiles and drones, QB-47s which were themselves drones (one of which was struck amidships by a Bomarc programmed to miss by not less than 100 feet), radio communications conversions, engine test-beds (one of which, with two Wright T49 turboprops derived from the Sapphire turbojet, sustained 597 mph, believed to be the highest level speed by any propeller-driven aircraft), special electronics trainers and many aircraft used to test systems and equipment, notably the YB-47J used to fly the MA-2 radar bomb-nav system of the B-52 and another that tested the B-52's spoilers.

One of the experimental conversions was highly relevant to bombing. In 1949 the Air Force contracted with Bell for one of the first stand-off missiles intended to be released by a bomber while still outside the enemy's most heavily defended zone in order not only to give the bomber a chance of flying another day but also of vastly increasing the enemy's interception problem. Bell was chosen because of the company's experience with the supersonic X-1 and in particular with the Reaction Motors liquid rocket engines. In 1953 the first full-scale GAM-63 (guided air missile) Rascal emerged, and the YDB-47B was converted to carry it. The Rascal was a cruciform canard with three superimposed rocket chambers and radio command guidance. It was found the B-47 could fly quite well with the big missile strapped low on its right side, and several inert, then hot and finally guided Rascals were launched under radio control from the B-47 down the Gulf Test Range operating from Eglin AFB. In the following year two E-model bombers were similarly converted, for service trials, but the Rascal paid the penalty of having been started too early in the state of the art and never saw production. Much later, in 1958, a B-47 was used to launch test vehicles leading to the feasibility studies for WS-199, the first proposal for an air-launched ballistic missile. But no B-47 ever actually served in a squadron equipped to loose any sort of missile, although the types of bombs changed and so did the method of delivery.

Many great flights were made by B-47s in service with SAC. I mentioned the unpremeditated 36 hours rectifying a landing truck malfunction, but for sheer endurance this was surpassed by a mission in 1954 which airline passengers may care to think about next time they suffer a bad-weather diversion. A B-47E of the 43rd BW took off from Sidi Slimane, Morocco, on 17 November to return to its base at RAF Fairford (now the UK Concorde base) in Gloucestershire. Fairford proved to be under a complete clamp, and the bomber flew all the way back to Morocco. Encountering extremely bad weather over Africa, the crew changed their minds and, learning of a better forecast over the UK, eventually set course again for Fairford. They landed at Fairford on 19 November, having covered

21,163 miles in 47 h 35 min. The longest point-to-point mission was made on August 10–11 1957, when a B-47 of the 321 BW took off from Andersen AFB, Guam, and flew 11,450 miles non-stop to Sidi Slimane in 22 h 50 min (it went eastwards, across the Pacific, the United States, and the Atlantic). And the biggest single SAC operation of all time was Operation Power-house, which occupied a two-week period ending on 11 December 1956. More than 1,000 aircraft, from 21 B-47 wings and 18 KC-97 tanker squadrons, flew simulated combat missions averaging 8,000 miles each over the whole area of the N. American continent and Arctic. As a demon-stration of global power it looked better than the deployment of the RAF's force of 45 Valiants to Suez the previous month.

Throughout the early years of the B-47 programme the year in which sharpening obsolescence would demand a replacement was estimated at 1957. But when 1957 came, the B-47 was at the very peak of its career. It equipped no fewer than 28 Medium Bomb wings of SAC, each with a combat strength of 45 aircraft. To this force of 1,260 could be added some 300 B-47s used in missions other than bombing plus a further 300 held in reserve for attrition. This immense force, almost all of it wearing the star-spangled blue band of SAC, was being worked very hard. In the considered view of an Air Force general, the B-47 had "become tired". The only visible replacement was the B-58 (p. 185), but in 1957 this was a long way from inventory service and promised to be so expensive that it could never replace the B-47 on a one-for-one basis. Some relief came in the growing force of long-range B-52s and their accompanying KC-135 tankers, which were to serve B-47 wings as well from the end of 1957, but it was clear the B-47 would have to serve in the front line until long after 1960. Budgetary considerations demanded that any necessary revision of the aircraft should be held to an absolute minimum.

Part of the revision was obviously going to involve updating the avionics, especially the communications and ECM equipment, and it was also planned to convert increasing numbers of B-47s for use in electronic reconnaissance, in multi-sensor reconnaissance (with the emphasis at first on research and then on operations) and weather reconnaissance, including hurricane research. But the biggest new requirement was to fly bombing missions at minimum altitude in order to penetrate under enemy radar screens, with the special capability of delivering nuclear weapons (not thermonuclear) by LABS toss-bombing. In this manoeuvre the aircraft, preferably under automatic flight control, is pulled up hard into an Immelmann turn over the target, releasing its bomb when passing through the 45° climb position so that, while the weapon is arching up to roughly 10,000 feet altitude and then falling again, the bomber can fly to a safe distance from the explosion. The B-47 had not been designed for such a manoeuvre, and calculations showed at once its structure would need local strengthening to withstand a further ten years of combat operation with the added stress of simulated LABS missions. This was something new in Air Force experience. It did not in any way reflect on the structural design at Boeing.

Later the B-52 was to need even more extensive structural revision, and similar modification was necessary on most of the other bombers in this book. But in the winter of 1957–58 the Air Force, in guessing a figure of $40 million for the B-47 modification programme, readily admitted it could be out by as much as 50 per cent. The true error was more like 500 per cent. At first it was thought that "design and weight limitations" would restrict the weight of added structure around the wing root and fuselage/wing attachments to a total of "60 lb added at critical points", while the job would be completed by "reaming out and replacing some 372 bolts". One of these bolts, at the front spar anchorage, was about the size and shape of a milk-bottle, and the programme soon became known, even officially, as Project Milk Bottle. At first planned to take two weeks per aircraft, done by Douglas-Tulsa and Lockheed-Marietta to Boeing drawings, it was reluctantly accepted by July 1958 that it was going to take at least a month per aircraft and would cost far more. The Oklahoma City and San Antonio Air Materiel Areas were brought in on a crash programme which involved reaming out and replacing 1,115 bolts on each aircraft and adding 238 lb of metal. Even then many aircraft were found already to have developed cracked forgings, and this meant not only costly replacement in those aircraft but also frequent inspection and repair of the others. With an 1,800-aircraft fleet this cost massive sums.

The strengthened bombers were designated B-47E-II, and many old B-47Bs were brought up to an almost identical standard by gross modification and emerged as B-47B-IIs. Gradually the pressure to fly airborne alerts and low-altitude missions eased, as the tension of the 1950s faded into history. LABS manoeuvres had been abandoned before 1960, not because of the "structural problem" alleged by SAC in its press release, but because the limiting safe distance the B-47 could reach at sustained full throttle was inadequate for the larger bombs SAC was planning to use. The last B-47 Bomb Wing did not de-activate until 1966, 21 years from the design of the Boeing 450 and 15 years from the start of combat service. Weather reconnaissance WB-47s of the Air Weather Service of Military Airlift Command were doing a great job, flailing their wings about in violent turbulence, until the end of 1969. Now this pioneer of the modern big jets—all of them, military and civil—is able to rest. It seems like yesterday that I counted 29 new ones on the flight line at Wichita, waiting to be collected.

Boeing B-52 Stratofortress

IT IS mainly because of the tremendous development of the aircraft gas turbine that long-range missions, that 20 years ago were only marginally possible with a huge aircraft, can today be flown by "fighters". Even the F-111, based on 1959 technology, showed itself capable of replacing all the early versions of the B-52 in the US Air Force Strategic Air Command, and if the payload was only a single SRAM or nuclear bomb it would be possible today to fly a B-52 mission with a single-engined aircraft weighing less than 30,000 lb. But when the B-52 was being planned it did not appear for three years that jet propulsion could be used at all, and when the design did finally go ahead it was the biggest and heaviest aircraft ever put into production. Although it used the most powerful engines available it needed eight of them. On purely technical grounds it is easy to write off the B-52 as no longer cost/effective, but as the later versions can fly missions that are still beyond the capacity of anything else actually available (whatever better things have been drawn on paper) this criticism is academic.

In any case, the B-52 is one of the greatest aircraft of all time, in every sense of the word. Despite its inception as long ago as 1948 it was planned on such a grand scale that it later served in a score of special programmes never remotely envisaged when it was designed. At Edwards AFB B-52s have thundered aloft carrying under their starboard wing an X-15 hypersonic aircraft weighing over 50,000 lb, various egg-shaped lifting-body aircraft, and the General Electric CF6-50A turbofan roughly nine feet in diameter and giving a thrust in excess of 50,000 lb. The B-52, the "long rifle" of SAC, was the supreme expression of the long-range subsonic bomber in the pre-missile age. Unlike the B-47 the giant B-52 was greatly developed over the years in order to carry bigger loads, different loads and different equipment over much greater ranges at all heights down to the minimum for safe terrain clearance. Many years have now gone by since this process of improvement ceased to yield cost/effective rewards, and it is sad to reflect that many of these noble aircraft have spent their twilight years trucking vast tonnages of iron bombs to hit targets nothing like those the designers had in mind. But the story began far from Viet-Nam in both time and place.

In 1941 the leaders of two great Western democracies met on a battleship in mid-Atlantic and, among other things, agreed that it would be a good idea for the United States to acquire the capability of bombing Europe in the event of Britain being defeated. Thus was born the first specification in history for air power to be exerted over intercontinental distances. Boeing submitted two proposals, but neither was judged so good as the remarkable six-engined pusher proposed by Consolidated-Vultee, and it was the latter that eventually went into production as the B-36. This giant bird in the hand gave the CV team at Fort Worth a big advantage when in 1945 the Army Air Force started a competition for a second-generation strategic bomber. Convair knew there was plenty of stretch in the B-36, and were assured by Pratt & Whitney of 4,500 horsepower and superior fuel economy with the planned compound (variable-discharge turbine) version of the R-4360 Wasp Major engine. Despite being plagued with gross mechanical problems, nearly all centred around the pusher R-4360 engines and their 19 foot Curtiss Electric propellers—so that to complete a mission without at least one fire or one propeller flying off seemed like letting the side down—the existence of the B-36 exerted a strong influence on this second competition.

The US government has liked if possible to alternate its big buys between different companies, and when Boeing was told it had won the competition in 1946 I think it was mainly to keep the pot boiling, rather than a definite conclusion that its submission was superior to the B-36F. Compared with the compound-engined B-36F the proposed Boeing Model 462 was vague in the extreme. It was essentially a scaled-up B-50 with six Wright T35 Typhoon turboprops each rated at 5,500 shp. Although an XT35 obtained a clearance for flight testing, and flew in September 1947 in the nose of a B-17, it was not a good engine and Boeing knew it. Even assuming Wright's optimistic specific fuel consumption, the Boeing 462 could not meet the range of 5,000 miles suggested by Wright Field, but in April 1946 Boeing was given a paid study contract, with the designation XB-52. Wright was not yet aware of its inability to develop gas turbines, and boldly schemed an improved T35 to give 8,900 shp. Boeing replanned the XB-52 around only four of these ambitious engines, secured acceptance from Wright Field and continued with paid detail design. But the swift emergence of the B-47 as swept-wing jet hardware, coupled with the disenchantment of the Air Force with very large propeller engines, caused Boeing to spend its own money in a detailed study of a pure-jet bomber to try to fly the same missions, using a completely new engine being designed at Hartford, Connecticut, by Pratt & Whitney.

Although most of the classic Boeing aircraft of the period 1927–35 had used engines from the young Connecticut company, the Boeing designs of 1935–45 were almost exclusively powered by Wright. I do not know if Boeing had the very deep insight that would have been needed in 1947 to assess the relative capabilities of the two piston-engine giants in the new jet era, but it would have found an almost unbelievable discrepancy. Whereas Wright never gained a production order for any aircraft gas turbine except for licence-built British Sapphires, Pratt & Whitney went from strength to strength. With dour and conservative philosophies and engineering skills of the highest order, Mr Pratt created "Turbo Wasp" engines fully equal to their reciprocating ancestors; as an Englishman I might suggest that this was in some degree due to close association with Rolls-Royce, and to the fact the first Turbo Wasps were based on Rolls designs. But the third Turbo Wasp, the JT3, was wholly home-grown. In 1947 it was awarded an Air Force development contract with the designation J57. Its features included the use of low-pressure and high-pressure axial compressors in tandem, each driven by its own turbine at its best speed. Initially planned to give 7,500 lb thrust, the J57 was designed to compress the air to a pressure-ratio of 12·5, then an unprecedented value. Although it was obviously going to be a big and heavy piece of machinery, its high pressure promised economy surpassing that of any previous jet engine, and it rapidly became the most important aircraft power-plant in the non-Communist world. Later it was to become the key to the Boeing 707 and Douglas DC-8 jetliners, and later still to form the basis for the JT3D fan engines. But the first airframe company to see what the J57 could do was Boeing, who considered this potentially powerful and economical turbojet might prove the solution to the previously impossible problem of driving a strategic bomber with jet engines.

It is important to try to recall the way in which most experts 25 years ago thought aircraft propulsion would develop. Notwithstanding high-pressure engines such as the J57, the prevailing expert view was that the turbojet would throughout the foreseeable future be drastically limiting in range. For a really long-range aircraft, such as the heavy bomber SAC was seeking, the propeller was considered the only possible answer. The turbofan, curiously enough, was generally either ignored or else drawn in on a graph between the turboprop and turbojet and dismissed with the opinion that it had the drawbacks of both and none of the advantages. I have a 1945 survey of future propulsion, written by great experts at the Royal Aircraft Establishment at Farnborough, which leaves one in no doubt that turbojets are useless for long ranges. It dwells at great length on whether a turboprop ought to have a heat-exchanger (to take heat from the exhaust and add it to the incoming air, to increase cycle efficiency), and uncompromisingly proclaims "For the most severe range requirements there is no doubt even the turbine-airscrew unit will prove inadequate and that some form of compound piston engine will be necessary".

Such statements could not be lightly dismissed. The conclusions of this report, and of its counterparts in the United States, represented the distillation of thousands of points carefully plotted on hundreds of graphs by people who were not mere narrow-track scientists but very full and complete men who in many cases were quite at home on the engine test-bed or in the cockpit. For a company of Boeing's stature, to put jets and swept wings on the XB-47 was fair enough, because this pioneer aircraft did not have to meet a numerical value of range; but for it to propose the same formula for the XB-52 looked like a fast route to a scandalous waste of federal funds. Not a few of the experts thought Boeing had simply been carried away by its own enthusiasm. I cannot do better than quote Leonard S. Hobbs, chief engineer of Pratt & Whitney, who in 1955 told me "We planned the J57 for a broad spectrum of missions. We had to take care the Pentagon did not get too worked up over it, because they tended to think high pressure was the avenue to solving all sorts of problems. . . . Boeing's proposal to use it for their heavy bomber was a case in point. Our own performance engineers were doubtful that a J57 airplane could fully meet this requirement, and it was partly with the SAC mission in mind that we pushed the big turboprop T57." The T57 was a J57 with extra turbine stages and a propeller reduction gear. Hobbs' off-the-record chat came at a time when the B-52 was flying hardware, but he emphasized the way such hardware was doubted in 1948.

I have dwelt at length on the propulsion problem because in 1973 nobody would dream of using anything but a jet engine for a long-range aircraft, and it needs a great effort of reorientation to imagine the environment of 1948. Indeed in October of that year, when a dozen or so Boeing engineers went to Wright-Patterson AFB (Wright Field now had a double dedication) to talk about the turboprop XB-52, the general consensus of opinion in the Air Force was that the future lay with the B-36F. Boeing's proposal had been fully evaluated and, though it promised to be about 50 mph faster than the compound-engine B-36, it offered no improvement in range/payload and might be inferior. A further consideration was the Air Force's mental picture of the future development of the Wright T35 and its giant propellers, which they saw as a nightmare of stripped gear-teeth, shed blades, fires, vibration, lubrication problems and a steadfast refusal to get "out of the wood". (Later the Air Force went through it all again with the T57 and a giant logistic freighter.) The bomber procurement staff were well aware of Boeing's unpaid study for a J57-powered XB-52; indeed it was done with their blessing. During the summer of 1948 they had drawn up a set of requirements for a jet strategic bomber. On this October Thursday they handed the document over to the Boeing team. It was not a formal RFP, because the procurement staff knew that no other company had anything like the expertise of Boeing in this field.

What they hoped was that Boeing would be able to come back quite soon and say it could come most of the way to meet the requirement. I doubt if they were prepared for Boeing's response. The team went back to nearby Dayton, holed up in one of their rooms in the Van Cleve hotel and absorbed the new requirement. Next morning they telephoned that their jet XB-52 proposal would be submitted the following Monday!

They were able to do this because they had with them, in their brains and briefcases, practically the whole world's detailed knowledge on how to plan a jet long-range bomber. From the start of 1948 Boeing's project staff had worked hard on the possibility, and their calculations had been backed up by many wind-tunnel tests and model rig tests to find the best and most valid answers. Taking the latest information on engines from Pratt & Whitney and other turbojet manufacturers they based their parametric planning on the paper "medium bomber competition" held in the winter of 1947–48 as described in the B-47 story. For this Boeing assumed the use of four engines each of 8,500 lb sea-level static thrust. They also assumed a fixed payload of 20,000 lb. On this basis they drew graphs of generalized performance for a variety of aircraft having different weights, ranges, speeds and altitudes. It was one of the classic parametric studies in aviation history, when "trade-offs" are made between conflicting variables to see how improving one worsens the others. The Boeing engineers, frustrated by the fact that on paper it is not possible to draw in more than two dimensions, transferred their plots to sheets of transparent plastic which were then stacked together to form a three-dimensional graph, with mission radius along the bottom of the flat front face, altitude up the vertical axis, and flight Mach number increasing through the depth from front to rear. The right hand side of the shining block was a smooth curving boundary representing the limit of the state-of-the-art. With this and a mass of supporting papers the Boeing team, scattered around the hotel bedroom, did a seemingly simple thing: they just doubled everything. Instead of a medium bomber with four 8,500 lb engines they began to draw a heavy bomber with eight 8,500 lb engines. They were able to do this because of the depth of the background studies, and their experience in understanding the pitfalls in scaling aircraft up and down. Eight engines was unprecedented for a bomber, although rather ill-planned aircraft of 1929–33 had had eight and even twelve engines. GE had the J53 turbojet planned to exceed 15,000 lb thrust, but this was seen as a supersonic fighter engine of lower pressure-ratio than the J57. Four or six giant engines did not look as attractive as eight of the economical Pratt & Whitneys.

By Saturday a detailed three-view drawing had been prepared of a completely new XB-52, the Boeing Model 464. One of the team went to a nearby hobby shop and bought some balsa wood. He could have told the sales assistant "I don't know exactly how much wood I'll need; I want to make a model of the B-52 and we haven't quite designed it yet!" But by Sunday evening the first B-52 ever made was resplendent in USAF markings, and Boeing's detailed written proposal had been typed by a public stenographer who may just have had an inkling of its security importance. On Monday the team appeared once more at Wright-Patterson and put the proposal on the desk of the astonished XB-52 project officer. The Air Force, to a man, was delighted. Despite its obvious enthusiasm for the jet, rather than the giant turboprop, and its clear invitation to Boeing to see if the XB-52 could be a swept-wing jet, it knew Boeing was a big enough company never to pretend to be cleverer than it was, or to bend the curve of a graph or add on a few vital percentage points. The little balsa model was a model of a giant bomber that Boeing could build, with a little more difficulty, full-scale.

It was back in January 1947 that Boeing had been awarded a contract for two prototypes, an XB-52 and a YB-52. This was a curious procedure because the two aircraft were similar and built in parallel. The reason was that Air Force Logistics Command had to help find the money and, as this command is not authorized to buy experimental aircraft, the second prototype was given a service-test designation! Preparations to build these two aircraft, each considerably larger than any previous bomber, went ahead at Seattle throughout the three years from 1949. Added impetus came from the start of the Korean war in June 1950. By this time Convair, loath to give up without a fight, had made a detailed proposal for a swept-wing conversion of the B-36 with the same propulsion system of eight J57 engines. On 15 March 1951 Convair Fort Worth was given a contract for two such aircraft, originally proposed as the B-36G but placed under contract as the YB-60. Despite the high cost of these two additional strategic-jet prototypes, funding the YB-60 appeared worth while because it simultaneously provided an insurance against any failure by Boeing, provided a quite different aircraft for comparative evaluation and kept the vital spur of competition at fever pitch. Boeing had the inside track, and on paper had the superior product, and this was reflected in the fact that in the same month that the YB-60 was placed under contract Boeing was given a Letter of Intent for B-52 production tooling, a most unusual award so far in advance of flight testing and testimony to its thoroughly documented and detailed submissions. But the whole game had not yet been played out. Convair's bold bid to update the 1942-vintage B-36 was probably the biggest redesign job in the history of aviation. The resulting B-60, which flew three days after the first B-52, was the biggest jet aircraft in the world until the C-5A flew more than 16 years later. The fact that it used almost the same fuselage, landing gears, systems and ground equipment as the B-36 meant potential cost savings of about $600 million initially and then some $200 million a year in SAC operation. In Britain such an argument would have carried great weight. In the United States it did not.

On 29 November 1951 the XB-52, serial 49-230, was covered in security sheets and towed from Seattle's Plant 2 to the new Flight Test Building at Boeing Field, where the king was A. M. "Tex" Johnston, the colourful character who after directing the B-52 flight-test programme at Seattle went to run Aero-Spacelines who make the swollen Guppy freighters. The XB was completed in January 1952, quietly rolled out by night on to an apron where few could see it and subjected to extensive systems testing. In March Johnston taxied it under its own power and conducted taxi tests on the runway at speeds up to 100 knots, but Johnston knew this aircraft was not to be the first to fly. It went back into Plant 2 for revision and further equipment installations, and the first into the air was the YB, 9231, which was rolled out on 15 March 1952. After brief taxi trials, and one stream of the vast 44 foot drag chute, Johnston, accompanied by Col Guy M. Townsend, flew the YB on 15 April. With eight YJ57-P-1 engines, each rated at 8,700 lb thrust, the noise of the monster was shattering. No 9231 climbed cleanly away on the four pairs of faintly smoky trails and, after 90 minutes of testing in the Seattle area, headed east to Larson AFB, at Moses Lake, where Boeing's Jet Delivery Center was being established. Here there were no community-relations problems. Johnston and Townsend did two more hours of work near Larson; even on the first flight there was plenty of fuel.

Named, fairly obviously, Stratofortress, the B-52 looked at a glance like an enlarged B-47, but there were significant differences. The wing was similarly swept 35° at the quarter-chord line but it had greater taper ratio and different laminar sections (Boeing 233 at the root and 236 at the tip), with relatively greater depth at the root. This made room for almost half the fuel load of about 29,645 gallons in flexible cells, and the section profile was biased in favour of its lifting rather than its high-Mach properties. Intrinsically the wing was less flexible than that of the B-47, but its tips were later bent through an incredible arc of 32 feet before the main wing box failed in static tests to destruction. In fact the sheer size of the aircraft gave rise to many structural and systems problems, and even the fuselage sagged an inch behind the rear landing gear.

There were two pairs of landing-gear trucks which folded up and inwards to lie diagonally in neat boxes on either side of the front and rear fuselage. The track of ten feet was enough for ground stability in most conditions, but for taxiing round corners a castoring outrigger was added in the outer wing, much further out than in the B-47, retracting inwards into the wing behind the main torsion box. The forward main trucks could be steered, and as cross-wind landings were expected to be frequent the production B-52 became the first, and I believe only, aircraft in which the landing gears could be rotated to the correct runway alignment while the rest of the aircraft crabbed down the glide-slope with wings level and zero drift.

There were four large flap sections of modified Fowler type, with the inner pairs of engines firing through the gap between them. Originally it had been intended to use the outer sections as flaperons, as in the B-47. This arrangement was fitted on 9231 when it first flew but it was abandoned before the XB finally took to the air on 2 October 1952. Instead two-thirds of the lateral control was effected by slotted spoilers of relatively small size hinged at 60 per cent chord above the outer wings roughly in line with the outer pods. Since the end of 1952 these have doubled as the primary lateral control and as the air brakes, but it took a long time to arrive at the final configuration. For the remaining one-third of roll control, and also for roll trim with minimum drag, small tab-operated ailerons were provided between the inner and outer flaps. These were first fitted to the XB, which also had three instead of six spoilers on each wing. Directional control was provided by the spoilers in conjunction with the very small (10 per cent chord) manual-tab rudder hinged to the enormous triangular fin which, because of its height of over 48 feet, folded to starboard to fit inside hangars. The sharply tapered horizontal tail again broke new ground in that it was of the all-flying type, the entire surface being hinged and driven by a live nut running on an irreversible hydraulically powered thread to provide fast and powerful pitch trim, the primary pitch control being the manual-tab elevator.

Although none of the control surfaces was powered, apart from the spoilers, the duplicated 3,000 lb/sq in hydraulic systems were physically the largest in history. The way aircraft accessory systems should be energized was very much in the melting pot around 1950. Several quite different schemes had become available and there was no slick way of finding which would be lightest, give greatest reliability or impose least penalty on aircraft range. One of the more radical ideas was to bleed hot, compressed air from the engines, duct this through thin-wall stainless pipe along the wings and fuselage and use it to drive small air turbines providing shaft power where it was needed. One of the front runners with this technique was Garrett-AiResearch. Boeing found their arguments convincing but hesitated to go the whole hog. But in the early B-52 versions there were no major airframe accessories shaft-driven off the engines. Instead bleed air from all four double pods was ducted to drive two pairs of 60,000 rpm turbo-alternators, one pair in each forward

B.O.W.—6

truck bay, which generated enough electrical power to drive everything else.

Seats were provided for a flight crew of five. Pilot and co-pilot were seated in tandem under a large canopy consisting of 12 separate windows, with a sharp slope from the high co-pilot seat down to the aircraft commander at a lower level. The cockpit was quite unlike that of the B-47. Further aft, on two levels, were the bombardier and navigator. In the extreme tail, 150 feet away, was to be the rear gunner who would actually sit inside his radar-directed turret (but this was not ready in 1952 and was replaced in the prototypes by a fairing). There was no flight station in the nose, which contained the forward and mapping elements of the radar bombing and navigation system (which, of course, was again absent from the first two aircraft). But despite their lack of combat systems the XB and YB kept Tex and his big team extremely busy; at a guess I would think the work load about double that needed to develop the B-47. These first two aircraft had empty and gross weights of 160,000 and 390,000 lb, a maximum speed of 556 mph at 40,000 feet (about Mach 0·85) and a still-air range of 5,200 miles. It looked good enough to predict that the ultimate B-52, with more powerful engines and flight refuelling, would fly all of SAC's missions.

Of the initial batch of 13 aircraft, which would normally have carried a Y prefix but were considered so costly and vital that they were regarded as likely to go into the inventory, the first three were completed as B-52As and the rest as B-52Bs. The A model was not an inventory aircraft and could better have been designated YB-52. All three were bailed back to Boeing as they were delivered and used to speed the development programme. It took a long time, and several hundred million dollars, to complete the production tooling, finalize the B-52A design and initiate production. The first A, serial 1952-1, written 2001, flew on 5 August 1954. Its most obvious change was the completely new flight deck, with an "airline-type" layout that was far superior. It took up less space, gave each pilot a better view (each could see downwards only on one side, but the B-52 was so big that from the original centreline seat one could not even do that) and made for a better arrangement of the controls, with every item reasonably within the reach or vision of both pilots. The eight throttle levers—which, with their thin disc-grips on top, were always likened to a stack of poker chips—and the rows of engine instruments and switches, all in eights, did not have to be provided in duplicate but were simply placed on the centreline and on the central pedestal in the usual way. The two pilots and the navigator had upward ejection seats. In the lower forward fuselage the bombardier and radar operator had downward ejection seats, while the tail gunner, now seated in his $4 \times 0·5$ in turret with Bosch Arma A-3A radar direction, could pull a lever and sever the whole turret from the fuselage. Further advances with the A were J57-9W engines, each rated at 12,500 lb with water injection supplied from a 360-gal tank in the rear fuselage, the cross-wind facility on the landing gear (not originally fitted to the prototypes), 833-gal non-jettisonable external tanks under the outer wings, and a receptacle for a Boeing refuelling boom in the roof of the crew compartment behind the flight deck. Gross weight of the A was 415,000 lb, and the Air Force paid $29 million for each of them because they were used to amortize much of the cost of tooling.

The first inventory B-52, the B-52B, differed from the A only in that the A still lacked the radar bomb-nav system, and one or two less significant items. With a 1952 order for 40, plus the last ten of the 13 "A" models, total procurement of the B was 50, all built at Seattle in 1955–56. Installation of the MA-2, also called Brane (for Bombing Radar And Navigation Equipment), added two tons to the weight and roughly $1 million to the cost, although the influence of the learning curve was such that the average price of a B model came down to $14·4 million. Gross weight rose to 420,000 lb, and the engines were the J57-19W or -29W of which many were made by the second-source for this fine engine, the Ford Motor Company at East Wacker Drive, Chicago. Of the 50 B models, 23 were plain bombers and the other 27 were contracted for as RB-52Bs with a removable pressurized pod filled with cameras, electronic sensors, counter-measures and two human operators. The RB batches came generally ahead of the single-purpose bombers, but pressure to have the dual capability soon cooled and all 50 aircraft were ultimately completed as plain bombers. The first B-52B, 2004, flew on 25 January 1955, and the type entered operational service on 29 June 1955 with 93 (Heavy) Bomb Wing at Castle AFB, California.

Learning how to use the eight-engined monster, with its equipment and systems quite different from those of the B-47, was no small task for SAC, which also had to do a great deal of airfield improvement because the demands of the B-52 were rather greater than those of the B-47 or B-36. The debut of the B-52 was satisfactory, and the 10,000 hour figure of only two aircraft lost (June 1956) set a record that has never been beaten. But by the end of 1956 four more aircraft had been lost. At least one broke up in the air after an exploding turbo-alternator had blown open the forward fuselage tanks, but two of the aircraft were lost through severe hydraulic fires. Skydrol and other less flammable fluids were by this time generally specified in new civil transports, but the B-52 was using mineral oil. Six write-offs at Castle in a few months was just what the Air Force didn't want, and it guardedly said the record was "grave, but not evidence of a defective weapon system". Defective the B-52 certainly was not, and just at this time the Air Force was particularly concerned over its strategic bombers. Apparently to the surprise of US intelligence, the Soviet Union had in July 1955 publicly exhibited several new types of aircraft including very important strategic bombers of three contrasting designs. Later it was to be judged that this was in some degree a hoax and that Russian concentration on bombers was deliberately emphasized (even to the extent of having the same six Tu-16s fly past nine times, to look like 54) to cause a faulty US response, while the real emphasis was applied to missiles. I do not subscribe to this view. The Soviet bomber forces were real enough, and I do not think the Americans were wrong when, early in 1956, they voted $547 million for a "crash program" to raise the production rate of the B-52 from 17 per month to 20, with Boeing's Wichita division as second-source. As discussed later, when it was discovered the Soviet bomber dubbed "Bison" was not being built in any quantity, the B-52 rate was cut back in 1957 to 15 per month.

The B-52 differed markedly from the B-47 in that there was continual pressure to improve its performance and equipment, so that instead of making 2,000 more or less identical aircraft the B-52 programme comprised relatively small batches of progressively improved models. In the B-52C the immediately obvious change was a startling increase in the capacity of the under-wing tanks to a record 2,500 gallons each. Less obvious was that there had now been time to re-think the water injection system and the water was moved from the rear fuselage to a 125 gal tank in each wing root. Gross weight climbed to 450,000 lb, but structural strengthening was confined to minor details. The first of 35 C models, which initially had the forward bomb bay equipped to carry the optional manned reconnaissance pack, was serialled 3399. It was the first to leave the factory with its undersurfaces protected by the special white anti-radiation paint that was already on SAC's B-47s and was later applied to nearly all B-52s. Several B-52s really needed this coating. The first air-dropped H-bomb in history was released from a SAC B-52B approaching a target near Eniwetok on 21 May 1956. Very untypically, a "human error" caused it to miss its target by four miles. Even without radiation burn, there were a few red faces that night.

The B-52D was essentially a C with the improved MD-9 tail fire control and without the provisions for the reconnaissance capsule. This was the first version built at Wichita, which delivered 69 in 1956–57 while Seattle delivered 101. By this time Seattle was becoming flooded with the vast orders for KC-135 tankers, which came on to the scene in 1956 and were assembled at the same rate—15 per month, then 20, then 15 again—as the B-52. By 1957 the great supersonic WS-110A, or "CPB" (p. 239) had emerged as the intended successor to the B-52, but this was obviously a long-term project that could not immediately influence B-52 production. On 3 October 1957 Seattle flew the first B-52E. This introduced a completely new bomb/nav system, the AN/ASQ-38. IBM was prime contractor and supplied the ASB-4 package comprising Raytheon radar, IBM displays, computers and interfaces, GPL APN-89 doppler radar, Kollsman astro compass, Kearfott true heading indicator and GE radar camera. Much of the crew compartment was rearranged to fit the new displays and greatly improve accessibility and convenience.

Despite the improved avionics the learning curve was by now operating to such good effect that the average price for the 100 E-models (42 Seattle, 58 Wichita) was a mere $6·08 million, the cheapest of all B-52 versions. The B-52F introduced the J57-43W engine, with a wet rating of 13,750 lb supplied with water from four tanks in the leading edge (thinks: why not have four wing tanks from the start?). The price was raised above that of the E by the titanium engine compressors. It was also raised by the extensive engineering work which followed the rather bitter decision that air-driven turbo-alternators had not, after all, been a good idea. After detailed parametric studies of the effect on aircraft range, the decision was taken with the F to use a more conventional shaft drive direct from the low-pressure spool of the left engine of each pair. The prominently faired package of the 40 kVA alternator and its Sundstrand constant-speed drive (the purpose of which is to keep all four alternators precisely synchronised, irrespective of fluctuations in engine rpm) was subjected to flight testing which involved 370 hours of B-52 flying, at a cost of $500,000. The first F was aircraft No 359 in the production run (excluding the two prototypes). A total of 44 was built at Seattle and 45 at Wichita. The last Seattle-built F emerged in November 1958. Immediately its major assemblies were out of the jigs the jigs themselves were torn out to make room for the expanding KC-135/707 programme, while elsewhere in Seattle the Bomarc missile was coming into volume production, parts of it having been moved from Wichita. Only the B-52 forward fuselage and "cab section" remained at Seattle, while all engineering support for the B-52 programme was bodily moved to Wichita. This saved the Air Force some tens of millions of dollars.

This saving eventually turned out to be greater than the Air Force had calculated. When AF Secretary Donald Quarles announced the stretchout in B-52 production to 15 per month, on 18 April 1957, the planned force was to be 603 aircraft, sufficient to support eleven wings each of 45 aircraft. The slow-down in manufacture was needed, according to Quarles, "to somewhat ease the training load and the problem of conversion from the B-36" as well as to allow a bigger proportion of the total buy to be of the planned final model, the dramatically improved B-52G. What nobody had predicted in 1957 was that procurement would go way beyond 603 aircraft and that the final version would be a very great further advance over the G. In 1957 it was planned that the new G model should equip three of the eleven wings, instead of the two that would have been the maximum with the 20-per-month production plan. In the event the final two models, the G and H, today equip six wings, and will remain the spearhead of SAC's manned force at least until 1977. In Britain the entire national capability in the field of combat aircraft was dealt an almighty hiccup, which seemed at the time to be near complete strangulation, by the 1957 doctrine that missiles would replace all future fighters and bombers. The US Air Force never even hinted at such a philosophy. In May 1958 General "Butch" Griswold had left his 3rd Air Division HQ at South Ruislip, England, and taken up the appointment of Vice-Chief of Staff at SAC. One of his first tasks at Offutt AFB was to host some English press-men, and he assured them "The day of the manned delivery system will never be over". Today, 15 years later, I doubt if any of those journalists would still disagree.

When the SAC general made this prediction six wings had been equipped with the B-52 and operational time was considerably in excess of 100,000 hours. On the whole the aircraft had performed very well. The first flexure of the giant muscles came in November 1956 when eight aircraft from the 93rd BW at Castle and the 42nd at Loring AFB, Maine, completed a non-stop mission that encompassed the whole North American continent and the North Pole and for some aircraft involved an aggregate air mileage exceeding 17,000 taking 32 hours. On 16 January 1957 the 93rd sent three aircraft on a mission that earned each crewman the DFC and gained the Air Force some of its biggest-ever headlines. In February and March 1949 a SAC B-50 had flown non-stop around the world in 94 h 1 min. The aim of the 93rd was to halve the time. On 18 January the trio came majestically in to March AFB, Calif, having flown further than the B-50, a distance of 24,325 miles, in 45 h 19 min, at an average of about 530 mph. One tail gunner insisted on spending the entire two days and nights in his own seat so that he could claim the doubtful distinction of having gone round the world backwards! Such missions were a severe test of the SAC delivery machine, and it stood up admirably. The J57 engine showed up particularly well, and several wings exceeded 200,000 engine hours without sending an engine off the base for overhaul. Admittedly the J57 was immensely robust, and when Pratt & Whitney produced a true airline version it was ultimately made almost 900 lb lighter, but the large-scale experience with the great bombers using engines eight at a time was a marvellous foundation with which to conquer the civil market.

By the mid-1950s it would have been very much within the state of the art to produce an engine with a dry rating in the 25,000 lb class, enabling the number of engines in a B-52 to be halved, with probable operating economies. This was considered, but the market looked limited, Pratt & Whitney was not enthusiastic and both Boeing and the Air Force told each other they were happy to go on as they were. But there was plenty that could be done with the B-52 airframe, and with the B-52G a whole series of improvements were introduced at once. These improvements can be summarized as: complete structural redesign; use of integral wing tanks; relocation of the gunner in the front crew compartment; elimination of ailerons; use of fully powered elevator and rudder; provision for launching ECM decoys; and provision for launching stand-off missiles. Any one of these changes would alone have been a major advance; taken together they transformed the targeting capability of SAC, opened the way to major operating economies and dramatically increased the ability of the B-52 to penetrate defended territory.

The structural redesign was obvious only in that the vertical tail was cropped in height by almost eight feet, which both reduced weight directly and also reduced the loads carried by the rear fuselage. Altogether almost 10,000 lb was taken out of the airframe, while actually increasing its safe life at the greater weights of the late-model B-52s. Compared with the F the G could carry about 40,000 lb more fuel, as well as 1,200 lb of water, because the lower empty weight was combined with an increase of 30,000 lb in allowable gross weight at 480,000 lb. The very large additional fuel capacity stemmed almost entirely from the completely new "wet wing". Integral tankage was far from new in the second half of the 1950s, but the B-52 wing was enormous. To build the wing of the G Boeing used extruded light-alloy panels each 80 feet in length, which were then sculptured by numerically-controlled millers and etched smooth in a chemical bath. When the wing had been assembled, mainly using large countersunk bolts, it was covered inside with fuel-tight sealant to make a secure tank that would not leak even when bent through an arc of almost 30 feet. Finally the inside was minutely inspected by a 15-strong skin-diving team who, clad in brilliant yellow rubber suits, cleaned off surplus sealant and carried out the final inspection prior to functional testing with fuel. It was no small task to develop this giant wet wing, but it gave the G a gain in operating radius over the F comparable to an air-refuelling by a KC-135. This meant that, for a given mission, the G either needed less tanker uplift or none at all. The Air Force tested and confirmed Boeing's claim that the considerably more expensive G model (about $9 million) would be cost-effective in increasing operating flexibility while reducing the need for tankers.

Moving the gunner out of the tail always seemed to me obvious. He sat up front in the B-47, and I could find no reason why he should have been consigned to the back end in the B-52. He could enter or leave his turret only in de-pressurized flight, and his presence in the tail imposed considerable weight and cost penalties in extending 130 feet aft the pressurization, air-conditioning, oxygen and intercom systems, besides adding over 1,000 lb in structure weight. With the G the B-52 at last got a sensible crew arrangement. In front sat the two pilots, and behind them were the defensive crew of gunner and ECM operator, both pairs of men having upward ejection seats usable at all heights over 700 feet. On the lower deck were the offensive crew of navigator and bombardier, these two having downward ejection seats with a height limitation of 1,000 feet. Cabin pressure differential was 7·5 lb/sq in, reduced by about half in combat zones. Surprisingly little difficulty was encountered in making room for the gunner and his radar display, and the new ASG-15 fire-control, in which the optical sight was replaced by a TV link, was actually improved in performance, though the radars and computer could not tell friend from foe (yet). Later a partial capability was acquired, as well as very much enhanced ECM performance which stemmed mainly from the fact that in May 1958 the ECM prime contractor, Sperry, brought in no fewer than eight additional companies to help a major updating in the whole system. The eventual total "defensive avionics capability" is still highly classified, although one element is obvious: the Quail.

Quail is a miniature jet aircraft that was originally designed by McDonnell in 1954 as the GAM-72 (guided air missile), the same category as for a missile with a warhead. Later decoys may have warheads but the purpose of Quail (which today is designated ADM-20, signifying air defence missile) is simply to create confusion among enemy defence systems by looking on a radar display exactly like a B-52. Quail is a mere 5½ feet across its wing-tips, and much of its 13 foot length is its GE J85 engine and ducting, but the purpose of it all is to carry passive and active ECM equipment in a way that simulates the B-52. Two Quails can be carried in the forward bomb bay; in the final qualification of the decoy system a B-52 in July 1960 released three within the space of a few seconds. Each Quail lights up as soon as it drops from the bomber and thereafter flies on a pre-programmed autopilot. In theory each Quail can do better than merely dilute the defences by doubling the number of targets, but this remains a security-sensitive area.

Most of the Quail development was done with a B-52D, but with this bomber the decoys would have drastically cut the bomb load. The major advantage of the G was that under each inner wing it carried a supersonic missile, either of which could carry a thermonuclear warhead to a separate target. The missile is Hound Dog, originally designated GAM-77 and now called AGM (air-to-ground missile) -28. Hound Dog's development began at North American Aviation in 1956 under yet a third designation, Weapon System 131A. Like Quail it is a miniature aircraft powered by a turbojet engine, but in this case it does anything but fly like a B-52. Hound Dog can cruise at all heights from 500 to 60,000 feet at a Mach number of up to 2·05; and it does all it can not to look like a B-52 to enemy radars. Its engine is a Pratt & Whitney J52, virtually a scaled-down J57 rated at 7,500 lb at sea level. This can be used to help the B-52 take off, the fuel burned by the missile subsequently being replenished from the B-52. Inside the Hound Dog is an Autonetics inertial navigation system which is continuously updated by the navigation system of the B-52 and by a Kollsman astro-tracker in the missile launch pylon. Missile targeting and mission profile (the flight path of the missile in the vertical and horizontal planes) can be altered by the B-52 crew at any time up to release. Depending on mission profile, Hound Dog range is 600–750 miles; the missile can weave and make feint attacks, and it can carry a very large thermonuclear warhead. The first production missile was launched on 1 March 1960 and since 1961 each late-model B-52 has been matched with a pair, camouflaged khaki and green. SAC has a force of more than 600 missiles which are not normally launched in training missions and stay on the bomber except when put through IRAN (inspect and repair as necessary) at the North American Rockwell Tulsa Division.

The first B-52G, 57-6468, flew on 26 October 1958. The number built, all at Wichita, was 193, making the G the most numerous of all B-52 versions. The last emerged on 23 September 1960. Already the enterprise and demonstrated cost-effectiveness of Boeing's product-development had extended the overall programme beyond 603 aircraft, an additional batch of 39 of the G model having been procured with 1959 funds. Despite all Boeing's blandishments this total of 642 would have been final had it not been for a completely new type of weapon, the air-launched ballistic missile. In the late 1950s the ballistic missile was widely regarded at least as the rival of the bomber for procurement funds if not its ultimate replacement, but early in 1960—as a result of favourable hardware trials in 1957–58—the Department of Defense contracted with Douglas Aircraft for a ballistic missile launched from an aircraft. The ALBM was not so much a stand-off missile designed just to penetrate the last, heavily defended bit of enemy territory as a delivery system in its own right. The carrier aircraft was not so much a bomber as a mere transport vehicle, and its sole purpose was to carry the ALBM aloft, so that it should be secure from enemy attack somewhere within 200 million cubic miles of sky instead of sitting helplessly on a fixed launcher. Ultimately there seemed no technical objection to an ALBM with intercontinental range, but GAM-87A Skybolt, the weapon placed under contract in 1960 with Douglas, had a design range of 1,150 miles. What made it particularly attractive was that, by setting modest targets for range and warhead size, Skybolt could be made small enough for a B-52 to carry four of them, each individually targeted, externally while still leaving the bomb bay for Quails and free-fall bombs. In 1959 this new weapon system played a part when the DoD placed an order for yet a further type of B-52, the H.

Apart from having provision for the twinned under-wing pylons and interface equipment tailored to the Skybolt, the B-52H introduced three main changes. The most obvious advance was that it had new engines. These marked a trend that today is common but in the 1950s was very unusual: it was developed first for the civil market. The possibility of modifying the pure turbojet into the ducted-fan or by-pass type of engine was studied by Whittle before World War 2, but little was done until Rolls-Royce produced the Conway in the mid-1950s. This was hardly more than a turbojet, the by-pass ratio being a mere 0·3; but technically it was much better than the rival JT3 (J57), and for a short time it caused Pratt & Whitney severe competition. Their answer was to devise a way of converting the JT3, both on paper and in terms of hardware, into a turbofan called the JT3D. With a more powerful low-pressure turbine spinning a huge fan added at the front the JT3D handled $2\frac{1}{2}$ times the airflow of the J57, giving more thrust with better propulsive economy. The result was swifter take-off, steeper climb and much greater range, with less noise as a bonus. By 1959 the JT3D had been very rapidly developed and was in production for the airlines. It was a natural to buy it for the B-52H. It conferred the biggest single improvement in mission radius of any B-52 version, to a value well over twice that of the B-52A. The TF33 also eliminated the need for the heavy and undesirable water-injection system.

The military JT3D for the B-52H is the TF33-3, rated at 17,000 lb static thrust or just twice the value assumed back in the hotel bedroom in Dayton. The engine installation, which was flight-tested in a converted B-52G in mid-1960, was made difficult by the fact the engines were installed close together in pairs. The solution was to discharge the fan air around only part of the fan periphery. By-pass and core streams were not mixed in this installation, it being considered preferable to eject the supersonic fan airflow through short "banana cowls" ending in nozzles close beside the core cowling. After much flight development the twin-TF33 pods were made to drive the B-52 27 per cent further for each pound of fuel than the already highly developed J57 installation of the B-52G. The only factor in the debit scale pan, and a major one, was that the big fan engines considerably increased the bomber's already very large radar cross-section. An engine, especially a turbofan placed close to its air inlet, is generally the most reflective component in any aircraft. With eight TF33s the new B-52 was going to need all the ECM help it could get. In fact it did get extra help of a kind I do not believe is used elsewhere: chaff and doubtless other ECM can be fired several miles ahead from small wing-mounted rocket pods.

The second obvious change in the H model was new tail armament. The fast-firing (up to 6,000 rds/min) "Gatling" developed for USAF fighters was picked for the B-58 in 1954 but left off all B-52s until this final model. The chosen 6 × 20 mm T-171 gun is lighter than the four 0.50 in guns it replaces and packs about 20 times the punch. Avco Crosley, which had displaced Arma as sole source of the ASG-15 system, fought hard to win the B-52H fire-control, and in view of its 1959 "Project Mongoose", in which the objective was a system that could intercept not only fighters but also all types of aerial guided missile, I thought it would succeed. But it was Emerson Electric that won, with the very advanced ASG-21 system developed from the Black Warrior concept. Today the B-52H has the latest type of defensive armament known to be in use anywhere. In future defensive avionics may be more important, as the B-1 (p. 262) shows.

The third change in the B-52H could hardly be discerned externally, but was actually even more significant than the new engine and gun. For the first time in the history of strategic bombing a new aircraft had been designed explicitly to fly low-altitude penetration missions. It required more than 120 structural modifications to withstand the greater forces and aeroelastic deflections encountered in flight through low-level turbulence. It also demanded the introduction of a terrain-avoidance radar and a different complement of ECM equipment.

When Skybolt was still at an early stage in development, in March 1960, President Eisenhower met with Prime Minister Macmillan at Camp David and concluded a Memorandum of Agreement under which the ALBM would be supplied to the UK for use by the RAF. It was an obvious way of prolonging the operational life of the Vulcan and possibly the Victor also, as outlined in the stories of those aircraft. But the missile programme continued to be marked by all the headwinds and diversions of an enterprise that is dominated by politics rather than mere technical problems. Skybolt suffered five sets of Requirements, three Demonstration Programs and at least 37 separate sets of Contractor Proposals, including several different ones from the same contractor at different times. Its selection as the main delivery system for the British deterrent was a matter of increasing concern to the new US President, John F. Kennedy, and also to the new man in the Pentagon, Defense Secretary McNamara. A further major consideration was that SAC already had, or was certain to receive, delivery systems for enough nuclear weapons to cover the whole of the Soviet Union and the whole of China several times over, without calling on the 656 Polaris SLBMs of the US Navy. There arose a new doctrine quite unlike "Massive Retaliation"; it was called Assured Destruction, and said that when this capability had been acquired, at astronomic expense, there was no point in assuring any destruction twice over. As JFK put it, "Enough is enough is enough". It was in this new and more considered atmosphere that during 1962 the political consequences of developing and deploying Skybolt, and alternatively of not doing so, were examined in great depth.

Some of the ground has been covered towards the end of the Vulcan story. Whether or not President Kennedy was wholly justified in suggesting that Skybolt was technically impossible, at that time, there is no doubt that by terminating its development in December 1962 he saved at least $1,000 million dollars over the subsequent ten years and inflicted no significant dent in the Assured Destruction capability of the United States. At termination the programme had passed many significant milestones. From the point of view of the B-52, four dummy missiles were visible on their twin pylons on the first B-52H, 60-006, which first flew on 6 March 1961 and began the Aerodynamic Flight Compatibility test programme in June. The flight trials aircraft was B-52F 57-038, which dropped inert rounds late in 1961. Full flight testing of hot, guided Skybolts began unsuccessfully, McNamara rating it nought out of five when he came to London on 10 December 1961 to find an atmosphere that can only be described as highly charged. This is not the place to rake over the curiously inept way the two governments handled the burial of Skybolt, which will probably remain a classic breakdown in intergovernmental communications, but it seemed to me ironic that on 19 December 1962, the last day of the Nassau talks that switched Britain to the naval Polaris, a Skybolt flew from the Eglin B-52F all the way down the Eastern Test Range far into the South Atlantic. The date for initial operational capability of Skybolt had been 30 June 1964 according to the original 1960 schedule. It was for this the first batch of 62 of the new turbofan B-52H model had been ordered under the 1960 budget, followed by a further 40 in 1961. These extra 102 aircraft, each considerably more powerful and longer-ranged than any previous aircraft ever built, extended the B-52 run to a grand total of 744 aircraft.

Total capital cost of these 744 aircraft was of the order of $7,500 million. The cost curve began steeply, with heavy R&D and tooling costs, flattened out to a slope corresponding to a unit price of close to $6 million, and finally steepened with the considerably improved G and H models. It was a curve typical of a good and well-managed programme, and at almost exactly $10 million a copy I do not think anyone could describe the B-52 as expensive. Put another way, look at how much aeroplane you get for your money! If this were the end of the story everyone would have a 100 per cent happy feeling about the B-52, but the end of the manufacturing programme was not much more than the beginning of some of the biggest problems.

One obvious problem—so a British observer might have thought as 1963 dawned—concerned the viability of the B-52 itself. In Britain the idea had become almost universally accepted that the whole future of the V-bomber force rested on Skybolt. When this missile vanished, so also was the V-force mentally written off, and replaced as the symbol of the deterrent by giant black submarines. The curious situation arose in which the strategic aircraft of RAF Strike Command became regarded by the public and press alike as coelacanthic left-overs that had no place in the modern world (last year a fellow holiday-maker, watching a Vulcan land at RAF St Mawgan, Cornwall, asked me "I suppose they are specially preserved for these Battle of Britain displays?"). In the United States, despite the awareness of enormous missile forces that are absent from the British scene, the manned bomber has yet to be mentally cast into oblivion. Arguments may rage about the B-1 (p. 262), because this hits citizens in the wallet and is planned for far in the future, but the designation "B-52" is known to every American as something very big, very powerful and very much here and now. Loss of Skybolt caused hardly a ripple of disturbance on the American scene. Cuba was only a few weeks in the past, China was fighting India and there were far more pressing things than some missile that wouldn't work properly.

The last B-52H had rolled from the Wichita plant in June 1962. It was not a good time for the Kansans. After building 1,644 B-29s, 1,390 B-47s and 467 B-52s the great plant has seen no more new aircraft go out of the door (but plenty of rebuilt ones, and hundreds of major bits of jetliners), and it was also in the throes of losing the acrimonious TFX (F-111) to General Dynamics. To make matters worse, their splendid run of the B-52H had all been delivered equipped to carry Skybolt pylons, and although some of the interfacial gear was missing the aircraft were closely matched to this weapon. The B-52H/Skybolt partnership would in my view have been practical and of great strategic value, and although its loss did not invalidate the B-52 any more than it invalidated the Vulcan I believe it could have given SAC a marked increase in targeting capability for a very long time to come. Without it SAC had to go back to Hound Dog, which has a shorter range, much bigger radar cross-section, lower flight speed and more weight and drag; and the switch cut the number

173

of stand-off targets per aircraft from four to two. During 1963 the two
B-52H wings progressively received their aircraft converted to fly with
two Hound Dogs as primary armament. Today the Hound Dog has also
been joined by SRAM, as described later.

The rest of the story of the B-52 relates how the biggest high-altitude
nuclear bomber in the world was made to fly at tree-top height, to fly
airborne alerts, to drop ordinary high-explosives, and, incidentally, to
fulfil a variety of non-military missions which no other aircraft could
perform. Hardly any of the story was envisaged when the B-52 was
designed, and it is not surprising to find that there have been big problems
and big additional costs.

Overwhelmingly, the main problem has been trying to make the great
airframe of the B-52 withstand sustained flight at low levels. It was never
designed for it. Neither was that of the B-47 or Vulcan or Mirage IV, but
only the B-52 ran into really massive structural difficulties. There were
several causes, among them the high air density, causing much increased
air loads, and the generally greater degree of air turbulence. At very high
altitudes the air density is so much reduced that turbulence, even of the
most severe "sharp-edged gust" variety, cannot load the airframe to
anything like its proof strength. Lower down any attempt to fly near full
throttle runs the risk of grossly overloading the structure, except in fighters
and strike aircraft for which this is a design case. Obviously in the B-52
the structural limits and the corresponding values of "q", the aerodynamic
pressure due to speed and air density, were calculated most carefully and
checked by various kinds of static and vibratory tests. When in the mid-
1950s it was accepted that the B-52 might have to operate at low altitude,
extensive structural research was undertaken both at Boeing and by the
Air Force to establish safe limits which could be written into the flight
manual. When the whole structure was re-engineered for the G model
the low-level mission was uppermost in everyone's mind. Yet the new G
and H suffered some of the worst structural problems of all, and the new
wing proved particularly difficult to modify.

In the early days of the B-52 I do not believe there was any gross
structural trouble, and although there were plenty of systems difficulties
the worst that happened to the airframe was quite local. When the engines
were fitted with water injection the increased jet velocity caused a sharp
increase in noise and ultrasonic energy impingement on the huge flaps,
and these tended to develop cracks in proportion to the number of take-offs
made. A difficulty that could be called structural was that numerous
landings were made with one landing gear truck retracted, and on one
occasion a more hairy arrival was made with one truck jammed at a steering
angle of 20°, which coated much of the undersurface of the fuselage with

rubber from the scrubbed tyres. But by the end of 1960 the intense utilization of airborne alerts and low-level missions had changed the picture. The notion of the airborne alert was that a B-52 fully laden with real bombs constituted a significant and flexible deterrent threat, whereas a B-52 on the ground could easily be knocked out by a missile before it could take off. Keeping a portion of the SAC B-52 force on airborne alert cost several million extra dollars every week, and proved tiring for man and machine. To give an indication of the costs involved, in 1961 an extra $45 million was voted merely to keep part of the B-52 force on 15-minute alert status, without actually flying. The airborne alert was considerably more severe, because by definition it was intended to keep aircraft airborne.

Not even SAC, with special Congressional appropriations, could keep the whole B-52 force on airborne alert status. The burden fell especially heavily on the latest versions, because these had the greatest flight endurance with minimum tanker uplift, and by the spring of 1961 potentially catastrophic cracks were being found in the primary structure of the wings. The integral-tank wing was designed with fatigue very much in mind, yet this problem reared its head when some aircraft had flown less than 300 hours. Two G models suffered major structural failure in flight, and an urgent external visual inspection on the flight-line showed evidence of cracking radiating from many of the wing-plank bolt-holes which in some cases extended right across a plank. The scurrying in the Pentagon and at SAC HQ in Nebraska can be imagined, and it swiftly reached Congress in order to raise extra funds. Lt-Gen M. E. Bradley, DCOS-Materiel, testified to the need for a "major modification program". It was planned to return 120 B-52Gs, and probably most of the H models, to Wichita for "gross rework". The programme was planned to take 12–18 months and was initially funded to the extent of $210 million. It also included extensive static testing, frequent surveillance of the aircraft in service and a blanket limitation on indicated airspeed and "g" in manoeuvres. This drastically reduced the effectiveness in combat of the B-52, especially in the vital low penetration role, although I suspect that in any mission "for real" such limits would have been ignored. It also reduced the effective size of the force, because most of the best aircraft were either being inspected or rebuilt. It didn't help when, in April 1961, an F-100 of the Air National Guard shot down a B-52 by mistake. It was afterwards thought that the offending Sidewinder missile was fired when "moisture seeped into the electrical connections".

Ultimately the structural rebuild programme, which involved replacing many wing planks and securing the remainder with new precision fitted bolts of increased diameter, incurred total costs in excess of $210 million.

It extended into 1963, by which time there was serious trouble at the tail end. By this time the Air Force was becoming touchy about bad publicity, and bad B-52 news in particular, and if it had not been for patient sleuthing by Marvin Miles, of the *Los Angeles Times*, this second round of failures might never have come into the public domain. The root cause was repeated overloading of the main rear-fuselage bulkhead during flight in turbulence. I have been unable to discover when the problem was first manifest but it was well before 1960. I found no evidence that there was any trouble before the B-52 was made to operate at low altitude, and the great size of the structure tended to complicate research into its aeroelastic behaviour, but the basic mode of failure of the bulkhead was compression buckling due to torsional loads from the fin. By 1960 the decision had been taken to add doubler plates and extruded stiffeners to the bulkhead as an in-service modification by Oklahoma City AMA. On 19 January 1961 a B-52 crashed near Monticello, Utah, and although the Air Force considered the cause "undetermined" it did think the circumstances sufficiently suspicious to accelerate the bulkhead-strengthening programme to prevent a repetition. What hit SAC between the eyes (again) was that early in 1963 two of the bulkheads that had already been strengthened failed catastrophically in flight. The first caused a B-52 to crash at Little Shanty Mountain, Maine, on 24 January; the second failure was at Mora, New Mexico, six days later. Yet another panic ensued, with Oklahoma City AMA, Air Force Systems Command and Boeing all analysing the mode of failure in greater detail and seeking a cost/effective fix. The result was a further round of frequent inspection and restriction on speed and manoeuvre at low levels, while the whole SAC force was given a totally new bulkhead and minor modifications to the autopilot and yaw-damper, to restrict fin loads, at a cost of $123,000 per aircraft.

There can be few more expensive pastimes than building huge stratospheric bombers of the character of the B-52 and then driving them around at high power close to the ground. With the B-52 force already in being, SAC had no real option; but the results could hardly have been worse. After the two crashes in January 1963 crews were carefully briefed on the structural problems and on flight limitations, while Boeing was given a paid research contract by Air Force Systems Command to explore the whole low-level operating environment and the way the B-52 responded to it. The objective was to obtain a proper basis of numerical data on dynamic structural loads, so that the B-52 operating envelope could be extended to more competitive speeds and powers of manoeuvre without compromising safety. For this purpose one of the latest B-52H models was bailed back to Boeing, heavily instrumented with hundreds of strain-gauges, transducers, accelerometers and recorders, and then flown with skill and precision by a four-man Boeing experimental flight-test crew under conditions appropriate to SAC missions, with Hound Dogs under the wings, bombs (inert) inside the bomb bay and ammunition for the Gatling gun. On 10 January 1964, with virtually no warning, the aircraft ran into turbulence of extraordinary violence, with one tremendous sharp-edged gust. In the B-52 the crew cannot see the tail, but they soon realized that practically the entire vertical tail had been torn off. The crew managed to make a normal landing at Blytheville AFB, Arkansas, where a new fin was later put on. The aircraft was flying at about 15,000 feet at a modest power setting, and was in no sense pushing its luck. This reinforces, yet again, the absolute need to treat the atmosphere—especially below 25,000 feet and over large land-masses, or in the lee of mountains—with the very greatest respect, unless you are flying a fighter.

Structural failure was not the only cause of expensive accidents. Even the highly refined technique of in-flight refuelling, using the Boeing High-Speed Boom specially developed for jet-to-jet contacts, exacted a toll which was doubly distressing because it often involved both bomber and tanker. The first fatal B-52 rendezvous came on 15 October 1959, high over Kentucky in one of the many thousands of B-52 contacts made at night. It was said at the time the two aircraft "exploded" in the air. Certainly the bomber broke up long before it hit the ground, scattering across the blue-grass country not only its library of 40 pounds weight of engineering manuals but also two live nuclear weapons. This incident was soon forgotten, except by people involved, but on 17 January 1966 there came a disaster that made headlines for months, suddenly highlighted (again) the problems of operating in the underwater environment that three years earlier had prevented aid being given the submarine *Thresher*, and altogether caused such prolonged excitement that it formed the subject of scores of feature articles and at least one full-length book. On that day the peaceful Spanish fishing village of Palomares happened to be directly below a refuelling contact between a fully loaded B-52 and a KC-135. Again, nobody will ever know precisely how the two great aircraft, carefully flown in the high blue sky, came into violent collision. The result was a sky full of frightening wreckage. What was not immediately obvious was that in that wreckage were four multi-megaton thermonuclear bombs, the most destructive things ever conceived by man. This is not the place to rake over the extraordinary story of how the frantic search found virtually all the parts of three of the bombs but not the fourth, while the US State Department consulted with the Defense Department to decide how much, if any, of the horrifying situation should be disclosed. Suffice to say that, after months of patient work, mainly by the US Navy, in the course of which deep-submergence exploration vehicles—the *Alvin* and the *Alumi-*

naut—were used for the first time in a real emergency, the bomb was found, secured, lost, found again and finally winched on to the Spanish shore.

After Palomares, while SAC recovered its lost poise and the Air Force opened its post one day to find a bill from the US Navy for $6 million, very carefully itemized, the Pentagon thought very hard about the pros and cons of flying around the world with live H-bombs. The matter reached the level of the President. It was still under discussion when, on 21 January 1968, a B-52 crashed on to sea ice on the approach to Thule AFB, the impressive SAC base on a bleak peninsula in north-west Greenland. The bomber had four bombs on board, each a thermonuclear weapon un-officially reported as having a yield of 1·1 megatons. Bits of three were found, but for some time it was thought the fourth bomb had gone through the ice into deep water and panic machinery went into action yet again. Eventually it was discovered that portions had been found of all four bombs, and ultimately there was little dangerous material unaccounted for. But the Pentagon had had enough. In almost his last act as Defense Secretary Robert S. McNamara cancelled all missions with live H-bombs. So far as I know, none has flown since.

This is less of a problem to SAC than it would have been 20 years ago. Increasingly, the scenario has shifted from great global wars with nuclear weapons to local conflicts with conventional weapons. Korea found the Air Force rather ill-equipped for such a war, and the same story was repeated with greater emphasis in Viet-Nam. American involvement in south-east Asia came at a time when the notion of "brushfire conflicts" and "Co-in" (counter-insurgent) operations had long been a matter of great interest to the Pentagon. Even before 1960 discussions had been held to see how the B-47 and other SAC bombers might be made more effective in the conventional (i.e., non-nuclear) role. Little was done to the B-47, which was considered to have insufficient life ahead of it. The B-58 was made to carry a considerable under-wing bomb load. The B-52, with its enormous lifting abilities, was obviously potentially able to carry huge weights of bombs, but only after considerable modification. On 27 January 1965 the US Air Force announced the greatest programme (in terms of cost) for modifying any aircraft in history. It affected the B-52 D and F, and the initial vote was $300 million. It was announced merely as a way of extending the useful life of these B-52s up to 1980, but in fact the decision had already been taken at that time to withdraw early models by 1970 (which itself was six years after the planned date of obsolescence of the entire B-52 force according to the original 1951 plan). Longevity of major equipment items is becoming a prime consideration in view of massive cost escalation, and the present B-52 effective life-span of 25 years is considerably more than double what was originally intended when the aircraft was designed. This alone has made possible great cost-savings, but it has been done (if I can get away with an Irishism that is hard to avoid) only at great cost.

By 1965 the Air Force had long-since cancelled the B-70 and had not been able to persuade itself, or Mr McNamara, of the need for a new long-range bomber. It had agreed to buy the FB-111A, a version of the Tactical Air Command F-111 strike fighter, to replace the B-52C to B-52F. Despite its much smaller size the FB-111 has a range comparable with that of the early B-52 models, needs less tanker support and can carry adequate loads of bombs (though not such big bombs, nor quite so many). The planned buy of the swing-wing bomber was 210, but the total force finally materialized at a mere 76 aircraft. Making up much of the balance is the fact that the B-52D and F have not been withdrawn from the inventory as planned. They are likely to soldier on alongside the wet-wing G and H until about 1980, in a primarily conventional role though they have been given equipment to mate them to Hound Dog. These two B-52 models were in fact the first and greatest beneficiaries of the major re-working programme begun in 1965. Much of the cost has been incurred in yet further structural improvement, based on the meticulous flight-test programme with the specially instrumented B-52H, which simultaneously lengthens safe life and allows missions to be flown at greater speeds in dense air low down. Some portions of B-52 structure have now been manufactured four times for the same aircraft! The rest of the money has been spent in increasing the general capability of the B-52 in conventional warfare.

Basically this means toting great loads of iron bombs. Early in 1965 the engineers at Wichita studied various ways of increasing both internal bomb capacity and external pylon loads. In the context of Viet-Nam some degradation in flight performance could be accepted, but considerable research was necessary to establish the optimum bomb configuration in terms of load carried, ease of loading and release, airframe modification, aerodynamic drag and airframe life. The best answer was found to be simpler than many of the arrangements studied. The bomb bays of the D models were structurally rebuilt to house up to 84 bombs each of 500 lb nominal weight (actual weight about 580 lb), while the existing inner wing strong point, used for the Hound Dog pylon in the G and H, was strengthened and equipped to carry the longest bomb rack in history, able to carry a row of four triple 750 lb bombs (actual weight 825 lb). This gave a total load of approximately 70,000 lb, which no other bomber yet built can rival. With very small penalties it increased internal capacity by 57 per cent and provided a previously absent external option, with much less drag and complication than some schemes. The corresponding engineering change (No 1208) for the F model added only the external racks, leaving the internal capacity at the original "conventional" limit of 27 × 1,000 lb. To prove that the modification worked Boeing-Wichita used two B-52s to drop more than one million pounds of inert and live bombs—1,497 bombs of six types—in 31 missions over ranges in Kansas and Florida. By March 1966 the trials were completed and Wichita was busy making field modification kits for Air Force Logistics Command.

Most of the first batch of aircraft to be modified were of the D model, and in 1966 these began to operate from Andersen AFB, Guam, on long nine- or ten-hour missions over Viet-Nam. Like RAF Bomber Command in World War 2 many of the first missions dropped nothing more lethal than leaflets, but before long the scene grew grimmer. Repainted in a khaki and green camouflage above, with black sides and undersurfaces again reminiscent of wartime Bomber Command, the giant B-52 settled down to almost six years of raining down high explosive and incendiary bombs on all sorts of targets in North Viet-Nam. It may have been an inglorious duty but it was no picnic for the crews or the aircraft, even though by the spring of 1967 the 5,000-mile round trip had been cut by three-quarters by a move to the new U Taphao AFB near Sataahip, Thailand. The Viet-Cong hated the B-52 more than any other aircraft, probably because nothing else could pour down such vast tonnages of explosive. Usually the bombardiers never saw the target; in fact it was frequently just a geographical co-ordinate on a map. In January 1967 the Secretary of the Air Force, Dr Harold S. Brown, made the startling admission that "the B-52 is not a pin-point bomber. It is suited only to pattern bombing. It can't hit targets in North Viet-Nam where civilians might get hurt." Some B-52 crews took a rather poor view of this assessment of their accuracy, but I think most had to accept the odd way the ghastly slaughter of that war was mixed with observation of political niceties, and that Viet-Cong troops by night might become law-abiding civilians next morning. In terms of cost/effectiveness the B-52 operations over Viet-Nam were poor. To hit an enemy like the Viet-Cong needs quite different methods. If it is to be done from the air it needs new —or rather resurrected—philosophies, with quite slow but very well protected aircraft capable of pin-point delivery of large loads of ordnance in the teeth of defensive fire. The B-52 could hardly be more inappropriate.

The one thing that favourably affected the B-52's performance in SE Asia was the generally primitive opposition, which mainly petered out above 20,000 feet. Yet during 1972 the Viet-Cong were able to strengthen and improve their defences, using large numbers of Soviet SA-2 missiles and many new radars and with both geographical mobility and rapid switching techniques used to avoid US defence-suppression raids such as the "Wild Weasel" operations of fighters armed with missiles which homed on to Communist radars. At the very end of the war the B-52 suddenly went back to work in a bold (and, as it turned out, successful) bid by President Nixon to make the cease-fire work. In the area of the main strategic target, Hanoi/Haiphong, no fewer than 17 of the giant bombers were shot down between the end of November 1972 and 4 January 1973. Before mid-December SAC was rather worried. A committee under Maj-Gen J. R. Allen, DCOS Operations, was urgently investigating ways of modifying the B-52 ECM systems, and before Christmas modifications were being made to the bombers' aerials. It so happened that the war was then nearly over (or so it seems in mid-1973), but continued B-52 operations would probably have been costly. For the more distant future SAC will introduce a completely new ECM device in the later types of B-52, as I shall describe.

A totally different kind of new technology has today enhanced the capability of the B-52G and H in their "proper" role of global deterrence. When Skybolt died it did not, as some imagined, leave a vacuum. The Air Force remained sold on the concept of a ballistic stand-off missile, but were politically encouraged to consider Skybolt not the best answer. After careful consideration of likely targets and missions it decided the optimum answer was a shower of small yet high-yield missiles with a range only a little over 100 miles. Although this is a long way for the defence it is short in SAC terms, and so the new weapon was called Short-Range Attack Missile or SRAM (with the designation AGM-69A). In October 1966 Boeing's Aerospace Group in Seattle was named prime contractor, since when the programme has gone fast and well. SRAM delivers almost as big a punch as any other airborne missile, yet it is only $17\frac{1}{2}$ inches in diameter and, with its fairing tailcone, 190·2 inches long. It weighs 2,200 lb, and its Lockheed two-pulse solid rocket motor drives it at very high supersonic speed. At such a speed it rides on body lift, without the need for wings, even though it can perform any desired flight manoeuvre upon command from its inertial system which incorporates a terrain-avoidance capability for a run home at tree-top height. Altogether SRAM is practically unstoppable. I believe its radar cross-section is closely comparable to that of a rifle bullet!

Not the least of its advantages is its small size. The B-52 rear bomb bay can be equipped with a rotary launcher which, if fully loaded, carries eight missiles. The bomb doors opened, the SRAMs can be released in quick succession if necessary, the launcher rotating exactly like the cylinder of a revolver. In addition, the inner-wing strong point can be fitted with a pylon (not the same as the Hound Dog or the conventional-bomb pylons) carrying tandem triplets of SRAMs, in this case with their aerodynamic tail fairings. Thus, the total B-52 load can be 20 missiles. Each can be launched against a separate target, which may be ahead of the bomber, far off to one side or even astern. SRAM can be used for defence suppression or for hitting primary targets. As the B-52 forward bomb bay can simultaneously carry two Mk 28 free-fall H-bombs, the targeting capability of a single B-52 wing of 45 aircraft is today greater than that of the whole B-52 force in pre-SRAM days. Since early 1972 the missile has been fully operational with the SAC force of B-52G and H aircraft, and has repeatedly demonstrated outstanding performance even in deliberately adverse conditions.

Matched with SRAM the B-52G and H ought by 1975 to be equipped with another new device, the AGM-86A SCAD (subsonic-cruise armed decoy). This is a miniature aircraft which, when folded up and hung in place of a SRAM on a rotary launcher, weighs slightly less than the missile (1,750 lb) and is a little shorter and fatter. Once in a very hostile part of enemy airspace the SCAD would be launched, unfolding its swinging wings and hinged tail surfaces, and would thereafter not merely fly like a B-52, with identical signature, but would carry all the B-52's ECM systems and other devices to serve in an extremely active role, over a range of several hundred miles at all altitudes. Moreover, SCAD is likely to carry its own nuclear warhead so that, even were the enemy to break the code and detect the SCAD was not a B-52, it would still have to be shot down. It is likely to form an essential part of the armoury of SAC bombers for many years, but it is chastening to learn that SCAD's R&D alone will cost at least $268 million, and production of a three-figure quantity a further $538 million. Everyone seems delighted that this little decoy will cost less than $500,000 a copy!

Today SAC's B-52 force, of sub-types D to H, are generally in fine shape. Major incidents are now rare although Maj Robert Winn and crew, from Wurtsmith's B-52H wing, lost all power on the right side one day in March 1969 after the right inner pod had blown itself clean off the aircraft; after this they cooled off burning 200,000 lb of fuel. The G and H aircraft look better than ever, the standard colour scheme being anti-radiation white underneath and with the sides and top camouflaged in two shades of dull grey-green and a purple-brown. Nose art, so prominent in World War 2, is worthy of the canvas; and, remarkably enough, the most splendid paintings withstand hundreds of hours of high-speed flying in all kinds of weather. The D and F models still wear their SE Asia night-flying paint scheme previously described, although in 1973 they left that theatre. But all is not well with these earlier models. By 1971 there was plenty of evidence of fresh fatigue cracking, although I do not believe there were any catastrophic failures. The House of Representatives

Defense Appropriations Subcommittee wanted to hear about it, and in June 1972 Charles McElhanon of the Air Force Maintenance Engineering Directorate told them in outspoken terms. He said the earlier B-52s had been built "under a great sense of urgency as a matter of national priority to get a jet-powered intercontinental bomber. . . . We were building the lowest safety factor into this aircraft of any one that we have ever built." He explained that many of the D to F models involved had flown longer than their expected lifetime of 6,000 hours (a remarkably long life for any combat aircraft), and stated the wing structural problem was of a kind "that cannot be detected by any routine inspection method that we have". I felt we had been here before, and was not a bit surprised to hear the Air Force decide it was not worth spending a sum of between $500,000 and $1 million on each of these tired aircraft, but would instead carry on flying with load, climb and turn limitations.

The only old B-52s that seem to have no problems are the oldest still flying. In 1959 the third B-52A was much modified to serve as the NB-52A, the carrier of the hypersonic X-15s. The launch crew in the NB-52 had an onerous list of duties in feeding, aligning and controlling their charge, and NASA added in an official report how little protection they had in their "0·040-inch-thick aluminium blockhouse". Later this aircraft was joined by the NB-52B used to launch all the egg-shaped lifting-body aircraft of NASA and the Air Force. These two workhorses may well go on at Edwards until the end of the century, one likely future duty being the launch of scaled Space Shuttle orbiters.

But the valuable work performed by the two "NBs" may be eclipsed by a truly remarkable programme being flown by a single B-52E at Wichita. On 2 July 1971 the Boeing division was awarded a $3 million contract by the AFSC Flight Dynamics Laboratory for a 32-month investigation as the biggest out-of-house effort in the CCV programme. The concept of a Control-Configured Vehicle very slowly grew over a long period as a result of industry studies, many research programmes at universities (notably at Cornell Aero Lab) and the severe design problems of future air-superiority fighters and low-level bombers. It has profound depth and wide scope, and will probably influence all future heavier-than-air aircraft for at least several decades.

Boeing's contribution involves four main concepts: stability augmentation, ride control, manoeuvre load control and flutter mode control. Stability augmentation essentially means doing away with traditional static stability, gained for example by large tail surfaces, and replacing it with light avionics governing a different flight-control system. The B-52 horizontal tail could be reduced from 900 to 500 sq ft by this means, but so far the tail of the CCV aircraft has been left alone and stability made neutral by adding fuel in the rear fuselage. To reduce wing bending moment the inner flaps have been turned into fast-acting flaperons, while outboard ailerons have been added to cancel extra flaperon lift. The aircraft also has a sensing system for all flutter modes which, via the new flaperon/aileron system, instantly damps out the wing-bending torsion mode (which has a frequency of 2·35 Hz). The Flight Dynamics Lab, at Wright-Patterson in Ohio, is itself doing the ride control which involves the addition of three canard surfaces, two horizontal and one vertically upwards, again controlled by an automatic sensing system. The overall result will be a B-52E that will teach designers how to make aircraft at least 20 per cent lighter, cheaper, longer-lasting and more manoeuvrable, besides giving its occupants a much smoother ride.

Of course the CCV concept is about 25 years too late to be of much use to the B-52, apart from the unique specimen at Wichita. But this B-52 will leave its mark on all the large bomber and transport aircraft, throughout the foreseeable future. It is a legacy of unparalleled magnitude, worthy of the great B-52.

General Dynamics B-58 Hustler

In 1955 the mighty US industry was labouring to create the B-58, the first supersonic bomber in the world. Of all the many secret new projects at that time this was the most futuristic, the most "far out", the most impossibly demanding. Today a great fleet of B-58s is parked in the clear desert air at Davis-Monthan AFB, Arizona. They have been there for four years, standing motionless. No more will their afterburner take-offs shake the countryside. They are in storage, removed from the active inventory because they are obsolete. I can think of no more telling testimony to the galloping pace of aviation technology than this.

The story of those hectic 15 years, and of the six years of study that preceded them, differs from some of the others in this volume in that it is little concerned with politics, muddles, disaster and change, but deeply concerned with technology. I cannot write it without discoursing at some length on structures, aerodynamics, propulsion and systems. In these four great areas, the main divisions of aero engineering, the B-58 marked enormous advances. At a time when supersonic flight was a rare and difficult goal achieved for periods of seconds or minutes by special single-seat research aircraft, the B-58 was built as a strategic bomber capable of being reliably and safely flown by crews of the US Air Force from ordinary bases in all kinds of weather, day or night, yet of flying at twice the speed of sound for hours at a time. It is characteristic of the United States that this immensely challenging programme, which posed large elements of risk and might very well have led to technical failure, was carried through at great speed and with complete success.

Of course it is always possible for the critic, sitting comfortably in his capitalist chair in the 1970s, to suggest that it was all a waste of two billion dollars. The B-58 force never went to war, and if it had not been built the history of the world would have been exactly the same. This is a superficially plausible argument, and certainly humanity must in future think of better reasons for spending vast sums than that it will automatically force a potential enemy to spend even more in setting up new defences. But I cannot forget that during the operational life of the B-58, when the US and its friends commonly called themselves "the Free World", as distinct from the Communist world which was thought to be enslaved, the notion of Communist aggression was certainly no mere invention of the powerful Washington lobby of aircraft makers and belligerent generals. And there is a second, more pragmatic, reason why the B-58 was not a

185

waste of money. The spin-off from this programme provided a broad technical base for all sorts of other aircraft designed to maintain speeds of up to Mach 2·2. If the B-58 had never happened, the research would have been more costly because it would have been done later; and in my view the great pressure to produce the B-58 to a tight schedule automatically minimized the cost. People like Anthony Wedgwood Benn would argue that if you want to create a Mach 2 technology you do just that, and not gain it as spin-off from a military weapon. Although it cannot be proved it is my belief that the fast-moving military programme does it quicker and therefore cheaper.

At the very beginning, however, in 1949, a supersonic bomber seemed an extremely long-term project. Nothing like enough was known for the Air Force to issue a detailed requirement, and even the value of such a weapon was a matter for conjecture. So in March 1949 the Air Research and Development Command (ARDC) held a competition for a generalized bomber study, called GEBO–II, to examine the feasibility of a manned supersonic attack system. Several firms took part, including Curtiss, Douglas, Martin and North American, and they drew some weird proposals having from one to eight engines and generally quite unlike anything that would be done today. The submission the Air Force considered the best came in January 1951 from the Fort Worth, Texas, division of Consolidated Vultee, creator of the wartime B-24 Liberator and at that time busily producing the giant B-36 for the newly formed Strategic Air Command (SAC) which was envisaged as the user of the supersonic reconnaissance-bomber if this should eventually prove to be feasible.

What is so difficult about a supersonic bomber? Perhaps the fundamental problem is that the L/D ratio, the ratio of the lift of the wing to the drag of the whole aircraft, worsens as speed is increased. At about Mach 0·85, the top speed of early jets, a good aircraft can attain an L/D ratio nudging 20. At Mach 2 the same aircraft would not reach an L/D of 4, because while lift would still equal the weight the drag would be more than five times as great. Obviously an aircraft designed for supersonic flight, of a more slender shape, would do better; but it could not do even half as well as the subsonic aircraft, and in any case 25 years ago nobody knew what the right shape was. Further complicating factors are that the supersonic aircraft needs big, thirsty engines (especially thirsty if they have after-burners, needed to boost speed beyond Mach 1) and a slim thin-winged shape that leaves little room for fuel. A further problem is that a long-range supersonic aircraft, if it could be built, would get hot through its swift passage through the atmosphere. It would also need a long runway, and be a rather "hairy" beast to fly when fully loaded, taking off and landing at speeds roughly twice the 100 knots or so of existing bombers in the late 1940s. This is mainly because the wing would have to be thin and sharp-edged and unsuitable for lifting the dense, heavy aircraft except at very high speeds.

Broadly speaking, dividing the L/D ratio by five divides the range attainable by the same amount. However clever a company may be there are times when the only possible answer seems to be to cheat. Convair could see no way of meeting SAC's medium and intercontinental ranges without cheating, and they boldly proposed the technique of "parasiting". The supersonic bomber was to be carried beneath a B-36 until within 1,500 nautical miles of the target. Then, at the maximum speed of some 500 mph attainable by the joined aircraft, and at not less than 30,000 feet, the supersonic aircraft was to be released, returning to the B-36 after its attack and hooking-on for a long free ride home. A lot of work was done on possible techniques that could make parasiting safe and repeatable. It was essentially the 1937 Short-Mayo Composite Aircraft brought up to date, but with the parent aircraft placed on top.

A second cheat was unusual if not unique: it was to carry the load outside the body. Chief engineer at Fort Worth was Raymond C. Sebold (he reported to another Ray, the FW general manager R. O. Ryan). In 1955 I met Sebold when he was vice-president engineering for the whole of Convair at San Diego. The B-58 was then highly classified but he told me a little of the difficulties encountered in the early feasibility study. One was that strategic atom bombs in 1949 were enormous. Everyone hoped they could be made smaller, but you cannot design a bomber on a basis of hope. In the case of the subsonic bombers it was possible to plan the fuselage around a huge bomb bay, but for a supersonic bomber the penalties seemed impossibly severe. Preliminary calculations showed substantial gains could be realized by making the body only just big enough to carry the crew and systems, and some fuel, and to clip on underneath a big streamlined pod carrying the warhead and possibly fuel also. Drag with the pod on, even at supersonic speed, seemed likely to be little more than drag of a fat body; with the pod gone the drag would be considerably reduced, giving an overall range increment of around 12 per cent.

With these two bold ideas as trump cards Convair examined a range of possible aircraft configurations. Most had sharply tapered wings with pointed tips, and of course this was long before the days of conical camber, ogival shapes, favourable vortex formation, compression lift, variable sweep or any other modern tricks. After very careful consideration the Fort Worth team chose the pure delta (triangular) wing, with a straight or slightly backswept trailing edge, of the kind that had been extensively investigated by the same company's San Diego division with the assistance of the German delta pioneer Dr Alex Lippisch. In September 1948 San

Diego had flown a full-scale delta aircraft, the XP-92A. This had con-
founded numerous experts who forecast disastrous aerodynamic behaviour
at high angles of attack; in particular it was thought the aircraft would flick
over in a roll, or a combined roll and yaw, on trying to land. Instead the
XF-92A behaved well, although its predictably nose-high attitude on the
approach spoilt the forward view. But the broad delta gave a wing of large
area, structural rigidity and interior space for a useful quantity of fuel.

Most GEBO studies from Fort Worth had two very big engines slung
just below the outer wings, but the final studies had a third engine in the
tail to make up for not having afterburners. Use of an afterburner is a
good way to boost thrust for supersonic acceleration but it makes the
engine heavy and long, and spoils efficiency in dry (non-afterburning)
cruising flight. Convair had no range to give away, so their final submission,
of 26 January 1951, had three dry General Electric J53 engines. It was a
pure delta two-seater to weigh 107,000 lb and fly a 1,500 n.m. mission
radius with a dash at Mach 1·7. The first specific design for a large supersonic aircraft in history, it was in a brochure designated FZP-110. In
March 1951 Convair was awarded a Phase I study contract for the FZP-110,
restyled MX-1626; Boeing received a rival contract for MX-1712. The
next eight months were crucial. The project increased in refinement and
in viability, and big changes were made. Proposal FZP-016, submitted
by Fort Worth on 11 December 1951, recommended two afterburning
J53s, a more conventional method of augmenting the range (flight refuelling) and the addition of a defence-systems operator to the crew. Points
of the very greatest importance that emerged at this stage were that the
aircraft could fly at Mach 2, that its penetration radius at high subsonic
speed at sea level would be the same as at high altitude at Mach 2, and
that the same aircraft could be a free-fall bomber, strategic missile carrier,
strategic reconnaissance aircraft, long-range intercepter and strike aircraft
for Tactical Air Command. For the rest of the programme's life Convair
was aware of this versatility yet never succeeded in selling more than one
version.

Another event of 1951 that was ultimately vital to the programme was
that the Air Force began to fund the General Electric X-24A, a radically
new and very advanced engine specifically intended for supersonic
applications. Despite the blandishments of rockets and ramjets the ARDC
plumped solidly for the supersonic turbojet, at a time when the massive
rightness of such a choice was far from obvious. GE were already running
the most powerful turbojet in the world, the Air Force's J53, which was
about to yield its peak reheat thrust of 23,750 lb on the bench (it never
flew). The J53 had been explicitly funded by the Air Force for possible
supersonic application, in the knowledge that engines take longer than

airframes. But by 1951 GE could see how to make a much better engine, using several rows of variable-incidence stator blades in the compressor to allow a single-spool engine—apparently simpler and lighter than the two-spool formula adopted by rival Pratt & Whitney—to operate at very high pressure ratio to give high thrust per unit frontal area (vital for supersonic flight) and good fuel economy at all speeds. GE had already, by producing the axial J35 and J47 turbojets that owed little to Whittle apart from the immediate availability of funds, shown that they were thoroughly competent in the new era of gas turbines. With the X-24A they strode ahead swiftly into the realm of Mach 2. Today, called the J79, this engine has more Mach 2 time than all other engines combined outside the Soviet Union.

This engine was much smaller and lighter than the J53, being sized to a dry thrust of 9,500 lb and a reheat rating of about 14,000 lb. It made the Convair MX-1626 proposal into a four-engined configuration, although precisely how the engines should be installed remained a matter of argument. The important feature is that the six months of study by Boeing and Convair beginning in March 1951 disclosed no design difficulty that appeared unlikely to yield to R&D effort, and the Air Force became convinced that a long-range supersonic aircraft ought to be bought for the inventory. In the autumn of 1951 Wright Field carefully reviewed the proposals and alternative options of the two companies, and on 8 December issued SAB-51, the first General Operational Requirement (GOR) in history for a supersonic bomber. On 1 February 1952 it followed with SAR-51 for a reconnaissance system. On 4 February Convair submitted at the Air Force's request a proposal for a complete development and manufacturing programme for the MX-1626 Phase I, together with estimated costs. In March the Air Force initiated a paid competition between Convair and Boeing to meet the two new GORs, the two MX numbers being changed to 1964 and 1965, respectively. This third round of competition was for possible hardware. Three rounds in the same programme is not unusual in the United States, and it is my belief that this sort of experience provides excellent training for the tough, resilient men who run that nation's industry. To survive at all, let alone win, one needs the ability to work day and night and possess nerves of cast steel. Perhaps one should not be dogmatic on this point, but I think the record shows that the United States and Soviet Union have demonstrated the immense value of competition in major programmes, and the former, at least, is reverting to the old practice of funding rival hardware for "fly-off" competition, having decided with the TFX programme that perhaps one ought not to make final choices (even after four rounds of competition on paper) until rival prototypes are in the sky.

Supersonic bombers come expensive, and despite the very high risk, the Air Force decided not to fund more than one design to the hardware stage. If Convair had lost it would have been a body-blow, because the Fort Worth division had just lost to Boeing the chance of building the world's first jet long-range bomber (B-52, p. 154). But Convair did not lose. They had begun first, devoted more effort (over 150,000 man-hours) and concentrated on this exceptionally challenging project in a way that showed their total belief in it (and such belief could not be taken for granted because in Britain nobody had even considered funding a supersonic fighter!). All this paid off in August 1952 when Convair was named the winner, although the fact was not announced and remained a supposed secret for four more years. In essentials MX-1964 was a bigger version of San Diego's F-102 intercepter design, with a plain delta wing, straight-sided body and a forward cockpit with a big vee windscreen. The four GE engines were to be in two side-by-side twin pods hung on pylons under the wings. Gross weight was put at 140,000 lb, and the proposal was that Convair should handle a package deal complete with four external payload pods: a free-falling bomb pod (FFBP), a reconnaissance pod (photo), a delta-winged rocket-propelled stand-off missile called the controllable bomb pod (CBP), and an electronic countermeasures pod (called either El Reco or the Ferret).

This award of the world's first supersonic bomber to Convair was a turning-point in the history of defence hardware procurement. Until MX-1964 military aircraft had been designed and purchased in a way that had grown up over the years along traditional lines. But the United States, especially under the pressure of a global Cold War and a bitter shooting war in Korea, was seeking ways of producing advanced military aircraft more rapidly and with fewer mistakes. In 1950–53 the Department of Defense, and ARDC in particular, made very great strides in military aircraft procurement which still provide the groundrules even today. One advance was the Cook-Craigie plan which attempted to get the best of all worlds by setting up a production line in advance of first flight but keeping down the rate of output until flight-test results showed that no major (or no further) modifications would be needed. An even greater advance was the Weapon System Management Concept. The Americans are very good at identifying abstract things and naming them, which makes subsequent progress much simpler than in countries where the problems and solutions stay ill-defined and anonymous. One of the greatest American achievements in this sphere was the treatment of defence hardware as weapon systems. Each new item for the inventory was henceforth treated as a complete "system" embracing the thing itself (an aircraft, a gun, an armoured vehicle or a portable generator of electric power), all the hardware needed to support it in service (tools, weatherproof coverings, spare parts, new plastic containers for fruit squash for the crew to drink) and all the hardware and software needed to create it and to train people to use it (manuals, films, computer tapes, mathematical formulae and mighty flight simulators). Under the WSM concept one "prime contractor" would be appointed to manage the whole system. The WS-prime would be charged initially with developing and then with delivering to the customer the entire system. He would decide which subcontracting firms would make which bits, would oversee the whole design and manufacturing programme (while being himself overseen by the customer) and would remain wholly responsible for the entire system in service. Such a concept has tremendous and far-reaching implications in practice. There is no doubt it has enabled the United States to create systems such as the Apollo for lunar voyages which would have been extremely difficult if not impossible to manage in the traditional way of lots of bits and pieces. In Britain the concept was amazingly little understood, even though it had been described in unclassified reports and magazine articles from 1953 onwards. Many top Britons as late as 1960 thought a "weapon system" was the armament carried by a military aircraft!

For the weapon system concept to work, a nation must have a choice of industrial prime contractors of enormous technical and financial strength, and staffed by thousands of engineers who understand the concept in depth and have the vision necessary to relate each bit to the whole. It appeared to the Air Force early in 1952 that the mighty challenge of a supersonic bomber was going to demand the application of this new scheme of procurement. MX-1964 thus assigned to Convair Fort Worth the role of the first WS prime contractor in history. With the sole exception of the engines, which like almost all propulsion systems have remained GFE (government furnished equipment), that document put Convair in sole charge of the entire system including such items as the filter panels for the ultra-clean rooms for base maintenance on inertial platforms and the special lofty rooms for drying and packing the big braking parachute. If Convair had wanted to, and could have convinced the Air Force it was a good idea, they could have made it all themselves. In fact, of course, the programme required the services of 16 major subcontractors, roughly 1,200 suppliers of raw materials and standard items, just over 2,400 suppliers of special items and facilities and more than 12,000 other companies throughout the United States to supply components or services. Convair jumped into the WSM concept very much at the deep end. Simultaneously, the San Diego plant was starting the F-102 supersonic intercepter, and the company soon formed an Astronautics division to manage a weapon system that transcended everything else conceived at that time, the Atlas ICBM. It was the Golden Age of new systems.

On 24 October 1952 ARDC completed its thick brochure outlining the military characteristics of the supersonic bomber (although the final approval was not forthcoming from the Pentagon until September 1953). In November 1952 Convair prepared a large document, FZP-4-008, in reply to a request by USAF Headquarters for a full explanation of how the aircraft had been designed, why it was that shape and how the decision-taking process had arrived at the proposed sizes and weights. While the customer often asks such questions in discussion round a table, I believe it is unusual for a formal question to be asked in the form "Set down on paper in detail how you designed this aircraft and justify your choices". It did not imply any lack of faith in Convair but merely reflected the fact that this programme was pushing very far into unknown areas where risks were as high as the costs. A contributory factor was the speed of the programme. Several of the most important men in Washington had to digest the document in a few hours, and by the end of November the Air Force had no further questions. On 10 December 1952 it notified Convair that MX-1964 had become the B-58—the name Hustler was officially bestowed four years later—and that the Fort Worth team would have complete weapon-system responsibility during the development stage.

Late in 1952 formal letter contracts were sent out to Fort Worth for 18 B-58 weapon systems and to GE at Evendale (Cincinnati) for the new turbojet engine, the J79. The J79, a classic among aero engines and the design which did most to put GE in the very forefront of the field of flight propulsion, was sized to a diameter of 38 inches and a maximum airflow of about 165 pounds per second compressed in a single spool of 17 stages. It was explicitly designed for the B-58, and GE had at least as much to do on the installation as to create the engine itself. Convair had from late 1949 elected to use four engines giving a total thrust with afterburner of about 60,000 lb. In 1950 the exceedingly bold decision was taken to aim at a "dash" Mach number of 2. Quite apart from the fact that a bomber flying twice as fast as sound is likely to be more difficult to intercept than one flying at, say, Mach 1·3, the propulsive efficiency at Mach 2 is significantly better, provided the engine installation is carefully designed for such a regime. GE and Convair had nothing to go on apart from model and rig testing, because although the Douglas Skyrocket and the Bell X-1 series were reaching out towards Mach 2 (reached by both in late 1953), these aircraft relied for propulsion at these speeds solely upon rocket engines. All that GE knew in 1952 was that the propulsion system would place the J79 engine in a duct starting with a clever intake that could change its areas and profiles and discharging through an equally clever nozzle that could do likewise. The prototype J79, with a simple fixed bell-mouth intake and plain jet-pipe without afterburner, ran for the first time late in 1953. In 1954 it ran with its afterburner and variable nozzle, and in 1955 flew in the first YF-104 Starfighter.

From late 1947 Convair's work on delta wings had been based on shapes about 5 per cent thick and with a leading-edge sweep angle of 45° to 60°. By 1952 the B-58 wing had settled at 60° and with the extremely low thickness/chord ratio of 4·08 per cent at the pointed tip and 3·46 per cent at the root. This wing gave the best lift/drag ratio at supersonic speeds, appeared to have excellent inherent stability and was structurally simple and light. On the other hand it was inefficient at low speeds and no way could be found to fit high-lift devices. It seems remarkable that the B-58 was not fitted with high-lift flaps and a flapped foreplane, like the Viggen. The chosen answer was to fit exceedingly powerful hinged trailing-edge surfaces of the type then becoming known as elevons, driven up and down together to act as elevators for controlling the aircraft in pitch, and differentially (one up, the other down) for roll control. The only other control surface was to be the rudder, carried on a swept fin on the end of the fuselage just above the trailing edge of the wing.

During 1953 about half the 15,000-odd contributors to the B-58 came into the programme. Most knew no more than that the B-58 was to be a supersonic bomber, and they were not helped by magazine articles which suggested the aircraft would be huge and have eight colossal engines (a leak from the 1949 study?). Better informed were the major subcontractors who devoted an enormous effort in partnership with the prime and discovered that the weapon system concept could be made to work well provided it was a partnership and not a master-and-man relationship. In terms of man-hours the biggest partner was Sperry, which had to create an unprecedented navigation and bombing system that was to make its marvellous K system of World War 2 seem prehistoric. Two others that must be named were Hamilton Standard, whose air-conditioning system was many times more important than in any previous aircraft because of the need to cool almost everything, and Bendix which faced formidable problems with the flight control system. By 1953 at least 12 Air Force aircraft, bailed to B-58 contractors, were being used in the development and proofing of the new bomber's systems, especially the flight control system. In 1953 the sort of problems posed by the Hustler were not dissimilar to those of today's aircraft. The new supersonic bomber was a new shape, demanded new structures, new materials, new systems and a bigger and broader awareness of the need to integrate much more into a smaller space in a harsher environment. Almost the only things that have changed in the subsequent 20 years are that today's aircraft must be self-checking and repairable in a matter of seconds by a man wearing a parka and fur mittens, and it must not offend the conservationists. When planning the B-58, nobody even thought about ozone, and the suggestion that it would be the noisiest flying machine in history would have been thought rather exciting.

Convair was bothered about noise but only because intense sound energy appeared likely to pose problems in the surrounding structure. From the original 1949 studies they had concluded the engines would have to be outside the airframe in the external pods that Boeing had shown were practical (B-47, p. 131), but it was very hard finding the best configuration. Twin pods slung under each wing caused excessive wing-surface heating, and pods above and below the wing had high transonic drag. Most engineers felt a conventional row of four single pods across the span the best answer, when suddenly, on 24 March 1953, Convair learned about the Area Rule. Richard Whitcomb at the NACA (forerunner of NASA) had discovered that a body's transonic drag is minimised if its plot of total cross-sectional area forms a smooth curve from nose to tail. Thus, the presence of a wing needs to be countered by reducing the cross section of the fuselage. It is so simple and elegant a rule it is remarkable it had not been discovered independently by a manufacturer. Later, in January 1954, Convair's San Diego division was to wish it had heard of the rule much earlier. The F-102 supersonic interceptor resolutely stayed below Mach 1, in one of the most dramatic shortfalls in performance in the history of aviation, until it had been completely redesigned to conform to the new rule. In the case of the B-58 there would have been no comparable situation, but Whitcomb's law was wonderful in making all the parts fit together correctly. The timing was perfect to avoid major revision of detail drawings, which in 1953 were just being started. By January 1954 the area-ruled B-58 looked as it does today. The main change was that the Siamesed engine pods were replaced by four single nacelles which, after a great deal of testing to establish the best locations, were very widely spaced. The inner engines were hung well below the wing as far forward as possible; the outers were snuggled close up near the wing tips as far aft as possible. The huge payload pod was slung well forward and the fuselage was "Coke bottled" to half its upstream cross-section to offset the wing and the array of pods, and also set at a 3° nose-down incidence relative to the wing. The wing itself was changed in shape. The leading edge was curved down increasingly towards the tip in what is known as 15 per cent conical camber, to improve off-design operation at the cost of a slight penalty in drag and in additional up-elevon deflection at supersonic speeds. The trailing edge was also swept forward to re-distribute wing volume axially. It all sounds easy but in fact Convair and the NACA spent most of 1953 extending the transonic Area Rule up to a Mach number of

2. The work was not completed until August 1954, one of the last decisions being the realization that on this aircraft the rule was incompatible with expendable wing drop tanks.

In June 1953 Convair submitted a detailed statement of how the B-58 would perform at sea level. In 1951 the Air Force had begun deep study of future penetrability of bombers and come to the logical conclusion that the only answer lay in very low flying, as related in earlier chapters. By 1952 a sea-level bomber competition was planned which by 1953 had resulted in a duel between Douglas and Martin. The result of the evaluation of the B-58 in this role was such that the separate competition was abandoned; it was clear the B-58 would be very good indeed in this role (in fact it proved to be outstandingly good, and the B-1 will be hard pressed to do very much better).

August 1953 brought one of the bigger milestones: the first engineering mock-up inspection by the US Air Force. The crucial moment in a crucial week came when a State Visit was made by the Commanding General of SAC, the redoubtable Curtis LeMay who, though a brilliant man, looked like a caricature of belligerent Top Brass. Convair didn't know exactly what LeMay thought of the B-58, and as he descended from the mock-up every pair of ears in his entourage strained to hear his first comment. Rather crossly LeMay removed his cigar and announced "It doesn't fit my arse". (As the B-58 survived this, to be replenished by KC-135 tankers, perhaps I can slip in the occasion when LeMay was actually admonished by someone who must have just joined the Air Force for smoking beneath a fully laden KC-135. "Why shouldn't I smoke?" enquired the thunderstruck general. "Well, sir . . . the plane might blow up." "It wouldn't dare," roared LeMay, who nevertheless stomped on his butt.)

In September 1953 Convair, which for a while had thought of making the front cockpit LeMay-size, decided instead to propose a new payload pod configuration. The original blended-pod concept had high drag after release, and as the CBP was being designed as a self-propelled missile with a range of 200 nautical miles it was agreed that this pod (but not the others) should be a pure body of revolution carried on a pylon well below the B-58 fuselage. Tunnel resting continued to show excellent results for the B-58 both with and without pods, but other USAF programmes intended to have supersonic performance were showing unexpectedly high drag. The classic case was the YF-102, which had been frozen as a design just too early to incorporate all the advantages of the Area Rule, and in the month this first flew, October 1953, Convair had to produce yet another big book telling the Air Force in great detail all about B-58 drag, just why there was no anticipated tanker-compatibility problem, why the operational concept was sound and exactly how the B-58 should best be used in practice. A month later, and very significantly, the first brochure describing the performance of a Long-Range Intercepter (LRI) variant of the B-58 was submitted to Air Defense Command, at ADC's request. Later, on 16 August 1954, a special 115,000 lb gross-weight version was presented to the HQ of Tactical Air Command. Convair didn't mean to miss a trick if they could help it, but I do not believe they actually spoke to any admirals.

In June 1954 the number of aircraft systems on order was cut from 18 to 13, plus 31 pods. Virtually all the detail design was finished by August, and in mid-September the configuration was frozen, approved by the customer for hardware go-ahead and drawings began to flow to the manufacturing department. Still keen for a broader programme Convair on 25 October 1954 submitted an ECM escort pod giving complete frequency coverage, and at SAC request soon afterwards proposed individual counter-radar and decoy missiles tailored to the B-58. The fact that a rudimentary decoy was developed for the B-52 and that a system resembling that proposed for the B-58 is now under development for the B-1 shows how far ahead was the SAC/Convair thinking 20 years ago. The reason why it never reached hardware was a mixture of shortage of cash and shortage of room in the densely packed B-58. At the end of 1954 Convair completed their first round of proposed additional versions with the only one that actually bore fruit: a pilot transition trainer.

By this time the Fort Worth team could see storms ahead. Although nobody cared to challenge any of the company's detailed proposals or actual test figures, the B-58 was being developed in an environment seething with rivals eager either to do their own Mach 2 design or else to disbelieve others. This was not serious, but what did jolt Convair very severely was the doubt cast on predicted B-58 performance by the two premier aerodynamic authorities in the nation, the NACA and the Wright Air Development Center. WADC Labs had a statutory duty to investigate contractors' proposals for the Air Force and they calculated the B-58 would not reach anything like Mach 2 and would also be deficient in range. August C. Esenwein, the new Fort Worth vice-president, promptly ordered a report to be prepared spelling out in clear terms the advances already made by the B-58 programme in aerodynamics, structures, propulsion and systems, and this was submitted to the Air Force at the beginning of 1955. A month later the Air Force set up a special Board of Review, under General C. S. "Sam" Irvine, to determine beyond doubt if the B-58 was going to work. Convair made presentations to the board on 9 and 10 February which included detailed submissions on the proposed LRI, TAC, SAC Growth (an improved strategic bomber) and Spl Reco (special extreme-altitude and electronic reconnaissance) versions. As late as May 1955 the board was still in session, and Convair was requested to submit formal proposal brochures for Mod 16 TAC, Mod 17 LRI and Mod 19, now called just "Spl". On 8 July 1955 the objective of the programme was redirected to R&D only, and the photo pod and flight simulator were deleted, support drastically cut and the Ferret ECM pod cut to a single specimen. At the same time it was made clear this was just a prudent middle-of-the-road course that would certainly be changed one way or the other as more was learned about actual performance. In fact the photo pod was reinstated within two months.

While the first elements of B-58 structure were loaded into the jigs Convair planned the first major MI (model improvement) intended to increase flight performance substantially. This work began in June 1955 with testing of a model wing having unchanged planform but supersonic camber and fold-down wing tips. By the end of the year a detailed proposal had been written summarizing tunnel and other tests on a "split mission" (part supersonic, part subsonic) B-58 growth version combining these changes with an extended fuselage and a two-component pod (TCP) comprising a small FFBP nestling between the B-58 and a much bigger fuel pod dropped first. Before the end of 1955 Convair had also submitted a revised TAC bomber, much better thought out than Mod 16, and had also defended the controlled bomb pod (CBP) against an Air Force which questioned why a Mach 2 bomber should need a stand-off missile. In January 1956 Convair proposed that the "Spl Reco" version should carry a high-resolution side-looking radar, which then was a new and highly classified device; in April an order was received for one such pod, designated APQ-69. What impresses me as much as anything else is the way the whole programme kept moving at a cracking pace even though the customer had been led to believe the basic flight vehicle might be no good. I wonder how fast it would have moved in these circumstances had it been British?

Through all this Convair kept a close eye on overall Air Force thinking and early in 1956 learned of the numbers written in to the WS-110A, which then was a split mission (part subsonic, part supersonic) for which Boeing and North American were competing (p. 236). Throughout the summer project staff at Fort Worth produced detailed reports outlining how the B-58MI would perform on the WS-110 split mission or in an all-supersonic mission with dry engines (but not cruising at the nonsensical Mach 3 later demanded for WS-110A with anything but dry engines). This work continued for well over a year—punctuated late in 1956 by an interesting proposal that the B-58 should be the flight test bed for the ANP (Aircraft Nuclear Propulsion) programme direct-cycle engine, a 40-ton package by General Electric which was popularly called the "hole in the head" engine. The B-58 was the only aircraft in sight that could begin to fly this in its proper flight envelope. Later, in March 1957 Convair made a formal proposal that the B-58MI should be the WS-110 split-mission aircraft, with the folding wing tips, four X-207 engines, side-by-side pilots, the TCP, longer body and additional ECM. But the Air Force chose to prefer the all-Mach 3 mission and charged down the highway that led to an almighty waste of money on the B-70.

This decision could well have gone the other way, making the B-58 a much bigger programme. As it was it stayed a programme for 13 similar R&D flight articles for a Mach 2 bomber, and the first of these, serial number 55-0660, left the giant assembly building on 31 August 1956. It is surprisingly uncommon for unauthorized photographs of secret American aircraft to be published, but in this case somebody—probably a GD employee—took a rather fuzzy picture from the roof and, via a news agency, revealed to the world what a remarkably small and compact thing the XB-58 was. It looked like a praying mantis because of its slim body held in a nose-down attitude on incredibly stalky legs that belied the old supposition that jet aircraft could be low on the ground. After intensive ground system tests B. A. Erickson flew 50660 (later written 5660) on 11 November, with no trouble at all. On 30 December he took the world's first supersonic bomber beyond Mach 1, still with no pod on board. Not very long afterwards I was able to spend a valuable hour with impressive Erickson, on the strict understanding nothing was published (it wasn't) and he even made me wish I could come for a ride. My abiding memory of this visit to Fort Worth is that the whole plant exuded an excited confidence about the still very risky programme on which their livelihoods depended.

Flight testing in 1957 went hand in hand with new proposals and concepts. It was a marvellous time to live in, with totally untrammelled brains thinking up at least one startling new scheme every day. At Fort Worth the brains went fairly racing ahead. In April 1957 the Air Force had terminated the CBP within a few months of its first rocket-powered flight, convinced the B-58 could penetrate without it. To replace it Convair dreamed up the then novel idea of an air-launched ballistic missile. The new Astronautics division's giant Atlas was a completely different beast, with tons of cryogenic liquid propellant in a vast thin-walled tank, but they told Fort Worth they could see nothing wrong in the idea of an ALBM. What the aircraft engineers had in mind was a slim solid-fuel, multi-stage vehicle able to be toss-launched from a B-58 at supersonic speed some scores or even hundreds of miles from the target. It could carry a SAC warhead and ought to be quite unstoppable. Convair made this radical proposal on 1 October 1957, having shortly before prepared detailed submissions on a requested quick-reaction capability and the way the B-58 showed up at sea level in a LABS manoeuvre. Every one of these developments was of profound importance and this was one of the most significant pioneering parts of the entire programme.

Nor was this all. Towards the end of 1957 there came three more proposals of equal significance. The first was to adapt the existing B-58 to a multi-weapon capability so that each aircraft could fly a wide spectrum of missions, not necessarily nuclear. The second was to use the B-58 as the basis for a supersonic transport for military and/or civil use. The third was to use it as a recoverable range-augmenting booster for a manned SAC system flying at Mach 4. This hypersonic dual-aircraft system was called the Super Hustler. All three ideas still seem eminently workable, and perhaps hindsight suggests the only thing wrong is that they were ahead of their time.

On 14 February 1958 Convair received a definitive contract for 17 production B-58 aircraft and 35 FFBPs designated MB-1, a ratio of two pods per aircraft and one spare. These 17 aircraft were planned to go into the SAC inventory but were initially regarded as backing up the first 13 to make an unprecedented fleet of 30 aircraft to handle the enormous flight and engineering development task. In the course of the next three years many changes and improvements were made to the B-58, but practically none showed on the outside and the ruling impression I have retained is the quite extraordinary degree to which Fort Worth had been "right first time" with this risky and radical programme. This is therefore a good point at which to break off from the history to describe the aircraft itself.

Walking round the B-58 one was impressed by its height off the ground but equally surprised by the small overall dimensions. This was a strategic bomber to fly SAC missions, and supersonic performance was not going to make it any smaller; yet it was under 100 feet long and had a span of less than 57 feet. This small size made people (probably not including the Russians) consistently under-estimate its capabilities. One generally authoritative book estimates that it had a "mission endurance (high altitude) of 2·7 hr" and a "tactical radius" of 1,200 miles. Both figures are about half the true ones. As the B-58 is technically of uncommon interest, with a specification hardly ever published accurately, I am including the figures in a box on the next page.

General Dynamics B-58A Hustler

Three-seat bomber and reconnaissance aircraft.

Four General Electric J79-5B engines with maximum (120 min) rating of 15,500 lb at sea-level at 7,734 rpm with afterburner.

Dimensions: span 56 ft 10 in, length 96 ft 9 in, height 31 ft 5 in, track (main leg centres) 13 ft 4 in, wheelbase 40 ft 8 in, gross wing area 1,542·5 sq ft, wing thickness/chord ratio 4·08 per cent at tip and 3·46 per cent at root.

Weights: empty without pod, 55,560 lb; payload drop weight (pods and other weapons), 19,450 lb; total fuel capacity (with TCP), 98,450 lb; design TO weight, 163,000 lb; max in-flight weight (after air fuelling), 177,120 lb; max landing weight, 95,000 lb.

Performance: max speed at altitude, with afterburner, Mach 2 or 1,147 knots; max speed at sea level, Mach 0·92 or over 600 knots; normal cruising speed at altitude, Mach 0·92 or over 525 knots; range without refuelling, over 4,450 nautical miles (5,125 miles); range at Mach 2, over 1,450 n.m.; range at sea level, over 1,900 n.m.; range with single refuel, over 7,400 n.m. (over 7,600 n.m. in ferry role); take-off ground run at 163,000 lb, 7,850 ft; take-off over 50 ft, 13,700 ft; initial climb at 163,000 lb, over 17,000 ft/min; SL climb at min gross weight, over 46,000 ft/min; sustained combat ceiling at normal combat gross weight, over 63,000 ft; landing over 50 ft, 4,890 ft; landing ground roll, 2,580 ft.

Dealing first with structure, Convair had a nice shape that was complicated by the need to try to eliminate interior structure (because there wasn't room for it) and accommodate severe heat-transfer rates from burning engines, freezing atmosphere, leading edges that could soak at 260° F and several hundred horsepower dissipated as heat by very dense avionics and hydraulics. Today a Mach 2 aircraft would have a lot of titanium, but over 20 years ago people were using it where it didn't matter (the exhaust manifold of the S-58 helicopter and nacelles of the DC-7B airliner) while shrinking away from specifying it for crucial structural parts of a supersonic bomber. Convair's main innovation was extensive use of honeycomb sandwich, a material only just coming into use. Martin used it in the Matador pilotless bomber and SeaMaster jet flying boat, but Convair had to devise their own honeycombs, production methods and infallible test procedures. Basically they developed cores of glass-fibre or metal, with skins of light alloy or stainless steel. Areas subject to severe loading or heating, such as the elevons, were made of brazed stainless-steel honeycomb. Elsewhere light-alloy sandwich bonded by organic adhesives were used, and to insulate the fuel from the outer skin most of the wing sandwich had a core of glass-fibre. Roughly 90 per cent of the wing surface was sandwich, and the result was a stiff, light structure well able to resist sonic fatigue and preserve a perfect exterior profile. This was instrumental in enabling Convair to achieve a percentage structure weight of 13·8. This figure was incredibly low for any aircraft, let alone one designed to sustain Mach 2; I cannot at the moment think of any aircraft that can beat it, but the losers might complain that Convair cheated by putting the bomb bay outside, where it wouldn't be counted as part of the airframe.

So successful were Convair with the B-58 structure that they were reluctant to believe the figures. Included in the 1952 contract for 13 flight aircraft was a static test airframe which, oddly enough, became the first B-58 to fly. Fort Worth did not have a static-test frame in which to bend it, and the Air Force decreed it should be tested at the ARDC headquarters at Wright-Patterson AFB in Ohio. To get it there Convair took off the nose, fin and engine pods and then fixed it under a B-36 from which the inboard pusher propellers had been removed. The B-36 found the light B-58 airframe child's play and flew it to Dayton on its remaining four piston engines and four jets in an odd parody of the B-36/B-58 parasite mission. The test results were satisfactory, but when I visited Fort Worth it was clear everyone had a deep-seated nagging fear about structural strength that was quite unfounded, provided the B-58 was flown according to the book (once or twice it was not thus flown, and did break). As a by-product Fort Worth gained experience with honeycombs, and with tape-controlled sculpture milling, that was essential for the airframe of the F-111.

For propulsion the first eight aircraft had the J79-1 engine which itself was under development; all the rest had the J79-5A (later modified to 5B and 5C standard), with a fully modulated afterburner capable of giving a maximum take-off thrust of 15,500 lb. The four engines are inside slim nacelles which nevertheless provide large flows of cooling air. Essentially all air is taken in through a sharp-edged circular inlet, in the centre of which is a large conical spike which moves fore and aft on a telescopic slide under the control of an automatic hydraulic system. The spikes are fully aft at take-off to give the maximum airflow; as flight Mach number increases, each spike gradually inches forward until at Mach 2 it is projecting far ahead of the intake lip, creating a conical attached shock and with an internal duct profile giving the best pressure recovery. Later supersonic installations suffered from such nasty-sounding troubles as inlet-unstarts, flame-extinguishing and buzz. The B-58 did not, and the engine buzzed—a destructive high-frequency airflow oscillation—only when made to do so by faulty spike position. Then the buzz nearly took the engine off the wing and, even at Mach 2, could be clearly heard by the pilot (the sound travelling through the air inside the aircraft?). The nozzles likewise adjust their profile and area, with minimum aperture in subsonic dry thrust and opening out to form a convergent/divergent ejector nozzle in supersonic flight. This is all commonplace today, but the B-58 did it first.

From the start the B-58 philosophy was one of minimum crew and maximum automaticity, with as much system redundancy as possible so that even a series of failures would not prejudice the mission. The irreducible minimum crew was considered to be three humans, called pilot, navigator-bombardier and defence-systems operator (DSO) and seated in separate tandem cockpits. The pilot, like his colleagues, gains his cockpit via a large mobile ladder (part of the weapon system) and the upward-hinged roof. His view is outstanding, with very deep, sharply raked transparent panels all round, and two more in the roof for vision in turns. The cockpit is small but very comfortable and well arranged, with a neat control column and exceptionally good night lighting. A unique feature is that the pilot seat is fixed to the floor of an escape capsule which can be bodily shot out of the aircraft. Normally the capsule is open at the top and front, but it can be closed in the event of oxygen or pressurization failure. The flight controls are inside the capsule and the pilot can see necessary instruments through capsule windows. For abandoning the aircraft the roof is jettisoned and the closed capsule is ejected in an automatic sequence. The capsule is stressed to withstand supersonic airflow down to levels giving a dynamic pressure greater than the B-58 limit of 1,240 lb/sq ft, and it provides a comfortable atmosphere in free fall and after the 32-foot main parachute is deployed at 15,000 feet. It cushions the shock of landing, is righted and made buoyant on water and provides food, equipment and shelter. Similar capsules are provided for the other two crew. Convair and Stanley Aviation of Denver took a long time to make the system work. The first live test did not take place until 28 February 1962. This was a subsonic ejection, but on 6 April 1962 a brown bear, with "organs and a spinal column like a man", survived 1,060 mph at 45,000 feet on a flight from Edwards. After that the capsules were fitted to the operational aircraft so that B-58 crews could fly in a shirt-sleeve environment, with no partial-pressure suit, no parachute and no Mae West or exposure suit. In Britain most bomber crews did not even have an ejection seat.

On the ground the B-58 stands tail-high on two main gears of amazingly long reach, necessitated both to facilitate loading the bomb pod and to allow a 17° incidence without scraping the tail. In fact the wing still gives plenty of lift at much higher angles, reaching its peak lift-force coefficient of around 1·3 at 35°, but this attitude is surely quite impractical (for one thing, the pilot could not see ahead) and the peak lift coefficient that can be used at 17° is around 0·65. The gears, made by Menasco and Cleveland Pneumatic Tool, consist of double gatefolds in high-strength steel which retract forwards to lie in big flat boxes projecting above and below the wing profile in long but shallow fairings. So thin is the wing that these fairings are needed even though the tire diameter is only 22 inches. Each gear has a four wheel truck with two tires on each wheel. Inflation pressure, wheel rpm and wheel peripheral speed (limit, 306 mph) were in a realm never before explored on aircraft. In normal take-offs the speed should not exceed 250 mph, but even then it was not unknown for a tire to throw its tread. The shorter nose gear likewise has an odd double-jointed retraction sequence to take it up past the nose of the bomb pod.

On take-off the fierce, thunderous acceleration brings the B-58 to rotation speed within 6,000 feet. Most of the run is made very nose-down, steering on the nosewheels and with the wing giving very slight negative lift which eliminates the strong dihedral effect of the delta and enables take-offs to be quite safe with a cross-wind component of 40 knots. At 90 per cent unstick speed the fuselage is brought level, steering on the rudder which from this speed onwards can handle an outer-engine failure. To lift-off, a very great rotation is needed, but the low engine thrust-lines and the fact that c.g. ought to be at or very near the aft limit means that elevon deflection is only about 5° up. These elevons are certainly the most powerful control surfaces yet fitted to an aircraft of this size, and it is understandable that in the early 1950s, when Mach 2 was a rather frightening and little known regime, Convair should have sought refuge in brute force. With a root chord of seven feet, they have one-eighth of the area of the wing, and the power units can move them 20° per second with a hinge-moment of 120,000 pounds-feet. At take-off the pilot can move them from 10° down to 23° up, but after the gear is retracted he selects the "automatic" mode for the flight control system which thereafter makes life almost simple and at least ensures he cannot break the aircraft.

At weights above 135,000 lb the allowable load factors are $+2/-0$ g, both rather severe limits but taken care of by the flight control system. B-58 pilots admitted one could not avoid transient negative loads, no matter what the gross weight, especially during cloud penetration; and, of course, low-level terrain following calls for very severe negative g at times. At low weights the limits eased, to $+3/-1$ g at below 100,000 lb.

As speed increases, temperature of the engine accessories becomes more bearable, helped by the multiple ejector-induced cooling airflows (the B-58 was the first production aircraft where the oil is cooled by the fuel). Cabin pressurization is from bleeds on the inboard engines. The heavily loaded B-58 climbs faster than most contemporary fighters (see data). The aircraft is climbed at Mil power (10,300 lb dry at 7,460 rpm) at between 400 and 500 mph until Mach 0·93 is reached. This figure, or sometimes 0·92, is then held for best range; engine power is eased as cruising height is reached and fuel burned off. There are two giant integral fuel tanks, one filling the front of the fuselage and wing and the other the rear. Total capacity, including a typical pod, is almost 100,000 lb. There is a small reservoir tank near the c.g. and a balance tank in the rear fuselage. Making the system work properly was one of the bigger B-58 tasks, just as designing the arrangement for proper balance had caused major headaches in 1952. Among the problems were gross sloshing due to sustained acceleration or sideslip, rupture caused by high dynamic fluid pressures, fuel running away to one side or end to leave pumps sucking air and the violent changes in fluid level giving rise to wildly inaccurate contents indications. But eventually, in 1958, the vast masses of kerosene were tamed and made to hold the c.g. automatically at or near the aft limit where the aerodynamic trim-drag of a tailless delta is at a minimum.

In subsonic cruise the B-58 does it all itself. This is the point at which to bring in Sperry's contribution, the ASQ-42V. In the design stage Sperry was more or less told to devise a bomb-nav system that would do everything, take care of every operational eventuality and fit a much smaller space than simpler systems already built. I could fill the book discussing ASQ-42V, but suffice to say it incorporated a set of seven major subsystems—vertical, heading, navigation, sighting, indicator, malfunction and bombing—among which were to be found a search radar in the nose, an inertial system near the c.g. with an astro tracker above it, a doppler in the tail, a radio altimeter at both ends and a computer to tie it all together. It was the first system in history to provide several interlinked navigation aids, automatic control of bombing and photography or radar mapping, automatic following of rhumb lines or great circles and, later, LABS and terrain following. It was conceived in the pre-digital days and the remarkable computer, the first ever designed for airborne use, still managed to cope with such variables as, in a nuclear bomb run, the height above ground zero, burst height, winds at various heights, air densities, precise aircraft attitude and vertical velocity at point of release, coriolis effects and "anomalies in navigation" (whatever they could be). Almost the only fault of ASQ-42V was that it broadcast its presence with electromagnetic emissions. In May 1956 Convair had proposed as a back-up a non-radiating system based on the radically new inertial hardware being developed by NAA Autonetics, but this had an incompatible timescale and came into its own rather too late for the B-58.

It was ASQ-42V that made me feel the military aircrew man was being paid more and more to have a free ride and watch complex systems do everything for him. In a lively discussion with an operational B-58 crew I probed their thoughts on the British 1957 Defence White Paper (no more manned aircraft) and reached a generally agreed conclusion that both the manned bomber and the unclever guided missile were obsolete and that the ideal was a mixture of the two. I still feel the same, and believe a highly supersonic flying vehicle could be created that, while leaving its crew on the ground, could carry out all sorts of bombing, reconnaissance, damage-assessment and other missions, including finding targets of opportunity, and come back to fly another day. In the B-58 the three men happened to go along for the ride, and a beautiful ride it was. Although the two rear men had no view except through a small rectangular window on each side, they found the Hustler very quiet and smooth and able to ride through rough air better than anything with long wings.

The third man was taken along to look after a set of ECM systems that began in 1958 with a mere chaff dispenser and ended up with about 12 separate avionic and other systems (which are sure still to be classified), as well as the bomb pod and the tail gun. The Air Force noticed the severe weight penalty of a tail gun and I was convinced they put it on the B-58 not so much to shoot down a budding Von Richthofen as to pump out special ECM hardware. The gun was the General Electric T-171 20 mm Vulcan six-barrelled device, which could have fired all its 1,120 shells in about 12 seconds. Every B-58 DSO I talked to assured me the gun really was intended to shoot down fighters. As it was fixed on like the sting of a wasp, and had rather less angular field of fire, it was obviously a relic of the days when fighters attacked in a curve of pursuit, which the US Air Force had overcome with their collision-course fighters of 1951. Puzzling.

In a high-altitude mission of the sort for which the B-58 was built, the change to supersonic dash would take place between 600 and 500 miles short of the target. Full afterburner would give gradual acceleration, with no particular buffet but a change in wing centre of pressure which would migrate outwards, increasing the wing bending, and then come in again at well over Mach 1 but at a point further aft (about 53 per cent chord instead of 33 per cent). Trimming this out would need the elevons to travel from subsonic $-1°$ to about $-3°$ as well as shifting fuel to a new rearwards c.g. location (as is done in Concorde). At Mach 2 the engines are placed in an intermediate afterburner regime and the autopilot put in Mach-hold so that the aircraft gently drifts up as fuel is burned. The ride stays pleasant, and noise not unpleasantly increased (except for the bang 60,000 feet below). The crew merely had to be sure of two things. The bomb pod had to be empty of fuel and the B-58 had to be going in the right direction. Erickson told me that to make a 180° turn at Mach 2 you put on full afterburner, rolled to a 2 g bank angle (which any pilot will tell you is the same at Mach 2 as for a Tiger Moth) and waited. After what seemed about ten minutes you saw your contrail come into view on the far horizon, many miles away.

Although the B-58 was never equipped with the self-propelled CBP, the pod trajectory was generally long enough to extend the power and definition of the search radar in finding the target sufficiently far ahead of the release point. Originally the B-58 was cleared for service with a single pod, the MB-1C, although this existed in at least five forms of bomb/fuel pod and also later as a photo/ECM/fuel pod for strategic reconnaissance. Outside the Soviet Union I think the MB-1C must be the biggest regular item ever dropped from aircraft, measuring 62 feet long and fat enough for a man to stand up in. At the start of the mission it would have contained one-quarter of the total fuel and might have weighed 40,000 lb. To preserve balance it was mounted well forward, calling for a major increase in the size of the vertical tail in the design stage to counter the pod's big side area far ahead of the c.g. Dropping a fully loaded pod would have caused an unstable nose-up pitch violent enough to destroy the aircraft. As the fuel is withdrawn from the pod the change in trim reduces to zero. When the ASQ-42V lets it go the crew merely feel a sudden $+\frac{1}{2}g$, followed by a steady longitudinal acceleration until drag once more equals thrust. Obviously, in SAC missions the ASQ-42V would be programmed to pull the aircraft into a level turn to escape the high-yield explosion. Before entry to service the B-58 was also cleared with the two-component pod (TCP) and multiple-weapons capability (MWC). The TCP comprised two pods: a small one containing the nuclear bomb and sometimes about 1,000 gallons of fuel, and a much bigger lower body, nested close around the upper one, containing nothing but fuel and dropped (empty) much earlier to give better speed and height over the target. Unlike the MB-1C the TCP had no stabilizing tail fins. The MWC comprised four wing racks on which could be carried any of the five types of small nuclear weapon externally, with a total weight of some 7,000 lb. If wished, all four could go on the same target as the centreline weapon, but dropping such complicated warheads into a fireball sounds unlikely to me.

Everything else was anti-climax. Subsonic deceleration could be done at any cold engine setting, although selecting flight idle at Mach 2 was most ungentlemanly and could injure the crew unless they were ready for it. This vicious deceleration could have obscured the odd fact that the

B-58 had no air brakes. The Air Force considered it, said Sebold, and thought the saving in weight more important. The crews never seemed to miss them. Going back through the transonic regime the pilot had to ensure he had the "subsonic" c.g., obtained by pumping fuel forward. Back in the circuit the B-58, weighing probably only one-third as much as at take-off, could fly at 175 knots, which to a B-58 is practically motionless. Compared with the B-47 the landing was easy: you just had to get lined up with the runway and keep the readings more or less right, finally streaming the drag chute near the point of touchdown. The ribbon-type arrester parachute was included as an emergency aid to stopping after a rejected take-off, but became standard on all landings to reduce brake wear and tire blow-outs.

Air Force pilots began to fly the B-58 in 1957 and, once they had overcome their awe, loved it. The ARDC test force comprised the 6592nd Test Squadron and, later, the 3958th Operational Evaluation and Training Squadron (I wonder how many clerical man-hours were lost by these big numbers?). The first bomb pod drop, with a simulated payload, was on 5 June 1957. Mach 2 was reached on the 29th of that month, and 1,380 mph, Mach 2·09, was reached before Christmas 1957. On 20 February 1958 a new KC-135 first stuck its boom into the flight refuelling receptacle on the upper left side of the nose. The B-58 rode superbly on tow by a tanker, and could accept fuel faster than a B-52. In December 1958 a B-58A flying at over 1,100 mph launched the first aerial ballistic missile, the first WS-199 flight round made by Lockheed in a programme that later led to the Skybolt. Despite various hairy incidents and mild pilot problems caused by such things as the flying-control ratio changers jamming with condensation ice and hydraulic reservoirs being ruptured by the explosion of retracted landing-gear tires, there was no doubt by 1959 the B-58 was very good indeed and a smashing success in practically every way. The one thing it had not done was demonstrate low-level penetration, and on 18 September 1959 Erickson flew a B-58 on a mission I hope will long be remembered (anyone under the line of flight certainly will not forget). He took off from Carswell AFB, adjacent to the Fort Worth plant, and flew over 1,400 miles to Edwards AFB, California, at the design sea-level limit of Mach 0·93 (a little over 600 knots) never more than 500 feet up. "We were travelling a little faster than a ·45 pistol bullet", he said, "no wonder people had trouble recognizing us." This flight demonstrated structural strength, long sea-level range (more than at Mach 2 at optimum high altitude), and the ability to stay under the US radars of 1959 in crossing four states. Erickson reckoned two hours to be near the reasonable limit for this sort of flying, although he said you soon got used to the intense level of concentration and were bothered only by

bad visibility caused by smoke or dazzling sunlight. The crew compartment of the B-58 was said to be located at a "node", a point in the structure
which stayed still while the rest flapped in turbulence (as the three cockpits
covered a considerable axial length I found this claim puzzling), which
was a bit of pure luck as low-level missions were not considered in the
original design. As a result the B-58 ride quality was outstanding in all
flight regimes including low-altitude penetration.

On 1 December 1959 Convair delivered the first production B-58A to
the Air Force, who assigned it to the 65th Combat Crew Training Squadron at Carswell. In September 1958 Convair had received an order for
another 36 aircraft and 41 pods, and looked forward to at least two more
small batches in the 1961 and 1962 votes. The single assembly line at
Fort Worth, nine feet off the ground, was bolting together the front
fuselage, centre fuselage and wing, and rear fuselage and fin at the rate
of two or three a month. This was slow by American standards, and one-
quarter the rate Fort Worth had achieved with the huge B-36, but each
B-58 was worth $9 million which in those days was astronomic. At the
end of 1959 ARDC de-activated the B-58 test force. The survivors of the
first 30 aircraft, and there were 26, were progressively brought under
fresh contracts at Fort Worth. Ten eventually emerged as standard B-58A
bombers, but eight were rebuilt as TB-58A conversion trainers, with dual
controls in two stepped pilot cockpits each having forward vision and with
the ECM and most of the ASQ-42V systems deleted; the first TB-58
flew on 10 May 1960 and was accepted by the Air Force the following
12 August. One aircraft was rebuilt as the NB-58A test vehicle for the
J93 engine of the XB-70 Valkyrie (p. 248), which was slung in a vast belly
nacelle.

In fact the Fiscal 1961 budget contained the last procurement of the
B-58, bringing up the total to 86 excluding the original 30. Soon after the
last contract was signed, the Air Force designated the 43rd Bomb Wing as
the first operational user, on 15 March 1960. The 43rd, a three-squadron
element of SAC's 19th Air Division, Second Air Force, was activated at
Carswell, and although they were excited they little knew how far the
B-58 would make them the most glamorous, and certainly the most
record-breaking, aviation outfit in history. On 23 March an Air Force
test crew made the longest B-58 flight up to that time, 11,000 miles with
two refuelling contacts, mostly flown at 0·92. On 1 August the B-58A was
officially declared operational with the 43rd, which 12 days later received
the first TB-58. Early in September a crew from the 43rd was the centre
of interest at Bergstrom AFB, near Austin, Texas, where SAC was holding
its annual Combat Competition. The grizzled veterans with their B-47s
and B-52s welcomed the sharp-looking newcomer, which they probably

all thought might come last. Its scores, however, were phenomenal, and on 16 September, when all the results were in, the lone B-58, operational just six weeks, took first place in both high- and low-level radar bombing. Such an achievement remains unique. Suddenly I wondered if Sperry's old press release claiming that the ASQ-42V, compared with the best previous bomb-nav system "weighs only half as much, occupies one-third less space and is improved in navigation accuracy by a factor of approximately 10 to 1" might actually be true.

With this quite unexpected achievement the 43rd were off to a flying start. With the encouragement of the Air Force they set about demolishing records and simultaneously demonstrating what their quite small Hustler could do. On 12 January 1961 Major Henry J. Deutschendorf and crew captured the world records, previously held by the Soviet Union, for flight round a 2,000 km (1,242 mile) circuit carrying payloads of 0, 1,000 and 2,000 kg; their speed was 1,061·8 mph. Two days later Major Harold E. Confer's B-58 showed it could go faster. With the same payloads it gained the world record for a 1,000 km circuit at a speed of 1,284·73 mph. This flight gained the first, and so far only, Thompson Trophy to be won by a bomber crew. On 10 May 1961 Major Elmer E. Murphy did something that M Louis Blériot may not have expected to happen quite so soon. In 1930 the pioneer aviator donated a trophy to the Aéro Club de France to be kept in perpetuity by the first pilot ever to exceed a speed of 2,000 km/h continuously for 30 minutes. There was now a new meaning to Murphy's law, because the SAC pilot knew it was in the bag if the engines kept going (and the J79 is a reliable engine). Flying B-58A-10 number 92451 he set up the ASQ-42V to describe a perfect circle of the required size, put on full reheat and waited. When the circle was complete he had flown 669·43 miles, or over 1,073 km, in 30 minutes 43 seconds, an average for the exact half hour of 1,302·07 mph or over 2,095 km/h. Naturally he still has the trophy.

On 26 May the same aircraft made what is probably the most famous B-58 flight and one of the most outstanding record missions by any military aircraft. Major William R. Payne and his crew took off from Carswell, flew at 0·93 across Washington and New York and then cruised at 1,300 mph across the Atlantic to the Paris Air Show, slowing to take fuel from KC-135 tankers east of Greenland and near 21°W. It landed in unseasonal weather after setting times of 3 h 39 m 49 s from Washington and 3 h 19 m 51 s from New York, the respective average speeds being 1,048·68 and 1,089·36 mph. This was certainly the first supersonic ocean crossing, and practically halved the previous best Atlantic time. Payne and his crew later demonstrated their B-58 to the assembled multitudes, and on 3 June I watched him roll rather rapidly into low cloud. Somewhere in that cloud

No 92451 disintegrated, unknown to all at Le Bourget save the radar plotters, and they were unable to suggest afterwards what had happened (I suspected failure of the elevon ratio changers). The crew did not escape, and never collected their coveted Mackay Trophy awarded each year by the USAF Chief of Staff for the "most meritorious flight".

In 1962 the 43rd continued to grab the limelight, based now at Little Rock AFB, Arkansas, even though they now had a rival in the 305th Bomb Wing at Bunker Hill AFB, near Peru, Indiana. On 5 March a crew of the 43rd took off from Carswell, flew to a point over the Pacific west of Los Angeles, raced to New York, raced back and then returned to base. The whole trip won them the 1962 Mackay Trophy, and the LA–NY leg, flown in a startling 2 h 0 m 56·8 s (originally reported as 2-0-58·7) at an average of 1,214·71 mph, won the Bendix Trophy as well. Westbound the B-58 really did outpace the Sun, a thing often claimed but seldom achieved at places remote from a pole, logging 2-15-48·6 for 1,081·77 mph. To me the round trip was the best figure, 4-41-11·3 for 1,044·96 mph, because this included the giant 180° turn around New York (and about half New York State). On 18 September 1962 the 43rd tried something new by carrying a load of 5,000 kg to 85,360·84 feet, thereby also breaking the world record for altitude with 2,000 kg. This was a zoom, in which kinetic energy of Mach 2 at about 60,000 feet is temporarily traded for height; from the apogee you fall like a brick, and it needs delicate handling in the thin air and near-zero control effectiveness to keep pointing the right way while speed builds up again. In a rather similar trajectory a B-58 test crew demonstrated the feasibility of using an aircraft to launch a satellite-inspection vehicle.

On 26 October 1962 the Air Force accepted the 116th and last B-58. By this time the 305th had long been operational, but not until 16 October 1963 did they at last make world headlines. They worked hard for it, making the longest supersonic flight in history. Taking off from Haneda, Tokyo, they flew to London in 8 h 35 m. The official distance between points on the globe is taken to be the great-circle distance, or minimum possible. In this case the figure was 8,028 miles, giving an average speed of 938 mph. This was a bit unjust on the 305th; the real average was over 1,000 mph because the crew flew far more than the great-circle distance—over singularly nasty terrain—to stay over friendly territory, avoiding the eastern extremity of Siberia. This flight netted five more world records to make the grand total for the B-58 no fewer than 19.

During the 1960s the two wings remained at readiness at their bases in the United States, from which they could reach their designated targets with a single refuelling. One accomplishment which could not be equalled by the B-52 crews that made up the rest of SAC's manned force was that from GAP (ground-alert posture) a B-58 could invariably be airborne within five minutes. Until about 1966 the B-58 wings also maintained airborne alert, as well as reflex deployment, quick reaction, and various kinds of missions in adverse weather. Many missions were also flown below 500 feet, and General Dynamics Fort Worth (as the Convair division was renamed in 1961) received several contracts to improve the flying-control system for low-level use, to upgrade the structure and to fit a terrain-following radar for use in autopilot or manual modes. Despite severe usage the well-liked B-58 maintained its reputation for reliability and trouble-free operation. In the first 10,000 hours in SAC service there were six major accidents, all fatal; beyond this point, reached in October 1961, the rate became appreciably lower, though not so low as for the B-52 or today's FB-111.

Having created a very capable aircraft that could fly for hours at over 1,000 mph, Convair/General Dynamics tried hard to find further markets for the same basic design or at least for the expertise they had gained. One development that very nearly came off was the "range-extension" B-58B, which materialized in January 1959 from a "reduced MI" configuration less ambitious than the original proposal for the WS-110 split-mission. The B would have had 20 per cent more weight and 30 per cent more power, a revised payload configuration of five separate stores and a big canard foreplane matched with a high-lift wing. A full development contract arrived in October 1958. By July 1959, when this project was cancelled, it had grown to 198,000 lb, with GE9 engines. The only other variant that received an award was the B-58C, which was approved in October 1959 as a feasibility test programme embracing the TAC and LRI versions mentioned earlier. The C model would have been an all-supersonic aircraft, with four Pratt & Whitney J58 engines and looking as if someone had taken it by the nose and tail and stretched the whole structure, wing and all. Despite weighing well over 200,000 lb it was intended as a multi-mission strategic/tactical/intercepter vehicle matched with a wide spectrum of weapons. Early in 1960 Convair prepared an analysis of how much better this would meet the SAC airborne alert requirement than the B-52, but the Air Force formally withdrew interest in April of that year.

All this time there had been a busy running fight between various special reconnaissance B-58 versions and the B-47. The latter won a major battle in May 1958 when the B-58 Ferret pod was cancelled and its highly classified Melpar ALD-4 system was repackaged to fit the B-47s that were lying around by the score surplus to SAC's inventory. This is a field outside the scope of this book, but it is possible that if the system had been carried by the B-58 fewer of these electronic probing flights around and over the Communist territories would have made headlines by being shot down.

In October 1960 the Air Force was sufficiently concerned to ask Convair to re-study the ALD-4 and ASD-1 Ferret systems as applied to the B-58, but no hardware was flown. Apart from reconnaissance, the other big development programme concerned the ALBM, which led to a proposal by Convair that the B-58 should support a joint Convair/Lockheed missile programme in February 1958. In June the Air Force signed a contract for a four-shot feasibility programme which was completed in September 1959 when the fourth round was launched at Mach 1·8 to inspect the Discoverer V satellite, as noted earlier. Earlier, in March 1959, Convair had made a bid for the WS-138A system that became Skybolt, to fit the B-58B as well as the B-52, B-70, KC-135, Camal (nuclear) and Vulcan; but the final hardware award went to Douglas.

Despite all sorts of investigations of airborne alert, low penetration, dispersal, hardening, the NATO market, multi-purpose conversions and fresh multi-weapons capability, Convair was never able to build beyond aircraft No 116. In 1963 Defense Secretary McNamara asked for proposals for a new Mach 2 strategic bomber, not because he believed in the idea but so that he could assess the Air Force's arguments. Rather to his surprise the Commanding General of SAC, Tom Power, tried to get the B-58 put back into production, calling the existing A model "One of the finest weapon systems in the world today". He lost, of course, but what Mr McNamara certainly did not expect was that a full decade later the Air Force would have the prospect of receiving a completely new and much bigger bomber, the B-1 (p. 262).

It would have been odd if Convair had not studied civil B-58s. Lockheed, North American and others had been exploring the SST market since 1954, and in 1960 Convair, feeling that it alone had usable hardware, proposed a minimum-conversion of the B-58 with the MB-1C pod furnished for five passengers, so that the US could gain civil experience. Convair also proposed the CV-58-9 which was a B-58A with a longer and fatter body seating 52 in 26 1 × 1 rows and cruising at Mach 2·4 on four J58 engines. In December 1960 the division said the 58-9 could fly in October 1963 and that the costs of building one-off would be £8·4 million in 1961, £21m in 62, £24m in 63, £16m in 64 and £1·33m in 65. In April 1961, when President Kennedy recommended $10m for the FAA to start off an American SST programme, Fort Worth published a voluminous market analysis with 324 major combinations of aircraft variable and numerous conclusions, most of which have not stood the test of time too well. General Dynamics is probably glad nobody took it up on a civil Hustler.

On 29 October 1969 the Department of Defense announced the retirement of the B-58 fleet from SAC, with effect from 31 January 1970. At that time the remaining aircraft were still with the 43rd at Little Rock and with the 305th whose Indiana base had been renamed Grissom AFB. A little later, on 7 November 1969, a General Dynamics plant at Waco, Texas, rolled out the last of the B-58s modified for SAC and bade it farewell. Unlike the previous modified aircraft, it was delivered not to the 43rd, whose aircraft it had been, but to Davis-Monthan for storage. I remember that the B-58 was the first aircraft to have automatic voice warning and trouble identification. Any significant system malfunction triggered a recording which told the crew exactly what had gone wrong. After a lot of research it was decided the voice should be "female, selected for its pleasant and soothing qualities". I heard this voice and can confirm it would take a man's mind right off the problem. I wonder if her voice is still inside those silent Hustlers parked out there in the desert?

McDonnell Douglas A-3 Skywarrior and B-66 Destroyer

ALTHOUGH it seldom made the headlines, the Skywarrior is notable on several counts. It is still the biggest and heaviest aircraft ever designed for use from an aircraft carrier, although small and light for its mission; it put the US Navy firmly in the strategic nuclear business and its presence played a significant part in the Cold War from 1956 until a decade later; and it happened by chance to be ideally suited to later development to meet totally different roles. As for the B-66, which stemmed from it, this goes to show that even the Americans can sometimes decide to buy an off-the-shelf aircraft and eventually, a few hundred modifications later, end up with something quite different.

Until after World War 2 the US Navy had equipped its carriers with only small, tactical aircraft (although on one memorable day, 18 April 1942, the USS *Hornet* had waved goodbye to 16 Mitchell bombers of the Army Air Corps in a raid on Tokyo that was certainly strategic). But the emergence of the atomic bomb, the jet engine and the Cold War combined to give the Navy an irresistible desire to flex some strategic muscle. Such a contention could be counted on to spark off a revival of the Army-Navy brushfire war that had simmered for 40 years, and from 1947 this strife was joined even more vociferously by the newly created Air Force. From the start the men in light blue had ample political strength, and Strategic Air Command in particular took a poor view of the Navy's proposal to build a fleet of giant aircraft carriers, bigger and more powerful than any previous vessels, to carry the instruments of "massive retaliation" that SAC considered to be its own exclusive mission. There was a clear reason for this bickering: a dollar spent on a giant carrier could not be spent on a giant bomber, and SAC's B-36 was the biggest and most expensive military aircraft in history.

Undaunted, the Navy BuAer went ahead with a specification for a very advanced bomber to operate from the first super-carrier that was nearing the funding stage in 1946. Boldly the bureau decided on a twin-jet weighing 100,000 lb. It had to be a jet to obtain the desired flight performance, and the Navy firm of Westinghouse had an engine in the advanced project stage, the big axial XJ40, that was sized to give an eventual 10,000 lb thrust and would thus make such a bomber practical. Early in 1947 the Navy sent out an RFP and by the end of the year had such firms as Douglas, Curtiss and North American locked in competition. From the start it was clear the new aircraft was to carry an atomic bomb, and the resulting secrecy was so total the design teams were most of the time groping in the dark. The main requirement was to carry "a device" measuring five feet by five feet by 16 feet and weighing 10,000 lb a distance of 2,000 miles radius; it was further stipulated that the crew must have access to the device, whatever it was, so that they could attach to it a further element in flight, a task taking some time and involving a number of operations, before the complete assembly was ultimately dropped. But BuAer refused to say what the large object was, and to ask for a drawing was to invite a probe by the FBI. At this time the technology of nuclear weapons was in its infancy. No expert, be he nuclear physicist or ordnance engineer, liked to predict what new atomic bombs might become possible by the time the proposed bomber was in service. In fact by that time the weight and volume of the nominal 20 kiloton bomb had been slashed to less than one-fifth of the values quoted in the specification, so whatever aircraft the Navy bought was far bigger, heavier and more expensive than it needed to be. But the same charge could be levied at most of the strategic bombers in this book; in any case, making a bomber carry a clumsy great fission bomb did at least enable it to carry great thermonuclear weapons, or smaller bombs further.

During 1948 North American withdrew from the competition, expressing the opinion that the specification could not be met with an aircraft weighing only 100,000 lb gross. Doubtless they were strongly influenced by the conclusion of the RAND Corporation, the first "think tank" to undertake technological forecasting for the Department of Defense, that this very important specification could not be met by any aircraft weighing less than 150,000 lb. At that time RAND had yet to achieve eminence, but their forecasts still carried tremendous weight and I think it a pity they cranked into their equations such pessimistic assumptions. NAA ought to have known better. I do not know whether Curtiss were also aware of the RAND 150,000 lb forecast but the Columbus, Ohio, project engineers did at least decide to have a go and late in 1948 they went in at the prescribed 100,000 lb. They simply had to win, because apart from the XF-87 Blackhawk all-weather fighter (which lost out to the F-89 Scorpion) they had no other prospect of work.

Their rival was the El Segundo plant of Douglas Aircraft, the former Northrop works on the edge of what was in the process of turning from old Mines Field into the new Los Angeles International Airport, and right next door to North American which had yet to put up its proud neon sign HOME OF THE SABRE JET. For many years the chief engineer at El Segundo had been tall, lean Ed Heinemann. He was one of those outstanding designers who exerted so great an influence that, like Sir Sydney Camm, it is difficult to discuss their aircraft without mentioning them. In 1948 Heinemann was up to his eyes with the Skyraider and its proposed turboprop development, with improving his B-26 Invader, with his fine new Skyknight all-weather naval fighter, which flew in March, and with the world speed record-breaking D.558-1 Skystreak and Mach 2 D.558-2 Skyrocket. He still found time to direct the design of a submission in the new bomber competition, and he was never a man content merely to meet a specification. He had begun a campaign to make military aircraft simpler, lighter, cheaper and more reliable, and he regarded 100,000 lb as too heavy. He had a particular reason in this case for doing his utmost to keep down the aircraft size and weight. The Navy had tailored its specification to the single giant carrier, CVA-58, later named *United States*, which was first funded in Fiscal Year 1948. He suspected that this ship would be torpedoed by the Louis Johnson Air Force Administration (Johnson became SecDef in March 1949), and that the only way the new bomber could survive would be to reduce its weight to 68,000 lb in order to allow it to operate from the three big *Coral Sea* carriers already in commission.

This was a typical Heinemann ploy, and when news of it reached the mathematicians at RAND their comments can be left to the imagination. Many failed to remember that Heinemann was an engineer, not a dreamer, and that he could not afford to base his calculations on mere guesses or vague assumptions. In mid-1948 he marched in to BuAer to be greeted with "Oh no, not you! You didn't come in here to sell us a 68,000 pound airplane and then have it over-run to 100,000 pounds—you know it can't be done for 68,000 pounds." Rather stung by this, Heinemann said "OK, give me the drawings. I'll go back home". To which Admiral John Murphy replied "No no, leave them here; we may as well take a look at them". That night Heinemann received a phone call from his boss, Arthur Raymond, Douglas v-p engineering, who asked "What have you been doing in Washington? The Air Force has said to get you out of town because you are making irresponsible claims". If anything could be calculated to make Heinemann set his jaw and make 68,000 lb this was it.

What made it much harder was that he was creating a "rubber" design to meet almost impossibly flexible requirements. Although the Navy stuck to their 100,000 lb target their own estimates had ranged from 62,000 lb up to 200,000 lb (a seagoing B-47), and they could never decide for more than a few days at a time what the new bomber had to carry. It was soon painfully clear that the dimensions and weights of the unmentionable device were as variable as everything else. Some unmentionable devices were very long and thin, others had strange projections, while others were very fat or had odd tail assemblies. Heinemann calculated that the growth factor, assuming "rubber" engines which could be sized to match the aircraft, was 6·4; in other words, one pound of weight saved in a detail saved 6·4 pounds in the gross weight. It seemed certain that, if no defensive armament were fitted, Heinemann could reach his target, and one of the El Segundo studies came out at a gross weight of just 50,000 lb. But the Navy stuck to its requirement for a twin-20 mm radar-directed tail barbette, which alone put up the gross weight by 12,500 lb. And it was not until 1950 that the weapon bay finally settled, and the chopping and changing here was a big handicap because this compartment was the basis of the whole aircraft.

At the end of 1948 Douglas and Curtiss were given three-month preliminary design contracts which served to convince the Navy that Curtiss was not going to succeed, even at 100,000 lb, thus bringing to an end aircraft manufacture by the first company ever set up in America to build flying machines. But at El Segundo there seemed to be a chance, so on 31 March 1949 Douglas was awarded a $14,650,000 contract for two XA3D-1 Skywarrior aircraft and a static-test airframe. The following week the keel of the *United States* was laid; but before April was out the great ship had been cancelled. BuAer suddenly realized how right Heinemann had been all along to try to match the new aircraft to the existing carriers.

The next three years were hectic. The big twin-jet was only one of the El Segundo programmes (another, equally radical, was the baby Skyhawk, to be discussed in a companion volume) and Heinemann held design meetings two or three times a week to maintain the necessary rate of progress. Today it is common for great teams of engineers, often from several countries, to hold a succession of solemn meetings at which vital decisions are persistently deferred. The result is massive escalation in man-hours and cost. At El Segundo such an accumulated backlog of design choices was never allowed to happen. Decisions had to be taken on a daily basis, and the luxury of "further study" or "additional evaluation" was hardly ever possible. Key men in the programme were Heinemann's assistant Leo Devlin, A3D project engineer Harry Nichols, Capt. J. A. Thomas who was BuAer head of naval aircraft, and the civilian head of the Navy attack branch Robert Francis. Other famous men on the team were L. Eugene Root, who was president of Lockheed Missiles and Space Co during the Polaris programme; K. E. Van Every, now with General Dynamics; Dr William F. Ballhaus, president of Beckman Instruments; and Nate Carhart, later vice-president at Douglas, Long Beach—a real first eleven! There were certainly plenty of design choices open to them, and it is important to remember how utterly new this aircraft was, even though it looks quite ordinary today.

It would have been nice to have used a stubby Lippisch-type wing of the kind Heinemann was putting on his XF4D Skyray supersonic fighter, flown in January 1951. This would have been structurally efficient, light, compact for carrier stowage and free from flutter. But the balance lay in favour of the difficult, heavy and complicated "conventional" swept wing of high aspect ratio, offering much higher cruise efficiency and thus more miles per gallon. The final choice, taken early in 1950, was a wing with straight taper, an aspect ratio of 6·75, a thickness/chord ratio of 10 per cent at the root and $8\frac{1}{4}$ per cent at the tip, and a quarter-chord sweep of 36°— apart from the rather sharp sweepback, not too different from what might be chosen today for an aircraft intended to fly at up to Mach 0·85. Heinemann chose high-lift flaps, conventional outboard ailerons and aerodynamically opened leading-edge slats. Boldly he made the main wing box an integral tank out to the wing-fold line. The two big J40 engines were ultimately hung in neat pods far below and ahead of the wing, then still a novel idea. The fuselage designed itself. The wing was placed in the high position, with the whole space under it being bomb bay. Fore and aft of this were huge fuel cells. In the nose was to be a great blind-bombing radar followed by a three-seat pressurized crew compartment, and Heinemann reckoned he saved 550 lb (equivalent to almost 4,000 lb off the gross weight) by fitting a crew escape chute instead of ejection seats, which in those days were not well developed in the US. Westinghouse contributed the tail barbette, the radar and the engines.

One of the constraints of the adopted layout was that the main landing gear had to fold into the fuselage, and many thought the track of only 11 feet would not be enough on a rolling carrier deck (it was). Another problem was the flight-control system. Heinemann believed in manual reversion, and designed the hydraulically boosted elevators and rudder (the latter folding flat, with the fin, to fit carrier hangars) to be moved by hand after total hydraulic failure. Dutch roll, a very new bogey, was countered by fitting a yaw damper system like that devised a little earlier for the B-47. The ailerons, however, were another matter. The hydraulic boost ratio had to be 40:1, and the only answer was duplicated hydraulics so that failure of one system still left a 20:1 ratio. For lateral control at high speed spoilers also had to be fitted, because tunnel testing showed the adverse wing twist would reduce the aileron effectiveness to zero well below the maximum speed of the aircraft. But on top of this Heinemann stuck to his guns and fitted a mechanical aileron control, giving a 2:1 ratio, that would enable a strong man to get back to his carrier with no hydraulic power. I thought it was asking a bit much, but a senior pilot of VAH-2 summed it up by saying "It's amazing what you can do when you have to". No regular squadron pilot was ever called upon to practise flight without aileron boost.

Potentially more serious was wing flutter. The A3D was designed to a moderate factor (6, I believe), and the slender wing looked like posing a flutter problem. The technique of flutter testing was not fully developed in 1949, but Douglas built a mechanical flutter model simulating the bomber structure, translated its behaviour into electrical signals and had these analysed by the new analog computer at Caltech. Disturbingly, the output demonstrated that the wing would flutter at high frequency at well below the maximum level speed. At once a special wind-tunnel flutter model was made and tested, first in the Galcit (Guggenheim Aeronautical Lab of Caltech) tunnel and then in the tunnel of the Southern California Co-operative. The model fluttered so badly it became a mere blur. There followed anxious months of structural redesign, beefing-up, re-arranged geometry and other palliatives, but the final and complete solution was brought about when the engine type had to be changed for a completely different reason, as related later. The tunnel testing also showed that at Mach 0·8 interference between the nacelle, pylon and wing would cause a local Mach number of 1·25. This was cured by extending and cambering the pylon.

Westinghouse was in bad trouble with the YJ40 engine right from the start, but until 1951 managed to convince the Navy that it was well ahead of the new two-spool J57 at Pratt & Whitney, and that a complete answer to the engine's misbehaviour was just around the corner. So it was on two under-rated 6,500 lb thrust YJ40 engines that George Jansen took the impressive new XA3D-1 into the air at Edwards AFB on 28 October 1952. Flying at Edwards, rather than El Segundo, showed how advanced and how important this new bomber was to the customer. It cost an extra few weeks in a programme that was already almost a year late. Heinemann had hoped to fly in 24 months from contract go-ahead, but he was defeated by the changing specification, by the protracted engine difficulties and by the fact that Westinghouse could not develop a workable radar either. Veteran Jansen found the midnight-blue giant pleasant to fly, but as long as the Westinghouse engines were installed it spent nearly all its time on the ground.

Fortunately the BuAer had faced up to the crippling engine situation in good time. In 1951 nearly all the new Navy fighters, and the Douglas bomber, were being planned around the disastrous J40. Early in 1952 the bitter pill was swallowed and all these aircraft were urgently found new engines. In the case of two Douglas aircraft, the big bomber and the Skyray fighter, the new engine was Pratt & Whitney's J57, the first really advanced American gas turbine and the foundation on which was built most of the nation's air power (and the world's civil aviation) from 1950 until the late 1960s. Compared with the J40 the J57 was more powerful, more efficient, and marginally heavier. But the hefty and robust two-spool jet, in a slightly more forward pod location, completely solved the flutter problem by taking the critical regime above the normal flight envelope. Preparations to fit the J57 began before the first flight, and the J57-powered YA3D-1 flew on 16 September 1953, again with pilot Jansen but this time at El Segundo.

By this time Heinemann had slightly mixed feelings about the pro-gramme. He had done what he said he would do: build the bomber to a gross weight of 68,000 lb. This alone took immense discipline and tough engineering management, even though towards the end of the project stage he held the weight by the simple expedient of taking out a pound of fuel each time the Navy added a pound of equipment! On the other hand the double failure of Westinghouse had cost over 18 months, the aircraft was sized to carry bombs much heavier and bulkier than those that it actually had to carry, and, to cap it all, the Navy had finally got its giant carriers—not just one but a fleet. The *United States* had been resurrected as the *Forrestal* (CVA-59), funded in 1951, after Johnson's departure, and laid down in July 1952. Behind her have come a succession of others, most of them even bigger and with the greatest of all still being built in 1973. So Heinemann could let the Skywarrior grow in weight, and despite its lean airframe, with not a pound of fat on it, he knew it had plenty of growth potential—not the unavoidable escalation BuAer had predicted in 1948 but a deliberate loading up with more fuel and weapons.

At the outset the ship designers insisted 68,000 lb was the limit, and that the carrier decks would not take any more. Heinemann figured the bomber could operate safely at 83,000 lb (more than three times the weight of Doolittle's Mitchells of 1942), and BuAer knew as well as he did what a tremendous difference this would make to the radius of action with maximum weapon load. But BuShips refused to sanction this great weight, especially as it would arrive on only two tires spaced a mere 11 feet apart. Heinemann could be relied upon not to take "no" for an answer. He obtained Navy authority to build a drop-test rig consisting of an A3D landing gear fixed to a container which could be loaded with lead blocks from 68,000 up to 83,000 pounds. He carted this up to Bremerton, Washington, and slammed it on to the deck of a real carrier in all the areas where an A3D might make contact. This proved the decks were sufficiently strong apart from one region which was easily strengthened. Thus, by a typically forthright procedure, the Navy's carriers were suddenly qualified for aircraft weighing 83,000 lb—which takes care of everything they have had to accept since.

In 1954 Douglas received a production contract for the A3D-1, re-designated A-3A in the revised DoD numbering system, and the following year I was able to spend some time aboard the sixth production machine.

The flight deck was reminiscent of a Lancaster, being about the same size, with glass all round and overhead, a pilot and co-pilot side-by-side and the nav-gunner facing aft on the left side. As there were no ejection seats the roof was strong and fixed, with just a ditching hatch aft. Acceleration to the limit of Mach 0·85 at high altitude resulted in Mach 1 airflow over this canopy, giving rise to deafening turbulence that temporarily made R/T or intercom impossible. The escape chute was long and smooth and sealed at top and bottom by interlinked doors opened by a solid-fuel cartridge that held the lower door open like a great speed brake to create a dead-air region. I was assured that any crew member could dive out through this chute no matter what gyration the aircraft might perform. Many years later Heinemann told me the system had worked admirably in practice, but I wouldn't use this as an argument against ejection seats.

Behind the chute was the secret access through which the unnamed part could be taken to the unmentionable device before the latter was dropped. The bomb doors were wholly conventional, and to ensure good store separation a large "buffet rake" in the form of a perforated speed brake was extended ahead of the open bomb bay while the bombs themselves were pushed out by powered ejectors. In view of the buffet rake and the even bigger escape door it was surprising to find that Heinemann had added on each side of the rear fuselage the two biggest speed brakes in the business, each 10 feet from hinge axis to trailing edge; but these were wanted to increase the engine speed on the approach and thus allow the pilot to get full thrust very quickly if he should suffer a "wave-off" and have to go round again.

Technically the Skywarrior was packed with interest. In some respects it was totally new. For example the main accessory power was bled from the J57s in the form of hot air through stainless-steel pipes, which spun tiny turbines that screamed stridently just ahead of the weapons bay. Douglas claimed these neat packages, each surrounded by flak curtains, were "125 lb lighter than a conventional shaft-drive system", and Boeing adopted the idea with the original models of the B-52; but nobody does it today. Structurally the new swept-wing bomber was remarkably conventional. Heinemann never allowed anything new unless someone could show him it was better. He knew all about tapered sheet, honeycombs and integrally stiffened machined panels when the Skywarrior was being designed, and not one of them got into the aircraft. He could have used high-strength alloys, but chose 7075S (even if it did mean three-eighths of an inch thickness above and below the wing box out to the fold). He could have used chemical milling, but allowed it for one small part only: a pair of very thin, sliding camera doors that were difficult to make by any conventional means.

Bleed-air pressure was used to force wing fuel, chilled by the high altitude, into the fuselage tanks where it sharply reduced the boil-off of light hydrocarbon fractions without the need for a heavy refrigeration system. The fuselage tanks were also pressurized, and the space above the fuel was purged by carbon dioxide, an idea considered novel 20 years ago. On each side of the rear fuselage could be clipped six Aerojet rocket bottles imparting a total mean thrust of 54,000 lb for five seconds. These were never needed, and were soon deleted, because the J57 grew in power and the C-13 steam catapult could launch the A-3 with nonchalance. The rocket bottles would have been needed only in an 83,000 lb launch from an *Essex*-class ship or in a free take-off from the deck.

With the A-3 Heinemann created a big, powerful, long-range bomber that fitted all the attack carriers in US Navy service. The original version became operational with VAH-1 in March or April 1956, and subsequently 282 were built. The bomber A-3A and A-3B really did wait at readiness, complete with an unmentionable device, on the catapults of the 6th and 7th Fleets on both sides of the world from 1956 until 1963. It has been said that this was "a very powerful deterrent" and that it "exerted a sobering effect upon the Soviet view of America's capability".

A bit of "spin off" to Douglas was that, despite the Navy passion for secrecy, the company inevitably built up a wide and deep knowledge of nuclear weapons and the associated aircraft requirements and hardware systems. So did Boeing and some other companies, but it was Douglas El Segundo division that won the contract to establish and operate a highly secret atomic bomb design, development and production unit for the Sandia Corporation, of Albuquerque, which in turn managed nuclear weapon hardware for the Atomic Energy Commission. This El Segundo offshoot designed and delivered many hundreds of air-dropped nuclear weapons in three different sizes, together with the associated control equipment and accessory components. And only a handful of people at El Segundo knew about it. Douglas also designed the shape for US external stores of all kinds (except guided missiles) and the special ejector racks to carry them.

In the course of its long operational life the A-3B, the main bomber version of the Skywarrior, was several times modified to upgrade its performance, versatility, countermeasures, low-level capability (especially by fitting a LABS) and structural life. One of the most significant alterations, made progressively as a field modification from 1961 onwards, was to throw out the weighty tail barbette that was so vital in the project stage and replace it by ECM systems including a chaff dispenser. Another was to fit many aircraft to carry a Flight Refuelling bomb bay pack, turning them into KA-3B tankers. But no tale of the Skywarrior would be complete without recording that the last 67 aircraft were of grossly altered models intended for quite different duties. All of them had a fully pressurized fuselage as far back as the main-gear bulkhead aft of where the bomb bay had been. The first of these new versions was the RA-3B five-seat reconnaissance aircraft, flown in July 1958. In December of that year came the first of the very important EA-3B electronic reconnaissance and countermeasures series, most of which had seven seats and were distinguished by a long Q-band SLAR under the belly; some of these can even double as tankers, with the designation EKA-3B. In August 1959 followed the first TA-3B bomber trainer with accommodation for pilot, instructor and six pupils each with his own navigation equipment and radar bomb-sight for level or LABS attacks. A small series was also made of the Aurora weather reconnaissance version used in hurricane studies and later also as a VIP transport. Altogether the A-3 family represented splendid value for money. Heinemann considers it would have been wise to build at least another hundred, because these aircraft have six times had their fatigue life extended and today, 23 years after contract go-ahead, are still in service, with fatigue tests still being conducted.

Only the first dozen or so Skywarriors were painted in the glossy midnight-blue livery of the Korean period, all later aircraft being originally pale grey and white. But the rest of the story concerns aircraft left in their natural metal finish: these were the B-66 Destroyers of the Air Force. It was in 1951 that Heinemann's bold project suddenly seemed to the Air Force to have a chance of success. Having initially laughed at the proposed weight the Air Force gradually came round to the view that the Navy bomber could do the work of a B-47 over tactical ranges for a fraction of the cost, and that an off-the-shelf buy of a slightly modified land-based version might be a very good idea. One or two changes were obvious. The airframe would be revised to take out local strengthening needed for accelerated take-offs and arrested landings, the wing-fold would be deleted, the Navy Westinghouse engine would be replaced by an Air Force one (the choice fell on the rather more powerful Allison J71, an engine the Air Force had slipped into the 1949 budget by calling it a version of the well-established J35, which it certainly was not), and some items of equipment would be changed to suit the Air Force mission and environment. The total number of predicted modifications was more than the "six" I saw reported in one reputable place, but it was not expected to exceed 28. Possibly the biggest change was that the Air Force bomber was to be built at an Air Force plant: the Douglas Long Beach division, today the hub of Douglas Aircraft but then a mere subsidiary.

Redesignated B-66, and given the name Destroyer (a name which turned out to be neither relevant nor memorable), the aircraft was the first

Navy design ever to go into production for the Air Force. It was also the first to come under the direction of Donald W. Douglas Jr, who had spent most of his post-war years at Long Beach managing major parts of the programme for the C-74 and C-124 Globemaster which in 1951 was the main Long Beach product. It was he who, in his new role of vice-president military sales, announced the B-66 in August 1952. It was meant to be a fast, trouble-free programme that would give the Air Force a really modern and effective multi-role tactical aircraft, something Korea had made painfully necessary and which had led to the unprecedented production by Martin of the British Canberra. John C. Buckwalter, chief engineer at Long Beach, was given what looked like a nice assignment in directing the swift conversion of the Skywarrior into the new Air Force machine. A contract was placed for 175 RB-66 reconnaissance bombers, with first delivery due in early 1954.

What followed was possibly predictable: the Air Force found they wanted to change practically every nut and bolt. One of the obvious modifications was that the wing was redesigned, with a kinked trailing edge giving lower t/c ratio at the root, a new flap system and different ailerons, as well as quite different detail structure. The engine pods, of course, were totally different, and the J71s carried shaft-driven accessories. The fuselage was new from stem to stern. In the original RB-66 the three-man crew was retained, but all had ejection seats, beneath big roof hatches, and the pilot sat by himself in front opposite an impressive instrument panel filling the right side from floor to roof; behind were the navigator and gunner/camera operator, both facing forward. The canopy was new. In the nose was the big APS-27 radar, utterly unlike the Navy system, and in front of it projected a Flight Refuelling probe. Unlike Strategic Air Command, Tactical Air Command had adopted the British FR system and the RB-66 was the first Air Force aircraft thus equipped from the design stage. In the redesigned mid-fuselage were a fan of three K-46 cameras and a giant K-38, two enormous equipment racks filling the upper regions and two vertical columns of photo-flash bombs in the rear half of the bomb bay. Further aft was about a ton of additional new equipment, while at the rear was a twin-20 mm gun barbette which looked like that of the Skywarrior but was actually a product of GE and completely different (it wasn't even the same as the installations in the B-36 or B-47). Other things the Air Force could not resist were a new electrical system, with a remarkable degree of fault-protection and automaticity, the Western Electric K-5 radar-navigation system, thermal cyclic de-icing for wings and tail and, to cap everything, a 2° reduction in wing incidence.

Whereas the objective of the Air Force had been to buy, almost off the shelf, "a versatile airplane to handle the bulk of the Air Force's tactical missions from the stratosphere down to minimum altitudes", with most of the R&D already paid for by the Navy, what it actually did was create a complicated bag of tricks that cost half as much again as a Skywarrior, carried so much equipment it had a marginal performance, and arrived too late for Korea or for it to be markedly superior to other equipment available concurrently, even though it was better than the ageing RB-45 which it replaced in most theatres. After about ten times the engineering effort he expected, Buckwalter got the first RB-66A out of the door in May 1954 —which was really an outstanding performance—and George Jansen flew it to Edwards on 28 June. Only five of the A version were built. The RB-66B, the main production version, first flew on 4 January 1955. This could carry a 450 gal tank under each wing, which was welcome because some of the original fuel space had been occupied by the incredible arrays of black boxes. The RB-66B entered service with Tac Rec squadrons in 1957, and in the same year a small number of the B-66B pure bomber version also entered service, one of them taking part in the "Redwing" H-bomb drop (by a B-52) at Bikini.

There were also two additional models of B-66, and to make sure the cost kept high the Air Force had these engineered and built at the Douglas Tulsa division, a World War 2 plant more than 1,400 miles to the east that had been re-activated in 1951 to make the B-47. The first to fly, on 29 October 1955, was the RB-66C specialized electronic reconnaissance aircraft; the final model, which was phased out of production in June 1958, to make total B-66 procurement only 209 aircraft, was the WB-66D weather reconnaissance machine. As only 36 of the last two versions were manufactured the overheads of the switch to Tulsa had a significant effect on the price. The WB was especially hard to understand. Previously the USAF had used conversions of existing bomber or transport aircraft for its Air Weather Service, an agency of Military Airlift Command charged with research and forecasting on a global scale. But the costly WB-66D, tailored for atmospheric research from the drawing board, was bought explicitly for getting "accurate weather data in combat areas", and was assigned to tactical units. It had a crew of five, the two systems managers in the mid-fuselage just managing to squeeze in among the special installations.

For sheer multiplicity of black boxes, however, the RB-66C beat the lot. It was the first aircraft ever designed from the start to sense, measure and analyse the electromagnetic environment over unfriendly territory, and also, in time of war, to lead strikes by tactical aircraft and ease their path with sophisticated countermeasures. It was the first type of B-66 to follow the Skywarrior in fitting countermeasures in place of the tail guns, and it also had prominent ECM aerials on the wing tips and beneath the pressurized ECM crew compartment in the mid-fuselage. Like the special ECM conversion of the B-47 the RB-66C was used for hazardous missions that probed the electronic radiation all round the frontiers of the Soviet world, although its more limited range tended to confine it to Europe, Turkey and one or two other countries. In a lot of these missions I think the crew knew they were pushing their luck, and that the US State Department would never admit that they had deliberately crossed a Communist frontier. Even after Gary Powers and his U-2 had knocked the whole US posture of innocence to the four winds there were several occasions when a USAF crew engaged in electronic reconnaissance fell before Communist guns, and the rest of the world would have to decide whose story to believe. For example—and I am picking one from a dozen similar incidents—on 10 March 1964 an RB-66C penetrated far into East Germany. It was "challenged" and, it failing to respond, "the forces of the Peoples' Democratic Republic took appropriate action"—in other words, Mig-19s shot it down. A USAF board of inquiry, which didn't have the wreckage, reported that the aircraft "inadvertently strayed over East Germany" because of "a gross navigational error caused by the compass system". Marshal Malinovsky, the Soviet Defence Minister, who happened to be in East Germany, said that careful inspection of the compass system disclosed no malfunction prior to the crash. He casually added that film recovered from the aircraft's cameras showed it to be "on an espionage flight". USAFE headquarters in Wiesbaden said the crew, who were returned, would "face a board of investigation" and would "*never* be available for a press interview". I think the last statement just about sums the whole thing up.

In 1967 I reminisced with Carlos C. Wood at Sikorsky. He had been chief of preliminary design at Douglas when the B-66 programme began, and I asked him whether he thought the Air Force had saved money by starting with the Skywarrior instead of a clean sheet of paper. It must have been a full half minute before he answered.

North American Rockwell A-5 Vigilante

THE VIGILANTE will not go down in history as a great bomber, and to the slick "whiz kids" Secretary McNamara imported into the Pentagon it was not very cost/effective either, for its costs were considerable and the increment in American striking power it brought was problematical. But it still has its place in history. From its sharp, lofty nose to its three-holed stern it was packed with new technology. Even today aircraft all over the world are being designed and built with materials, techniques, systems and equipment that had their genesis in this dramatically advanced machine created in the heyday of the US industry in the mid-fifties before pacifists, conservationists and the man in the street began to take a critical interest in the aerospace scene.

At this time, when the design offices of the world's biggest aerospace industry were brimming with immaculate white-shirted engineers and the giant corporations were extending their floor-space to areas exceeding the peak reached in World War 2, the biggest giant of all was North American Aviation. It vied with Boeing and, later, with Lockheed for the coveted role of top defence contractor, but it had more varied aerospace programmes than either. In 1950 it had set up a Columbus Division by taking over from unhappy Curtiss a vast wartime plant near the Ohio city of that name and transferring to it all its Navy programmes: the piston-plus-jet Savage carrier-based bomber and reconnaissance tanker, the pugnacious XA2J 11,000 hp turboprop machine that was developed from it, the excellent series of Fury fighters derived from the land-based Sabre, the T-28B Trojan trainer and, later, the T-2 Buckeye jet trainer. Columbus also became the second-source plant for the F-100 Super Sabre for the Air Force, and made its contribution to various missile and research projects. This was all fine for the immediate future, but the embryonic design staff at Columbus had to look ten years and more ahead. After much thought the chief of preliminary design, Frank G. Compton, was allowed to challenge Ed Heinemann and propose a carrier-based attack bomber more modern than the Skywarrior and Skyhawk.

By the end of 1954 the Columbus Division had schemed NAGPAW, North American general-purpose attack weapon. This was to be a compact, single design-point, high-subsonic strike/reconnaissance aircraft so bristling with radical yet demonstrably good ideas that Compton had high hopes. In particular it had a small radar cross-section and could fly at maximum speed right on the deck for attacks under the enemy radars.

By May 1955 BuAer had evaluated NAGPAW and decided it made sense. It was practically a carrier-based TSR.2 in many respects, with ideas and systems that could rightly be called futuristic. But the customer, who had too many experts, called for two changes which profoundly affected the design and ultimately the size of the programme. Within the Navy, especially within BuShips, there was stiffening resistance to the introduction of aircraft with smaller wings and greater weights which fell into the sea when they were catapulted on a calm day in the tropics. "Wind over the deck" was deemed to be the crucial design criterion, and it was decreed that the NAGPAW must be capable of full-load launch with this parameter equal to zero. I can think of few sillier decisions. Naval air strikes are not usually mounted in absolutely still air with the carrier at anchor, and I have never been on a carrier deck (and not often on a land airfield) when the relative wind was zero, yet this quite unnecessarily harsh requirement was solemnly agreed to. Outside the Navy, in the Department of Defense, it was equally solemnly decreed that subsonic aircraft were out of date and that Columbus must come up with supersonic performance, preferably Mach 2. The comment here is that the two subsequent attack aircraft in production for the US Navy today are both subsonic.

Compton and his team spent the rest of 1955 trying to reconcile irreconcilables. They had to design an aircraft with a very small, stiff wing for high speed at sea level. It also had to have a very big wing to lift the aircraft with zero wind over the deck. The aircraft had to be optimized for high-subsonic cruise at high altitude for maximum radius of action, with slender, long-span wings; except that the wing had to be short and stubby for supersonic speed. Compton did some sums for Mach 2 at sea level and gave up. In the vital low-level role NAGPAW could not go faster than the Mach 0·95 of the original proposal, but it was going to be much more difficult and expensive in order to fly at Mach 2 at the tropopause (where a missile could shoot it down). Of course it was a clear case for variable wing sweep, but nobody had produced a happy solution here and the Grumman XF10F Jaguar had put the Navy off this approach. That the Columbus team succeeded at all is a marvel.

The wing they chose was an extension of the type used in the Fury and Super Sabre, with sharp sweep and taper, a hinged leading edge and a thin section. It broke new ground in being even thinner (3·5 per cent), in having powerful blown flaps but no ailerons, and in being an integral tank out to the fold with machined skins, chemically etched panels and aluminium honeycomb secondary structure. Its area of 700 square feet was roughly 50 per cent larger than could have been accepted for a Mach 0·95 low-level aircraft, but was the smallest that could handle the still-air take-off. Only in the body was NAGPAW not greatly altered, and here the shape was quite new. Previous high-speed aircraft tended to look streamlined, with smooth tapering curves. Compton appeared merely to have drawn parallel lines, with a pair of lateral jet intakes with inclined edges which, instead of curving back to the original body profile, kept at their full enormous width right back to the tail. The result was a box-like centre and rear body in which the width was twice the depth, with a flat top and bottom. Inside, it was like a three-barrelled gun. In the outer barrels were two General Electric J79 variable-stator turbojets with afterburners. In the centre was a linear weapon bay from which the bomb was to be shot out rearwards, between the jet nozzles. Non-integral fuel cells filled all available space above and ahead of the three barrels.

In 1955 aircraft design had for ten years been advancing by leaps and bounds as the jet engine opened up the Mach scale and the global confrontation between East and West, and especially the Korean war, loosed the purse strings. Today each new technological possibility is critically examined and may be rejected on grounds of cost/effectiveness, but in 1955 little was rejected that seemed to make for a superior weapon system. So the NAGPAW specification bristled with new ideas. The high-lift wing and shot-out bomb have been mentioned. The flight-control system comprised extraordinary upper and lower wing spoilers, slab tailplanes and a slab fin/rudder. Roll control was solely by the spoilers, which were arranged in outer, mid and inner sections on each wing. Each outer unit comprised a spoiler, hinged at its leading edge, under the wing, and a deflector, hinged at its trailing edge, above. The mid and inner sections were the other way round, with spoilers on top and deflectors below, each spoiler and deflector being arranged so that when they were open there was a huge open duct right through the wing to divert the airflow from the top to the bottom or vice versa. Pitch control was by the hydraulic tailplanes, which could be inched together for pitch trimming and differentially for trimming the aircraft in roll. I never understood why the Columbus designers, having fitted these powerful left and right slabs that could move independently, used them differentially only for trim and not as the primary roll control as was done later on TSR.2.

Controlling these unconventional surfaces was an automatic flight control system of unprecedented scope which, more than in any previous aircraft, introduced the concept of a totally integrated system for every flight manoeuvre or operational situation. Prior to this aircraft the US Air Force had set out along this path with the F-86D and F-102 intercepters, but the North American proposal took it right up to the technology of the 1970s. The single system linked navigation, weapon preparation and delivery, reconnaissance data handling and aircraft flight control. Each sub-system in turn was new through and through. Another NAA division, the infant Autonetics, had begun to pioneer inertial navigation, and although this was not yet ready for use as the sole aid for long aircraft missions, the new bomber was planned to use REINS, radar-equipped inertial navigation system, and was the first production aircraft in the world to have such a system. In the nose was a very advanced multi-mode radar, by GD/Electronics, and linking everything together was Verdan, a name formed from "versatile digital analyser", (or "Very Effective Replacement for Dumb-Ass Navigators" to the crews) the first miniature digital computer ever to go into production for an airborne application. It was likewise a product of Autonetics and, like REINS, was possible largely because of the massive research undertaken for North American's great Navaho missile. The whole bombing system, called ASB-12, could find targets by comparing what it saw beneath the aircraft with pictures and magnetic tape of target appearance, radar signatures and other data and fly the aircraft so that the weapon would hit the target. The radar and computer were easy to get at, if you had a ladder, and in the early days in 1959 this was important because the mean time between failures was 15 minutes. By 1961 the MTBF had been improved to 240 hours (about nine months' flying) and it later reached 500 hours—a truly great achievement.

Structurally the design ran true to form. Although 78ST light alloy was still much in evidence, the severe intensity of loading and the high temperatures encountered by major parts of the airframe made new materials attractive, and one can write off scores of millions of dollars from this programme on perfecting ways of using these new materials and thus of freeing later aircraft programmes from a mighty research burden. For example, the big integrally stiffened skins of the wing and tailplane were made of Alcoa's new 2020 aluminium-lithium alloy which was good up to 400° F, besides offering increased strength, greater elasticity and reduced density compared with such traditional alloys as 7075 (and in those days "traditional" meant it had been used before). The 2020, at first produced only for this application, was costly, so that a machined set of wing skins cost as much as a squadron of World War 2 Fortress bombers. But this was nothing; most of the engine bays were made of titanium alloys, and surfaces facing the engines were sprayed with a heat-reflective gold coating which was then baked on. The press copy-writers had to add "low cost" in front of the word gold, and I eventually discovered this meant that "the original gold used is not of the high-carat type used in fine jewelry" (*sic*). It was a relief to find that the landing-gear legs were not platinum but US Steel's new STRUX, and that the wing/main-gear and main tail frames in the fuselage were made of H-11 hot-work tool steel, which only cost a few score dollars per pound. Even the proposed windscreen was priced at some $15,000, Libby-Owens-Ford believing it to be the biggest piece of curved, laminated aircraft glass ever made. It was a bit of a come-down when, in 1961, the technology of stretched acrylics had progressed far enough for a new screen to be produced for half the price.

One could go on and on about the feast of futuristic goodies in the NAGPAW design as it finally crystallized late in 1955, with its beautifully neat folding refuelling probe, its automatically controlled variable-ramp intakes and engine nozzles, its main power system filled with pure nitrogen instead of hydraulic fluid, its oil-cooled alternators generating paralleled a.c. electric power, the 8-hr liquid-oxygen converter and the rocket-assisted NAA seats. Suffice to say the Navy was overcome by sheer technical interest. On 29 June 1956 Columbus received an instruction to proceed with the detailed engineering, tooling and long-lead items, and the NAA division was assigned the status of weapon-system prime contractor to the fullest degree. Only the two J79 engines were to be GFE (government furnished equipment), NAA Columbus having total system responsibility for every other item of hardware in the aircraft and its ground-support, checkout, training and auxiliary equipment. By this time the techniques of weapon system management had been brought to a fine art in the United States. In Britain the very notion of what a weapon system was was little understood, and when the management technique was at last attempted with the TSR.2, the management structure was imperfectly designed.

In September 1956 a contract followed for two flight prototype aircraft, designated YA3J-1 Vigilante, plus a static-test airframe. Bearing in mind the fact that Columbus was still a very new organization, grossly over-worked, I do not think I need comment on their performance in achieving a first flight on 31 August 1958 with an incredibly complicated aircraft that probably incorporated more new features than any other flying machine in the history of aviation (a bold claim, but I think a true one). It was partly this swift development that made the costs reasonable, although the true R&D bill was several times greater than the original 1956 contract for $86 million. On the other hand the Vigilante was obviously going to be a mighty programme involving a wide spectrum of Navy bureaux, test establishments and laboratories and many hundreds of industrial con-tractors, and with Korea receding the Navy was looking more keenly at how it should spend its funds. By 1957 a major faction, led by Garrison Norton, Assistant Navy Secretary for Air, was campaigning against the Vigilante on the hoary old ground that strategic bombing was no part of the Navy's business—a belief with which the Air Force found no fault at all. This seemed odd, because the Navy had had a strategic role since the first carrier, and in any case the missions of the Vigilante were no different from those of the widely deployed Skywarrior. The contrary faction supported the Vigilante for the rather secondary reason that it could fly a low-level mission and carry conventional weapons. In the end it was the latter group that carried the day, and many at Columbus must have torn their hair as they realized how Navy policy in 1955 had made them veer away from the low-level conventional role in favour of Mach 2 at high-altitude with a nuclear weapon.

Obviously there would have to be some rethinking (again); but what mattered was that production funds were included in the 1960 fiscal year, and between then and 1963 Columbus delivered 59 bomber Vigilantes, originally designated A3J-1 but under the 1962 Department of Defense system re-numbered A-5A. These differed remarkably little from the original 1956 NAGPAW. One of the few really severe hardware problems was that the clever weapon delivery steadfastly refused to work. The idea had been to make better use of restricted space by doing away with bomb doors. Instead a large chemically milled 14 foot non-structural panel could be unscrewed from the belly of the aircraft to gain access to much of the crowded interior and, in particular to the front end of the weapon tunnel. To load the bay a standard Air Logistics trolley was used to hoist a 275 US gal drum of fuel into the bay until rollers engaged with two rails running the length of the bay. The tank was then rolled rearwards to the next store station while a second, identical tank was raised into place ahead of it, located on the rails and joined to the first tank both mechanically and by fuel connections. Finally the linked tanks were moved to the rear and the weapon, either nuclear or conventional, raised into the first store position and coupled up to make a single rigid "train" carried on rollers and more than 30 feet long. To launch the assembly the signal from the bomb/nav system would first blow off the tailcone and then, having released the latches that previously prevented axial movement, catapult the great tube out rearwards with a towing system energized by a solid-fuel cartridge. The pressurized tanks, emptied early in the mission to help trim the aircraft for supersonic flight, were intended to remain attached to the bomb to improve its stability. Suffice to say the system did anything but run on rails and at times people at China Lake, the Naval Ordnance Test Station, were thinking of telling NAA to fit ordinary bomb doors.

By 1959 NAA, though in the midst of this and other development problems, was looking hard at what could be done with this unique aircraft. It had a wing much too big for the specialized low-level role, but it was a fine wing for a fighter. By mid-1959 the Columbus division had prepared a submission to the Navy and to the Air Force for a long-range fighter Vigilante. The main interest centred on the land-based version, which would have had a number of modifications including one of NAA's own HTP/JP-4 rocket engines, already flying on an FJ-4 Fury, to boost an already outstanding high-altitude performance. On 13 December 1960 a standard A-5A set a world zoom-climb record by reaching 91,446 feet with a payload of 2,205 lb. This was nicely timed to influence the detailed submission, made under the name Retaliator, that was being evaluated by the USAF Air Defense Command. Various Retaliators were examined, some armed with guns and Sidewinders for in-fighting but most carrying long-range Falcons, Sparrows or projected AAMs having ranges up to 100 miles (such as the Eagle, about to be turned into hardware by Bendix). No decision was taken in the first evaluation, but ADC came very near to ordering a further upgraded Retaliator in a second evaluation early in 1962. Had they done so it would have made a big difference to what had become one of the few US military programmes of the period to suffer from low-rate production. The 59 A-5As were the only bombers ordered, and the unit price varied from $6 to $9 million. NAA had great plans for developed versions, but these bore fruit only in the field of reconnaissance, as presently related, and the company had a hard time making a profit from the very low-rate manufacture and modification needed between 1960 and the mid-1970s.

Development of the Vigilante was generally quick and free from trouble, apart from bomb delivery, and by the summer of 1960 carrier qualification had been completed aboard *Saratoga*. Hatron 7 (Heavy Attack Squadron 7 or VAH-7), commanded by Cdr Louis B. Hoop, was busily learning the technology of the most complex and advanced aircraft ever to reach any navy; indeed, it had few rivals anywhere, and in most respects was later than the B-58. By the autumn of 1961 the 12 aircraft of this unit were working up at NAS Sanford, Florida, and in August 1962 they became one of the first units to go aboard the nuclear-powered super-carrier *Enterprise*, as part of Air Group 6. Hatron 7 were proud of having had no flying accident in two years, and took a leaf from SAC's book in calling themselves "Peacemakers of the Fleet", although fortunately they were never called upon to demonstrate their brand of peace even when later in 1962 they joined the Sixth Fleet in the Mediterranean. Aurally the A-5A was marginally more peaceful than some of the other aircraft on board in that, with a good 35 knots blowing over the 4½-acre deck, it did not need afterburners for a full-load launch at about 56,000 lb. The pleasant run up from Norfolk to the great ship's first port of call, Boston (where she was open to visitors on Independence Day, 1962), demonstrated that the catapult crews could fire the Vigilante at 160 mph at the rate of four per minute per catapult. I doubt they could have kept this up for many minutes!

On 29 April 1962 NAA Columbus had flown the first A3J-2 (A-3B) after three years of further development. The key to this aircraft was the abandonment of the zero-wind stipulation, which opened up the possibility of a major increase in weight. Proportionately it was one of the largest increases in history, from an original design gross of 50,000 lb to a new figure of 80,000, and it shows the penalty the Navy imposed by their demand for still-air launch. NAA kept the propulsion system unchanged but increased the wing lift at low speeds by almost 30 per cent by increasing the span and chord of the flaps and, in particular, by blowing the drooped leading-edge flaps. They assured me they had meant to do this even before they saw the British Blackburn NA.39, and I think they scored in weight and cost over the British aircraft in making the six new blowing ducts out of titanium alloy (5 per cent Al and 2·5 per cent tin) instead of Nimonic. Having done this the aircraft was given a hump-backed fuselage, the bombardier-navigator sitting about two feet higher and the space behind him housing about 1,000 gallons more fuel (the weight of which was said to be largely cancelled out at high speeds by the increased fuselage lift), as well as two more underwing pylons each capable of carrying a 400 US gal (330 gal) tank. This practically doubled the payload/range of the Vigilante, and every bit of it was put to use in the reconnaissance role for which all subsequent Vigilantes were bought. These machines, designated RA-5C, are outside the context of this book, but are notable in their range of sensing and communication systems which even in 1973 make them unexcelled by any other aircraft. Here again the Vigilante broke a tremendous amount of new ground, and the maker did get some reward in a succession of production contracts for the RA-5C ending with 36 new aircraft ordered in 1968–9, to make the RA-5C total 140, as well as contracts to convert all remaining A-5A aircraft up to this very different standard. Today NAA is part of Rockwell International.

Of course the four wing pylons of the RA-5C do give it the ability to deliver a wide range of weapons, even though the troublesome linear bomb tunnel is now packed with avionics and fuel, but the aircraft have not been bought for the attack role. In 1962 Defense Secretary McNamara concluded that "the information-gathering capability (of the RA-5C) could not be duplicated by any other vehicle . . .". Perhaps I can illustrate this capability. Early in the US involvement in Viet-Nam, in 1965, persistent navigation and bombing errors were traced to inaccuracies of up to four miles in existing maps. In two weeks a flight of RA-5Cs had carried out a detailed aerial survey of the whole of South East Asia from which new maps were speedily produced. And to check the accuracy an RA-5C took an oblique of a football field (which as every American knows is 100 yards long) at a range of 60 miles. When the photograph was scaled, the image yielded a measured length of 100·1 yards (thinks: did they check the accuracy of the field?)

So the RA-5C brought much more than a local naval capability, and the Pentagon was not too concerned that, even though they came some way down the learning curve, they were at least as expensive as the original bombers: in fiscal year 1963 the RA-5C cost about $5·5 million, not including several of the complex new sensing systems. Small numbers and resulting high costs have always been the basic problem with the Vigilante. I think it is only fair to this aircraft to bear in mind that, because of the unparalleled amount of R&D accomplished in the programme, every subsequent combat aircraft—in the Western world at least—has been a little cheaper.

North American B-70 Valkyrie

On Monday 11 May 1964 a roll-out ceremony took place at Palmdale. Into the hot California sun emerged an "air vehicle"—to use the correct parlance—that established more "firsts" than any other in history. For almost the first time since the Wright Brothers it had a foreplane instead of a tailplane. More significantly, for the first time since the Wright Brothers it was simultaneously the world's heaviest aircraft, the most powerful, the most costly and, except for the special air-launched X-15s, the fastest. It only just missed also having the longest range. Its flight deck, 25 feet up on the end of a fuselage like a giant serpent extending 80 feet ahead of the "nose" landing gear, controlled the biggest fuel system, the most powerful accessory systems, the largest variable-geometry surfaces and a thousand other record-breaking devices, all of them specially developed to run not at the normal 250°–275° F temperature limit of earlier aircraft but at 550°–630°. The vast airframe was likewise built in a new way, from new materials, by new machines using technology that had been specially created for this monster aircraft.

It was the first XB-70A Valkyrie. Painted dazzling white, it bore no insignia other than the letters USAF and the serial 20001. But the hundreds of invited guests who sought the shade of the vast wing, with its fantastic root chord of 110 feet, knew very well that, whatever the Air Force might wish, the XB-70A was no longer a bomber. Secretary of Defense McNamara had introduced a new evaluation criterion called cost-effectiveness, and in his opinion the XB-70A showed up badly. The mighty structure had been gutted of its military subsystems, and had posed such severe technical problems that even at the roll-out No 5 fuel tank could not be used because it still leaked. What had begun quietly a decade earlier as the greatest bomber in history could now be seen as a watershed. It separated the time when a big and powerful nation could develop almost any military hardware it wanted, from the tough modern world when it must pick and choose most carefully. It happened to reach fruition just at the time when the choice seemed to be to buy either missiles or bombers, and the choice fell on the new missiles. Creating the B-70 was perhaps the most difficult assignment ever given to any industry, in my view even transcending the creation of the ICBMs that defeated it. Deciding what to do with it generated heat and rhetoric rivalled only by the decision not to build a supersonic transport (which owed so much to the B-70) in 1971. It was a time when intelligent and personally uninvolved patriots emotion-

236

ally called for diametrically opposite courses of action affecting the security of the nation and billions of dollars. Today the United States is going through it all again, with a quite different bomber that happens to be made by the same prime contractor. But this time the programme is based on a much fuller understanding of the roles and limitations of missiles and bombers.

Such understanding was impossible 20 years ago. In any case, in 1954 it seemed to Curtis E. LeMay, Commanding General of SAC, only prudent to press for a new strategic bomber. He had a huge force equipped with the B-47 and would later have the much more capable B-52 and the supersonic B-58. But while the B-52 could carry huge loads long distances it flew at subsonic speed and seemed likely soon to experience difficulty in penetrating defended airspace. The B-58 could probably penetrate more assuredly, but it was deficient in bomb load and range. It seemed reasonable to hope that industry would shortly find a way to combine the attributes of both aircraft. LeMay asked the Secretary of Defense to consider a follow-on to the B-52 having at least the same range (5,500 nautical miles without air-refuelling) and able to operate from the same bases, yet possessing "as high a speed as possible". The clue to the demand lay in the last bit, which implied something in excess of Mach 1 and hopefully greater than Mach 2. ARDC in February 1955 issued a Requirement for two major weapon systems to meet SAC's need. One was WS-125A for a Nuclear-Powered Bomber. The other was the more conventional WS-110A. Like 125A this described a split-mission, with a cruising speed of Mach 0·9 but "the highest possible speed and altitude" in a 1,000-mile dash across enemy territory. LeMay had suggested the new bomber should be in use in 1965-75, but the WS-110A timescale envisaged the first SAC wing becoming operational in 1963.

These were stirring times, with gigantic programmes being awarded to gigantic companies. Six of the giants made bids for WS-110A on 13 July 1955. One, Convair, had already won the prime contract for the first ICBM, the challenging WS-107A that was later named Atlas, and had also won one of the study contracts for WS-125A. Lockheed was the other WS-125A finalist, and Martin was in negotiation for WS-107A-II, a follow-on ICBM that later was named Titan. Only Boeing and North American appeared to be wholly suited to tackling the job, despite their massive existing commitments, and each was awarded a Phase I design contract on 11 November 1955. Both needed every ounce of technical strength to meet what I suppose was an impossible demand. Although supersonic speed means a better engine pressure-ratio it also means dramatically increased drag and a heavier airframe and greater fuel load. To get off a standard SAC runway with a supersonic aircraft able to fly over 6,300 miles, including 1,000 miles at something like Mach 2, was demonstrably impossible. Really it required two different aircraft, so North American blandly hit on the idea of making their WS-110A take off as one aircraft and penetrate enemy airspace as another.

At take-off their proposal was a huge Mach 0·9 aircraft with a large delta foreplane filling the entire front end and the wing and engines at the back. The wing comprised a stubby tapered centre section and long-span drooping tips each carrying a fuel nacelle almost as big as a B-47. Overall length was about 150 ft, span about 260 ft and gross weight 750,000 lb. The trick lay in the fact that the 80 ft outer wings were freely hinged to the rest of the aircraft, so that each carried just the 190,000 lb weight of its fuel pod. When 1,000 miles short of the target (in fact it would have had to be closer) the pilot jettisoned the outer wings and was left with a vehicle nicely tailored to Mach 2·3. Back home again the gross weight would have fallen to under 220,000 lb and the stubby canard arrangement could provide enough lift for a normal landing. All very ingenious, except that when LeMay was shown an artist's impression of how the aircraft would look on the outward journey he exclaimed "This isn't an airplane, it's a three-plane formation". He didn't think it was exactly what SAC wanted, and when the two studies were submitted in October 1956 they were promptly rejected, as the companies had been given to expect, and replaced by six-month feasibility studies of other approaches.

Both companies re-thought the requirement. Significantly both reconsidered variable-sweep and again rejected it. Both had by now fully applied supersonic area rule and explored the furthest limits with gas-turbine engine cycles, structural materials and aerodynamic design. The only obvious thing left was "zip fuel". Gas turbines do not have to burn petroleum. It would be possible to make them run on salad oil if necessary, but this would give poor performance. In 1946 the NACA had begun somewhat academic research on high-energy fuels, mainly based on the element boron, which in theory could give considerably greater propulsive impulse than the same weight of kerosene. By 1952 the Air Force and Navy had both begun their own study programmes, and now at last it looked as if the imminent advance in combat Mach number from 2 up to the region between 3 and 5 was going to demand a widespread use of zip fuel. At the end of 1956 the DoD authorized the Air Force to build a $45 million plant at Model City, NY, to produce about 10,000 lb of boron-based zip fuel (mainly ethyl borane) per day, the plant manager being Olin Mathieson Corporation, and the Navy to build a $35 million facility at Muskogee, Okla, to be run by Callery Chemical. This decision was one of the utmost gravity. It was taken after careful analysis of future combat needs had shown, seemingly beyond doubt, that supersonic aircraft were going to make zip fuel a permanent large-scale logistic commodity. Pratt & Whitney and General Electric each received a design contract for a supersonic afterburning turbojet to use the new fuel, and WS-110A became popularly known as the chemically-powered bomber or CPB.

Very soon the greatly intensified research into the use of the exotic fuels threw up severe problems, as I shall later describe, which seemed likely to restrict their use in the initial stages to afterburners and ramjets and to prohibit an all-zip turbojet installation. The airframe contractors were concerned to learn this, because it obviously meant that the future generation of supersonic aircraft would have to have two separate fuel systems, one filled with conventional petroleum-derived fuel and the other with a boron zip fuel. This promised to be complicated and unattractive. The most sanguine prediction for the extra range the zip-fuelled after-burners might confer was a mere 9–10 per cent of the overall mission, and this did not seem a big return for the massive extra cost and difficulty. Then, early in 1957, one of the competing firms, North American Aviation, stumbled on something that seemed to offer far bigger benefits for hardly any penalty at all.

Big aerospace companies are always involved in R&D programmes, bids and feasibility studies that call for a constant effort to keep abreast of the state of the art, and this means—among many other things—conducting a ceaseless search through the published and classified literature. During one such search the NAA Los Angeles Division, where WS-110A was centred, came upon a classified paper of March 1956 entitled "Aircraft Configurations Developing High Lift/Drag Ratios at Supersonic Speeds". The authors were Alfred J. Eggers and Clarence A. Syvertson, of the NACA Langley lab in Virginia. The paper explained how a highly supersonic aircraft, flying at a Mach number of between 3 and 5, could be shaped so that it could make the most favourable use of the pressure distribution created by its own shockwaves. Essentially the shape comprised a long, slender delta wing with a substantially flat top and a half-body underneath it, rather like a mid-wing aircraft from which the top half-body has been removed. With careful juggling it was possible to obtain an optimum interaction between the wing leading-edge shockwave and the flow pattern around the half-body on the underside. The result was to increase pressure under the wing, without affecting the pressure above it. One popular report erred in precision, but hit the right descriptive picture by saying such a shape could "climb atop its own shock wave much as a speed boat rises on to its step". Eggers, who hit on the idea as he was mowing his lawn, called it "compression lift". It was like manna from Heaven.

NAA re-shaped their tunnel models, and within a week had got the first simple compression-lift shape up to a Mach number of 3·5. When the L/D ratio was plotted against angle of attack there was found to be a gain of well over 100 per cent at small angles and a peak L/D 22 per cent higher yet reached at a lower angle. The gains could fairly be described as fantastic. I suppose they rivalled in importance the discovery by another NACA researcher of the Area Rule three years earlier. Even the most cursory calculations suggested that, with further refinement, the application of compression lift could turn an impossible split-mission aircraft into a possible all-supersonic one; in other words, the bomber, instead of just making a relatively short supersonic dash, could fly supersonic all the way. In terms of meeting the WS-110A numbers this was marvellous, and probably the biggest unexpected bonus ever dropped in a planemaker's lap. Lt-Gen C. S. Irvine, DCOS for Materiel, called it "a major technical breakthrough" and said that "even a year ago optimists like myself said such a thing was impossible in so short a time". In such a situation the Air Force would always secure the maximum advantage of an open competition by passing on the "breakthrough" to rival bidders, even if the discovery had been made by one of the companies involved (which might receive a cash award or be able to patent the discovery). So Boeing were told to read the NACA paper, and very soon they also had a smaller, more practical design able to fly all the way at Mach 3. The WS-110A competition suddenly looked good.

In retrospect this was the time when the requirement should have been examined with a very critical eye. But the environment was unique. Against a background of intense competitive and political pressure from the Soviet Union the United States had made advances in aircraft flight performance that have never been paralleled either before or since. The introduction of jet propulsion in World War 2 had added only about 150 mph to bomber speed, but in the five short years between 1952 and the end of 1956 the speed of US Air Force strategic bombers had risen from 400 mph to 550 mph and thence to over 1,100 mph in a flying prototype and now to 2,000 mph in this new design. Multiplying flight speed by five in as many years had never happened even in the earliest days of flying. Military planners had always wanted more flight performance, and now at last they had it in abundance. So great had been the urge to fly faster that it seemed logical to expect the trend to continue indefinitely. The dramatic emergence of the ICBM as a practical weapon merely served to reinforce the notion that there was no obvious upper limit on speed. Many experts with whom I talked in 1956–57 took it for granted that fighters and bombers would within three or four years be flying at Mach 3, and that hypersonic air-breathers in the Mach 5–7 range would then quite soon merge into the wingless area of rocket propulsion and controllable body lift. Beyond the Century-series fighters and the Atlas missile could thus be seen a never-ending spectrum of flight vehicles extending from existing Air Force runways out through the atmosphere and into space, with the ability to boost and glide, cover vast distances, skip in and out of the fringes of the atmosphere and pull high g in atmospheric manoeuvres, while carrying all the avionics and weapons needed for useful combat missions. It was all very exciting, and science fiction all but gave up the struggle of competing with incredible reality.

Whenever the WS-110A specification was re-evaluated the main nagging doubt was "Is it bold enough?" Obviously SAC was not going to get a combat wing of these aircraft before the planned date of 1963, and even this looked optimistic in view of the magnitude of the development task. The chief worry was that further dramatic advances might make the bomber prematurely obsolete. In the old days it was easy to bring in a "Mark II" with significant improvements, but in the new breakneck race of fundamental aerodynamics, structures, systems and propulsion it was going to be almost impossible. WS-110A was in the summer of 1957 upgraded to Mach 3, 2,000 mph. Engineers and generals alike were elated, but tempered their enthusiasm with the knowledge that history might show they should have chosen 3·1. This sounds a trivial change, but it means an airframe of a slightly different shape, with slightly different engines, and with everything designed to soak at a temperature just over 100° F hotter. Having built the bomber it would be practically impossible suddenly to bring in a Mark II version capable of Mach 3·1. This sort of problem was very real and understandable. It was perhaps simpler to comprehend than the more fundamental issues, which were: why should a bomber fly at Mach 3 (or 3·1, or whatever) rather than Mach 2, or Mach 0·9; why should it fly at 65,000 ft altitude (or 78,000, or whatever) rather than at 1,000 ft or at 200 ft; how vulnerable will it be against the likely defence systems of the late 1960s; how vulnerable will it be on the ground, and how does it compare with the ICBM?

Undoubtedly these questions were asked, but the answers were either bent or ignored, because a fair analysis of any of them ought to have been enough to cause major changes or even stop the programme. Hindsight suggests the WS-110A was a little like the giant bombers of the past. General "Hap" Arnold, US Army Air Force chief in World War 2, described the Barling of 1923, the B-15 of 1937 and the B-19 of 1941 as "examples of the full-scale method of securing data". All were huge bombers which I do not believe could have withstood the modern criterion of cost/effectiveness for five minutes, yet all were built and flown. The Barling cost $500,000, and was built in a special hangar that cost $700,000,

adding up to a sum greater than the total book value of all aircraft in the
Army Air Corps in 1923! The lumbering B-15 and B-19 took the bill into
the millions, yet either could easily have been shot down by a single round
from a German flak-88. With the WS-110A the research-cost alone ran
up a bill exceeding a billion. Undoubtedly the research, into new materials,
structures, tools and many other areas, would have been done anyway;
much of it had been started when the Air Force first aimed at Mach 3
and a 600° F soak temperature in 1952, and it would be unfair to charge
all of it against this one programme. The point I am making is that by
the time WS-110A came along the costs had reached astronomic levels,
and one needed to be very sure indeed that one was spending wisely.

Today the whole concept of a giant bomber flying at supersonic speed
at high altitude but still within the atmosphere has been discredited.
Mach 3 means it cannot suddenly depart from a straight and level trajectory; it is very simple to plot its future position within quite a narrow cone
extending ahead of it, and this dramatically simplifies the interception
problem. Its radar signature is likely to be large and distinctive, and its
attempts to confuse the defences by ECM are severely handicapped for
reasons which all stem from its high speed. There are countless other inter-
related factors, but it is not too much to claim that the WS-110A might
not have been much more difficult a target to the ultimate radar-directed
AA guns than would a B-17 taking evasive action at 20,000 ft. Shooting
it down by even an early SAM, such as Nike-Hercules or Bloodhound,
would in my view have been no trouble at all. Some people still strongly
dispute such an assertion; they might refuse to listen to General John B.
Medaris, USA, who was first commander of the Army Missile Command,
but they could hardly ignore the views of impartial Secretaries of Defense.
The relevant argument is not that the bomber had been made obsolete
by the missile. This trite belief was the cause of a decade of sadly wrong
decisions, especially in Britain, from 1955 to 1965, largely because governments and their advisers had not done their homework properly. When
WS-110A was about to move into hardware development in 1957 many
people, including senior officials in the Pentagon, thought the big argument
was "Does the ICBM make the manned bomber archaic?" In fact the real
question was "Is WS-110A the right sort of strategic bomber?" Curiously,
hardly anyone seems to have asked this. The notion that the right sort of
bomber might have been smaller and slower, and flying very much lower,
would have seemed retrograde and unbelievable.

So WS-110A stayed the fastest and highest-flying bomber it was possible
to imagine. I even saw a classified report which said that a supersonic dash-
capability (in the original split-mission) sufficed to give "over-target
invulnerability". I cannot help thinking this belief stemmed from the very

early 1950s and was somehow insufficiently questioned later on. Certainly by 1957 the sharpening visibility of SAM systems was making bomber proponents a little less anxious to talk about over-target invulnerability or over-target anything. Instead the new bomber became increasingly viewed as a carrier of a stand-off missile, a launcher for ballistic missiles, a parent vehicle for hypersonic devices such as the Dyna-Soar, and a flexible transport system that could fit the existing SAC bases and attack an enemy from any direction, or fulfil any of the duties—such as reconnaissance, damage-assessment, strike on mobile or imprecisely known targets, or post-ICBM "gap filling"—that could not be performed by the otherwise valuable ICBM. There is no doubt that it would have been grossly foolish to abandon WS-110A (as many experts suggested when it could be seen the Atlas was going to work), because the need for a manned bomber was just as great in 1957 as it had ever been. All that the ICBM brought was a much more effective, and much more certain, method of delivering a modest-size nuclear warhead to a particular geographic location in some enemy country. Practically the only target suitable for an early ICBM was a city; with much better accuracy the later ICBMs have learned how to attack smaller fixed targets such as an ICBM silo or an aircraft runway, but its position must be accurately known in advance. Even today there is a very great deal the ICBM cannot do, and a long-range bomber forms its ideal partner. But it was a very big mistake indeed to plan WS-110A as a mere extension of the traditional bomber mission to "speeds in excess of 2,000 mph above 70,000 feet" in the hopeful belief that this made it able to penetrate defended territory.

Of course, the US Air Force knew all about low flying as a means of trying to penetrate underneath an enemy's early-warning umbrella of powerful radars. Like the RAF, which had looked at studies for special low-flying bombers from six companies in 1952-55, the USAF had conducted very extensive research and study programmes into precisely this area and was most concerned to find ways of improving the ability of its existing B-47 and B-52 to operate in the low-level role. WS-110A was not conceived in ignorance of what could be done at low level but in the belief that 2,000 mph at 70,000 ft was the lesser of two evils. It just happened to be an unfortunate fact of life that an aircraft designed to cruise at this speed and altitude crystallized into a design extremely unsuitable for the low-level mission, unless it could be made to incorporate extensive variable geometry. Today this is being done with the B-1, but in 1957 the WS-110A stayed inflexibly optimized to the extreme speed at extreme altitude. The only variable geometry that North American incorporated (apart from the retractable landing gear) was the very advanced engine inlet system and the hinged wing-tips which could be folded down to 25° or 65° to improve directional stability and cut down the lift generated far aft of the c.g. and thus reduce the lift needed from the canard foreplane. Although these folding wing tips were the biggest variable-geometry surfaces on any aircraft they did not help the bomber much at low level. From the start it was thought to be impossible to devise a useful WS-110A submission that could fly at low level except at subsonic speed.

North American were always the leading bidder on the programme and had several times in 1950–57 been top defence contractor in terms of total value of military business. The company's best-known products were the F-86 Sabre and F-100 Super Sabre fighters, but in fact the biggest single contract of the whole of the early 1950s was NAA's $691 million to develop and test the XSM-64A Navaho. Today few people remember Navaho, which was to have formed a bridge between the bomber and the ICBM. A canard delta like WS-110A, but designed to 1952 aerodynamics that were extensively explored with the X-10 research vehicle, Navaho was a pilotless supersonic bomber of great size that took off vertically riding on the back of a booster driven by three huge rocket engines. What made it so expensive was that it was the principal vehicle for the development of the entire first generation of large-rocket technology in the United States. Upon the back of Navaho came two giant new divisions of NAA, the Autonetics division which for a vital decade spearheaded the technology of inertial guidance and the Rocketdyne division which did the same in the field of large liquid rocket engines. Having built up a huge organization to develop and build Navaho, NAA watched with mixed feelings as the even more radical Atlas ICBM rode into the sky on its Rocketdyne engines that, but for Navaho, would not have existed. Obviously the Air Force considered the ICBM made all winged missiles obsolete, and in July 1957 Navaho was cancelled. Although NAA saw it coming, it had no option but to dismiss more than 5,000 technical staff and shake up the Los Angeles division violently. If Navaho had lived, the WS-110A might have been won by Boeing; with Navaho cancelled I think NAA would have had to be singularly inept not to win. The Air Force evaluation team descended on NAA on 14 October 1957 and the award of the potentially giant programme to NAA was announced on 23 December. On 6 February 1958 the programme was redesignated B-70, and—following a SAC contest in which 20,000 (presumably different) names were submitted—the name Valkyrie was chosen for the bomber on 3 July 1958.

In fact I am being mischievous in suggesting that NAA won the B-70 simply because they lost Navaho. Their submission received the unanimous vote of SAC, the Air Materiel Command and the ARDC (which was about to be renamed Aeronautical Systems Command). The Air Force Chief of Staff was General Thomas D. White, the Secretary of the Air

Force James A. Douglas and the Secretary for Defense Neil McElroy, and all concurred with the choice. At the prime contractor the top man was James H. "Dutch" Kindelberger, NAA founder and board chairman. Unlike the situation with the ICBMs, which were being managed as systems by a separate *ad hoc* organization, NAA was judged capable of managing the whole of WS-110A just as Convair had managed the B-58 programme. Primary responsibility devolved upon the company's Los Angeles division, the general manager of which was Raymond H. Rice who as chief engineer had led the design of the F-86 Sabre and F-100 Super Sabre. Rice had also been deeply involved in the top management of the incredible design that had won the division the B-70, the biggest and most challenging programme any aircraft manufacturer had ever been awarded. It was marvellous, and promised to do far more than merely replace Navaho; but it was a bit daunting. Kindelberger said "I've been in this business for more than 40 years, and I've never seen anything like the engineering solution to this problem".

This engineering solution has been described many times and is far too involved to deal with in much detail here. In my view the best technical description of the B-70 is that written by Iain Pike and published in *Flight International* for 25 June and 2 July 1964, when the engineering design had been declassified but before the aircraft flew. The only point Pike did not make is that the B-70 was rendered possible only because of the immense wealth of fundamental research previously accomplished into Mach 3 structures and systems, much of it funded by the Air Force and started in 1952 when even Mach 1 was a challenge. Nearly all the system development was done by industry, but a great deal of fundamental research into propulsion and aerodynamics was accomplished by the NACA. Dr Hugh L. Dryden, Director of the NACA, said in February 1958 that "About a year ago a strange and wonderful thing happened. It was as if the pieces of a jigsaw puzzle began falling into place. Almost simultaneously research programs that had been underway at the NACA labs in Virginia, California and Ohio began to pay off . . .". The NACA contribution to the B-70 was immense. Before 1958 was out the organization had vanished into the far larger NASA, and Dryden had become No 2 to the first NASA Administrator James E. Webb. Since then NASA has instantly conjured up "space" rather than "aeronautics", but its title contains both words.

NACA's compression-lift discovery brought about total redesign of the NAA aircraft. The discardable outer wings were abandoned, the wing was made a 65·5° delta of almost pure form, the afterburning turbojet engines were packaged in a colossal box under the wing, and the foreplane was carried on a slender fuselage cantilevered ahead of the apex of the

245

wing and tapered off rearwards to leave an unimpeded dorsal surface. Flight control was assigned to trailing-edge elevons for roll, the elevons were geared to a flapped canard surface (foreplane) for pitch, and two vertical slab rudders were used for yaw. The basically conventional bogie landing gears all retracted into the engine box. Fuel, planned to be about three parts a special hydrocarbon for the engines and two parts zip fuel for the afterburners, was arranged in enormous integral tanks filling the wing and rear body. Between the engine inlet ducts, immediately behind the nose gear, was a weapon bay tailored to the biggest free-fall 20-megaton bomb in SAC use, covered by a rearward-sliding door; there were also several projected ways of carrying ballistic missiles and other devices externally. The flight crew of four were to be housed between the canard and the radar-filled pointed nose. As there was nothing but clear space behind it upward-ejection seats seemed practical. Even then the seats were far from ordinary, for each was to be rocket-assisted and arranged to close up into a sealed capsule during the ejection sequence to protect the occupant against what might be a 2,000 mph slipstream; but the relative ease of abandoning ship contrasted with almost everything else about the B-70 that was difficult in the extreme.

The extensive use of digital and analog computers merely made the B-70 possible; it still needed more R&D man-hours than any previous aircraft. General Anderson, ARDC Commander, put the figure at 14,500,000 and noted this was 70 times the work-load needed to design the B-17. In fact, although the B-70 combat equipment was abandoned at an early stage, the number of engineering man-hours actually exceeded 21 million. This is a very conservative estimate because with over 800 major industrial suppliers involved it is impossible to calculate a comprehensive total. What is interesting is that the design effort was greater than that needed for the first ICBM. (When they checked this chapter the former B-70 engineers pointed out that, on a basis of man-hours per pound of gross weight, the B-70 total was "lower than that for the B-52, B-58 and several supersonic fighters".)

Perhaps half the total engineering load was expended on the airframe structure. Old-time stressmen—who are the real "designers" of aircraft—will be glad to learn that even in the computer age everything has to be recorded in vast books. Admittedly in these the computer print-outs are more numerous than the typewritten sheets and the typescript is more common than handwriting, but the principle of having a written record remains. I once saw some of the books on B-70 elastic analysis, just one facet of dozens on the airframe design, and gave up counting at 54 volumes. Each contained literally millions of complex calculations, and even these ignored the sums done elsewhere to relate the stress results to commercial and timing considerations. For example, an extra thousandth of an inch on the wing skin would have added a ton to the structure weight; other people had to work out the correct skin gauges and tolerances in the light of what appeared to be the best compromise in terms of cost and timing. What made it so much harder was that the materials were largely new ones, or at least never before used in such big pieces. Where do you get it from? What ought the price to be? Never before had such questions been so difficult, nor applicable to the whole of such a huge aircraft.

Roughly 69 per cent of the structure weight was brazed sandwich in a relatively new stainless steel known as PH 15–7 Mo which, to make life harder, had to be either hot-creep formed at 1200° F or deep-freeze formed at −100° F. Each panel, perhaps 10 or 20 feet long, comprised a fine honeycomb core with a facing sheet bonded on each side. The core material thickness was generally about 0·006 in, as thick as the paper of this page, and although it came in huge sheets no wrinkle was allowed anywhere. The core was often far from flat, but had to be accurately profiled, often using a skin-mill taken off F-100 production and converted to profile the honeycomb by electrochemical means. Every part of the core and skins had to be exactly the right shape, and fit with an air gap less than 0·002 in; then it had to be tack-welded or tack-brazed and finally brazed all over in a giant furnace, retort, salt bath or electric blanket (methods were devised of using all four techniques with extreme precision). It seemed appropriate that a major ingredient of the brazing alloy was large ingots of sterling silver. These stainless honeycomb panels were works of art, with surfaces like mirrors, immense strength and rigidity at temperatures around 600° F and extreme dimensional accuracy. They cost a great deal of money, and I doubt that they would be used so extensively today, but to NAA they were the best answer to the formidable problems of strength, lightness, rigidity, low heat-transfer, immunity to intense noise, good fatigue resistance and a smooth exterior skin.

There were about 100 main honeycomb panels, the only other major parts of primary structure being the sine-wave corrugated spars, made by Convair, and the sharp machined leading and trailing edges. Everything was fastened together by extremely advanced welding, the main method being machine fusion welding by the TIG (tungsten/inert-gas) system. A seemingly endless succession of clever machines and devices helped towards perfect welds, including several using remote TV control, numerical control and even intelligent computer control. One of the simplest yet most effective devices was the Skate, which ran along a precision track while simultaneously welding, milling or grinding, and inspecting. Thousands of problems in distortion, cracking, loss of material properties and other illnesses had to be overcome.

Some of the hottest parts of the airframe were even made of René 41 refractory alloy, while the most highly stressed fittings were of H-11 tool steel. Another very special stainless steel was selected for the hydraulic piping, operating at 4,000 lb/sq in which in the United States is still a very unusual level. The only part of the airframe that was in any way conventional was the snaky forward fuselage, and even this was almost wholly of special alloys of titanium.

GE was the winner on the great propulsion system. It comprised a battery of six J93 single-shaft variable-stator engines arranged side-by-side and fed with air through what is still by far the biggest inlet-duct system ever created. The engine box measured roughly 7 ft deep, 37 ft wide and 110 ft long. At the front was a vertical knife-edge like the bow of a supersonic battleship that split the airflow into right and left ducts and also bled off boundary layer into a chute underneath. Each inner wall, about the size of the wall of a large room, was perforated and movable and adopted a profile that was varied according to the Mach number. The inlet control system was assigned to Hamilton Standard, who a week earlier had begun work on the equally vital environmental control system. HamStan's Charles Kearns told me "It's just the sort of job we like, a real challenge. . . . In fact I'd rather not say too much until we've done it." Making the vast walls of the duct shape themselves exactly according to the engine demands, with split-second reaction, was indeed a massive challenge. In fact it was too much for poor HamStan, and in the end NAA had to take the control system back and develop it "in house". It was easily the most advanced air inlet system ever created, and is still unsurpassed.

The J93 itself was a fairly conventional single-shaft turbojet with a variable-stator compressor operating at what was in 1957 a high pressure-ratio and an air-cooled turbine operating at what is still a high temperature even today. The J93-5 was planned to burn JP-6, a specially prepared and filtered kerosene-type fuel that could soak at 450° F without depositing "coke" and "sludge", while the afterburner was designed to use a zip fuel, principally ethyl borane. It was never my lot to hear a J93 running at full power on zip fuel, but I am told it was the noisiest turbojet in history. Six of them would have made the B-70 an environmental problem that not even HamStan and NAA together could have cured.

Secondary power systems were nothing short of fantastic. The hydraulic system, filled with 260 gal of a new fluid called Oronite 70, served 85 linear actuators, 44 hydraulic motors and many other items, with total horsepower measured in thousands and all made of new materials capable of operating at 630° F. Seals were metallic, and an idea of the scope of the four systems is provided by NAA's estimate that—leaving aside temperature considerations—a system made of conventional parts would have weighed 10,000 lb *more*. For electrics, each of the six engines drove a 60 kVA brushless rotating-rectifier generator feeding 240/416V current for over 600 services! A "flood-flow safety system" was installed so that, should the pressure cabin be damaged, ram air could keep it at full pressure (but, as it would roast the crew and electronics, the aircraft would have to slow down). The environmental system, fuel system, flight controls and many other systems were all packed with interest and by far the biggest and mostest the world had ever seen. Contracts were placed with Boeing-Seattle to make the wing, Lockheed-Georgia to design and build the aft fuselage, Chance Vought to produce the rudders and elevons, Cleveland Pneumatic to make the landing gear (with each bogie having a fifth wheel serving as an anti-skid reference), Sundstrand to manage secondary power systems, IBM to handle the bomb/nav system, GE the "unjammable" radar, Sperry the radically new twin-gyro platform, Autonetics the stellar-inertial navigation system, AiResearch the central air-data system, John Oster the engine-instrumentation system (of a totally new form), Westinghouse the highly classified electronic shield (what today would be called defensive avionics) that was to protect the B-70 against missile interception, and Beech the unique "alert pod" which was to accompany the B-70 everywhere and enable it to make quick getaways in three minutes without external aid (but which was so secret that Beech could only claim they had won the job of making "a special power device"). Perhaps the most impressive thing about these awards is that every one was the result of competitive bidding, usually in a battle between six and 14 companies but in one case (Chance Vought's tail surfaces) involving 21. Bearing in mind the formidable challenge posed by every single nut and bolt on the B-70 —and I mean this strictly literally—could there be any more telling testimony than this to the United States' industrial power?

By the spring of 1959 Ray Rice was able to announce that all major subcontracts had been let, both for the B-70 and for the North American F-108 Rapier long-range intercepter that was virtually a twin-J93 scale of the B-70 stressed to serve as a long-range missile-armed interceptor. He thought 70 per cent of the funds for the B-70 would be channelled to the "more than 20,000 firms . . . which will participate in the program to strengthen this country's capability to deter an atomic war". Early in March 1959 more than 200 of the Air Force's top engineers spent ten days at NAA Los Angeles division to check the most minute details of the design and the programme at the first Development Engineering Inspection (DEI). A month later came the first Mock-up Conference, when 20 technical teams examined the B-70's operational suitability. The conference chairman was Col John J. Smith, ARDC Deputy Chief of Strategic Systems; conference recorder was Col Ted L. Bishop, who had chaired the DEI. One point that emerged forcefully was the magnitude of the SAC training programme needed, in view of the fact that just over half the men who would look after the B-70 in service would have less than 18 months' experience. I felt such experience would not be of particular help because everything learned before, even for the B-58, would have to be unlearned for the B-70.

While these two milestones were being passed, General White was testifying to the need for the B-70 before the Senate Armed Services Committee, and President Eisenhower was putting his signature to a Fiscal 1960 budget making increased provision for the B-70 and F-108 and naming these two aircraft as leading the new types on which "much of the effort in 1960 will center". Outwardly these two programmes seemed the biggest and best things in manned aircraft, but in fact behind the scenes there were the greatest possible problems. One concerned zip fuel; a second concerned the need for a Mach 3 fighter; a third concerned the viability of the B-70; and a fourth stemmed from the success of the Atlas and Titan, the funding of the newer Polaris and Minuteman and the astronomical rate at which these huge missile programmes could eat up the budget. Both aircraft were about to experience an agonizing period of reappraisal, the first of many occasions when decisions had to be taken contrary to the success achieved technically and the strongly expressed wishes of the customer. Americans were in for a bad time. They still saw themselves as leaders of the Free World, and in this context were almost unanimous in promoting American armed might, American technical dominance and a seemingly natural belief that if a new fighter or bomber could be built then built it should be, and fast. Today after years of self-questioning mainly triggered off by Viet-Nam there is no unanimity at all over such fundamental matters.

The first casualty was zip fuel. On 12 August 1959, a matter of days before the USAF and Navy plants were about to go "on stream", the Department of Defense terminated the whole programme. At first it looked as if nobody need do more than tear up the invitation cards for the opening ceremonies, but although the decision never made big newspaper headlines —because it sounded technical and so could not be understood by the public—Congress immediately wanted to know a bit more of the background. Overton Brooks, Chairman of the House Committee on Science and Astronautics, called in some top people to explain; and I am obliged to him, because otherwise I doubt that much of the tale would have got on the public record. Rear-Admiral Bob Dixon, Chief of BuAer (then just being merged into the new BuWeps), explained how zip fuel was no longer needed by the Navy in view of the decision (soon reversed) to buy slow fighters designed as launch platforms for fast intercepter missiles. Joseph V.

Charyk, Air Force Assistant Secretary for R&D, dwelt at length on the increasing technical problems encountered with boron-based fuels, which had made it ever more apparent that "the early promise . . . could not be realized on a timely and economical basis". Numerical data were left to Emerson W. Conlon, Assistant Director of Research of the new NASA, who explained the way boron compounds tended in a microsecond or two to turn into a solid during combustion, passing as a sandy dust out of the jet pipe when only partly burned; or, if they did burn, they generated fresh compounds that condensed to liquid at about 3,000° F and became solid around 850°, leaving the most horrible deposits it was possible to imagine. This was on top of problems due to toxicity and extreme difficulty of handling, pumping and injection. Representative Brooks called the hearings to find out "why it took the service five years and more than $200 million to determine that they have no requirement for the fuel". After the hearings he must have wondered why the zip saga was ever begun.

Of course the elimination of zip from the B-70 was a major reason for the dropping of the whole boron programme, not a consequence of it. It was early in 1959 that the decision in principle to use only conventional petroleum-derived fuel in the B-70 was taken, without much regret (but it was not announced). GE had already built a J93-3 with an afterburner designed to use conventional fuel, and the division of the airframe fuel system to handle both liquids had not progressed far into hardware. Compared with the far from finalized J93-5 the -3 engine gave about 3 per cent less thrust, and the decision to drop high-energy fuel in theory cut about 10 per cent off the aircraft range; but Charyk told Congress the improved flight efficiency (really a matter of higher L/D) of the B-70 made range-extension by using zip fuel much less important than it had been a year previously. Today, some 14 years later, high-energy fuels are conspicuously absent from the announced future plans of any air force in the world. These 14 years have seen the entire emphasis placed on consolidating the gains made in 1950–55 up to Mach 2·5, and in improving the hardware of structures, propulsion and systems (especially those for avionics and guidance). The great momentum of the advance up the scale of flight Mach number has been dissipated, and although both the US Air Force and Navy continue to fund small study programmes into high-energy fuels these are not narrowly concentrated upon boron and, unless I am grossly in error, are not likely to lead to any imminent service use. Overton Brooks was only doing his duty in questioning the sudden abandonment of what had seemed a good idea, and which the Congress had liberally supported, but in work on the frontiers of technology under the spur of potential military threats it is impossible to avoid the occasional big mistake. Hindsight shows that zip fuel should have stayed in the laboratory and not become a reason for huge production plants. Around 1957 I doubt if anyone had the combination of knowledge, second-sight and self-assurance to say so, but by 1959 the scene was very different.

Loss of zip fuel was really no great hurt to the B-70, and in terms of cost/effectiveness probably improved it. But this same rather slick yard-stick was already hurting the programme very much indeed, especially as the torrent of dollars flowing into the ICBM programmes had already dramatically slashed the money available for military aircraft. The first two ICBM programmes, Atlas and Titan, had gone extraordinarily fast and well, but the setting up of a whole new industry involving hundreds of suppliers skilled in new fields, using new tools and materials, and with final assembly at enormous plants on what had been virgin territory, jacked up the bill the Air Force had to face until by 1960 it handsomely exceeded three billion dollars. By this time plans were far advanced for a completely new and radically different ICBM, Minuteman, again to be created by a new industry housed in totally new plants. Throughout 1959 it looked touch and go as though the B-70 would be cancelled. Its stable-mate, the F-108, was abruptly stopped in September 1959, automatically increasing the B-70 bill by throwing on to the bomber the whole development burden of the J93 engine and much of the structural and systems tech-nology. Many people in Washington were surprised that the B-70 did not accompany the Mach 3 fighter into oblivion. That it did not was largely because of the sincere and urgent fight put up by General White, in what was probably the most difficult of all his battles in the political arena.

He did not really have a very convincing case. Most of the leaders of the Air Force felt in their bones it would be a grave mistake to leave the whole burden of the deterrent to the new ICBMs, because of the strictly limited range of missions these could fulfil. But the B-70 was now in-creasingly being regarded as an ineffectual competitor, and some thought it merely an extremely expensive way of getting shot down. It was quite unsuited to conventional warfare, did not look half as attractive as the ICBM in a nuclear war, was very difficult to alter, and could not launch an ALBM any better than could the B-52. It was burning up money at a prodigious rate, and the mind boggled at the cost of putting it into the SAC inventory. On 1 December 1959 Thomas S. Gates Jr replaced Neil McElroy as Defense Secretary and found the decision had already been taken to drop the B-70 as a bomber. A few days later it was announced that the programme had been "reoriented" to a single prototype, to fly in December 1962 and to be flight-tested until 1966. Plans for production were shelved, and all work on the military subsystems was terminated. The Fiscal 1961 budget of $365 million was cut to $75 million. This seemed a fair compromise, in that it saved a lot of money while keeping open the option of one day having squadrons of B-70s if this should later appear desirable. But the decision generated a furious reflex action by the Air Force Association, which said the word "reorienting" really meant "gutting". So it did, and the patriotic cry to restore the B-70 was echoed by a thousand editors across the United States who angrily implied— sometimes in very direct wording—that those who had gutted the B-70 were thoughtless if not traitorous people whose sole concern was to balance the defence budget by sacrificing vital weapons. Usually the Americans are very good at communicating, but I think on this occasion a little more might have been done to explain that the B-70 did not appear as attractive as it had three or four years earlier and that the public's money could be better spent.

I greeted the news with relief. Although it was obvious SAC would one day have to have a completely new and versatile bomber, the B-70 was not the right aircraft. Having taken the painful decision, I thought the Air Force would now take a fresh look at the strategic scene and eventually fund a quick-reacting, short-field, highly efficient low-level penetrator that could also do a good job in conventional war. To my amazement, when the Skybolt missile went ahead in 1960 the B-70 was named in the list of carriers, and late in January that year the Air Force released a further $95 million for work on the prototype B-70 and on the bomb-nav system which was one of those that had been explicitly terminated. Obviously a good bomb-nav system is a great national asset that could be transferred to a later aircraft, but it gradually became evident that the Air Force was at pains to portray the B-70 as an ongoing bomber programme. In May I was informed, by letter, "The B-70 is in active development for Strategic Air Command. . . . It will be the Air Force's primary strategic manned weapon system after 1967 . . . The bombing and navigation subsystem is one of its most vital parts. This already has been flight-tested for several hundred hours, and is designed to incorporate a future capacity for accurate missile launching . . . The Air Force is continuing to fund the other subsystems you mention . . ." I wondered if anyone had told the Secretary of Defense. Clearly there was a big cauldron bubbling, and it was anyone's guess how long it would simmer before cooling off. Suddenly, in October 1960, the Pentagon put out a short statement blandly announcing that the B-70 had been "restored to full weapon-system status". IBM, Westinghouse, Beech and all the other suppliers could stop hiding their military systems, and the only subcontractor really hurt seemed to be Boeing which had given back the B-70's wing to North American (it seemed preferable to clear the Seattle decks for the new 727 and the development of the Minuteman ICBM). In November the DoD bumped

253

up the FY61 funding to $265 million, pointing out how useful the B-70 would be to the SST programme which was then a burning issue. I could not see why a B-70 bomber would be of any greater help to the SST than a B-70 research aircraft, especially as no attempt was made to regain the year's slippage in the timing.

It was an extraordinary programme by this time, fully worthy of Britain in that it seemed to have become just too difficult to take a decision and stick to it. On 20 January 1961 John F. Kennedy entered the White House and Robert S. McNamara the Pentagon. McNamara was well briefed on the B-70. He had perhaps begun to suffer slightly from having made up his mind, so that he did not want to be bothered by the facts, but I think he usually made it up very well. From the start he told the Air Force he was unconvinced about manned bombers. The Air Force tried to sell him what it said was a totally new animal called the RS-70, the new initials standing for "reconnaissance-strike". It was to be a multi-sensor carrier capable of rushing across an enemy land hit by an ICBM strike and of dropping bombs or missiles on anything that had been missed. But it was different from the B-70 only in the subsystems, and at no time did McNamara show enthusiasm. In April President Kennedy announced the programme was being cut back to three prototypes, without military subsystems, and he pointed out that even this would cost $1,300 million before completion in 1967 or some $500 million more than had already been spent. (Later the estimate was put at $1,500 million; NAA never accepted such high estimates, claiming that the assumed learning-curve was unreasonable.)

But the argument continued to rage. McNamara, whose lightning brain had not endeared him to generals and so-called aviation lobbyists, soon became Enemy No 1 to the still powerful and vociferous forces that clamoured for fleets of B-70s to darken the sky. Warren E. Swanson, who today is v-p engineering for the North American Rockwell Aerospace Group, was the XB-70 programme director. He believes the XB-70 high-altitude mission "is valid today"; he reminds me that the B-70 could fly at a sustained Mach 0·9-plus at sea level for a useful range, could do a LABS manoeuvre and would have had a structural-mode ride control (which was tested at the time, but not on an XB-70); and he also reminds me about radar-absorbent material to reduce the barn-door cross-section, of the belief that an intercepting missile would have to fly at "Mach 4 to Mach 6" and that there were no adequate infra-red windows through which an IR-homing missile could look. But Hawker Siddeley Dynamics will certainly quarrel with the last claim, and I am afraid I still side with the antis.

I am in good company. In January 1962 McNamara was called before

Congress to explain why he opposed the B-70, and it is worth recalling
what he said:

". . . We have again re-studied the role of the B-70 in future strategic
retaliatory forces, and again have reached the conclusion that the B-70 will
not provide enough of an increase in our offensive capabilities to justify
its very high cost . . . The principal advantage of the B-70 is its ability,
in common with other manned bombers, to operate under positive control
and to deliver a large number of nuclear weapons in a single sortie.
Considering the increasing capabilities of ground-to-air missiles, the speed
and altitude of the B-70, in itself, would no longer be a very significant
advantage. Furthermore, it has not been designed for the use of air-to-
surface missiles such as Hound Dog or Skybolt, and in a low-altitude
attack it must fly at subsonic speeds. In addition, the B-70 is not well
suited to an era when both sides have large numbers of ICBMs. It would
be more vulnerable on the ground than hardened missiles, and it does not
lend itself to airborne-alert measures.

"Nevertheless, we plan to complete the limited development programme
outlined to the Congress last year—namely, to demonstrate the technical
feasibility of the aircraft structure and configuration, as well as certain
major subsystems required in a high-speed, high-altitude environment.
This approach would still preserve the option of developing a manned
bomber if we should later determine that such a system is required.

"The Air Force has studied the reorientation of the B-70 to a
reconnaissance/strike vehicle. Such an aircraft might be useful in providing
damage-assessment and reconnaissance information for the retargeting of
the missile force during the attack period. It would also have a capability
to attack previously unlocated, undetected or incompletely destroyed
targets. Obviously this proposal will require a great deal more study to
determine whether the advantages to be gained from such an aircraft are
worth the great costs involved."

To me this was only common sense, but in March 1962 the powerful
House Armed Services Committee, chaired by formidable Carl Vinson,
"directed" the Secretary of the Air Force to spend $311 million, on top
of the $180 million already voted, to pay for three fully equipped RS-70s.
I do not believe Congressional committees have the authority to "direct"
the actions of the executive; anyway McNamara at once issued a detailed
statement demolishing the RS-70. After noting that the Air Force, having
urged production of the B-70 bomber, was now "implicitly rejecting" that
programme by switching to the RS-70, the Defense Secretary observed:
"We calculate that the strategic retaliatory forces programed through 1967
could achieve practically complete destruction of the enemy target system
—even after absorbing an initial nuclear attack. The addition of a force of

either 200 B-70s, which was proposed last year by the Air Force, or the 150 RS-70s now being considered, either of which would cost about $10 billion, would not appreciably change this result. . . .

"With regard to the wartime reconnaissance capabilities of the RS-70, we have other means of performing that function and with any adequate high-processing-rate radar system which may be developed, the B-52s and B-58s could have a considerable reconnaissance and bomb damage assessment capability incident to their principal mission. We think that the B-52s and B-58s, arriving after our missiles have suppressed the enemy's air defense, could penetrate as well, or almost as well, as the RS-70.

"A decision by the Soviet Union to produce and deploy an anti-ICBM system could not significantly change this over-all picture, and in any event would be no less effective against the B-70 and its missiles . . .". He went on to doubt the capability of developing an RS-70 high-resolution radar by 1970, to doubt the ability of communications to transmit the reconnaissance data and to doubt that humans could interpret it fast enough. Not forgetting the strike role, he opined the RS-70 would "require the development of new air-launched strike missiles . . . because of their limited size and warhead yield would have to be far more accurate than any strategic air-launched missile now in production or development". McNamara was altogether too brilliant for a lot of Congressmen.

According to former colonel Ted Bishop, whom I mentioned earlier, the Lockheed A-11/YF-12A/SR-71 played a significant role at this time. Kelly Johnson's secretly produced family had a demonstrated Mach 3 performance and their presence "in the wings" was McNamara's trump card against such people as Curtis LeMay and Carl Vinson. In any case the Defense Secretary promised "a thorough review" of the RS-70 proposal. This gave the Vinson Committee an "out"; they took it, and withdrew their so-called directive. For FY63 Congress voted a large $362 million, with the intention that this would help fund three RS-70 flight vehicles plus a static test airframe, but in fact by this time the programme had been agreed between the Air Force and the prime contractor as two two-seat aircraft called XB-70A and a four-seat aircraft with military subsystems called XB-70B. In December 1962 the cancellation of the Skybolt ALBM drew sour comments from several senators—and doubtless from many other Congressmen—who argued that they had accepted the denial of the production B-70 only on the understanding that the B-52/Skybolt combination would become available. Worse was to come (worse for them, that is); in February 1964 Congress voted to hold the whole programme to a total of $1,500 million, and whereas three years earlier $1,300 million would have bought three flight vehicles, by 1964 $1,500 million would buy only two. The XB-70B was eliminated, and the

sole return for the huge outlay was two aircraft devoid of military equipment and equipped solely to gather flight data for pure R&D purposes.

By this time the first XB-70A had been almost completed. It should
have been finished more than two years earlier, but tens of thousands of
unforeseen man-hours were expended in trying to seal the fuel tanks. As
described earlier, the fuel was to be carried in huge bays formed by the
precision welded panels of brazed steel honeycomb sandwich. Nearly all
of these panels were Armco PH 15-7, but many of the interfaces were of
H-11 tool steel or, near the jet-pipes, René 41. When the supposedly
finished fuel tanks were heated to Mach 3 temperatures, around 470° F
over most of the skin but much hotter near leading edges, and then flexed
to simulate flight conditions while internally pressurized to 20 lb/sq in
by nitrogen, fuel seeped from all the joints and vaporized in huge smoke
clouds. A year of intense research and the fuel was still seeping. Part of
the trouble was corrosion caused by water during ultrasonic cleaning and
inspection, but the root cause was that the faying surfaces of the joints
were too narrow, and spot welds caused minute pin-holes. The cure was
Viton sealer, cured at 350–400° F. Ultimately, by May 1964, only the
narrow U-shaped No 5 tank, at the extreme rear of the almost vanished
"fuselage", remained impossible to seal properly and it was left empty, as
noted early in this chapter. No attempt was made to rework the tank even
though four months were spent after roll-out preparing the monster in the
hot sunshine with its seven tons of instrumentation. Finally, on 21 September 1964 the Air Force project pilot Col Joe Cotton and NAA chief test
pilot Al (Alvin) White walked out to No 20001 knowing this time they
weren't just going up and down the Palmdale runway; this time they were
going to fly, and incidentally deliver the B-70 to its owners at Edwards.

Long before that date I had seen a flight plan which gave the rotation
speed, at which the pilot lifts the aircraft off the ground, as 150 knots.
On the first flight V_R was actually set at 183 knots, and this was described
as "within three knots of the planned take-off speed", so somebody had
second thoughts, perhaps on the consequences of losing an outer engine.
Everything seemed fine as the 30 miles to Edwards were covered, still in
the take-off configuration. Then, in preparation to going upstairs for a
possible run at over Mach 1 (to earn NAA a bonus of $250,000), the
canard flap and landing gear were raised. Unfortunately the main gears
stayed resolutely down, and the agreed drill in this eventuality was to
lower the nose gear and proceed with an alternative flight plan at low
speeds. After shutting down an engine which showed as overspeeding, the
B-70 was brought across Edwards at 50 feet to evaluate low-speed handling.
Finally a good landing was made, with excellent directional control helped
by the pull of three 28-foot braking parachutes while hindered by the

fact that a malfunctioning brake system locked the two left rear main tires, which blew with loud reports within two seconds of touchdown. The B-70 flight programme, which had for so long seemed almost a dream, had actually begun.

Supersonic speed on flight No 2 would have earned + $125,000, but this mission was cut short at Mach 0·85 at 28,000 feet as a result of a fluid leak in a utility hydraulic system. Not until the third flight did the aircraft exceed Mach 1, in the course of directional control and stability evaluations at Mach 1·1 both with and without yaw damper; unfortunately, delay in exceeding Mach 1 until the third flight entailed a penalty of − $125,000, which was invoked. On flight 4 the wing tips were folded to the 25° position and on No 5 to the full 65° inclination. On flight 6 Lt-Col Fitzhugh (Fitz) Fulton, Cotton's back-up pilot, was in the right seat, and on No 7 he and White gathered a fantastic 72 million points of data in a superb flight which involved a record 62 minutes of continuous supersonic operation. On the eighth mission White was teamed with his own back-up, Van Shepard, and they went to Mach 2·14 while exploring the operation of the huge multi-shock engine inlets. Mach 3 was demonstrated on Flight 17, earning a bonus of $275,000—a sum which would have been debited from NAA's account had this achievement proved impossible.

What was the "70" like to fly? Probably the worst part was the perilous climb up to the flight deck. Once there one found regal appointments and superlative comfort. General handling was fine, and anyone who really wants to go into the question is referred to "Airline Management & Marketing" for March 1967 where all the B-70 pilots were cross-examined (Joe Cotton likening Mach 3 in the B-70 to "driving a Greyhound bus 200 miles an hour around the track at Indianapolis"). The only real problem was obviously the landing, and the problem was caused by its smoothness and by the fact that it happened a long way from the pilot. The smoothness stemmed partly from the flatness of the dry lakes in the Antelope Valley around Edwards, and partly from the very powerful ground effect which made a firm arrival practically impossible. When I first wrote this chapter I quoted White as saying he could "easily use up half the runway trying to determine if I was down", but today he thinks this gives a false impression of undue difficulty. What is indisputable is that one's touchdown target had to be something like 2,500 feet from the threshold, because the pilot's eyes followed an approach trajectory some 110 feet ahead of the main gears and more than 40 feet higher—distances even greater than those of today's 747. Another thing that I think is indisputable is that with just two pilots the workload on a typical B-70 mission was extremely high.

The second XB-70A joined the flight programme on 17 July 1965, reaching Mach 3 on its own 17th flight, on 3 January 1966. On its 39th flight, on 19 May 1966, the No 2 aircraft put up what I consider the best performance of the whole programme, reaching Mach 3·08 and holding at least Mach 3 for 33 minutes in the course of a 2,700-mile mission over eight Western states. By this time the B-70 was playing its part in the National Sonic Boom Program based at Edwards in which various types of aircraft trailed carefully measured boom carpets over predesignated routes across Nevada and California. North American's Phase I flight contract was scheduled to terminate on 15 June 1966, to be replaced by a Phase II programme funded jointly by the Air Force and NASA and with the objective shifted slightly to the gathering of data on the behaviour and effects of large Mach 3 aircraft to support the American SST programme which by then was very much under way.

On 8 June 1966 the No 2 aircraft was scheduled for a general "clean-up" mission, preparatory to completing the Phase I programme, with various tasks (mainly subsonic) to which a sonic-boom run was added at the final flight-plan conference. As it was a flight making only modest demands on the co-pilot Joe Cotton let Major Carl S. Cross have his first familiarization ride. About a week beforehand GE had obtained approval, on the usual "non-interference" basis, to organize for publicity purposes a formation of GE-powered aircraft around the B-70 at the conclusion of its mission. The B-70 took off at 7.15 am, worked through its tasks and then formed up with a T-38, F-4, F-5 and F-104, looking like minnows in contrast, while a Learjet (likewise GE-engined) took some splendid pictures. By 9.30, after 20 minutes of good formation flying, the job was over. But for some reason that will never be known the F-104, flown by NASA chief research pilot Joe Walker (long-time king of the X-15 programme and probably the world's most experienced supersonic research pilot) tucked itself very close under the right wing of the B-70. His tail struck the underside of the tip (which was in the 25° position), and the 104 then pitched up, rolled on its back and slid across above the B-70 carrying away most of the two rudders. The almost demolished F-104 exploded in a ball of flame, leaving little for the Edwards investigators to piece together later. The B-70 kept straight and level for several seconds. Then, with majestic lack of haste, it entered a sickening rolling and yawing manoeuvre that eventually carried it outside the design flight envelope. As it suffered further structural failures White ejected, but Cross did not emerge. It finally hit the ground with immense vertical velocity in an almost flat attitude. It was subsequently found that Cross had not even begun to initiate the ejection sequence.

The ensuing storm was tough for GE, who were portrayed as the PR-seeking cause, and even more so for an Air Force colonel who was

259

dismissed from Edwards with a written reprimand. As far as I could see, the whole idea of tagging other GE-powered aircraft on to the B-70 at the end of its mission had been properly authorized and properly conducted, and the unfortunate colonel on the ground was in no way responsible for what seemed to be a dangerously close approach by one of the aircraft after the conclusion of the photographic session. He would not normally exercise authority over a NASA pilot, and had no reason to suppose that the formation flight would endanger the B-70. I read the testimony of the "corollary board" headed by the DCOS of Systems Command and formed the view that it had simply been told to find a scapegoat, to placate Congress and the public, and so chose the nearest officer in a responsible position.

Months later, when the No 1 aircraft had been much modified, with a new bogie forging and extensive instrumentation duplicating that lost in No 2, the Phase II programme began, and in March 1967 its management was assigned to NASA. By this time the B-70 was running on ordinary JP-5 fuel, thus completing a move to conventionality which had progressed from borane compounds via proposed special hydrocarbons (mainly aromatic mixtures) stable at 600° F, JP-6 with special additives and straight JP-6. NASA had hoped in Phase II to test a podded SST engine and representative SST structures (which would be most unlikely to resemble B-70 structure), but funds were inadequate. Despite the severely limited programme the remaining B-70 accomplished a great deal before the termination in January 1969. By this time it was far removed from being a bomber so I will not dwell on the countless undiscovered phenomena, pilot techniques and invaluable experience that Cotton, Fulton and Shepard gained (White had left to join TWA). Hopefully none of it will ever be lost or left unused in future programmes.

On 4 February 1969 Fitz Fulton and Lt-Col Ted Sturmthal felt considerable regret as they completed the 83rd mission of XB-70A No 1. The log book merely records "Subsonic, cruise Mach 0·91, ILAF and exciter-vane data, 33,000 ft. Landed Dayton, Ohio." From the runway at Wright-Patterson the most futuristic aircraft in the world was towed to the Air Force Museum, where you can marvel at it today. Many visitors regard it, rather literally, as a white elephant. Others keenly regret that SAC never operated the planned force of these enormous machines. Probably almost all of them regret that the Mach 3 SST, to which the B-70 was to make so big a contribution, was killed in 1971 by a wave of conservationist feeling whipped up by a campaign that attributed to the SST harmful qualities almost as terrifying as those attributed to steam railways 150 years earlier. Rather defensively the builders of the B-70 have pointed to the countless suppliers and industries that have benefited, very greatly and very directly, from this otherwise unprofitable programme. The number of patents filed as a result of B-70 research exceeds 700. Reading about the fantastic spur the B-70 gave to the technique of precision welding or the vacuum-refining of steel is one thing; discovering the endless spin-off of B-70 hardware and materials on to the everyday scene is another. To me one of the lasting advantages of the B-70 is that in future, whenever a harassed aircraft engineer feels something is too difficult, he can derive solid comfort from the B-70. Compared with that, his problem—whatever it is—is a pushover.

North American Rockwell B-1

B-1, one of the shortest of designations, identifies one of the greatest weapon systems in the world. To the US Air Force it is a vital, indispensable part of the Triad, the weapon mix that is to deter war until possibly the end of the century and hopefully much longer. Without it the United States and its allies would labour under a very grave strategic disadvantage and by 1978 would probably not be in a position to deploy a credible deterrent to all would-be aggressors. But to millions of ordinary folk, as well as to many highly intelligent people who think they understand the military scene, the B-1 is an anachronism on an unprecedented scale. The notion of a giant bomber penetrating to the depths of an enemy country seems to them utterly unrealistic in the future world of fast-reacting, unfailingly lethal defensive missiles. B-1 to them is the biggest possible waste of money, and they explain its existence as a mere continuation of the habit of the aerospace/defence lobby of organizing weapons that are ever more dreadful and ever more expensive. As this one has an estimated programme cost of something like $12,000 million they cannot believe it will be allowed to happen. Is the B-1 really nonsensical? Is the Air Force really just thinking up highly technical arguments to try to win over a puzzled Congress and milk the helpless taxpayer (again)?

If this were indeed the case not even their most ardent critic could accuse them of rushing things. It was in 1960 that the B-70 (p. 236) was halted as a weapon system. Probably most of the world's population that thought about it at all considered that this was the end of the manned bomber. It superficially looked like it. All that the Air Force did was maintain two small study groups, one in the Pentagon in the office of the DCOS Research and Development and the other at Systems Command a few miles away at Andrews AFB. Here in a think-tank atmosphere knowledgeable men tried to look at the world scene as it might be 20 years in the future and avoid being handicapped by too many preconceived notions. One of the most powerful of these notions was the supposed obsolescence of piloted vehicles as instruments of strategic attack. In the United States the ICBM was now the primary carrier of the deterrent, backed up by the Polaris, the first SLBM. These, the first two elements of the Triad, could deliver a nuclear warhead to targets on the other side of the world, with accuracy and reliability that was already very good and was getting even better. The warhead was tiny in comparison with a bomber, difficult to detect and practically impossible to intercept. Missiles on land could (it was thought) be hardened to withstand nuclear attack, and the SLBM was lurking in a submarine lying silently somewhere in a million cubic miles of ocean. In contrast the old-fashioned aeroplane, with its relatively long flight time, slow speed, huge radar signature and need for unhardenable airfields and the support of tankers seemed merely a supremely costly way of committing suicide. At last the penny seemed to have dropped. The stirring vision of a bomber flying like an arrow through the stratosphere unerringly to its distant target was nonsense—missiles would shoot it down, as they had shot down Gary Powers' super-stratospheric U-2 on that traumatic May Day of 1960. The only possible way to penetrate seemed to be at low level, and here there was no evident way of doing significantly better than the excellent B-58, which gave its crews a smooth ride at Mach 0·93. But the studies continued. They embraced almost every sort of supersonic and hypersonic manned vehicle I can think of. Most had air-breathing engines and a wing loading of about 250 lb/sq ft, and were intended to blast through the dense air at about 500 feet altitude—or whatever the minimum height might be to avoid too many changes of trajectory—at Mach 2 or above, getting extremely hot in the process and posing formidable engineering development problems. It was at this time that Systems Command wondered hard whether they ought not to pour a lot more money into the development of hardware, such as structures and accessory power systems and avionics, capable of functioning at 500° F or more. Such hardware had first been studied in 1953, when it was customary to add about one whole Mach number a year to the speed of aircraft, and hypersonic combat seemed just around the corner.

Fortunately the work stayed mostly on paper. The first big study to emerge, in 1961, was called AMPSS, for advanced manned precision-strike system, intended primarily to hit Soviet ICBMs—the one job that can be done better by a missile! It was followed by LAMP, low-altitude manned penetrator (not to be confused with the more recent LAMPS helicopter, the naval light airborne multi-purpose system), which I was assured required the crew to cage eyeballs before starting their dash to the target. Another scheme, which I thought looked even more marvellous and improbable, was SLAB, the strategic low-altitude bomber. In the midst of these, in 1962, the SecDef, Robert S. McNamara, told the Air Force to bring the low-altitude stargazers right down to earth and take a completely fresh look at what was, after all, of the very first importance to the United States and possibly to the story of man. Instead of rather narrowly trying to plan clever new strategic bombers perhaps the correct procedure would be to consider the real present and a range of possible futures. Project Forecast attempted to do just this, and in a back-up study a panel of general officers was convened to look at all the consequences of having, or not having, a new strategic bomber. These two 1962 study groups were of profound importance. In a way that I will later outline they showed with great clarity that a new strategic bomber was becoming more important every hour, and that instead of sacrificing everything to increasing the speed over the target the main efforts should be applied to quite different objectives such as short field-length, quick reaction time and an aerial armada of avionics and defence systems. In 1963 the studies led to a much more conventional, yet more likely, sort of bomber. It was called AMSA, which really stands for advanced manned strategic aircraft and not, as some humorist suggested as the years went by, America's Most Studied Aircraft.

AMSA was studied for eight years, or the same time that it took to design the B-24 Liberator, develop it for service, build over 19,000 and phase it out as obsolete. It may well be that in the next century it will take a man's working lifetime to produce a new weapon system, and the B-1 is apparently a giant step in this direction. The incredibly long gestation of this bomber was due not to any lessening of tension in the world, but to the sheer magnitude of the concept, of the great and increasing difficulty of finding enough money for it, of the need to be absolutely sure (in so far as this is possible) that it was a viable concept and not a monumental mistake, and of an increasing and—some would say—possibly overdue wish by the Pentagon to avoid troubles by making haste more slowly. It was a worrying gestation, because with each week that went by the Air Force could appreciate the need for a new bomber better, yet there were strong divisions of opinion on the form it should take, what its missions should be and how it should be deployed, and there was a need to spend years proving the underlying technology before even considering a full-scale development programme; and nagging always in the back of the mind was the vague fear that the Soviet Union suffered from no such time-consuming preliminaries and could put a new bomber into production practically overnight. Throughout all these years, from 1962 to 1970, Congress continued to vote what in the context of the US budget were small sums to fund paper studies and, increasingly, hardware development to provide requested capabilities. A detailed weapon system was still a long way off, but as early as 1963 several major firms were at work on vital tests with laboratory rigs to lead the way to new avionics, new engines and new subsystems.

In the first half of the 1960s some of the major areas of disagreement were: should AMSA be designed for conventional, as well as nuclear, war; should it be only a precision-strike system or should it have the capability of carrying mighty thermonuclear bombs to destroy cities or large areas; should it have sensors and weapons for finding and striking targets of opportunity; should it be able to fly at supersonic speed at low altitude; should it cruise at high altitude supersonically or subsonically; should it be designed to operate from relatively short, austere airfields (or even from highways); and should its unrefuelled range be 4,000 miles, or 5,500 or 7,000 or 10,000?

In 1964 the decision was taken to go ahead with a new missile for launching from SAC bombers, and this became a full programme the following year under the designation SRAM, for short-range attack missile (short, in this context, means over 100 miles). From the start of this weapon programme it was matched to the proposed new bomber, which in an apparent security leak in November 1964 was said to be planned to carry 25 of them. In January 1965, in a conference at the New York Academy of Sciences, Brig-Gen Howard A. Davis said that from the mid-1970s SAC would "concentrate on AMSA", using low-altitude penetration and releasing either gravity bombs or stand-off missiles. He confirmed that funds had already been approved for research into the engines and avionics. In September 1965 Gen John P. McConnell, whom I had known in Europe, had become USAF Chief of Staff, and he told Senator John Stennis of the Senate Armed Services Committee that an AMSA contract "should have been let for fiscal year 1966". But the following January SecDef McNamara testified before the House Armed Services Committee that "the strategic missile forces recommended for 1967–71 will provide more force than is required for assured destruction against both the USSR and China simultaneously". He had a strong personal identification with the FB-111, the SAC variant of the F-111 swing-wing tactical aircraft, and considered "a large spending on . . . a new advanced strategic aircraft does not at this time appear justified".

McNamara certainly put a few uniformed noses out of joint by his brusque methods and lack of respect for tradition, but over AMSA he was sweet reasonableness itself. He believed—and he was backed up by President Johnson—that missiles could achieve better and more certain results than could manned bombers, and that as SAC's bombers wore out they should not be replaced. But, he insisted, as soon as anyone could convince him of the need for a new manned bomber he would have one built, and he kept his options open by continuing to request funds for supporting advanced bomber capability. In March 1966 the Secretary of the Air Force, Dr Harold S. Brown—who as the former Director of Defense Research and Engineering in the Pentagon knew the whole programme backwards—said that "the two types of war the US has to prepare for make it entirely possible that two types of bomber will be needed in the years ahead". It was he who disclosed that, while the proposed FB-111 would be able to replace the B-52C to F models, and the

B-58, there was no replacement for the B-52G and H apart from AMSA, which he obviously supported wholeheartedly. He said the two basic requirements were long range and penetrative capability for nuclear war (which was not new) and a large and varied payload for conventional war (which was). As soon as I saw the Air Force no longer thought of the new bomber only in terms of nuclear war I considered they could eventually win their case against any open-minded Congress.

Most of 1966 was spent by the Air Force deciding whether or not it really wanted AMSA and, if it did, precisely what it was for. In the spring of that year McNamara told Congress, during the budget hearings, that the generals were not in agreement over its most basic characteristics. I thought he said it rather gleefully. So the Air Force put its house in order, and on 8 November 1966 presented the Defense Secretary with a carefully considered proposal for AMSA, and Gen McConnell assured him that the service at last spoke with one voice on the agreed specification. The document called for a versatile aircraft capable of carrying 25 SRAMs or a very heavy load of other ordnance an unrefuelled distance of 6,100 miles on a typical hi-low mission, with the ability to fly just below the speed of sound at low level and at Mach 2·5 at high levels. Though the report was detailed, and classified secret, *The New York Times* gave it comprehensive coverage on the morning of its transmission to the Defense Secretary. Apparently the Air Force thought publication would help its case, although I have always felt the "arranged leaks" that are part of the American heritage make their extremely detailed security arrangements rather pointless. In this case a Pentagon spokesman merely tried to make the newspaperman's story seem pure guesswork by saying it contained "some facts and some fiction", but so far the DoD have not told me which bit was fiction. Reading between the lines of this and other US reports I wrote an outline of AMSA in my regular review of aircraft development for the 1967 volume of *Brassey's Annual: The Armed Forces Yearbook* that stands up even today. In it I suggested "an R&D budget of $1·5–2·0 billion and a production run of 100 to 200 at some $25–30 million each (almost certainly an underestimate) . . ." This got me into trouble with a very eminent Briton who poured scorn on such figures. He considered it "grossly misleading" that I should suggest that there was any likelihood of a new bomber being procured, "and even if there were, the cost figure quoted is ridiculously high". To him, I can now say, "please read on".

Admittedly, the money involved back in 1967 was seemingly more reasonable: the Fiscal 1967 budget provided for only $26 million. It was a far cry from this to the 200-aircraft force that the Air Force wanted, with the first 15 becoming operational in 1974. Indeed it seemed self-evident that such a timescale could not be met; neither the US government nor the public were prepared for a giant, fast-moving programme for a new strategic bomber, and it was pretty obvious that before such a programme could go ahead there would have to be a passage of some years while people re-adjusted themselves to the idea. Indeed, some could never make the adjustment. I have several intelligent friends who would instinctively consider military men trying to "educate the public" into voting more money for new weapons as an old confidence trick on an astronomical scale. To them there never could be justification for a new bomber. Their attitude is not the traditional polarization among Europeans into left-wing and right-wing, because they would (I think) disapprove of the new Soviet supersonic swing-wing bomber called "Backfire". Rather is it based on the belief that military men, and especially American ones, have for 20 years spent sums that are colossal even in the context of national budgets on weapons that history shows (in their opinion) to have been unnecessary. When in November 1966 it was clear the USAF really meant to campaign for AMSA they took refuge behind the oft-repeated arguments—until recently the Air Force's own arguments—that such a weapon was nonsense. Unlike the true experts, they are unable or unwilling to examine fresh situations and come up with a different answer. And I might interject at this point a basic fact that my anti-weapon friends simply refuse to believe. The Air Force had no *prima facie* wish to buy a new bomber. Generals really do give credence to factors other than self-aggrandisement and the joy of flying off into the wild blue yonder. In fact their thoughts tend to revolve around fiscal appropriations, and a costly new bomber means tightening their belts everywhere else. In any case it is no longer easy to get money out of Congress, if indeed it ever was. The only way to do it is to present a Congressman with arguments he can understand and agree with—not only the hawks but also the growing ranks of the doves. That the Air Force succeeded in doing this is itself testimony to the fact that the new bomber is not as silly as it seems to the uninformed.

What are these arguments that have made a strategic bomber a good investment for the rest of the century? There are really two sets of considerations, one dealing with possible events over the United States and the other with possible events over the territory of a future enemy. I'll try to skate over some of the more obvious arguments quickly. Over the enemy country the US president can send 1,000 Minuteman ICBMs, many with MIRV warheads, plus 656 Polaris SLBMs. None of these is any use in striking the most hardened fixed target or any mobile target, and these missiles are fully effective only in a nuclear war against cities, which means civil populations, or against known fixed military installations which the enemy has probably discounted and inactivated. The only way of hitting superhard enemy missiles or mobile forces is with a bomber. This alone

267

is a considerable reason for having a bomber, but a reason for having a bomber with very long range is that it can attack any target in any potential enemy's territory—whoever he may be—from any direction. This enormously complicates the enemy defensive problem; in fact, the Pentagon concludes no complete defence against such a bomber is economically possible, although I think I could provide such a defence if I ruled a small but rich island such as the UK or Japan.

What about the situation over the United States? Without bombers the US is committed either to all-out war against humanity, using missiles, or it can have its bluff called. The ICBM and SLBM are practically useless in conventional war, and that is the only war America has had to fight for almost 30 years. But suppose another country did launch a nuclear attack on the United States? The US government has said it will not assume it is being thus attacked until a hostile warhead has exploded over the US. Without bombers, the US must wait until enemy warheads are exploding on the SAC missile silos before retaliating with whatever is left; and if the enemy is accurate in his timing, all his warheads will explode simultaneously, obliterating the ICBM force before it can be fired. But with the existence of US bombers the enemy problem is more difficult, if not impossible. Hitting SAC bases is an ideal task for enemy SLBMs, fired on depressed trajectories from close offshore so that their time of flight is only ten minutes or less. But, no matter whether the enemy plans his attack so that all his warheads are detected at the same moment or so that all impact at the same moment, there is no way he can destroy the ICBMs and the bombers. If he times his attack for simultaneous impact, the US bombers will be "flushed" 20 minutes earlier, on first BMEWS sighting of the enemy ICBM warheads, so the SLBM strike on airfields will catch nothing. If he times for simultaneous detection the attack on airfields will explode ten or fifteen minutes before that on the Minuteman silos, so the latter can be fired unhesitatingly in plenty of time. Bombers are the essential ingredient to such an enemy dilemma. It was this very basic scenario that threw up the vital importance of two factors in the design of the bomber: the ability to operate from dispersed bases; and the ability to take-off unfailingly with no delay.

Without a bomber the United States would have to decide which was the lesser of two terrifying evils: being annihilated; or firing its ICBM force as soon as the BMEWS detects what appears to be an enemy attack. In fact, the missiles would not have to be launched as soon as this happened, and SAC has determined with some precision the exact point in time at which it must launch a Minuteman in order for it to escape the effects of an enemy ICBM strike on its silo (it is a distressingly long time in advance, because the missile travels quite slowly during its first minute or so of flight). Clearly, if the US were to adopt a policy of "fire on warning" it would be open to a horrifying mistake if another country chose to send over some ICBMs carrying nothing but the Thoughts of Mao. Only the possession of a bomber could remove this fear. And a bomber could counter the sudden increase in vulnerability of the SAC missile force caused by the massive build-up in Soviet ICBM strength, with SS.9 and later missiles carrying large silo-destroying warheads. Only the bomber could likewise counter any new technical development that could reduce the effectiveness of American missiles. But the bomber had to be credible, which means it had to reach its target. I am not a party to the innermost secrets of the Pentagon, but I have strongly formed the view that in 1973 a bomber can be made at least as credible as the B-52 was in its timescale. I have been privately told as much by people who ought to know and have no axe to grind. Indeed by 1968 I had myself come to the view that it was technically possible to create a bomber that might survive in any foreseeable environment. But it would have to be large and expensive, and to be worth its immense cost it would obviously have to be a rather difficult compromise. It would have to meet the needs of nuclear and conventional war, attack at high level or low and be equipped with a remarkable array of clever devices. What it certainly could not do was follow the B-70 and try to compete with the ICBM on missions where the missile is obviously supreme. Later I will outline how the new bomber works, insofar as this is permitted, but I left the reader in 1967 when even the paper studies were changing daily.

At this time the study funding was running at about $25 million a year, and although several million was being consumed "in house" in the broad study and management programmes, at least three-quarters was finding its way to industry where upwards of 30 companies were contributing to a process described by Felix Rogers, then a brigadier-general and now DCOS for Development Plans, as "buying capability". At least ten of the companies were engaged in electronics, and others were involved in all kinds of systems and other hardware. Two vital participants were Pratt & Whitney and GE, who worked on the ATEGG (advanced turbine engine gas-generator) programme to provide supporting technology for improved engines that could achieve higher work-per-stage (more compression of the airflow for each row of compressor blades and more horsepower for a given area of turbine blades) and operate reliably at much increased gas temperatures. Three airframe companies were also involved: Boeing, General Dynamics and North American Rockwell. Their feelings can be imagined: each stood to land one of the biggest, if not the biggest, of all the contracts in the history of aviation, yet none of them could dare to believe it would really happen. Of the three airframe contractors, Boeing superficially appeared to have the inside edge, not so much because it had provided the backbone of SAC in the past, in both aircraft and missiles, but because it was airframe prime contractor for the American SST. But the Air Force is not greatly influenced by such considerations. Everyone to whom I spoke was careful to emphasize the gross differences between the SST and AMSA, and when Boeing had to give up the swing-wing for the civil machine the differences multiplied because AMSA very strongly suggested such a configuration, for reasons I will explain. In many ways the bomber superficially seemed easier than the SST: the payload is less bulky and can be distributed in the right places, the engines and landing gear can if necessary be hung on the fuselage (something the FAA did not permit for the SST) and calculations showed from the start that the bomber would not have to cruise at Mach 3, and so would not get so hot as the SST nor have to be made of steel and titanium.

To a million schoolboys it probably seemed odd that the USAF should throw away the B-70 that could cruise at Mach 3 and then spend years pondering a bomber that could not cruise much faster than Mach 2. The simplest answer is that the B-70 was trying to compete with the ICBM and was planned in the days when it was thought a high-flying bomber could penetrate better by flying as fast as possible. AMSA was based on much deeper study. As far as manned aircraft are concerned I think it is generally agreed that at high altitude speed is not a significant factor in determining penetrability; with no ECM or penaids a bomber is equally at the mercy of missile defences no matter whether it flies at 200 knots or 2,000. Only in the so-called "damage limiting" role, in which the bomber's task is to destroy an enemy's strategic attack forces before they can be used, is high cruising speed of vital importance; and in this duty the ICBM or SLBM are so much faster that no bomber shows up well at all, even if flying so fast it becomes red hot. Indeed, after some nine years of calculation, the final decision was made in 1969 to cruise the new bomber subsonically, at Mach 0·85. This gives the best figure of ton-miles per hour, considering the aircraft simply as a transport vehicle, and very substantially eases the problems and the cost. Even at low level, where high speed helps in surprising the defences, it was decided in 1969 to pull back from Mach 1·2 to 0·85–0·95. According to General Rogers, quoted by "Air Force/Space Digest", when one plots penetration capability against on-the-deck speeds, "there isn't much of a wiggle on the chart" between Mach 1·2 and high-subsonic speeds. This is partly, of course, because the reduction in speed enables the bomber to fly lower. One of the few real threats to the low-level bomber is the snap-down missile fired from above by a fighter equipped with radar that can see the bomber against the Earth's surface immediately below it. It was rather pleasing for the USAF to discover that even the Mig-21 and Mig-25 are subsonic at low altitude; in fact the Pentagon thinks these fighters are red-lined at Mach 0·85, so the new bomber could just outrun them if it wished. It could not outrun Soviet AAMs, but it would be no better off in this regard at Mach 1·2 either. For defence it uses guile, not fleetness of foot. So much guile, in fact, that I was almost surprised when Bob Seamans, then Secretary of the Air Force, managed to persuade Deputy SecDef David Packard in November 1969 that the new bomber should be able to fly at supersonic speed at altitude if it wished.

It is a measure of the unpredictability of aircraft design that, whereas in 1954 the USAF would scarcely look at any combat aircraft unless it was supersonic, by the end of the next decade the pros and cons of particular flight Mach numbers, and their equivalent costs over a 20-year service life, were being argued and analysed in computers for months and years. I even heard the view expressed that, by not calling for Mach 15 and controlled thermonuclear propulsion, the Air Force might get Congress off-balance and get funds for what would appear a surprisingly ordinary aircraft. This is, of course, utter nonsense. The performance of AMSA was worked out in great detail by balancing accomplishments against the goals and the costs to a degree never before attempted with any aircraft. It is very much a job for computers. Although in the study stage the Air Force did not have an actual aircraft design—indeed the successful contractor could have come up with a biplane if he could prove it was right—it knew with great precision the sizes and weights and power consumptions of the avionics, the sizes and weights of the weapons, the volume and weight of the fuel and the likely miles-per-gallon on different mission profiles. Typical of the problems that had to be solved is "find the most cost/effective combination of CEP and weapon load for an attack on a point target with conventional weapons". CEP, circular-error probability, depends on the navigation and offensive avionic systems, and changes to these can vary the space they need and even the shape of the aircraft. Degradation in CEP means a bigger weapon load to accomplish the mission. The sums are unbelievably complex, even when many of the variables and interactions are omitted. Undoubtedly, in this programme the sums were done more fully than in any other aircraft programme in history.

Although this prolonged study paid dividends, so that General Otto J. Glasser, DCOS for R&D, could in 1970 describe the programme as "in better technical shape than any previous Air Force program—going all the way back to the B-29 of World War 2—has ever been at this juncture", it posed formidable problems for the main industrial participants. It costs about $100,000 a week to be a major partner in such a project, far more than the fees paid for the study accomplished, and companies do it in order to win the later contracts for hardware. But only one can win. In 1967 Boeing, then enjoying a boom in commercial aircraft, disbanded its AMSA team because it needed the engineers elsewhere. In 1969, with the 747 design peak over, it came back in an all-out attempt to win the AMSA. Just at this time North American Rockwell, whose participating Los Angeles Division was having a lean time and was sinking to a total strength of below 4,000, cut back its team from 500 to about 80. It did this in order to put maximum effort on the F-15 fighter; if it failed there, it considered it could still switch its effort to win the AMSA, which was in many ways related to their F-15 submission and used the same blended wing/fuselage design. Only General Dynamics steadfastly kept a full team on the bomber, and I know that their study funds did not cover half the total costs incurred.

As 1969 dawned the industrial participants were eagerly looking forward to the RFP stage, from which it might be only six months or so to the crucial process of source-selection and the signing of contracts for engineering development. But the whole DoD contractual process was thrown into disarray by the bad public image of the F-111, C-5A and other giant programmes, and early in 1969 the Pentagon was in the final stages of devising a completely new way of doing things that—it was hoped—would somehow avoid cost escalation and most of the severe management problems of future large programmes. No programme was potentially larger than the new bomber, so there was a year's delay in issuing the RFP while a new "management package" was devised. Hopefully the British government and industry has studied the form of this package because in my view it would do Britain more good than the irrelevancies of successive aerospace investigations that merely make amateurish generalizations. The principal feature of the package is the "milestone technique" in which hard technical accomplishment must be demonstrated before moving on to the next stage. The idea is ascribed to David Packard, and the action in the event of any milestone not being met at the correct time and for the agreed expenditure is a stern-lipped Pentagon review at which the decision is taken to (1) stop the whole programme; (2) trade-off performance to get back on timetable and budget; or (3) accept a controlled escalation in cost. To me it looks like a lot of (3), but accepted in a planned and deliberate way; whether this will help the taxpayer is problematical. The European MRCA is run the same way.

Certainly in the autumn of 1969 AMSA seemed well on the way to big political and financial trouble, with a million noisy critics all rubbing their hands in glee. In June the DoD had put the total programme cost (R&D plus production, but not service) at "about $9,000 million". By September Congress was shouting that it had already escalated to "between

$12,000 and $15,000 million", and that in any case the bomber would "become a museum piece in the missile age". What such critics are apparently anxious to do is influence the ignorant, because in this case anyone who was not wholly uninformed could see such a claim to be arrant nonsense. But this did not stop the Senate from forcing a division on the project, which the bomber survived by 56 votes to 31. AMSA thus lived to become the B-1 on 3 November 1969, when the RFPs were finally sent out to the three airframe and two engine firms. All five by this time had detailed designs, and the engine makers had both run extremely advanced reheat turbofan engines having a size and thermodynamic cycle matched to the B-1. These demonstrator engines had cost some $72 million. An additional $44 million had been spent on advanced avionics, including flight testing of "brassboard" systems in such major areas as IR surveillance, multi-mode radar and radar location homing and warning. By this time the programme had consumed more R&D effort and money than all the bombers in American history up to and including the B-52, and yet the B-1 was still a mere proposal.

It had been expected that the successful airframe and engine contractors would be announced on or about 18 May 1970, but the Source Selection Board, which began its gruelling session on 12 January of that year, took until June to complete its separate evaluations of the airframe and engine proposals. In the case of the airframe I think they could have made a choice earlier than they did, because the winner, North American Rockwell, "was the lowest bidder, received the highest weighted score and was the unanimous choice at each reviewing level" throughout. Rarely can a bidder have received such universal acclaim. One wonders idly how far the choice was influenced by the fact that NR, having lost the F-15 to McDonnell Douglas, simply had to win the B-1 or face a shut-down of its famed Los Angeles Division. Certainly the published costs for the B-1 engineering development are clear enough: NR reckoned it could do the job for $1,346 million, whereas GD and Boeing respectively thought the bill would be $1,450 million and $1,560 million. But history shows the man who needs the business most, usually turns out to be the one universally agreed to have submitted the best proposal. In the case of the engine, P&W, having won the important propulsion contracts for the F-14 and F-15 supersonic fighters, lost out to GE who had no parallel military programme and had lately lost the prospect of powering the SST. I have no doubt the GE F101 engine will be a world-beater, but the way contracts are awarded in the United States nevertheless seems in sharp contrast to what happened in Britain in 1956–1966, when the weakest were deliberately driven out of business in a successful attempt to reduce the number of British aerospace companies.

Having won potentially the most valuable contract in the history of military aircraft, NR were able to move with urgency and assurance, even though the development programme initially had only $25 million for the airframe and $10 million for the F101 engine out of Fiscal 1970 funds. Altogether the Air Force had received $100 million from Congress for the B-1 in that year and asked for the same sum in 1971. Both NR and GE are working on incentive-fee contracts. NR was committed to design, develop, build and test seven B-1 aircraft, five for flight and two for static test, for a target price of $1,230 million; if there is no short-fall in performance or timing they stand to gain a fee of $115,750,000, bringing the total to the budget figure quoted earlier. Likewise GE contracted to deliver 40 of the advanced F101 engines for $406,650,000, including their maximum fee of $30,120,000. It is appropriate here to list the programme milestones (with the original June 1970 dates in brackets): engine parameters fixed, November 1970 (same); aircraft configuration fixed, January 1971 (November 1970); cost schedule control system criteria (CSCSC) approved, February 1971 (same); preliminary design review, August 1971 (not included); mock-up review, November 1971 (January 1971); design validation, October 1972 (two phases, October 1971 and July 1972); critical design review, June 1973 (March 1973); engine PFRT, November 1973 (not stated); roll-out, February 1974 (not stated); first flight, May 1974 (summer 1974); production decision, May 1975 (not stated); complete structural testing, June 1976 (December 1975); complete flight testing, May 1977 (January 1977); complete contractual testing, May 1978 (December 1977). Although some of the early dates slipped almost a year, the first flight has actually been brought forward and altogether the milestones look like being not unrealistic. In passing I cannot help musing on how impossible it would be for Britain to publish such a schedule, if there were any purely British combat aircraft, because apparently to do so would harm national security. Am I then to conclude the Americans are fools, bent on assisting their enemies?

As soon as NR were chosen the Pentagon released a series of artist's impressions of the B-1, and pictures of a mock-up F101. Subsequently each engineering change has been fully reported, apart from a number of crucial items that really would help an enemy and remain classified. Even these are automatically declassified with the passage of one or three years unless positive action is taken to continue to protect them, which is again the approximate opposite of what happens in Britain where the public is told nothing unless some positive action is taken to wring out a piece of information. I will not repeat details of the B-1 that can be looked up elsewhere, but will describe a hypothetical mission to indicate some of its capabilities and techniques.

Although a great deal of effort has been devoted to making the B-1 outstandingly effective in a conventional war, most of the design choices have had to be biased in favour of nuclear warfare. It is because of this type of conflict that the aircraft has been designed to operate from runways no longer than 6,000 feet, of which there are many hundreds in the United States, with no special facilities. This made a swing wing almost mandatory, especially as the unhappy weight-management of the F-111 and C-5A has been taken to heart by the Air Force. As I write, the policy is to design the B-1 to fulfil its mission to the uttermost, and if it grows—say, to 420,000 lb—the outstandingly efficient wing and the power of the F101 will suffice to meet the field-length restriction. Incidentally, the design gross weight is barely ten tons less than the 385,000 lb of Concorde; aggregate engine thrust is in most flight regimes also slightly less, but the bomber has considerably greater fuel capacity. Maximum Mach number for the bomber exceeds the 2·05–2·1 of Concorde, but only marginally. It is in the matter of field length that the two aircraft differ most sharply, the B-1 being able to spread its wings to a span of almost 137 feet to cut runway requirement by half.

I believe the B-1 will be one of the first combat aircraft to look like a contemporary civil transport. I know some bombers began life cloaked in the guise of airliners, but when they shed their false plumage there was scant resemblance. But the B-1 could easily be an SST, particularly as future designs may well dispense with passenger windows. Apart from the relatively small fuselage there is little to proclaim the B-1 a bomber except to the expert who could tell from the avionic aerials. But not even the expert could tell the remarkable way the aircraft has been designed to "survive in a nuclear environment". The effects of a nuclear weapon explosion are complex. Except for the obvious case of an explosion near enough to be devastating, the B-1 is designed to remain fully serviceable in conditions of overpressure, radiant heat, nuclear radiation, neutron flow (flux), ionization and electromagnetic pulse (EMP) more severe than the criteria laid down for the Minuteman ICBM. Special electro-optics enable the bomber to "see" throughout the intense flash of a nuclear explosion. This merely means adding new equipment, but the basic nuclear hardening has called for immense technical development, especially to the avionics and above all to the crucial digital computer that links all the main variables and in particular controls the penetration process as later described.

Crew of the B-1 comprises pilot, co-pilot and two systems operators. At a time of extreme political tension they would be able to "live" in their crew module, which serves as a self-contained emergency escape system and survival shelter as is now standard for multi-seat combat aircraft. If they are outside the B-1 they can all board and connect themselves up in 30 seconds, the first man hitting the APU start button on the nose gear (this button will be on the back of the leg, because in its original position on the front it could have suffered from air blast at high IAS), which saves a full minute in energizing all aircraft systems as the crew climb aboard. Obviously all four main engines must be started together, rather than in sequence, calling for high starting energy input without external supplies. The system also must be as reliable as humans can make it, using some of the philosophies and techniques of manned-space programmes, because there is every reason to believe that a pre-launch snag costing more than two minutes will prove fatal. Pity that this notion of utterly reliable operation cannot spin-off on to consumer goods used by the rest of us!

Special measures, almost certainly based on the digital computer, will enable the B-1 to take off without the crew reading through long checklists. It will be instructive to learn, when security permits, how far this is done by checking everything out in advance and how far by high-speed computerized checking after the "flush on warning" alarm has sounded. I am also eagerly wondering how many faults that today are a dispatch criterion on civil airliners will be tolerated in B-1 operations. By the 1980s it could be that this highly specialized military aircraft will indirectly have done something to improve the dispatch reliability of the airlines.

At take-off full reheat will be used, raising static thrust from about 18,000 lb to 30,000 lb per engine. This is just double the thrust of GE's classic J79 engine, which is considerably longer and less efficient. The F101 has a two-stage fan, with solid titanium blades. Although it may seem a retrograde step, this fan is preceded by inlet guide vanes and struts, and these were included not so much to improve tolerance to inlet airflow distortion as to decrease the likelihood of losing an engine through impact with birds (or the tops of trees?) during low-level penetration. Undoubtedly the B-1 could hold its penetration speed with one engine out; it may be able to with two, but this would cut its range and altitude performance on the return flight. Other features of the F101 are a nine-stage HP spool, giving an overall pressure ratio of about 23:1 for good subsonic economy; a highly loaded HP turbine with thoria-dispersed nickel/chrome guide vanes and air-cooled blades of the new René 120 alloy operating at a temperature in excess of 1,650° K; reheat in the jet pipe behind a fan/core flow mixer (which gives a cooler exhaust than the alternative duct-burner technique, and thus reduces the IR signature); and extensive use of graphite (carbon fibre) and epoxy or polyimide resin composite construction in the cooler parts.

These engines thrust the B-1 off a 6,000 foot runway at gross weight with ease. On the assumption the runway needs to be as far as possible from the sea, those westwards from Chicago to the Rockies and the Canadian border (and perhaps north of the border?) look the most suitable. It is likely that the B-1 force will be dispersed in pairs throughout these states, where most of the Minutemen already stand at readiness, accompanied by pairs of KC-135 tankers. Although it needs far less tanker support than the FB-111, the B-1 will need air-refuelling on most missions at present envisaged. Congress and anti-war experts set up a noisy campaign in 1971 claiming that the B-1 was the reason why the USAF wants a new tanker fleet. In fact the B-1 is fully compatible with the KC-135, and new tankers are needed because the KC-135 itself has shortcomings, such as an inability to disperse to short runways and flush inside four minutes. Rolls would be happy to supply cartridge-started Super VC10 engines, which would make a big difference on both counts, but it is more likely SAC will live with today's tankers until a completely new fleet can be bought.

The KC-135 would thrust its high-speed boom into the B-1's receptacle immediately in front of the very large pilot windscreens, and in some missions would probably top up the bomber to more than the maximum take-off weight. The outward legs would then normally be flown at Mach 0·85 at a height rising from 45,000 to about 60,000 feet, with wings close to the fully spread position. With an advanced enemy the B-1 would come within surveillance distance of an AWACS aircraft, such as "Moss", patrolling at great height when it was still several hundred miles away. I doubt that it could escape detection, with nothing but space as a background, but from this point onwards the B-1 will have full need of its incredible defensive and offensive avionics. These systems may be expected to grow in capability with the life of the aircraft, and the B-1 has been designed to carry a modular avionics payload which, as and when potential enemy capabilities increase, can readily be extended until the system weight is about double that of the original "fit". The Air Force does not want a repetition of the B-52 story where the avionics grew by 500 per cent in a difficult and unplanned way.

Both the B-1 and the AWACS will try to see each other while themselves remaining invisible. Even if the B-1 is unaware of any such sentry it will probably fold its wings and work up to Mach 2·2 as it approaches the enemy frontier. If it detects an AWACS it will try to destroy it, something no bomber has ever before attempted. To do so it is planned to have an "active defence capability" involving two types of air-to-air missile, each unlike anything previously available. To counter the AWACS the ideal would be to carry several SCADs (the AGM-86A subsonic cruise armed decoy). Not yet subject to full development, the SCAD would be a small aircraft capable of flying ahead on the B-1's course, while the bomber sharply changed direction to confuse the enemy, maintaining a speed of Mach 0·55 to 0·85 at all heights down to sea level. It would weigh about 1,350 lb and have a cheap turbofan engine. Most of its payload would be powerful ECM devices, but it would also have a 200 lb warhead and could be made to home on to the enemy AWACS. As an alternative to an optimized SCAD the B-1 could carry much cheaper Teledyne Ryan drones to do the same task, or possibly a flock of purely passive decoys such as modified Northrop MQM-74A drones. Probably by 1980 a fully optimized SCAD will be available, and this may even prove to have mission capabilities on its own.

The second B-1 missile is BDM, the bomber defence missile. This again is not yet designed, but several contractors have been studying two versions, one for short-range use against interceptors (fighters or missiles) at about eight miles' range, and the other for killing enemy fighters and SAMs as much as 250 miles distant. The concept of a giant bomber carrying fighters for its own defence is almost as old as flying, and in August 1948 McDonnell actually flew the XF-85 Goblin intended to fit inside the forward bomb bay of the B-36. But today technology allows the job to be done by an unmanned fighter, and the BDM (LR) is intended to have high kill probability against any anticipated enemy aircraft (and missiles?). It would be nice if it could do so without blowing itself up, so that it could engage a succession of targets, but this does not appear possible. It is still uncertain how many BDMs the B-1 could carry, but with a maximum load of other ordnance the total cannot be much greater than one. In the AMSA specification provision was to be made for a gun in the tail, but I doubt that this will be fitted. In a nuclear environment it is policy to prevent enemy hardware approaching within the range of accurate gunfire.

For the heaviest defences, the B-1 may be profiled to penetrate at minimum altitude. Just how a strategic bomber can best penetrate the defences of a sophisticated enemy is a 64 billion dollar question. Like the B-58, the B-1 flies roughly the same distance at Mach 0·85 at 400 feet as it does at Mach 2·2 at 65,000 feet, and the extra distance due to dog-legs and weaving is likely to be about equal. The wing sweep for "lo" penetration is a compromise not previously encountered, with manoeuvrability and range calling for less sweep and the quality of ride and the possibility of hitting the ground calling for more. Minimum altitude is classified, but I believe the specification said 250 feet. One of NR's big bidding advantages was its deep research into low-altitude ride control (LARC), which the company now calls "Softride". Stemming from the XB-70 programme, this uses accelerometers in the fuselage to sense the up/down and left/right accelerations as the strong but flexible airframe responds to its passage at high speed through rough air. I see no reason why these accelerometers should not be the same ones already used in the inertial navigation system. Their output signals pass through one of the central computers and drive the lower rudder panel, the elevators and the Softride vanes—small foreplanes just ahead of the crew compartment—to bend the fuselage the opposite way and thus cancel out the turbulent motion. To me it seems amazing that the system can respond fast enough. That such a system is needed has been obvious since the B-52 began to fly low, at a lower speed than the B-1, and according to the USAF the teeth-jarring ride without Softride would even affect hardware, especially the avionics. But its main purpose is to make the crew compartment fly in a straight line. N. D. Showalter, B-1 operational suitability manager at NR, says the main trouble is simply "discomfort and increased probability of error due to difficulty in monitoring instruments and carrying out basic tasks". Ideally the crew compartment ought to be at a "nodal point" so that, when the B-1 is viciously shaken, the crew stay more or less still. The designers of passenger trains have overcome their tradition of putting the driver at the front, and it may be that designers of bombers ought to do likewise.

Enemy radars will obviously be placed on towers, hilltops and in aircraft. How well will they see the oncoming B-1? Probably no part of the early study programme was more exhaustive than finding ways of minimizing the bomber's radar and IR cross-sections. The so-called "invisible bomber" made of glass or whatever else is permeable to defensive radiations is simply unattainable. For example, if the B-1 really were glass it would show up beautifully to a powerful passive IR system, and no glass is transparent to all useful radar wavelengths. Much more can be done by tinkering with the design of the aircraft. Although it is roughly as big and heavy as a B-52, the B-1 will have a radar cross-section approximately one-twentieth as great. This is because the radar energy will almost all be reflected from acutely sloping surfaces in the new bomber, and very little will be returned along its outward path. One of the most reflective components is the engine, and radars will not be able to see the B-1 engines unless they are sighted directly into the long inlet ducts. Leading edges and intake lips are sharp, and there are no external tanks or weapons.

There remains the problem of the bomber's own radar emissions. B-1 avionics were initially studied by many companies under the overall industrial direction of NR's own Autonetics division, now called the NR Electronics Group, and IBM. This rather ground to a halt in December 1971 when the Air Force, from Secretary Seamans downward, decided the B-1 avionics were looking too airy-fairy and ought to be brought down to earth sharply. Previously the objective had been "an enormous challenge" calling for "a high degree of creative initiative"; General Glasser said "contractors should earn their fee by bringing to bear their utmost ingenuity". Then, suddenly the cry was "austerity". On 23 February 1972 contractors were briefed on the new approach, which calls for maximum use of off-the-shelf hardware; if someone simply has to design something new it must be "highly advantageous" and backed up by a second parallel development in case of trouble. The change of course has undoubtedly been occasioned by cost rather than timing, and many avionic engineers are feeling sick that splendid new concepts derived after years of study and "brassboard" development—and even, in many cases, flight testing—should now be thrown out. In the case of the vital computer there has been a further change in policy. As the potential of enemy radars and other defences is continually being changed and up-graded, a separate computer must now be fitted to manage the B-1's defensive avionics that blanket, twist and confuse the enemy radiations and make the B-1 seem to be elsewhere and moving in a different trajectory. Thus the defensive software can be taken from the bomber separately, up-dated and put back without touching the software for the one or two other computers that control the penetration and weapon delivery. The need to use existing hardware drastically reduced the choice of computer. My money was on either the IBM AP-1, already far along in development for the F-15 Eagle fighter, or the Univac 7532 used in the Navy S-3A Viking anti-submarine aircraft, which is more costly but can be used as a multi-processor and has a plated-wire memory that is hardened against nuclear radiation. To my surprise the choice eventually fell on the SKC-2000 developed by Singer-Kearfott for the Swedish Viggen. This again rams home the lesson that little Sweden is no slouch in specifying for combat aircraft. As for the terrain following radar, which tells the bomber the configuration of the land and obstructions in its path, this could only be a modification of the TFR used in the FB-111, and in December 1971 Texas Instruments were awarded $640,000 to see how best this could be done. The only new item seems to be that, according to Maj-Gen Douglas T. Nelson, B-1 System Program Director, "We are very interested in the laser. We are watching it closely. It is very promising as a possible weapon system for the B-1." Lasers are available off the shelf as accurate sighting and range-finding devices for aerial weapon delivery, but this could be the first time the words "death-ray"—which inevitably crept into the reportage of General Nelson's statement—might have a germ of truth. There are ways in which a laser of very high pulsed power could play an active role.

By this time our B-1 ought to have arrived over or near its target; indeed in an earlier comment General Nelson said "there is no technology in sight that can prevent it from penetrating to target". In some missions the bomber would stand-off and release pre-programmed, inertially guided SRAMs (see B-52 story), of which it can carry no fewer than 24 in its three bomb bays. SRAM is the B-1's chief weapon, and as the weapon bays were tailored around it all other stores, including the defence missiles, are in turn to be tailored to SRAM. Unlike all other SAC bombers the B-1 will carry its full load internally and thus can do so at supersonic speed, even with its maximum load of about 50 tons of conventional bombs. The USAF has emphasized that, despite its price, the B-1 is a good buy for conventional warfare. Compared with the B-52 it could reduce the time for flying from Guam to South Viet-Nam from $4\frac{1}{2}$ to $1\frac{1}{2}$ hours while carrying roughly twice the load. To deliver the same weight of ordnance "more than ten F-4s, F-105s or A-7Ds are required"; even SAC's FB-111 shows up poorly in comparison, because it takes six of these swing-wing attackers to do the work of one B-1, each of them needing as much air-refuelling off-load as the bigger aircraft.

Except to my friends whose minds are made up and don't want to be bothered by the facts, all this is convincing testimony to the belief that the B-1 makes sense so long as arms of any kind make sense, and that the USAF would be foolishly short-sighted not to try to buy it. It is certainly no bad thing that the B-1 is being procured in an atmosphere of public and Congressional opinion that ranges from a need to be convinced, through various degrees of cynical supposition that this will turn out another technical or cost scandal, to blind paranoic hatred. As the generals and the planemakers can no longer do no wrong they are trying harder to make sure they do right. The management of the B-1 probably interests me more than it does most readers of this book, but it is a model of the best that humans can devise for a large programme today. The System Program Office (SPO) is not at Wright-Patterson AFB, the HQ of the Aeronautical Systems Division (ASD) but at NR's plant at El Segundo. Thus, says General Nelson, "the individual reporting requirements have been reduced from several hundred to forty, which is saving many millions of dollars. . . . What we are doing on this programme . . . is adapt our way of doing business to that of the contractor." Duplication has been swept away, the liaison between contractor and customer is intimate, and Nelson's deputy, Col M. M. Bretting, learns of problems as they arise and makes decisions on the spot. Another innovation is that the Commander of ASD, Lt-Gen James T. Stewart, has hired systems engineering and technical assistance from Cornell Aeronautical Laboratory "simply because we can't assign any more of our own engineers without hurting other programs".

Hopefully, the new bomber programme will not be hurt too much itself.

Early in 1972 one of the key men in US defence, Dr John S. Foster Jr, the DoD Director of Defense Research and Engineering, claimed "In terms of constant 1970 dollars there has been no cost growth in the B-1 program . . .". But to some degree this has been achieved by lopping bits off the programme. Early in 1971 the number of flight aircraft on order was cut from five to three, and the two static-test aircraft were cut to one, saving about $300 million. Obviously making the best of a bad job, General Nelson commented "This involves an element of risk since loss of one of the three test aircraft would have considerable impact on the program. But on balance I believe it is a good trade-off. With good supervision we can live with the increased risk, and I think we will wind up doing a much more efficient job during the flight-test phase. . . . Previously, flight testing was done first by the contractor and then again by the Air Force, resulting in duplication of more than fifty per cent of the effort." Like all the ASD programme managers, Nelson holds the policy of "disengagement" in vogue in the 1960s as a prime factor in causing, or allowing, the massive technical difficulties and cost overruns. The new policy of togetherness is meant to do better.

Based on a projected buy of 241 aircraft, the currently (1972) estimated B-1 programme cost is $11,100 million. Adjusted for inflation, this is $100 million below the estimate of 30 June 1970. Allowing for all R&D, the cost per aircraft, with supporting equipment and initial spares, works out at $45.6 million. This makes the B-1 the most expensive production aircraft in history. It is tempting to find reasons for not building it. Senator Allen J. Ellender, Chairman of the Subcommittee on Defense Appropriations, claims the Soviet Union is "not building bombers to any extent. . . . The moment we start building the B-1 . . . they are going to go back and try to imitate us." This seems convincing, until one remembers the "Backfire".

I have not been able to visit Los Angeles recently, but John W. R. Taylor, Editor of *Jane's All the World's Aircraft*, has told me his impressions of wandering round the engineering mock-up. "Despite its size," he says, "it is like a fighter. The flight deck reminds one of the F-111, although the forward view through the incredibly deep windscreen is better than anything I've previously seen. Each pilot has a stick control, and flying the B-1 should be a wonderful experience. When I saw the mock-up one bomb bay had a revolving SRAM dispenser, another had two thermonuclear cookies, another a SCAD and another a huge load of conventional h.e." This mock-up is impressive. Colonel Bretting, who is also president of the 208-man mock-up review board, called it "the most Hi-Fi and true-to-life mock-up I've ever seen", and many industrial subcontractors have affirmed its great value to them in giving them a detailed "feel" for their contribution that one cannot acquire from drawings. General Nelson recently praised the "outstanding program visibility . . . we are finding out things on the B-1 that didn't surface in the old days until the Category II flight tests". As I write, late in 1972, the news comes through that the wing-pivot structure has passed its static testing at Ling-Temco-Vought, while the pivot bearing itself has successfully completed three B-1 simulated lifetimes at Boeing—a company just named as an associate contractor (the same status as GE) responsible for a new role called ASIC: avionics subsystems interface contractor. They will manage the defensive and offensive avionics and make everything work harmoniously inside the densely packed airframe.

At this stage in the programme the only adverse comment I can make is that the "control-configured vehicle" programme, mentioned at the end of the B-52 story, has unfortunately crystallized several years too late for the B-1 to take advantage of it. It seems indisputable that, if the B-1 were being designed today, it would be a different shape and would be markedly smaller. There is fairly general agreement among CCV experts (outside the B-1 programme) that the B-1 requirements could now be met by a bomber powered by only two F101 engines instead of four. Probably they would be above the wing. All this is technically interesting, and if true must be annoying to the Air Force Chief of Staff when he thinks how many twin-engined B-1s he could buy for the same money.

There are enough factors influencing, and influenced by, the B-1 to write a book on this programme alone. What will be the long-term outcome of the SALT nuclear disarmament talks? Is B-1 worth having purely to fight future conventional or limited wars? How far will it help the United States get back in the SST picture? In a democracy, how far must the public understand the reasons underlying complex defence procurement? Perhaps above all, how will the B-1 look twenty years hence? At present it just seems a big step along the road of cost escalation in defence systems. Soon nobody will be able to afford more than one bomber; and if it has a flat tire the war won't be able to start.